BERLITZ®

DISCOVER
BRITAIN

Edited and Designed by
D & N Publishing,
Lambourn, Berkshire.

Cartography by Hardlines,
Charlbury, Oxfordshire.

Although we have made every effort to ensure the accuracy of all the information in this book, changes do occur. We cannot therefore take responsibility for facts, addresses and circumstances in general that are constantly subject to alteration.

If you have any new information, suggestions or corrections to contribute to this guide, we would like to hear from you. Please write to Berlitz Publishing at the above address.

Photographic Acknowledgements

Copyright © All Sport 318 (Russell Cheyne); Berlitz Publishing Co. Ltd 10–11, 13, 16, 19, 23, 25, 34–5, 36, 42, 50–1, 52–3, 54, 96, 101, 103, 107, 108, 109, 112, 116, 117, 119, 132, 135, 136, 138–9, 140, 142, 145, 150–1, 157, 160, 161, 165, 166, 174–5, 182–3, 184–5, 188, 190–1, 198, 206, 211, 214–15, 221, 222–3, 232, 233, 234, 240–1, 244–5, 248–9, 252–3, 254, 256–7, 258–9, 260, 268–9, 274–5, 277, 278, 280–1, 285, 286–7, 290–1, 294, 301, 303, 308, 309, 323, 324, 326; Colorific 122; Ecublens 62, 94 (both), 95 (André Held); Frank Lane Picture Agency 320 (Peter Dean); Roy A Giles 44, 290, 306, 313, 314–15; John Glover 27, 120; David Price-Goodfellow 41, 111, 162, 187, 242, 311; Martin Gostelow 39; Jeremy Grayson 290; Hulton-Deutsch Collection 57, 59, 66; Erling Mandelmann 6, 216–17; Natural Image 152 (Robin Fletcher), 1, 74, 148, 180, 282 (Bob Gibbons), 32, 126, 130, 133, 219, 229, 270, 289 (Jean Hall), 239 (Peter Wilson); Nature Photographers 296 (Brinsley Burbidge), 224 (Ron Croucher), 47 (Geoff du Feu), 20, 30, 201, 230 (Jean Hall), 156, 172 (lower), 178, 321 (Paul Sterry), 202 (Roger Tidman), 134 (Derek Washington); Steve Nevill 110, 115, 155, 196, 228, 263, 329; PRISMA/Telegraph Colour Library 298–9; Neil Ray 21, 170, 172 (upper), 186, 246; Swift 300 (Martin King), 147, 192, 272, 305 (Mike Read).

Front cover photograph: Church of St Mary, Stoke By Nayland
(©Telegraph Colour Library)
Back cover photograph: Stratford-upon-Avon
(Berlitz Publishing)

Photograph previous page: Montacute House, Somerset.

Phototypeset, originated and printed by C.S. Graphics, Singapore.

The Berlitz tick is used to indicate places or events of particular interest.

BERLITZ®

DISCOVER
BRITAIN

Martin Gostelow

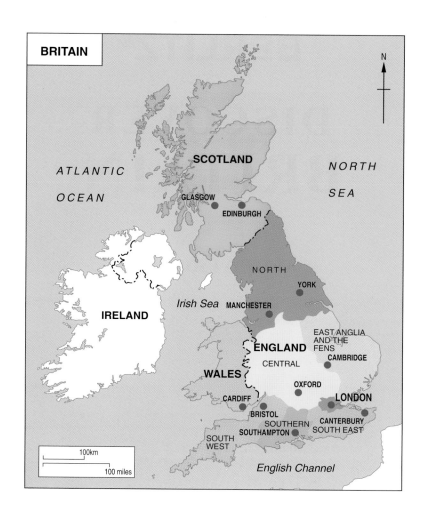

Contents

BRITAIN: FACTS AND FIGURES   7

When to Go   9
Climate and Clothing   9
Time Differences   10
Getting to Britain   10
Customs and Entry Regulations   13
Money Matters   14
Getting Around   14
Tours   19
Tourist Information Offices   20
Maps   22
Disabled Visitors   22
Keeping Children Happy   23
Health and Medical Care   24
Embassies, Consulates and High
    Commissions   24
Accommodation   25
Communications   28
Religious Services   30
Complaints   30
Crime and Theft   31
Lost Property   31
Electric Current   31
Emergencies   31
Opening Hours   32
Public (Legal) Holidays   32
Eating Out   33
Tipping   40
Toilets   41
Weights and Measures   41
Festivals and Events   41

THE COUNTRY, ITS HISTORY AND ITS PEOPLE   47

ON THE SHORTLIST   72

LEISURE ROUTES AND THEMES   75

LONDON AND ENVIRONS   97
BRITISH ART   124

THE SOUTH-EAST   127

SOUTHERN ENGLAND   143
BRITISH ARCHITECTURE   164

THE SOUTH-WEST   167

EAST ANGLIA AND THE FENS   193

CENTRAL ENGLAND   207
A SENSE OF PLACE: THE ENGLISH COUNTRY TOWN   232

WALES   235

THE NORTH OF ENGLAND   261

SCOTLAND   291

WHAT TO DO   319

HOTELS AND RESTAURANTS   332

Index   346

MAPS: Britain 4, 8; South-East 128; South 144; South-West 168; East Anglia and the Fens 194; Central England 208; Wales 236; Northern England 262; Scotland 292.

Town Plans: Bristol 171; Cambridge 195; Canterbury 129; Edinburgh 293; Glasgow 297; London 98/99, underground 100; Manchester 264; Oxford 209; Stratford-upon-Avon 213; York 271.

Planning to Get the Best Out of Your Visit

A trip to Britain is like a walk in the country. You can make rapid progress towards a goal or simply meander. You will find it easier to improvise outside the peak summer months, when pressure on accommodation and transport eases, but even in the high season you can travel with relative freedom away from the more heavily touristed zones. Few first-time visitors deviate from the London–Edinburgh axis with York the natural halting place en route. Other magnets, Oxford, Stratford and Bath, are popular day-trips from London, although there is plenty of scope to stay overnight in or near them.

This guide includes all regions of mainland Britain and some of the offshore islands. Some may already be familiar to you—although we hope you'll see them in a new light—while others deserve to be better known.

Try to visit the north as well as the south of England. According to local folklore, northerners are friendlier and more open. The landscape, too, is different—rugged and austere, as opposed to the gentle greenness of the south. You should also spend some time in Wales or Scotland. Moodier scenery and the reputedly more romantic nature of the people make for some striking contrasts with England.

Wherever you go, there will be castles, cathedrals, museums and great country houses to visit. Many attractions remain open until sunset, which means well into the evening in summer, allowing you to fit a lot into a day. You will have to be much less ambitious in winter, when night falls early.

One way to organize your trip is to follow some specialist interest, perhaps concentrating on gardens, great cathedrals, industrial archaeology, birdwatching or steam railways. We offer a broad spectrum of ideas in LEISURE ROUTES (*see* pages 75–95).

How many kinds of sweet flowers grow in an English country garden?—so the old song goes. This garden is carefully cultivated to look "natural".

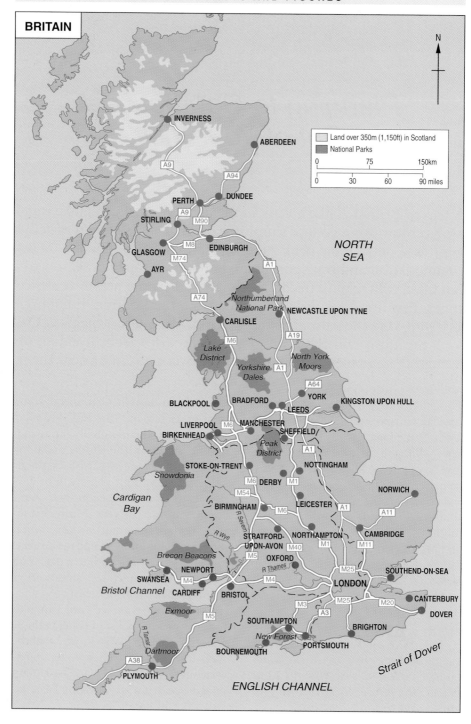

BRITAIN

N

Land over 350m (1,150ft) in Scotland
National Parks

0   75   150km

0   30   60   90 miles

INVERNESS

ABERDEEN

A9

A94

PERTH   DUNDEE

A9

STIRLING   M90

M8   EDINBURGH

GLASGOW

M74

AYR

A74

*Northumberland
National Park*   NEWCASTLE UPON TYNE

CARLISLE

M6   A19

*Lake
District*

*North York
Moors*

*Yorkshire
Dales*   A1

A64

BLACKPOOL   BRADFORD   YORK   KINGSTON UPON HULL

LEEDS

LIVERPOOL   M6   MANCHESTER
BIRKENHEAD   SHEFFIELD

*Peak
District*

STOKE-ON-TRENT   A1

Snowdonia   NOTTINGHAM

M6   DERBY   M1

M54   LEICESTER   NORWICH

*Cardigan
Bay*   BIRMINGHAM   M6   A1

R Severn   A11

R Wye   STRATFORD-   NORTHAMPTON   CAMBRIDGE
UPON-AVON   M40   M1   M11

Brecon Beacons   M5   OXFORD

SWANSEA   NEWPORT   *R Thames*   M25   SOUTHEND-ON-SEA

M4   A4   LONDON

Bristol Channel   CARDIFF   BRISTOL   M25   CANTERBURY

Exmoor   M3   M20   DOVER

M5   A3

SOUTHAMPTON   BRIGHTON

R Tamar   *New Forest*   PORTSMOUTH

Dartmoor   BOURNEMOUTH

A38

PLYMOUTH

Strait of Dover

ENGLISH CHANNEL

*NORTH
SEA*

Temperature Chart

°F		Jan	Feb	Mar	Apr	May	Jun	Jul	Aug	Sep	Oct	Nov	Dec
Cardiff	max	45	45	50	55	61	66	68	70	64	57	50	46
	min	36	36	37	41	46	52	54	57	52	46	41	37
Edinburgh	max	43	43	46	52	57	63	64	64	61	54	48	45
	min	34	34	36	39	43	48	52	52	48	45	39	36
London	max	43	45	50	55	63	68	72	70	66	57	50	45
	min	36	36	37	43	46	54	57	55	52	46	41	39

°C		Jan	Feb	Mar	Apr	May	Jun	Jul	Aug	Sep	Oct	Nov	Dec
Cardiff	max	7	7	10	13	16	19	20	21	18	14	10	8
	min	2	2	3	5	8	11	12	13	11	8	5	3
Edinburgh	max	6	6	8	11	14	17	18	18	16	12	9	7
	min	1	1	2	4	6	9	11	11	9	7	4	2
London	max	6	7	10	13	17	20	22	21	19	14	10	7
	min	2	2	3	6	8	12	14	13	11	8	5	4

Minimum temperatures are measured just before sunrise, maximum temperatures in the afternoon.

When to Go

The local holiday season is July and August, when schools take their summer break, but despite the millions who leave Britain in search of more reliable sunshine, many roads and attractions are crowded and you will scarcely hear an English voice in London. June, September and October can be beautiful, but May has the best track record for fine weather.

The entertainment scene is more active outside the summer months— apart from the festivals (*see* FESTIVALS AND EVENTS, pages 41–43), and out of season you will also be able to take advantage of travel and accommodation bargains.

*Map of Britain
showing the main roads, towns
and features.*

Climate and Clothing

The butt of endless jokes, Britain's weather will probably be wetter, milder and even more capricious than you might have expected. Rain falls in every season, and the humidity is generally high, especially in autumn and winter. But come prepared with your raincoat and umbrella, and a heat wave may ensue. Britain's weather is nothing if not fickle. There is considerable regional variation, too, from the relatively warm south-west (the "English Riviera") to the brisker north-east. The chart gives maximum and minimum daily temperatures for the three national capitals.

So what to pack, apart from the raingear? Woollens, even in summer, comfortable walking shoes, a few lightweight things for a hot spell and a heavy coat for the depths of winter. When it comes to style of dress, informality is the rule, apart from in the better hotels and restaurants.

Time Differences

In winter, Britain is on Greenwich Mean Time (GMT). From the last Sunday in March until the last Sunday in October, clocks are put ahead one hour (GMT + 1). For most of the year, therefore, when it's midday in Britain, it's 7 a.m. in New York, 4 a.m. in California, 1 p.m. in Amsterdam, 9 p.m. in Sydney, and 11 p.m. in Auckland.

Getting to Britain

By Air
As well as the usual first-, business- and economy-class, there is a complex series of special fares, discounts for families, children and students, as well as charters and package tours. Only a travel agent familiar with the latest changes can give you up-to-date information.

Thatchers keep ancient skills alive, fixing nature's own roofing material to a house in Exmoor.

Airport Information

Although London, served by Heathrow and Gatwick and the smaller Stansted, Luton and London City airports, is the principal gateway to Britain, many direct intercontinental flights land at Manchester or Glasgow. Other cities with international airports include Aberdeen, Birmingham, Cardiff and Edinburgh.

Heathrow, mainly used by scheduled flights, is 24km (15 miles) west of central London. Terminal 1 serves mostly British and Irish airlines; Terminal 2, other European airlines; Terminal 3, intercontinental traffic; and Terminal 4, mainly British Airways intercontinental flights.

The Piccadilly underground line links Heathrow to central London in about 45 minutes. The Flightline bus runs direct from the airport to Victoria Coach Station in about 40 minutes (depending on the traffic). London Transport Airbuses, routes A1 (to Victoria) and A2 (to Euston Station), stop at all the main hotel areas and take from 50 to 85 minutes, according to area. Taxis can be expensive: consider sharing to keep costs down.

For connections to other parts of southern England, take the Railair Link bus from Heathrow to the railway station in Woking. To reach towns in the far west of England and Wales, take the Railair Link bus to Reading station.

Tour operators offer a wealth of different packages (with air fares and various combinations of accommodation, meals and sightseeing tours included), as well as hiking, biking, boating, birdwatching, riding, golfing, language and other holidays. The British Tourist Authority (BTA) offices can supply you with lists of tour operators and a booklet on special interest tours.

Coaches also link Heathrow to Gatwick and Stansted airports.

Gatwick is 45km (28 miles) south of central London. North Terminal handles mostly British Airways flights; the majority of other airlines use the South Terminal. The rail journey to or from London's Victoria Station by the Gatwick Express takes 30 minutes.

London City Airport lies 10km (6 miles) east of the City of London in the Docklands area. Flightline buses run every 30 minutes between the airport and Victoria Station, and a Thames riverbus service links London City Airport Pier and the City and West End.

Stansted airport in Essex and **Luton** Airport in Bedfordshire are further out of London: they have their own bus and rail connections to the capital.

Birmingham International Airport, 14km (9 miles) south-east of the city centre, has its own railway station. Buses also make the journey into town.

Manchester International Airport lies some 16km (10 miles) south of the city centre.

In Scotland, most long-haul flights land at **Glasgow** Abbotsinch Airport, 13km (8 miles) to the west of the city, a 20-minute bus ride away. Prestwick Airport, 51km (32 miles) south-west of Glasgow, is less used. **Edinburgh** Airport, served by European and domestic flights, is 13km (8 miles) west of the city centre. Buses go to the city terminal at Waverley Bridge. **Aberdeen** Dyce Airport is just north of the city.

Cardiff-Wales Airport, serving South Wales, is about 16km (10 miles) south-west of the city centre. Buses link the airport to Cardiff, Swansea and Newport.

By Sea

From Mainland Europe

All the main North Sea and cross-Channel ferries apart from jetfoils carry cars. Vehicle space should be booked in advance during July and August. Out of season, the operators offer special deals. Some of the many routes are (in north–south order): Bergen/Gothenburg/ Esbjerg–Newcastle-upon-Tyne; Esbjerg–Harwich; Rotterdam–Hull; Hook of Holland–Harwich; Ostend/ Calais–Dover (about 35 minutes by hovercraft, 75 to 105 minutes by ferry); Boulogne–Dover; Dieppe–Newhaven; Le Havre–Portsmouth; Cherbourg–Weymouth; Roscoff–Plymouth.

From Ireland

The choice of ferry routes includes Rosslare–Fishguard, Dublin/Dun Laoghaire–Holyhead and Cork–Swansea. Services from Northern Ireland connect Larne to Cairnryan and Stranraer in Scotland and Belfast to Stranraer.

You can buy through-tickets for travel by train/ship/train on many of these routes.

From North America

The *Queen Elizabeth 2* makes about a dozen round trips a year from Southampton to New York, a journey of five days each way. Certain return trips call at Cherbourg, Cork, Baltimore or Boston. Fares are high, but less expensive packages enable you to travel one way on *QE2* and return by air. A premium package offers return flights by Concorde. Some freight-carrying ships also take a few passengers across the Atlantic.

Customs and Entry Regulations

Nationals of European Community (EC) countries need only a valid national identity card to enter Britain. Nationals of other Western European countries, the USA, Canada, Australia, New Zealand, Japan and South Africa must have a valid passport. Visitors from other countries may need a visa; check with your travel agent or the nearest British consulate before you leave home. No vaccinations are required to enter Britain from any country. Citizens of countries outside the EC usually have to fill in a landing card, and may have to convince the immigration officer that they have not come to work or to stay permanently.

At most British ports and airports, Customs Control is divided into two channels, green for "nothing to declare" and red for "goods to declare". Green channels are subject to spot checks.

Goods obtained duty and tax *paid* in the EC may be freely taken from one EC country to another, provided they are for personal use. The single market of the EC means that customs barriers have practically disappeared from the borders between member countries.

To keep out rabies, very strict laws, including quarantine of up to six months, are in force for the import of dogs, cats and other animals to Britain. Smuggling of pets is severely penalized, along with the probable confiscation and destruction of the animal. If you intend to take your pet with you, permission must be obtained at least six weeks in advance.

Severe penalties are imposed for drug smuggling. Travellers are warned never

*H*ow do you keep *these buttons clean? Yeoman warder in Elizabethan uniform and guardsman in bearskin compare notes.*

to carry baggage or packages through customs for someone else. Items subject to import control include weapons, fireworks, horror or pornographic material, plants and meats.

Money Matters

Currency

The eccentric world of shillings and half-crowns is now a distant memory, and the pound sterling (symbolized £) is simply divided into 100 pence (p). Coins are of 1, 2, 5, 10, 20 and 50 pence, plus a chunky gold-coloured £1 and a rarely seen £2. Banknotes (bills) are in £5, £10, £20 and £50 denominations. Several different banks in Scotland issue their own notes (including £1) but Bank of England notes are valid in Scotland too.

Changing Money

Exchange rates can fluctuate daily and vary considerably—banks give a better rate than most exchange offices, many of which also charge more commission. Try to find the rate you should be getting from the financial pages of the newspapers. Traveller's cheques are readily accepted by hotels, some bed-and-breakfast places, restaurants and stores. Again, banks may give a better rate. Eurocheques can be used anywhere, up to the set limit. You will need your passport or national identity card to cash a cheque.

Credit Cards

Most hotels and many shops and restaurants honour the major credit and charge cards. Look for their symbols displayed at the entrance. Even the police accept "plastic" to bail out cars impounded for illegal parking. If you know the Personal Identification Number (PIN) of your card, you may be able to obtain cash from the automatic teller machines outside many banks. Check before leaving home.

Getting Around

Although distances in Britain look relatively short on the map, journeys can take more time than you think. Roads in and near the cities are crowded. However you choose to travel, and wherever you stay, resist the temptation to turn a tour into a marathon, covering too many miles or sights in a day. Relax and enjoy the trip.

By Train

British Rail's trains are comfortable and usually punctual; most have first- and standard-class compartments. InterCity express trains are quick, travelling at up to 200kph (125mph). They can take you from London to Edinburgh in well under five hours, Plymouth in three and York and Cardiff in less than two. Other trains are usually much slower.

Seat reservations on long-distance trains are not normally necessary, except at rush hour and on popular routes in holiday periods. On night trains, sleeping-car berths must be booked in advance. Rail rover tickets, various travelcards and cheap day-return (round-trip) tickets are available at any British Rail station or Travel Centre.

By Coach/Long-distance Bus

Coach (bus) services are probably the cheapest way to get around, although time-consuming over longer distances.

National Express (England and Wales) and Caledonian Express and Citylink (Scotland), account for most inter-city connections. In London, you can book tickets at the British Travel Centre (12 Regent Street), at the National Express Coach Travel Centre across the street (13 Regent Street) and at Victoria Coach Station, the terminal for express motorcoach services. For information, contact:

National Express Central Enquiry
  Bureau
Victoria Coach Station
Buckingham Palace Road
London SW1W 9TP
Tel. (071) 730 0202.
(*Open*: Monday to Saturday 8 a.m. to 10 p.m., Sundays 10 a.m. to 8 p.m.)

By Plane

British Airways and several other airlines fly to some 60 domestic airports, linking major cities (worthwhile only for the longer routes) and connecting the mainland with Orkney and Shetland, the north-western islands, Northern Ireland, the Isle of Man, Isles of Scilly and Channel Islands. Shuttle services include those from London to Edinburgh (one hour) and to Glasgow (one hour). Check-in time is 30 minutes before departure.

Cycling

Several organizations, both in Britain and overseas, arrange package tours for cyclists. Brochures and leaflets are available from BTA offices.

You might prefer to take your own bike. Most airlines will accept them as part of the luggage allowance—check when you book your ticket. You might have to pay a small charge on ferries. Trains will carry them free of charge.

The Cyclists' Touring Club, Britain's national cycling association, organizes cycling holidays and provides information on individual bicycle routes. For further details, write to the CTC (enclosing a stamped self-addressed envelope/international reply coupon):

Cyclists' Touring Club
Cotterell House
69 Meadrow
Godalming
Surrey GU7 3HS.

Hitchhiking

In theory you can thumb a ride anywhere in Britain except on motorways, but don't depend on it as a method of travelling around the country unless you have plenty of time to spare. If you must hitchhike, do it in pairs.

Car Hire (Rental)

For independent travellers, a car offers freedom to roam and freedom from timetables. You can combine modes of travel, for example by taking the train to any mainline station and hiring a car there to explore the local area at your leisure.

Rates are high by world standards, but local firms compete with the international companies, so it is worth shopping around. Weekend and weekly unlimited-mileage rates are usually available, as well as various deals and packages. It is usually more economical to book your car at the same time as your travel tickets, or to order it in advance through a company in your home country. Chauffeur-driven cars are available for hire through most major companies.

To hire a car in Britain, you need to show your passport and driving licence (generally one that you have held for at least one year). The minimum age varies from 21 to 25, and a maximum of 70 or 75 may be stipulated. A substantial deposit is required unless you pay with a recognized credit card. Third-party liability insurance is included in the rental charge; a CDW (collision-damage waiver) charge covers your liability towards the rental company in case of an accident.

Driving in Britain

With the exception of London, driving in Britain doesn't require any special prowess, whatever people say. Remember that traffic keeps to the left, overtaking (passing) on the right. If you are not used to driving on the left, you will need a few hours to become accustomed to it. Think twice every time you

set off, and pay special attention at junctions and roundabouts (traffic circles).

All but the most minor roads are given numbers, prefixed by *M* for motorways (expressways); *A* for main trunk roads, often dual carriageways (divided highways); *B* for paved secondary roads.

Regulations

Drivers and passengers are required by law to fasten their seat belts. Dipped (low-beam) headlights should be used whenever daytime visibility is reduced by rain or fog.

Motorcycle drivers and passengers must wear crash helmets. A driving licence is required even for mopeds under 55cc. The minimum age for operating a moped is 16; for motorcycles, scooters and cars, 17.

Whether you bring your own vehicle or hire one, you should buy a copy of the *Highway Code*, which gives details of the rules of the road. This is available at most ports of entry and from book shops in Britain.

Cars already in a roundabout have priority; when entering, give way to vehicles coming from the right. At junctions, signs and markings indicate who has priority. Pedestrians have priority on zebra crossings—broad white stripes painted across the road, marked by flashing orange beacons.

Speed limits are, unless otherwise indicated, 48kph (30mph) in towns and

*F*ootsore shoppers in the Cotswolds won't be taking the tour to Oxford or Stratford today.

built-up areas, 112kph (70mph) on motorways and dual carriageways and 96kph (60mph) on other roads. For cars towing a caravan, the maximum speed on motorways and dual carriageways is 96kph (60mph) and on other roads 80kph (50mph). These vehicles are banned from the fast lane of motorways that have three lanes in each direction.

If you plan to drink more than half a pint of beer or a tot of whisky, you had better let someone else drive or leave the car behind. Penalties for driving with more than a very low level of alcohol in the blood are severe.

Parking regulations are strict in cities and town centres. Never park on white zigzag lines along the kerb (which indicate pedestrian crossings), on a double yellow line, on a single yellow line during working days (times are given on nearby signboards), on spaces marked "Permit Holders Only", in "Control Zones" or "No Stopping" areas. In some places, offending cars are towed away or, especially in big cities, their wheels may be clamped.

If you intend to bring a car into Britain, you should carry with you, as well as your driving licence, the vehicle registration document, insurance cover (the green card is recommended but not obligatory for vehicles registered in western Europe; drivers of vehicles registered in other countries must show proof of public-liability and property-damage insurance) and a nationality sticker. Before leaving home, check with your own automobile association to see if they are affiliated with one in Britain.

Fuel

Petrol (gasoline), priced in litres (.25 US gallon) and sometimes in imperial gallons as well) is sold in leaded (4-star), unleaded and super-unleaded grades. Ask which your rental car needs. Diesel fuel is also widely available. Few petrol stations stay open at night except on the motorways.

Getting Around London

Single- and double-decker buses, under- and overground trains, taxis and boats, can all help you to get about in London. There are travel Information Centres at Oxford Circus, Piccadilly Circus, King's Cross and Heathrow, and Victoria and Euston main railway stations. Dial (071) 222 1234 for travel information (24 hours).

The **underground** (or "tube") is the quickest means of public transport in London. ("Subway" in Britain means an underground walkway.) Maps in the stations and trains show the various lines, colour-coded for easy reference. Buy your ticket in the station entrance hall, either from a vending machine or at the cashier's window. As you go through the turnstile to your platform, insert your ticket in the slot and retrieve it when it pops out. You have to hand in your ticket at your destination. Trains run from 5.30 a.m. to midnight on weekdays, from 7.30 a.m. to 11.30 p.m. on Sundays.

London has a dense and complex **bus** network. Free route maps and time-tables are available at underground stations. Buses run from early morning to around midnight. On the red double-deckers, the conductor circulates to collect fares (tell him your destination); on single-decker Red Arrow buses, put the exact fare in the slot as you board. At "Request" stops, you must wave down your bus; at all others, every bus must stop (unless full). Ticket prices increase with the number of zones to be travelled. There is a selection of money-saving cards, available from underground ticket offices and from London Transport Travel Information Centres (*see* above).

Green Line buses connect central London with the surrounding countryside. The main terminal is at Eccleston Bridge, behind Victoria Station; tel. (071) 668 7261 for information. Special rover tickets are available.

You can also travel between certain points by **boat**. On Regent's Canal, a waterbus service runs between Camden Lock and Little Venice (buy the ticket on board). On the Thames, a riverbus operates regularly between Chelsea Harbour Pier and Docklands, with stops at both banks. Other services go further up- and downriver.

You can hail a **taxi** on the street when the "For Hire" or "Taxi" sign is on, or one can be ordered by telephone—look in *Yellow Pages* for the numbers. Taxi ranks are found at main rail stations, ports and airports. Should the cab have no meter, ask the fare to your destination before setting off.

Good Deals

Buy the appropriate reduced-rate tickets, passes and cards and you can cut costs substantially. On most public transport, senior citizens (women over 60 and men over 65), children and students can travel at reduced fares, while children up to 5 travel free.

Here are the main bargains for anyone who plans to travel widely in Britain.

The **BritRail Pass** (British Rail's equivalent of the Eurailpass, which is not valid in the UK) offers unlimited rail travel in England, Scotland and Wales for periods of 4, 8, 15 or 22 days, or one month in first class. Over 60s can buy first-class passes at reduced rates. For young people 16 through 25, there is a BritRail Youth Pass (standard class only). These and several other sorts of pass are sold in Europe at accredited travel agents, main railway stations and BritRail Travel International offices (Amsterdam, Basle, Brussels, Copenhagen, Dublin, Frankfurt, Milan, Paris); in North America, at BritRail accredited travel agents and BritRail Travel International offices; in other countries at appointed travel agencies— lists are available from your local BTA office. They cannot be bought in Britain.

In the Highlands and islands of Scotland, the **Travelpass** is good for travel on Caledonian MacBrayne ferries, P & O Ferries to Orkney, Scottish Bus Group coaches, Scottish Citylink coaches and on Scotrail. The pass is valid for 7 days' travel in 8 days or 13 days' travel in 15 days between 1 March and 31 October. It is on sale at principal British Rail stations, the British Travel Centre in London, Scottish Citylink and Scottish Bus Group offices.

Various passes to give you reductions on journeys by bus on National Express coaches in England and Wales and most Caledonian Express coaches in Scotland are on sale at National Express, Caledonian Express and Citylink Travel Centres in Britain.

British Airways' **Highland Rover** offers eight separate flights within a 21-day period on the Highlands Division network. The ticket must be obtained seven days before the first flight and is only good for one return journey between any two points. Available from British Airways offices.

The **London Visitor Travelcard** gives 1, 3, 4 or 7 days' unlimited travel on London Transport buses (except the Heathrow Airbus) and most of the underground railway network (including Heathrow). You have to buy it through a travel agent or BritRail Travel International office abroad.

Tours

First-time visitors to London will get the best introduction to the principal sights on a guided panoramic tour bus,

such as the 90-minute "Original London Transport Sightseeing Tour" (frequent daily departures). You see the sights from the top deck of a red London bus (open-deckers in fine weather). Several companies also organize half- and full-day bus tours of London and its environs. Guided walking tours of London are advertised in the newspapers and what's on magazines. You can also see the city from the water— Thames cruises are organized up- and

If this is your first visit to London, find your bearings by taking one of the sightseeing tours.

*E*ach part of the country uses its own building materials in its own distinctive way. These are Tudor cottages in Essex.

downriver; more offbeat are the narrowboat tours of Regent's Canal. Inquire at the London Tourist Board (*see* page 21).

Packages available, mostly starting from London, include fully escorted tours by express train and coach (entrance fees included). They can be booked through travel agencies and BritRail Travel International offices.

The national bus companies and many private tour operators also offer escorted tours of the country. Travel agencies will tell you which tours are available, and they can also arrange personally conducted tours.

Tourist Information Offices

The British Tourist Authority (BTA) office in your country will provide information before you leave home.

Australia
University Centre
8th floor
210 Clarence Street
Sydney NSW 2000
Tel. (02) 267 4555

Canada
111 Avenue Road
Suite 450
Toronto
Ont. M5R 3J8
Tel. (416) 925-6326

Eire
123 Lower Baggot Street

Dublin 2
Tel. (01) 6614 188

Japan and **Korea**
246 Tokyo Club Building
3-2-6 Kasumigaseki
Chiyoda-ku
Tokyo 100
Tel. (03) 3581-3603

New Zealand
Dilworth Building
3rd floor
Suite 305
corner Queen and Customs streets
Auckland 1
Tel. (09) 3031-446

USA
2580 Cumberland Parkway
Suite 470
Atlanta GA 30339-3909

625 North Michigan Avenue
Suite 1510
Chicago IL 60611
Tel. (312) 787-0490

350 South Figueroa Street
Suite 450
Los Angeles CA 90071
Tel. (213) 628-3525

551 Fifth Avenue
New York NY 10176
Tel. (212) 986 2200.

In Britain
More than 700 Tourist Information Centres can help you find out what to see and where to stay.

In **London** the British Travel Centre at 12 Regent Street, near Piccadilly Circus is open seven days a week, 9 a.m. to 6.30 p.m. Monday to Friday, and 10 a.m. to 4 p.m. Saturdays and Sundays (9 a.m. to 5 p.m. from mid-May to September). It provides information on the whole of Britain and can reserve accommodation and tours. Telephone information is on (071) 730 3400 during Centre opening times except Sundays.

British Tourist Authority
Thames Tower
Black's Road
Hammersmith
London
W6 9EL
Tel. (081) 846 9000

Scottish Tourist Board's Travel Centre
19 Cockspur Street
London
SW1Y 5BL
Tel. (071) 930 8661

Wales Information Bureau
Wales Centre
12 Regent Street
London
SW1V 4PQ
Tel. (071) 409 0969

London Tourist Board and Convention Bureau telephone information service: (071) 730 3488, Monday to Saturday 9 a.m. to 6 p.m.
Accommodation and Tour reservations: (071) 824 8844.
Artsline telephone information service for the disabled: (071) 388 2227.
London Tourist Board has information centres (TICs) at: (1) Victoria Station Forecourt SW1 (*open*: daily 8 a.m. to 7 p.m., from Easter to end October; 9 a.m. to 7 p.m. Monday to Saturday,

and 9 a.m. to 5 p.m. on Sundays, November to Easter); (2) Selfridges department store basement Oxford Street, W1 (*open*: store hours); (3) Heathrow Airport terminals 1, 2 and 3 underground station concourse (*open*: daily, 8 a.m. to 6 p.m.).

Scotland
Edinburgh Information Centre
Waverley Market
3 Princes Street
Edinburgh
EH2 2QP
Tel. (031) 557 1700
(*Open*: Monday to Saturday 8.30 a.m. to 8 p.m./9 p.m. July and August, Sunday 11 a.m. to 8 p.m./9 p.m. July and August.)

Scottish Tourist Board
23 Ravelston Terrace
Edinburgh
EH4 3EU
Tel. (031) 332 2433.

Walk Right In
If you plan to do a lot of sightseeing, buy a Great British Heritage Pass. Valid for a period of 15 days or one month, this pass admits visitors from abroad to over 500 stately homes, castles, gardens and historic sites in England, Wales, Scotland and Northern Ireland, including privately owned, National Trust and English Heritage properties.

Savings are considerable, not only in money but in time, as pass-holders can often bypass queues (lines) at ticket windows. The pass comes with an atlas of the sites covered and it is on sale at British Tourist Authority offices abroad and in Britain at airports, seaports and many tourist information offices.

Wales
Wales Tourist Board
Brunel House
2 Fitzalan Road
Cardiff
CF2 1UY
Tel. (0222) 499909
Telephone and written inquiries only.

Maps

You can pick up basic local maps and street plans at any Tourist Information Centre. Look in bookshops, service stations and major newsagents for the good road atlases of Britain published by the Automobile Association and the Ordnance Survey. These are on a scale of 3 miles to the inch (about 2km to 1cm), and include many city street-plans. For hikers and cyclists, the most detailed maps are Bartholomews (1:100,000) and Ordnance Survey (1:50,000 and 1:25,000).

Disabled Visitors

Although much still needs to be done, great progress has been made in helping people with special needs, particularly in providing wheelchair access to hotels, public buildings, toilets and tourist sites. Free information on accommodation and facilities for disabled visitors to Britain is available from the Holiday Care Service
2 Old Bank Chambers
Station Road
Horley
Surrey
RH6 9HW
Tel. (0293) 774535.

Keeping Children Happy

Donkey rides and Punch and Judy at the seaside, safari parks and theme parks, miniature towns and steam railways—there's plenty for children to see and do on holiday in Britain. Here are some ideas:

In **London**, a ride on a double-decker bus; a boat trip on the Thames; Egyptian mummies at the British Museum; dinosaurs at the Natural History Museum; Madame Tussaud's famous waxworks (Marylebone Road, NW1); Bethnal Green Museum of Childhood (Cambridge Heath Road, E2); the London Toy and Model Museum (23 Craven Hill, W2); and Pollock's Toy Museum (1 Scala Street, W1). Older children might enjoy the London Dungeon, a horror museum (28/34 Tooley Street, SE1), or Rock Circus, the world of rock and pop in wax at the London Pavilion, Piccadilly Circus.

Around Britain, some of the possibilities are the theme parks at **Alton Towers** (Staffordshire), **Thorpe Park** (Chertsey, Surrey) and **Chessington** World of Adventures (Surrey); **Beaulieu** (Hampshire) National Motor Museum of vintage cars, mini-car and motorbike race circuit; **Chatham** (Kent) Historic Dock-yard, with traditional rope-, sail- and flag-making and carriage rides; and **Beltring** (Kent) Whitbread Hop Farm rural museum and crafts centre with shire horses and a nature trail. There are many miniature towns, such as the one at **Beaconsfield** (Buckinghamshire), and various toy and doll museums, including **Edinburgh** Museum of Childhood.

*F*rom traditional fairgrounds to the latest theme parks, Britain can offer you a hair-raising ride to compete with the best.

Health and Medical Care

Visitors from EC countries or those with which Britain has a reciprocal health agreement (including New Zealand, Norway and Sweden) are eligible for free emergency medical and hospital treatment through the National Health Service. Other visitors can benefit from free emergency treatment but will have to pay for overnight stays in hospitals. A charge is made for medicines. If your general health insurance policy does not cover foreign travel, make sure your travel insurance includes medical cover.

Pharmacies (Chemist)

In every large town, at least one pharmacy (called a chemist) stays open until 7.30 or 8 p.m., and 24-hour prescription service may be available. Look in the local newspaper or the window of any pharmacy for the name and address.

If you have a minor ailment, a pharmacist can advise about treatment. You can get the address of a local doctor or hospital from the telephone operator by dialling 100 (free) or, in an emergency, 999.

Embassies, Consulates and High Commissions

All embassies, and the high commissions of Commonwealth members are in London. Many countries also maintain consulates in other cities in Britain.

Most diplomatic representatives are listed in *Yellow Pages* under "Embassies, Consulates, High Commissions and Legations".

Australia
High Commission
Australia House
Strand
WC2B 4LA
Tel. (071) 379 4334

Canada
High Commission
1 Grosvenor Square
W1X 0AB
Tel. (071) 629 9492

Eire
Embassy
17 Grosvenor Place
SW1X 7HR
Tel. (071) 235 2171

Japan
Embassy and consulate
101–4 Piccadilly
W1V 9FN
Tel. (071) 465 6500

New Zealand
High Commission
New Zealand House
Haymarket
SW1Y 4TE
Tel. (071) 930 8422
      (071) 235 7151

South Africa
Embassy and Consulate,
South Africa House
Trafalgar Square
WC2N 5DP
Tel. (071) 930 4488

USA
Embassy
24 Grosvenor Square
W1A 1AE
Tel. (071) 499 9000.

Accommodation

You can stay in a castle, a friendly bed-and-breakfast, a farmhouse or a hotel. From London's grand traditional establishments to the elegant informality of certain country house hotels and the convenience of the national and international chains, the range is enormous.

Hotels, guesthouses, inns, bed-and-breakfast establishments and farmhouses that participate in the British Tourist Authority's (BTA) standards scheme are inspected regularly by the national tourist boards. Those that pass are classified, from "Listed" through one to five crowns. A low-crown classification does not imply low standards, but indicates that the facilities and services provided meet an acceptable minimum.

Our list of selected hotels and restaurants (*see* pages 332–345) will help you choose places in your price range. For a comprehensive listing, consult the accommodation guides published by the English Tourist Board and Scottish Tourist Board and by the Automobile Association. Shorter selections are given in several other annual guides. Some of these books can be ordered through BTA-nominated agents abroad; for addresses and procedure, contact the BTA office in your country.

T he streets of Clovelly in north Devon may be jammed, but not by cars. You have to leave them at the top and walk.

Reservations and Rates

It might be difficult to book rooms in summer and at Easter and Bank Holiday weekends. Try to reserve well in advance, either through your local travel agent or by contacting individual hotels or hotel chains. Many local Tourist Information Centres (TIC) can make reservations on the spot. TICs in Scotland and Wales ask for a deposit. In London, the British Travel Centre at 12 Regent Street, a two-minute walk south of Piccadilly Circus, provides a national reservation service.

Accommodation in London may be reserved in advance through the London Tourist Board, 26 Grosvenor Gardens, London SW1W 0DU. Your request must reach London at least six weeks prior to your date of arrival.

Hotels with four or more bedrooms are required to display a notice at the entrance or reception showing minimum and maximum overnight rates and whether they include service charges and value added tax (VAT). Full or half-board terms may be available, especially in the country. Breakfast (English or continental) is usually included in the quoted rate; in addition, some hotels provide tea- and coffee-making facilities. A service charge of 10 to 12 per cent (15 per cent in some larger hotels) is usually added to the bill. In autumn, winter and spring, hotels all over Britain offer bargain rates and short-break deals.

Alternatives to Hotels

Throughout Britain, but especially in villages in the holiday areas, **bed-and-breakfast (B&B)** houses generally cost much less than hotels. They can be private homes or farmhouses, or small, family-run, budget hotels, and usually have a warm, friendly atmosphere. A private bath is the exception rather than the rule. You don't usually need a reservation. Just look for a sign saying "B&B" and ring the doorbell.

Guesthouses have more rooms and often better bathroom facilities than B&Bs, and many serve an evening meal. They are slightly more expensive, but still cheaper than most hotels.

Ask the BTA for information if you would like to stay on a **working farm**, or in **self-catering accommodation** run by the National Trust, the National Trust for Scotland or the Landmark Trust—you might find yourself in a restored fort, mill or manor house. Early reservation is essential. If you would like to stay in a **private home** with a local family and gain an insider's knowledge of British life, or participate in a **home-exchange scheme**, again, the BTA will be able to advise.

Youth and **student accommodation** includes youth hostels, YMCA/YWCAs and also college and university halls of residence, which offer both B&B and self-catering arrangements during student holiday periods. Britain's 260 youth hostels are open to everyone, but you will need a national or international membership card, or a guest card that you can buy on arrival in Britain.

Camping and Caravanning

Britain has thousands of caravan and camping parks, many with stationary caravans (trailers) or lodges for rent. Details of licensed sites, their charges and amenities—graded from one to five—are available from BTA offices. The best caravan parks are awarded symbols by the tourist boards: a rose in

A canal narrow boat that once used to carry coal is transformed into a floating country garden.

England, a thistle in Scotland and a dragon in Wales. Most are open from end-March to October. During July, August and September, the more popular ones tend to fill up early in the day, so it is usually best to reserve a space in advance. If you want to camp outside official sites, you will need to obtain the permission of the landowner or tenant. The Camping and Caravanning Club, and the Caravan Club, publish directories of sites. Campers can be rented from most car-hire companies, but the rates can be high.

Holidays Afloat

You can hire a traditional canal narrowboat (a kind of houseboat) or another suitable vessel and cruise Britain's inland waterways. No special permits, licences or previous experience are required, but the "skipper" must be at least 21 years of age. The minimum rental period is normally one week. Narrowboats have from two to eight berths. You could cover about 160km (100 miles) in a week at a leisurely pace, depending on how many stops you make and the number of locks you have to negotiate. You may also be able to pick up the boat in one place and leave it in another. Local TICs can direct you to rental agencies. However, for the July–August holiday period, you should reserve in advance; the BTA office in your home country will have the brochures.

Communications

Post Offices

Main post offices open from 9 a.m. to 5 or 5.30 p.m., Monday to Friday, and from 9 a.m. to noon or 12.30 p.m. on Saturdays. Smaller offices may have shorter hours. Post offices don't just handle mail: they operate the Giro banking system and act as a government agency by handing out welfare payments and collecting various taxes. Stamps can be bought at post-office counters, vending machines outside post offices, and many stationery shops and supermarket checkouts. Letter boxes are painted bright red.

If you are not sure where you'll be staying, you can have letters addressed to you in any town c/o Poste Restante. In places with more than one post office, it will be sent to the main branch. You need to show identification to retrieve your mail.

Telephone

The system is modern and efficient, with direct dialling practically everywhere in Britain and indeed to most of the world. The majority of public telephones are part of the British Telecom (BT) network. For some you need coins, while Phonecard phones accept only cards. The rarer Mercury phones take cards only. BT and Mercury phonecards can be bought at post offices and many shops. Prominent signs say where they are on sale.

Coin-operated payphones can be used for direct domestic (minimum charge 10p) and international calls (deposit at least 50p and have more ready). Unused coins are returned.

Credit Call payphones accept Visa, MasterCard (Access), Diners Club and American Express cards, as well as British Telecom's Phonecards, and have a 50p minimum charge.

From private telephones only, reduced rates apply from 6 p.m. to 8 a.m., Monday to Friday, for both local and long-distance calls, and from 8 p.m. to 8 a.m. for some international calls. The cheap rate also applies all day Saturday and Sunday.

Hotels usually add a surcharge to the normal rate. If you are going to make many calls, it will be worth finding out how they calculate it. A public payphone may cost less. A reverse-charge (collect) international call (dial 155) can be expensive. If you have the appropriate US phone company's card, you can call the USA from Britain by dialling a US operator.

To call a subscriber in Britain from abroad, dial the international prefix used in your country followed by 44, then the number (omitting the initial 0).

To make a direct international call from Britain, dial 010, then the country code, the area code (omitting any initial 0) and the subscriber's number. Some country codes:

Australia	(010) 61
Austria	(010) 43
Belgium	(010) 32
Canada	(010) 1
Denmark	(010) 45
Eire	(010) 353
Finland	(010) 358
France	(010) 33
Germany (former West)	(010) 49
Germany (former East)	(010) 49

India	(010) 91
Japan	(010) 81
Netherlands	(010) 31
New Zealand	(010) 64
Norway	(010) 47
Singapore	(010) 65
South Africa	(010) 27
Sweden	(010) 46
Switzerland	(010) 41
United States	(010) 1

Telegram, Telex and Fax

Telegrams arriving in Britain from abroad are communicated via the telephone (telemessage); a copy is sent by mail the following day. Telegrams from Britain can be sent from post offices or over the phone—dial 190. Telex and fax services are listed in the *Yellow Pages* under "Telex" and "Facsimile Bureaux".

Newspapers and Magazines

In addition to many national and local publications, from lurid to learned, big news-stands in London and other major cities sell newspapers and magazines from Europe, the US and the Middle East. The *International Herald Tribune* and *Wall Street Journal* are widely available. Entertainment and special events are publicized in the daily papers. In London, happenings are listed in magazines such as *What's On in London*, *Time Out* and *Where to Go in London*.

Radio and TV

On radio, you have a choice of five BBC national stations—everything from pop music on Radio 1 to classical on Radio 3 and news, comedy and plays on Radio 4. Commercial stations include Classic FM (popular classics)

A Common Language?

You may not catch the quick fire cockney of a London cabbie, but neither does the average Yorkshireman. Quite apart from problems of accent, even the words themselves may not mean what you expect. Transatlantic differences, for instance, are so numerous that full-scale British-American dictionaries have been published. A sampler:

British	American
bill	check (restaurant)
bonnet	hood (of car)
boot	trunk (of car)
caravan	trailer
chemist	druggist, pharmacy
fag (slang)	cigarette
first floor	second floor
flat	apartment
ground floor	first floor
lay-by	roadside parking spot
lift	elevator
lorry	truck
nappy	diaper
off-licence	liquor store
pants	shorts (underwear)
pavement	sidewalk
pram	baby carriage
pushchair	stroller
petrol	gasoline
public school	private school
to queue	to stand in line
reception	front desk
rubber	eraser
single/return	one-way/ round-trip (ticket)
surgery	doctor's or dentist's office
sweet	candy
torch	flashlight
underground	subway

and local services. The BBC World Service's excellent international news coverage is not so easy to pick up in the UK itself.

British television broadcasts on four main channels. The two BBC channels are state-owned and financed by a yearly licence-fee payable by each TV-owning household. There are no advertisements (commercials). The independent channels, ITV and Channel 4, have advertising, as do various satellite and cable channels. Newspapers carry details of the day's viewing.

number of Roman Catholics in all parts of Britain.

Of the non-Christian faiths, Muslims are the most numerous, followed by Jews, Buddhists and Hindus. Virtually every major religious grouping in the world has some adherents in Britain. Hotel desks and Information Centres can give you details of local places of worship.

Religious Services

The Church of England has been the established state church in England since the Reformation, and has the highest nominal membership, although the percentage attending services is very low. In Scotland, the Presbyterian Church of Scotland has official status and the largest following, while the Methodists and the Baptists predominate in Wales. There is a substantial

Complaints

In shops, hotels and restaurants, talk to the manager or proprietor first—the personal approach is usually the most

T he towers and spires of village churches define the English landscape. St Mary's, Uffington, is unusual for its octagonal tower.

effective. If there is something you can't sort out, report it to the British Tourist Authority. They will investigate the matter or suggest what action to take.

A defective article or one which doesn't correspond to its description may be returned or exchanged. (It helps if you keep your sales receipts.) You may be offered credit, but you have the right to ask for a refund. If you need further help, contact the local Citizens' Advice Bureau (listed in *Yellow Pages*).

Crime and Theft

While Britain remains a relatively safe country, crime is on the rise here as elsewhere. Be on your guard after dark in the cities, and watch out for pickpockets in crowds—especially at street markets, in cinema and theatre lines, in department stores and on public transport—especially crowded tube trains. Put items of value in your hotel safe. Lock your car (and caravan) when you park, and remove all property from view. Avoid leaving your car in the street for long periods.

Lost Property

Finding a lost object depends on where you lost it. Check with officials at the train or bus station, airport or store, or at your hotel. For property left behind on London's underground or buses, go, or write to, London Transport Lost Property Office (forms are available at bus and underground stations) at 200 Baker Street, London NW1 5RZ.

Report the loss of your passport or identity card to your embassy or consulate. Any other major loss or theft should be reported to the nearest police station; unless you do, and ask for a copy of the police report at the same time, your insurance company at home may not pay up.

Make photocopies of your tickets, driving licence, passport and other vital documents in case you have to obtain replacements. Keep these separately from the originals. Report any loss or theft to the nearest police station; your insurance company will need to see a copy of the police report.

If you lose a credit card in Britain, call:
American Express: (0273) 696933 (0800 521313 for traveller's cheques)
Diners Club: (0252) 513500
MasterCard/Access/Eurocard: (0702) 352211
Visa/Barclaycard: (0604) 230230.

Electric Current

The standard is 240-volt, 50-cycle AC. Most hotels have sockets for shavers that operate on 240 or 110 volts. Voltage transformers and adaptors for the British three-prong square sockets are available at hardware stores.

Emergencies

For police, fire brigade or ambulance service, dial **999** from any telephone (no coin required). Tell the operator what you need and give the telephone number shown on the phone. Wait on the line. When the emergency service replies, give the address where help is needed and any other vital information.

Opening Hours

Banks are normally open from 9.30 a.m. to 4.30 p.m. Some open on Saturday mornings. Branches in Scotland generally close for one hour at lunchtime.

Museums, art galleries, castles, sites. Standard hours are from 9 or 10 a.m. to 5 or 6 p.m. on weekdays, and from approximately 2 p.m. on Sundays. Sites in the open air usually close at sundown. Off season, there may be a severely reduced schedule. Hours do vary, so check with the local Tourist Information Centre before you set out.

Offices and **businesses** operate from 9 or 9.30 a.m. to 5 or 5.30 p.m., Monday to Friday. Few open on Saturday morning.

Post office hours are generally from 9 a.m. to about 5.30 p.m., Monday to Friday, and from 9 to noon or 12.30 p.m. on Saturdays.

Pub hours can vary, but are usually from 11 a.m. to 11 p.m., Monday to Saturday, and from noon to 3 p.m. and 7 to 10.30 p.m. on Sundays. Some keep shorter hours.

Shopping hours are normally from 9 or 9.30 a.m. to 5.30 or 6 p.m., Monday to Saturday. Shops in smaller towns may close for an hour during lunchtime and some close on Saturday afternoons. Newsagents and some corner stores open for much longer hours, and on Sunday mornings.

In London, the shopping area in Covent Garden is open until 8 p.m. Shops in Knightsbridge and Chelsea close at 7 p.m. on Wednesdays, while those in the West End and Kensington High Street stay open till 7 p.m. on Thursdays.

Public (Legal) Holidays

Banks, most shops and many museums close on the following holidays.

If any of these holidays falls on a Saturday or Sunday, the usual practice is to take the following Monday off.

1 January	*New Year's Day*
2 January	*Bank Holiday (Scotland)*
March/April	*Good Friday*
	Easter Monday (except Scotland)
First Monday in May	*May Day Bank Holiday*

Last Monday in May	*Spring Bank Holiday*
First Monday in August	*Bank Holiday (Scotland)*
Last Monday in August	*Summer Bank Holiday (except Scotland)*
25 December	*Christmas Day*
26 December	*Boxing Day*

> **Fish 'n' Chips**
> If Britain has a national dish, this is it. Batter-dipped fillets of cod, plaice or haddock deep fried and served with chips (French fries) in a greaseproof paper bag, traditionally sprinkled with brown vinegar and wrapped in newspaper for taking away and eating messily in the street with your fingers. The evocative smell still wafts from takeaways and vans, but you'll find fish and chips on the menu in plenty of pubs and restaurants too.

Eating Out

The British may not live to eat, as the French and Italians do, but they know how to eat well. The best British food is traditionally based on top-quality ingredients uncomplicated by fancy sauces, but habits are changing, and food is getting more varied all the time. The ethnic influence has been decisive, introducing flavours and spices from the Far East, India and the Caribbean. And the lifting of frontier barriers in the European Community has brought an influx of Continental products, from French cheeses, pâtés and wines to Greek yoghurt.

Where to Eat
The proliferating fast-food chains need no introduction. More typically British are sandwich bars and cafés catering to office and other workers, open for breakfast, lunch and dinner, where food is sustaining and cheap.

The pub or "local". It's a club, a bar, a home from home, a meeting place, a social centre and, increasingly, a restaurant.

Pubs, many of them historic landmarks, are everywhere. In addition to snacks and drinks, you can have a hot meal at many of them—sometimes mass-produced and microwaved, sometimes as good as any restaurant.

In the cities, wine bars provide hot and cold food, perhaps a salad bar, along with wine by the bottle or glass. They are especially popular with young professionals.

Restaurants range from rustic inns to elegant gourmet spots, but expensive menus don't guarantee quality. Try to take local advice. Look for fixed-price menus if you want to know just what the bill is likely to add up to.

Carveries, often attached to hotels or pubs, specialize in roast meat carved from the joint, with potatoes, vegetables and salads.

Ethnic Variations
You'll find many Italian and French restaurants in the cities, and even small towns have their Chinese and Indian restaurants and takeaways. Other economical options may include Turkish, Greek, Lebanese, West Indian, Hungarian, kosher, Indian vegetarian... the choice is wide, and so is the range of quality.

Times

Breakfast is usually served between 8 and 9.30 a.m. (sometimes from 7 to 10.30 a.m. in hotels), and lunch from noon to 2 or 2.30 p.m. Teatime may extend from 3 to 5 p.m. and dinner from 7 to 9.30 or 10.30 p.m.

Breakfast

A Continental-style start to the day may keep you going until "elevenses", mid-morning tea break, but a true British breakfast is a real meal. Typically this consists of juice, cold cereal or porridge (oatmeal), followed by bacon and eggs, or sausages and grilled tomatoes, or kippers (smoked herrings), with toast, marmalade and tea or coffee.

Pubs

In the countryside as in the city, the local pub (Britain has more than

Not only London's Chinatown, but practically every town in Britain has at least one Chinese restaurant, and probably a fish-and-chip shop too.

relish). Other pub staples served cold: meat pies (pork or game); Scotch eggs (hard-boiled eggs wrapped in sausage meat and deep fried); and Cornish pasties (pastries filled with potato, onion and meat).

By way of hot food, there are soups; the traditional "shepherd's pie" (minced beef or lamb with herbs and onions, topped with mashed potatoes); steak and kidney pie; chicken and mushroom pie; "bangers and mash" (sausages and mashed potatoes); or "toad-in-the-hole" (sausages in a batter base).

Tea

It is no longer quite the rule that "everything stops for tea", but the ritual still holds sway in restaurants and hotels across the land. A "cream tea" involves the sinfully good combination of scones spread with jam and a lavish helping of thick or "clotted" cream. Otherwise, cakes and thinly sliced sandwiches of egg, cucumber, tomato, cress and smoked salmon are served. In Scotland and the north of England "high tea" means a complete evening meal.

All this, of course, accompanied by strong Indian or Ceylon teas, perhaps smoky Lapsang Souchong or scented Earl Grey. The English usually drink their tea with milk, but serve lemon when asked.

70,000) is a centre of social life. Only people 18 years or older can buy or consume alcoholic drinks in a bar or pub. However, where a special dining room has been set aside, children are admitted and if they are 16 or older may drink beer, wine or cider with their meals.

Lunchtime fare includes the "ploughman's lunch"—a plate of cheese, bread, salad and pickle (a kind of spicy

Dinner

A more elaborate restaurant meal may start with smoked salmon, a prawn (shrimp) cocktail, terrine or salad. In season you may find green asparagus, hot with hollandaise sauce or cold with vinaigrette. Rainy, raw weather calls for warming soups—thick and creamy or a light consommé laced with sherry.

Oysters and mussels from clean Atlantic waters are widely available. Grilled Dover sole and seabass can be excellent (and expensive). Trout and salmon (usually farmed) are on many menus.

For meat-eaters, roast beef comes with Yorkshire pudding, puffed-up portions of batter (like American popovers). Leg or saddle of lamb (usually well-done, so ask for it pink if you prefer) is traditionally served with tangy mint sauce or redcurrant jelly. Americans, Australians or South Africans may find steaks are sometimes small and disappointing. In the game season, wild duck, partridge, grouse and pheasant appear on some menus.

With main courses come seasonal vegetables—green beans, peas, Brussels sprouts, carrots, courgettes (zucchini), parsnips or cauliflower—and potatoes, perhaps roasted, "creamed" (mashed) or "jacket potatoes" (baked).

Dessert

Fruit of all kinds appears in tarts (with pastry below), pies (pastry above and below) or crumbles (with a top crust of crumbly pastry). "Fool" is a confection of cream and raspberries or gooseberries. "Summer" pudding lives up to its name: a concoction of stewed raspberries and redcurrants poured into a breadlined mould, chilled and dished up with whipped cream. Trifle is a complex compilation of sponge cake soaked in

A summertime favourite among adults as well as children, the ubiquitous cornet. Try it with a chocolate flake, known as a "99".

sherry, topped with fruit or jam, custard and cream. A winter treat is the rich dark Christmas pudding, studded with raisins, sultanas, and candied fruit. Other hot favourites: bread-and-butter pudding (baked with egg custard, sugar, cream, vanilla, sultanas and apricot jam), or its cousin, queen of puddings (bread crumbs mixed with milk and egg, flavoured with lemon or chocolate and baked with a meringue topping).

Cheeses traditionally follow dessert (though some people reverse the order) and are eaten with biscuits (crackers), or bread. Among the best: blue-veined Stilton, tangy mature Cheddar, red or white Cheshire and crumbly white Wensleydale.

Regional Specialities

Many dishes are much the same throughout the country, but each region has its local favourites:

London is generally too cosmopolitan to favour any speciality, but if you have a taste for eels, head for the East End markets where they are served stewed or jellied.

In the seafaring **West Country**, you can't go wrong with lobster, crab, or smoked mackerel. Fertile **East Anglia** yields a wealth of vegetables and fruit—strawberries, asparagus, peas, parsnips and new potatoes. Geese and turkeys are raised by the million. Seafood is plentiful: herrings and whitebait from Yarmouth and Lowestoft, or flat round oysters from Colchester, considered among the world's finest.

In the **Midlands**, Melton Mowbray is famed as the home of the pork pie—cuts of pork, veal, ox-tongue and hard-boiled egg baked in a pastry crust. Elvers (baby eels that look like bean sprouts) are served fried with onions and herbs as a spring delicacy. Derbyshire has its Bakewell tart: a rich almond-flavoured filling cooked in a deep-dish crust spread with raspberry jam.

The **North** is the home of potted seafood, preserved by a covering of clarified butter and eaten cold. Potted Tweed salmon or potted shrimps from Morecambe Bay are delicious spread on wholemeal bread or toast. Lancashire hot-pot is a beef and onion casserole topped with sliced potatoes and slowly oven-simmered.

Decoding the Menu

Many foods have different names in British and American English.

British	American
aubergine	eggplant
banger (slang)	sausage
bilberries	blueberries
biscuit	cookie cracker
black pudding	blood sausage
chips	french fries
courgettes	zucchini
crisps	potato chips
endive	chicory
fillet of beef	tenderloin steak
fizzy/still	sparkling/plain
jacket potato	baked potato
jam	preserve/jelly
main course	entree
marrow	squash
minced	ground
neat	straight (alcoholic drink)
pudding	dessert
spirits	liquor
starter	appetizer
sweet	dessert
wholemeal bread	whole-wheat bread

It may now be universal, but they thought of it in **Wales**: cheese melted with ale and mustard, piled on hot buttered toast and browned under the grill and called Welsh rarebit.

Welsh lamb is excellent and prepared inventively—barbecued or stuffed with apricots or walnuts and roasted. The leek is the national symbol of Wales. It crops up in soups (cream of leek), in pancakes, and in "flans" (cousins of quiche) with cheese. Soft, unripened Caerphilly is the main Welsh cheese. Laver, a reddish seaweed, can be served as a vegetable or mixed with oatmeal into a bread and fried for breakfast. *Bara brith* is a Welsh currant bread, best eaten warm from the oven.

Cock-a-leekie, **Scotland**'s national soup, is a hearty brew of chicken, leeks and prunes: Scotch broth is made with vegetables, mutton or beef and a thickening of barley. Scotch woodcock is no bird but a delicious "savoury" of toast spread with anchovy butter and topped with a creamy sauce. Salmon and seatrout come wild or farmed, fresh, smoked or as *gravadlax*. Look out for excellent langoustines, mussels, oysters and scallops. The land of the Aberdeen Angus is proud of its beef—a lot goes to London.

The grouse season opens on the "glorious 12th" of August. Other game, farmed or wild, includes pheasant, guinea fowl, quail, hare and venison.

If you have never tasted haggis, you should—before you consider what's in it. Scotland's most famous dish contains chopped sheep's innards, onions, beef suet and seasoning, stuffed into a sheep's stomach bag and boiled. Eat it as the Scots do, with "chappit tatties and bashed neeps"—mashed potatoes and turnips—and wash it down with a tot of whisky.

Crusty bread, scones, bannocks, pancakes and baps are a Scots delight. Old-fashioned oatcakes are eaten with butter, pâté, jam or crowdie, Scotland's centuries-old version of cottage cheese. The renowned buttery shortbread keeps so well that it's exported all over the world.

Cheeses to watch for: "Caboc", a Highland cream cheese coated in oatmeal; and "Hramsa", a cream cheese with herbs and garlic. Dundee, the birthplace of bitter-orange marmalade, also contributes a popular fruit cake ("Dundee cake").

Drinks

A casual pub crawl might convince you that beer is *the* national drink, but there's much more to lift the spirits, including excellent London gin and Scotch whisky.

Sherry is a popular apéritif, and some of the greatest brands are a legacy of the enterprising British families who emigrated to Jerez in southern Spain nearly two centuries ago.

Port was created in the 17th century when a heavy tax on French wines forced the British to turn to a Portuguese variety. This proved too harsh for their palates, and was eventually "fortified" with brandy and then aged. Port may be served with the cheese course or after a formal dinner for the toasts.

Gin evolved about the same time as port, and for the same reason—the prohibitive wine tax. Originally a medicinal brew from Holland, it became such a rage by the mid-18th century that

*E*normous copper
stills bubble away around the
clock to produce the golden
spirit that will eventually be
turned into Scotland's most
famous product—whisky. Many
distilleries run tours for
visitors, explaining the
whole process and offering
a "wee dram" or two to sample
at the end. Drivers should be
warned!

addicts were killing themselves with
spurious substitutes. Today English gins
are clear and pure spirits, with secret-
formula flavourings from such ingredients as coriander, cassia bark, orange
peel and—above all—juniper. Specify
your proportions of gin to vermouth if
you want an American-style dry martini
(or you may get all vermouth).

Beer remains the favourite. There is a
bewildering variety of brews, depending
on what region, town or pub you happen to be in. The preferred English beer

is "bitter", light amber-coloured with body and distinctive flavour given by malted barley, hops and yeast. Its alcoholic content is higher than American beers, and it is drunk at cellar temperature, which can also be disconcerting to Americans. Best when unpressurized, it should be "pulled" from the cask by a pump handle. Another type of beer known as "mild" is reddish in colour and tastes rather sweeter. "Stout" is heavier and almost black. What Americans and Germans call beer is "lager" to the British. Nowadays, with stiff drink-driving laws and health concerns, you can get bottled low-alcohol and no-alcohol beers in most pubs.

If you hit Scotland's **whisky** trail (*see* page 310), you will be regaled with all the folklore involved in its production, although it is generally conceded that the Irish invented whisky and set up distilleries in Scotland and Wales in the 16th century. Then the Scots, of course, did it their own way, producing spirits of such finesse that Scotch became the world's most famous whisky. Scotch is most often a blend of two kinds: malt whisky, meaning the barley is germinated and then dried before fermentation, and whiskies from other unmalted grains. While there are excellent blends, the purists and especially Highlanders recognize unblended malt whisky as the choice of discerning drinkers.

A speciality of the West Country, English **cider** is not only thirst-quenching but can pack a terrific punch. Golden-amber, sometimes sparkling, it may contain up to 8 per cent alcohol.

A number of intrepid English growers make acceptable white wines, but their output is just a drop in the barrel compared to the enormous quantity needed to satisfy the growing British taste for **wine**. You will not have any trouble finding a decent claret, as the British call red Bordeaux, as well as Burgundy and Beaujolais, Alsace and many other regional wines from France, mostly sweeter whites from Germany, and reds and whites from Italy and Spain. These traditional sources have been successfully challenged by reliable, and often superb, wines from Australia, New Zealand, California, Chile and South Africa and good, economical table wines from eastern Europe. Champagnes and other sparkling wines are very widely available.

Post-prandial **brandy** used to be offered with cigars to men at dinner parties, after the ladies had left the table to sip coffee in another room, but that custom is dying out. Restaurants offer a range of digestifs from cognac to liqueurs (including sweet, whisky-based varieties).

Tipping

A service charge of 10 to 15 per cent is included in most hotel bills. Many restaurants also add a service charge. Those that do not may add a note on the bill saying "Gratuities at your discretion", in which case a tip of 12–15 per cent will be expected. There is a growing tendency to leave spaces on credit card slips for you to enter a tip. (This practice is not unknown even where service has already been included.) Pub bar staff are not usually tipped. In informal eating places, you can just leave a few coins on the table.

Toilets

Look for the sign "Public Conveniences" or "WC" in railway stations and in museums and parks. If asking directions, simply inquire about the "toilets" or the "lavatory" (pronounced *lav*-a-tree) or the "loo". In Britain a bathroom is a room with a bathtub in it; a restroom means nothing at all; and if you should ask to "wash up", your hostess will refuse to permit it— "washing up" in Britain means washing the dishes.

Weights and Measures

The metric system is slowly inching its way into every walk of life, though many people still prefer the old Imperial weights and measures. Decimalization was adopted in 1971 for British currency, and those young enough to have been brought up with the system generally don't know what a shilling was. Cloth is sold by the metre and wine by the litre, but you always ask for beer in pints or "halves". Temperatures are officially quoted in Celsius (centigrade), but understood in Fahrenheit. Food is sold in both metric units and pounds (lbs) and ounces (oz). The gallon is disappearing, being replaced by the litre.

Festivals and Events

Most festivals and celebrations coincide with the summer season, though there is bound to be something going on

M orris dancers with bells, sticks and ribbons are supposed to bring luck by performing a ritual dating from pagan times.

whenever you visit. Local festivals feature some or all of the following cultural offerings: classical music, jazz, opera, drama, exhibitions, fringe events. A sample of annual events:

January *London International Boat Show* (Earl's Court Exhibition Centre, London SW5). *Cruft's Dog Show* (Earl's Court Exhibition Centre, London SW5).
March *Chelsea Antiques Fair* (Chelsea Old Town Hall, London SW3), *Cheltenham Gold Cup Meeting* (horse racing; Cheltenham).

*C**hoir practice in St David's Cathedral. Singing comes naturally to the Welsh, and is not reserved for Sundays. There's plenty at soccer and rugby matches too!*

March–April *Oxford and Cambridge University Boat Race* (River Thames, Putney to Mortlake), *Grand National Meeting* (horse racing; Aintree Racecourse, Liverpool). *Edinburgh International Folk Festival* (Edinburgh).
March–January *Royal Shakespeare*

Theatre Season (Stratford-upon-Avon). **April** *London Marathon* (Greenwich to Westminster).

May *Brighton International Festival* (Brighton), *Chelsea Flower Show* (Royal Hospital, London SW3), *Guineas Stakes* (horse racing; Newmarket), *Mayfest* (Glasgow), *Perth Festival of the Arts* (Perth).

May–June *Bath International Festival* (Bath), *Exeter Festival* (Exeter), *Malvern Festival* (Malvern), *Nottingham Festival* (Nottingham).

May–August *Glyndebourne Festival Opera Season* (Glyndebourne).

May–October *Pitlochry Festival Theatre Season* (Pitlochry).

June *The Derby* (horse racing; Epsom), *Trooping the Colour* (Horse Guards Parade, Whitehall, London SW1), *Greenwich Festival* (Greenwich, London SE10), *Royal Ascot* (horse racing; Ascot), *Aldeburgh Festival of Music and the Arts* (Aldeburgh), *Sevenoaks Summer Festival* (Sevenoaks). *Royal Scottish Automobile Club International Scottish Rally* (start and finish in Glasgow).

June–July *Wimbledon Lawn Tennis Championships* (Wimbledon, London SW19), *Henley Royal Regatta* (Henley-on-Thames), *Ludlow Festival* (Ludlow).

July *City of London Festival* (London), *Birmingham International Jazz Festival* (Birmingham), *British Grand Prix* (Silverstone), *Cambridge Festival* (Cambridge), *Chelsea Antiques Fair* (Chelsea, London), *Cheltenham International Festival of Music* (Cheltenham), *Chester Summer Music Festival* (Chester), *Chichester Festivities* (Chichester), *King's Lynn Festival of Music and the Arts* (King's Lynn), *Lichfield Festival and Fringe* (Lichfield), *Warwick Arts Festival* (Warwick), *York Early Music Festival* (York). *Open Golf Championship (moveable)*. *Llangollen International Musical Eisteddfod* (Llangollen).

July–August *Buxton International Festival* (Buxton), *Harrogate International Festival* (Harrogate).

July–September *Henry Wood Promenade Concerts* (Royal Albert Hall, London SW7), *Summerscope on the South Bank* (South Bank Centre, London SE1).

August *Three Choirs Festival* (Gloucester). *Edinburgh International Jazz Festival* (Edinburgh). *Royal National Eisteddfod of Wales*.

August–September *Arundel Festival* (Arundel). *Edinburgh International Festival* (Edinburgh), *Edinburgh Military Tattoo* (Edinburgh Castle).

September *Salisbury Festival* (Salisbury), *St Leger Festival Meeting* (horse racing; Doncaster). *Braemar Royal Highland Gathering* (Braemar), *Pitlochry Highland Games* (Pitlochry). *North Wales Music Festival* (St Asaph).

September–October *Cheltenham Festival of Literature* (Cheltenham), *Windsor Festival* (Windsor).

October *Horse of the Year Show* (Wembley Arena, Wembley), *Canterbury Festival* (Canterbury), *Norfolk and Norwich French Festival* (Norwich). *Swansea Musical Festival* (Swansea).

November *Lord Mayor's Procession and Show* (City of London), *London to Brighton Veteran Car Run* (from Hyde Park, London, to Brighton). *Royal Automobile Club International Rally*.

November–December *Cardiff Festival of Music* (St David's Hall, Cardiff).

December *International Showjumping Championships* (Olympia, London W14).

Distance Chart (miles)

	Aberdeen	Bath	Birmingham	Bristol	Cambridge	Canterbury	Cardiff	Dover	Edinburgh	Exeter	Glasgow	Inverness	Liverpool	London	Manchester	Oxford	Penzance	Plymouth	Southampton	Stratford
Bath	523																			
Birmingham	430	97																		
Bristol	511	13	85																	
Cambridge	468	174	101	178																
Canterbury	610	177	186	187	114															
Cardiff	532	56	107	45	213	218														
Dover	626	200	203	198	121	16	233													
Edinburgh	127	384	293	373	337	451	393	457												
Exeter	584	85	157	81	255	233	120	246	446											
Glasgow	149	384	291	372	349	472	393	490	45	444										
Inverness	105	544	453	532	500	632	558	648	159	610	171									
Liverpool	361	195	98	178	205	281	200	295	225	250	221	385								
London	537	116	117	119	60	61	155	77	401	199	400	569	210							
Manchester	354	181	88	167	153	268	188	283	218	239	214	378	34	197						
Oxford	498	66	63	74	80	131	109	148	362	152	355	518	165	56	154					
Penzance	690	213	278	195	368	345	232	365	556	121	563	722	370	312	358	265				
Plymouth	624	141	199	125	297	275	164	287	488	45	486	651	294	244	281	193	80			
Southampton	567	64	128	75	132	131	122	155	433	121	429	596	237	78	224	65	227	149		
Stratford	461	71	24	75	99	171	99	188	324	150	319	478	124	95	116	48	264	192	107	
York	332	236	128	221	157	258	241	274	195	291	208	360	101	209	71	185	406	340	252	154

A popular event at the Highland games is tossing the caber, a tapered fir pole 5m (17ft) long and weighing 40kg (90lbs).

Island of Traditions—and a Host of Surprises

Once, you knew what to expect of Britain and the British. Dull cooking, polite policemen, bowler hats, and rain alternating with fog. The supposed national character came in clichés too: "stiff upper lip", "the old school tie", "it's not cricket, old chap", "it just isn't *done*". A lot has changed. You can eat much better these days. People are generally more casual and relaxed, but many of the old certainties have recently been thrown into doubt, starting with the role of the royal family. Even the British weather won't fit the standard image—there have been a few violent storms lately, and some hot, dry summers.

Although average standards of living have risen steadily, Britain today is a more fragmented society than it once was, with whole groups and regions asserting their differences. Particularly in England, the quality of education provided by the state has not kept up with the rest of western Europe. Parents who can afford it tend to send their children to private schools, perpetuating the class-consciousness that pervades British society. You may be oblivious to the workings of the system

*T*he circle and avenue of giant stones at Avebury, Wiltshire, are even older and more mysterious than the better-known Stonehenge.

at first, but once aware, you will find it as endlessly fascinating as do the British. Yet the British are far more tolerant than they used to be. Increased travel on their part, visitors and immigrants, and television exposure to other customs mean that differences won't cause the raised eyebrows they once did.

Change for its own sake strikes the British as a highly subversive notion. They like clutter, comfort and things with memories attached to them and hate most modern architecture. There's still resistance to metrication, initiated back in the 1970s. The drinking man, for one, has no intention of giving up his pint. Most fraught of all is the issue of integration into Europe, a place that begins, in the British view, on the *other* side of the Channel, tunnel or no

What's in a Name?

Where are you going? Is it to England, Britain, Great Britain or the United Kingdom? Or the British Isles? What about Wales, Scotland and the different parts of Ireland? Some of the British themselves get into a mess about this, and seriously annoy the others. To pass through the minefield, remember:

1. The United Kingdom (UK) is the political entity made up of England + Wales + Scotland + Northern Ireland.

2. The first three of these comprise Great Britain, so called long ago to distinguish the island from Brittany in France. People shorten this to Britain, many mistaking the "Great" for a reference to world status. "The British Isles" is a geographical term, meaning Great Britain and the whole of Ireland.

3. England means England and does not include Wales or Scotland.

4. Most inhabitants don't mind being called British, but the Welsh must not be called English; nor must the Scots (not "Scotch"—a word restricted largely to whisky, broth and mist).

tunnel. If they refer to "Europe", they usually do not mean to include the UK, and if they talk of "The Continent", they certainly don't. The newspaper headline "Fog in Channel, Continent Cut Off" may be apocryphal, but it embodies a real attitude.

Take your Pick

For visitors, Britain's many attractions are cast on an epic scale. A five-hour train journey from south to north traverses a whole continent of landscapes, from England's smoothly contoured expanses to the rugged grandeur of the Scottish Highlands.

In the South-East, millennia of cultivation have tamed the land. Orchards, fields of hops and wheat stretch across the Weald from Kent into Sussex, and flocks of sheep graze the chalk downs.

More rolling downland and rich farmland exists in the counties of the South—Hampshire, Wiltshire and Dorset—full of memories of Thomas Hardy's rustic characters. It's all perfectly pastoral, but you don't have to travel far to feel London's commercial and cultural pull.

Windswept moors, rocky coves and sea-battered headlands add to the appeal of the south-western peninsula. Little visited by foreigners, Somerset, Devon and Cornwall live from farming, fishing—and British tourism.

Eastern England's wide skies and flat Fens—marshland reclaimed, like coastal areas of Holland, from the sea—inspired John Constable's art. A rural peace reigns inland, far from the container ports of Felixstowe and Lowestoft.

The country's heartland takes in Oxford and its colleges and Shakespeare's Stratford, the industrial cities of the Midlands and the peaks and dales of Derbyshire. Wales, in turn, offers the contrasts of its Celtic language and customs, while castles, mountains, valleys and a 965km (600-mile) coastline make for a change of scene.

The craggy Pennines—England's spine—slope away to the Lake District's "bare grey dell, high wood, and pastoral cove" (in William Wordsworth's words), and to the bleak yet beautiful North York Moors. Hadrian's Wall near the Scottish border is a coast-to-coast monument to the Roman conquest.

Scotland's lowlands claim the big cities of Edinburgh and Glasgow and 75 per cent of the population. The Highland glens, lochs and snow-capped heights are, by contrast, wild, remote and romantic.

Heritage Business

The British revel in the countryside, although the overwhelming majority live in towns and can only dream of a country cottage, let alone a country estate. "The stately homes of England", run the words of a Noël Coward song, "How beautiful they stand". Today you have to be a rock star or an Arab prince to afford the upkeep on one of the really great houses, and many hereditary owners have had to sell up—or open up. The late Marquess of Bath, pioneer of the "stately homes" business, hit on the idea of opening his 16th-century Longleat House to the public shortly after World War II. Hundreds of other aristocrats followed suit.

The British may not have exploited their considerable inventiveness as dynamically as the Japanese, or with German efficiency, but they are brilliant at marketing their heritage. They have sold the Americans everything from the *Queen Mary* to London Bridge (not the original, medieval structure, but a rather ugly Victorian replacement). Demand is also high worldwide for second-hand black taxis and red phone boxes, for chintz, tweeds, shooting sticks and all the accoutrements of the country-house lifestyle.

Old stereotypes die hard—the bluff, warm-hearted Yorkshireman, chipper Cockney, eloquent Welshman and canny Scot, but with more than 2 million Commonwealth and other immigrants Britain has become a multicultural society.

The Empire may be only a memory, but the nation of Shakespeare and Dickens, the King James Bible and Oxford English Dictionary has never relinquished cultural leadership of the English-speaking world. British publishing and broadcasting set international standards of excellence. The same goes for opera, dance and theatre, and the dynamic pop scene has been evolving ever since the heyday of the Beatles.

The very concept of sport is virtually a British invention, though the country that taught the world to play everything from cricket to tennis is often beaten at its own games. No longer in the first division of the economic league either,

---

British People

Successive waves of invaders and settlers populated the British Isles: Celts in prehistoric times; empire-building Romans; Angles, Saxons and Danes; conquering Norman French in 1066 (the best-known date in English history); Huguenots fleeing religious wars; and Dutch engineers and farmers. Later, Jewish refugees came from Russia and Eastern Europe, and did spectacularly well in business, the professions and the arts. Britain traditionally offered sanctuary, and only in recent decades put up obstacles, pleading shortage of space and jobs.

The most recent immigrants came from the former empire, in particular the West Indies, India, Pakistan and Bangladesh. Their communities have been established long enough for there to be a large, British-born, second generation, and the big cities are indisputably multiethnic. Racial or religious discrimination is illegal, and people get on well enough face to face, but you may hear jokes or disparaging remarks aimed in any and every direction. It is safest to be non-committal yourself.

An English ideal home. Cottages can be draughty and impractical, with low beams and oddly shaped rooms, but their charm is legendary.

the British can only be philosophical. Despite perennial balance of payments problems, a shrunken share of world trade and other disappointments, they take their occasional successes as proof that, after all, they are still a world power. A blind faith, in turn maddening or amusing to foreigners, reassures them that things will turn out all right in the end. They are quite sure that their TV is the best, their advertising the most ingenious, their countryside the most beautiful in the world. Unlike some other countries, you will rarely be asked how you like Britain.

History

Britain was not always an island. Until as recently as 7,000 years ago, it was joined to the rest of Europe by a land bridge. Nomadic hunters had followed this route for several hundred thousand years, venturing ever farther in search of game. They wandered the tundra and the great forests that evolved in its place—opening a network of trackways as they went. Some of the tracks survive as footpaths to this day: Wiltshire's Ridgeway Path, for example, and Peddar's Way in East Anglia. At the close of the Ice Age, rising seas made Ireland and then Britain into islands.

Around 4000 BC, newcomers from Europe began farming and breeding cattle. Pottery-making and weaving developed and trade evolved, along with a tribal organization of society. By 3000 BC Britain's first monuments were going up: megalithic chambered tombs, standing stones and the circular constructions known as henges.

Britain emerged from the Stone Age some time in the 2nd millennium BC, when the technology of bronze-smelting was introduced. Local deposits of

copper and tin were mined early on, and a lively trade grew up with the Continent. Powerful chieftains in the Salisbury Plain area organized ambitious building works at Avebury and Stonehenge, great stone circles that remain an enigma to this day. Were they temples, burial complexes or astronomical observatories?

From the 8th century BC onwards Britain experienced a flood of Celtic immigration from mainland Europe, as one tribe followed on the heels of another. By the 7th century BC, some of the incomers were brandishing weapons of iron. Hill forts proliferated as settlement—and conflict—spread and the Celts put down roots in every part of Britain and Ireland too.

A final incursion of Celts began around 200 BC as warriors of the Belgae tribe overran the south-east. Superior horsemanship and the skilled use of the chariot in battle ensured their success. These were troubled times for Britain. The Celts, a notoriously quarrelsome lot, fought constantly with each other. Nothing could bring them together— not even the Roman threat.

Roman Britain

Julius Caesar himself led the first Roman expedition to Britain in 55 BC. The Belgae met his advance on the beach near Deal, but they were no match for the legionaries. After a second campaign the following year, the southern tribes submitted to Rome and made tribute payments. Caesar sailed back to Gaul in triumph. In the short term little changed for the warring Britons, but the Romans returned to stay when Emperor Claudius mounted a large-scale invasion of Britain in AD 43. They built roads and founded cities such as *Camulodunum* (Colchester), *Londinium* (London), *Glevum* (Gloucester) and *Eboracum* (York). They introduced a money economy, expanded agriculture (sheep-farming was a Roman innovation) and encouraged the leather, timber and wool industries.

Initially, imperial rule was confined to south and central England. Control of Wales and the north of England came later, after more than 30 years of campaigning. The Scottish lowlands

Clouds gather over the poetic ensemble of Stonehenge. Its builders (starting nearly 40 centuries ago) directed its axis precisely to the rising sun at the summer solstice.

were subdued, too, but not for long—the fiercely independent Celts saw to that. By AD 122 the Romans withdrew to the line marked by Hadrian's Wall, which lies close to the present Scottish-English border.

At its peak, Roman Britain had a population of around 2 million, with 50,000 concentrated in London. City dwellers enjoyed paved streets, a piped water supply, temples and public baths. On hundreds of rural estates, great villas like Lullingstone and Fishbourne went up, all with central heating and baths. Prosperity continued into the 4th century, a turbulent period for the rest of the empire. Christianity slowly gained a foot-hold.

Saxons, Angles, Jutes and Danes

Roman rule in Britain was challenged in the year 367, when Picts from Scotland and Scots from Ireland breached the northern and western defences. In the century that followed, as Roman power declined, raids were stepped up. The Romanized Britons appealed for help to the "barbarian" Saxons, who were only too happy to oblige. They made quick work of the Picts and Scots, with a little help from their friends the Angles and Jutes. Success was so easy that they went on to call in other Saxons and subsequently expanded their hold on the island.

No mean architect, Emperor Hadrian himself designed the wall that sealed off rebellious Scotland from the north of 2nd-century Roman Britain.

Local forces rallied under the command of a leader called Artorius—model for King Arthur of Round Table fame, or so they say. But it was a lost cause. The barbarians stayed and settled, mixing with what remained of the native population. (Many Britons had been killed and many more fled to Cornwall, Wales and distant Brittany. The cities the Romans founded fell into decay. After a while, few remembered who had built them.)

In the 6th and 7th centuries, several Anglo-Saxon kingdoms rose to power in England. Kent in the south-east achieved an early dominance, then Northumbria and midland Mercia.

Arthur: Man or Myth?

Yes, there really was an Arthur, although he may not have been a king. A general, perhaps, or more romantically, a resistance hero who defended Britain to the death.

The historical facts are few and disputed. It seems that a war leader named Artorius—a Briton, a Christian and a Roman citizen—raised troops to fight the pagan barbarians in the aftermath of the Anglo-Saxon invasion. He probably directed the great victory at an unidentified place called Mons Badonicus around the year 500, stemming the Anglo-Saxon tide for several decades. A final encounter with the invaders took place at the Battle of Camlan, and ended in defeat for the Britons and death for Artorius. The date, 537, appears in the history books with a question mark.

The legendary court of Camelot was the creation of the medieval writers Geoffrey of Monmouth and Chrétien de Troyes, and their tales of adultery, incest and murder inspired Sir Thomas Malory's 1469 *Morte d'Arthur*.

Wales and Scotland stayed independent, though often influenced by events in England. The house of Gwynedd had begun to assert itself over the lesser kingdoms of Wales, while Picts and Scots vied for control of Scotland.

Christianity made inroads in England, thanks to the work of St Augustine. The kingdom of Kent was the first to convert (597); consequently Canterbury became the seat of the archbishop. Celtic missionaries spread the gospel to the north, founding the great monasteries of Iona, Lindisfarne and Jarrow, and by 650 or thereabouts most of the Anglo-Saxons had been baptized.

Raids from northern Europe were far from over. At the end of the 8th century, Viking sea-rovers—Danes and Norwegians—descended on Britain's coasts, creating havoc and terror. The Danes concentrated on the east, spreading inland during the 9th century to establish a region known as the "Danelaw". Alfred the Great, King of Wessex, contained Danish expansion at Edington in 878 and his son, Edward the Elder, and grandson, Athelstan, reconquered the Danelaw. Athelstan (d. 939) was the first king to rule all of England. Even Welsh and Scottish sovereigns swore personal allegiance to Alfred and his heirs, setting a precedent of Anglo-Saxon supremacy. Long before the word "democracy" entered the vocabulary, the Anglo-Saxon kings were consulting with their nobles, or "thegns", at meetings of a council called the Witan. The kings standardized coinage and administration, dividing England into shires (precursors of today's counties), each of which had its own officials and courts. The villages, churches and manors of rural England took shape in Anglo-Saxon times, and merchants and artisans came together in towns.

England suffered another round of Danish raids late in the 10th century. Unprepared to fight, the ineffectual King Ethelred the Unready followed a policy of appeasement. His attempts to buy off the Danish king, Sweyn Forkbeard, bankrupted the country. Ethelred fled into exile and Sweyn briefly took over. Sweyn's son Canute subsequently became King of England (1016–35), ruling also over Denmark (from 1018) and Norway (1028). But the Scandinavians lost hold when Canute died, making way for yet another invasion.

In 1066 the Normans, who were led by William the Conqueror, stormed across the Channel and defeated the forces of Harold, England's elected king. Since the Normans' victory at the Battle of Hastings, no foreign power has ever succeeded in conquering this island kingdom.

Normans Take Over

Duke William was crowned King of England at Westminster Abbey on Christmas Day, 1066, but not many people took gladly to his rule. English resistance was fierce at Exeter, Durham, York and, last bastion to fall, Ely in East Anglia (1071). The Saxon hero Hereward the Wake held out here for months—until William built a causeway through the marshes and flushed him out.

With the Normans came a new Latin influence that profoundly affected Anglo-Saxon culture. French became the official language and it remained supreme in court circles until the late

14th century. William's survey of land tenure for taxation, the Domesday Book, provides a unique record of the times. Success in England fuelled William's hopes of conquest in Wales, but he hadn't reckoned on the mountainous terrain and Celtic resolve. For decades Welsh princes and Norman barons struggled for control of the border territory, or Marches.

On his death, William the Conqueror entrusted England to his son, William Rufus. Normandy went to another son, Robert. Their younger brother Henry eventually ended up with both, thus joining England's fortunes to those of

William, Duke of Normandy led the last successful opposed invasion of England in 1066, possibly the best remembered date in English history.

France. But Henry left no male heirs. Only after years of bitter civil war was the right to the throne of his daughter's son, another Henry, established.

House of Plantagenet

Henry II (1154–89) was not only King of England and Duke of Normandy, but also Count of Anjou, through his father Henry Plantagenet. As such he ruled all of western France down to the Pyrenees. Coupling a strong Norman monarchy with the Anglo-Saxon traditions of local rule at shire and borough level, Henry brought peace and prosperity to England.

It wasn't all easy going for Henry. There was the public outcry over Thomas Becket's murder in 1170 (*see below*)—and the private conflict with his own family, who conspired against him. Henry weathered the Becket incident: however much he may have wished the Archbishop of Canterbury dead, he hadn't held the "dripping knife". He went on to new victories with the conquest of Ireland (1172). However, the rebellions of his wife, Eleanor of Aquitaine, and their four sons became a source of permanent grief towards the end of his life. Henry's preference for his youngest son, John, instigated one last revolt by Richard, his oldest surviving son, in 1188. The old king died, defeated, and Richard (the Lionheart) gained the throne.

The English developed the habit of governing themselves during Richard's ten-year reign. The king spent most of his time abroad, on the Third Crusade and at war in France. It was almost inevitable that Richard would die in battle. His autocratic brother John (1199–1216) was derided as John "Lackland",

Murder in the Cathedral

Thomas Becket was a worldly cleric when Henry II made him his Lord Chancellor in 1155. An old and trusted friend, Becket served the king well—so well that Henry promoted him to archbishop seven years later. To Henry's surprise, Becket took his new job seriously, becoming an avid champion of the Church. The specific issues—the king's right to try clergy who had committed civil offences in civil courts, for example—were less important than the broader principle of absolute royal authority. A power struggle between Church and state was on.

Henry never expected anyone to take him literally when he asked, "Who will rid me of this turbulent priest?" Unfortunately, four knights acted on the king's words, murdering Becket in cold blood in Canterbury Cathedral. With a few sword thrusts, they created a martyr and a saint. To this day, the date—29 December 1170—is commemorated in the Christian calendar.

The deed sent shock waves through medieval Christendom. Henry visited the scene of the crime and did public penance. Scourging—a symbolic punishment in the king's case—didn't hurt half as much as the concessions forced on him by the pope. Overnight Canterbury turned into a place of pilgrimage. People came by the thousands to visit the martyr's tomb. Just touching it could cure disease, they said. Miracles were reported until 1547, when Henry VIII ordered the shrine destroyed.

T S Eliot has the last word in his play *Murder in the Cathedral*, a dramatization of Becket's assassination performed for the first time in the Chapter House at Canterbury Cathedral in 1935:

For wherever a saint has dwelt, wherever a martyr has given his blood for the blood of Christ,
There is holy ground, and sanctity shall not depart from it
Though armies trample over it, though sightseers come with guide-books looking over it.

the inept king who lost the Crown's Norman possessions in a series of disastrous campaigns. By 1204, with only the Channel Islands left to his name, John returned to England and clashed with both Church and his barons.

Unreasonable taxes and disregard for feudal custom endeared John to few of his subjects. When a new expedition to France was a failure, rebellion erupted. In 1215 the king was forced to bow to the noblemen assembled in the meadow of Runnymede, near Windsor, and set his seal to the Magna Carta. This historic breakthrough in the struggle against absolute power subordinated the Crown to the law. The document eventually came to be regarded as England's charter of liberties.

Parliament, that great British political institution, developed into a representative assembly during the 13th century. Under Edward I (1272–1307), a total of 45 sessions were called. Increasingly, participation was extended not only to the nobility and the Church, but also to the burghers and yeomen—the "commons".

The forceful Edward moved the country a step closer to becoming a United Kingdom with his conquest of Wales (1281). To control the rebellious Welsh, Edward ordered construction of a string of castles: Conwy, Caernarfon, Criccieth and Harlech. His son, the young Edward, born at Caernarfon, was named Prince of Wales, a title granted to the heir to the throne ever

Romanticized by Shakespeare, Henry V and his archers with their longbows won a famous victory over the French at Agincourt.

since. Edward I also brought Ireland under tighter control but Scotland fought to stay free of English domination. It was a great day for the Scots when Robert Bruce triumphed at Bannockburn (1314).

The Welsh and Scottish campaigns were the prelude to a century of conflict on the Continent. The Hundred Years' War between England and France broke out in 1337. Edward III's claim to the French throne was the main bone of contention. Edward and his son, the Black Prince, masterminded several stunning English victories in the 1340s and '50s: Crécy, Calais, Poitiers; and Henry V and his archers prevailed at

Agincourt (1415). But the French finally won out in 1453.

More devastating than any war, the Black Death invaded Britain in the 14th century, taking an appalling toll of lives. The first epidemic of 1348 spread from the seaports in the south to Wales, Scotland and Ireland. It was followed by three more outbreaks later in the century. In a few decades, the population of Britain fell by perhaps 40 per cent. Landowners blanched at the high wages they had to pay a vastly reduced work-force. The Peasant's Revolt of 1381 was suppressed, but not before the poor of England had run riot from Kent to Yorkshire.

Lancaster vs York

Henry Bolingbroke, Duke of Lancaster, a grandson of King Edward III, deposed the tyrannical Richard II. Richard died in prison, probably on Henry's orders, and the duke ruled as Henry IV (1399–1413). Once he had gained the throne, Henry was forced to defend it by force of arms. Shakespeare immortalized Henry's struggle with the words: "Uneasy lies the head that wears a crown."

By this time, people of all classes had begun to converse in English—derived from Germanic and Scandinavian dialects, with an admixture of French. John Wycliffe's translation of the Bible did much to popularize the language, along with Geoffrey Chaucer's medieval best-seller, *The Canterbury Tales*, although literacy continued to be the prerogative of the aristocracy and the Church.

With the accession of Prince Hal (Henry V) and his son Henry VI in turn, the Lancastrian line seemed set for a long run, but the dynasty proved as unstable as Henry VI's mental health. When Henry suffered a complete breakdown in 1453, a rival, Richard Duke of York, took the reins of power. A bloody civil war known as the War of the Roses (1455–85) pitted the House of York (the white rose) against the House of Lancaster (the red rose). Richard of York died before he could gain the throne, but his son Edward continued the struggle. He imprisoned Henry in the Tower of London in 1461, and had himself crowned Edward IV.

The Lancastrians managed to spring the befuddled Henry from his cell in 1470, forcing Edward into exile. He in turn made a swift comeback the following year, and held on to power until his death 12 years later. His ambitious brother Richard, Duke of Gloucester, was appointed Protector and took custody of his young nephews, Edward and Richard, the "Little Princes in the Tower". When shortly afterwards the boys died in suspicious circumstances, most people pointed the finger at their uncle, the new Richard III.

Against a backcloth of foreign wars, plague and dynastic struggles, England grew to economic greatness. Agricultural land was fenced in for sheep-farming in Suffolk, the Cotswolds, the Welsh Marches and the north of England. The wool industry generated fabulous wealth, creating a new class of rich merchants and landed gentry. This commerce in wool also contributed to the nation's developing maritime power. It was English ships that carried raw wool, and later finished cloth, from the ports of Bristol and London to markets in the Low Countries.

The two-year reign of the hunchback Richard III ended with Henry Tudor's victory at Bosworth Field in Leicestershire in 1485. The winner joined the red rose to the white through his marriage to Edward IV's daughter, Elizabeth of York. The Tudor dynasty were to rule the kingdom of England and Wales for the next 118 years.

The Tudors

A shrewd statesman, Henry VII forged an alliance with Spain, Europe's rising power, through the marriage of his eldest son Arthur to Catherine of Aragon, youngest daughter of King Ferdinand and Queen Isabella. Another marriage, between Henry's daughter Margaret and King James IV of Scotland, brought a thaw in relations with England's northern neighbour. A good manager, Henry harnessed the power of the nobility and streamlined government. To his second son and namesake went the considerable fruits of Henry's labours.

Henry VIII (1509–47) was a playboy of 18 when he came to the throne, but he matured into a ruthless ruler with a talent for choosing ministers of the stature of Cardinal Wolsey, Archbishop Cranmer and Sir Thomas Cromwell. From the start, Henry developed a taste for power politics. He joined the Holy Alliance against France and distinguished himself in the field in 1513. The Scots, honouring their "auld alliance" with France, attacked England through the back door. The ensuing battle at Flodden saw the English crush the Scots. About 10,000 were killed, including King James IV himself. His wife (and Henry's sister) Margaret took over as regent for her year-old son, James V

The Marriage-Go-Round

Henry VIII literally moved heaven and earth to dispose of his first wife and marry his paramour, Anne Boleyn. Alas for Henry, Anne turned into a shrew once they'd tied the knot. Henry's patience with her ran out after less than three years of life together, when a miscarriage followed the birth of a daughter. Arrested on trumped-up charges in 1536, Anne ended her career on the executioner's block.

With her successor, Jane Seymour, Henry was third time lucky. Not only did she make a loving wife, she also produced the desired son, Edward, in 1537. Unfortunately, complications from the birth claimed Jane's life 11 days later.

Marriage number four, to Anne of Cleves, was an affair of state: Henry couldn't conceal his loathing for the "Flanders mare". By refusing to consummate the misalliance, he simplified annulment proceedings. Free again, Henry rushed the flirtatious Catherine Howard to the altar, but their love soon went sour. The king took exception to the adultery of his 22-year-old bride and ordered her beheaded.

The following year a widow named Catherine Parr came into Henry's life. She was 31 and no beauty, but by then the ageing king needed a nursemaid as much as a wife. Their marriage—her third and his sixth—lasted until his death did them part in 1547.

the king with a male heir. Obsessed with the succession, and infatuated with Anne Boleyn, Henry decided to have his marriage dissolved. Negotiations with the Church quickly foundered. It so happened that the pope was taking orders from Catherine's nephew—and Europe's most powerful ruler—the Emperor Charles V. About this time, the teachings of Martin Luther began to spread to England. Precipitating events, Henry rebelled against Rome. Parliament, meeting over a seven-year period from 1529, saw to the legalities. The king was declared head of the Church of England. For members of the government, refusal to sanction the crucial Act of Supremacy was a life and death matter. The principled Lord Chancellor, Sir Thomas More, for one, was tried for treason and beheaded.

In 1536, England's monasteries began closing their doors under provisions of the Act of Suppression. Monks and nuns were pensioned off, and Church property was seized and sold piecemeal to pay for Henry's military adventures, unleashing a social revolution. Great manor houses rose on former abbey lands, vast tracts of which were committed to sheep pasturage.

The famous divorce was granted by Archbishop Cranmer in 1533. It came just in time. Within months Anne Boleyn gave birth to a daughter, Elizabeth.

Henry VIII's reign marks a watershed in English history. Suddenly, or so it would seem, people emerged from the Middle Ages into the light of modern times. The intellectual ferment of the Renaissance had reached England, setting the stage for a flowering of letters and the arts.

of Scotland and an uneasy peace settled on the English-Scottish border.

Henry's choice of Catherine of Aragon for a wife (the pope annulled her marriage to Arthur, who had died as a boy of 15) was as calculated as his decision to divorce her 16 years later. By 1525, it had become painfully clear that Catherine, then 42, would never provide

Henry VIII by Holbein.

Protestant regents were the power behind the consumptive boy-king Edward VI (1547–53). One regent, Lord Northumberland, attempted to secure the succession for Lady Jane Grey, a Protestant granddaughter of Henry VIII—and Northumberland's own daughter-in-law. Edward colluded in the plot, but when he died, the rightful heir, Catherine of Aragon's daughter Mary, pressed her claim and cut short Lady Jane's nine-day "reign" on the block.

A devout Catholic, "Bloody Mary" tried to turn back the clock. She restored the Roman confession and had hundreds of Protestants, including several bishops, burned at the stake. Against all advice, the queen pursued an unpopular (and loveless) marriage with a Spanish prince, the future Philip II, involving England in another costly war with France. Relief was universal when she died.

An outpouring of affection greeted Elizabeth I on her accession in 1558. The Virgin Queen was only 25, but she knew how to survive. Raised in an atmosphere of political intrigue and constant peril, she looked first to security—her own and that of her country. Elizabeth had one serious rival for the crown: her Catholic cousin Mary Stuart, the deposed Queen of Scots. Exiled in England, Mary inevitably became involved in Catholic plots to overthrow Elizabeth. Although stability was returning to religious and political life, Elizabeth wasn't taking any chances. She put Mary under permanent house arrest in 1569. Eighteen years later, with a Spanish invasion threatening, the queen reluctantly consented to the execution of her cousin. Mary's 21-year-old son, the Protestant James VI of Scotland, moved to the top of the queue of Elizabeth's potential successors.

The struggle with Spain dominated Elizabeth's reign. Despite public denials, the queen gave tacit support to the freelance activities of England's privateers—the illegal slaving expeditions of John Hawkins and Sir Francis Drake's raids on the Spanish Main. In 1580 Drake went on to circumnavigate the globe, ending Spain's monopoly of the seas. The turning point for England came in 1588 with the defeat of Spain's fleet, the Invincible Armada. The outcome depended as much on adverse weather conditions as naval superiority, but it was no less decisive for that. England took on the status of a world power, and London, developed into a great commercial centre with interests in Europe, America and the Orient. A golden age of literature had already begun, marked by the achievements of Francis Bacon, Ben Jonson, Christopher Marlowe and, above all, William Shakespeare.

Revolution and Restoration

James VI of Scotland ascended the English throne as James I (1603–25), joining the two realms under one crown, although separate legislatures would be maintained for two centuries. James is remembered mainly for his narrow escape from death by assassination in the abortive Gunpowder Plot (1605). Guy Fawkes was within hours of blowing up Parliament with the king in attendance when the conspiracy was uncovered. The plot was religiously motivated: Fawkes was a Catholic, and for a long time afterwards Catholics in Britain were subject to persecution for their "papist treachery".

There was discrimination, too, against Protestant extremists, especially the Puritan Separatists. Thousands of members of this religious splinter group left for a new life in America. The *Mayflower* led the way in 1620, sailing from the West Country port of Plymouth, with the Pilgrim Fathers on board. About this time, Protestants from England and Scotland began to move into Ulster. They settled on land confiscated from Irish Catholics, with consequences that are felt to this day.

Like his father James, Charles I resisted Parliament's growing power and plunged the country into civil war. In 1642 the Royalists or "Cavaliers"—supported by the aristocracy and the Church—fought Parliamentary forces (the Roundheads), backed by the merchants, tradesmen and Puritans. The sympathies of the landed gentry were divided between the two.

After some early successes, Charles went down in defeat at Naseby in 1645. Four years later he was publicly executed outside his palace at Whitehall. The man behind the coup, the dour Oliver Cromwell, seized power and forced the warring factions together, declaring himself Lord Protector. But the country grew disenchanted with Cromwell's dreary Puritan rule. After his death the monarchy was restored under Charles II (1660–85), the "Merry Monarch", a great theatre-goer and art collector.

Anxious not to be sent "travelling" again, Charles proved an amenable (if dissolute) king. He restored the Church of England and came down on the side of reason. After decades of strife, theological debate gave way to science, led by Isaac Newton with his contributions to the fields of mathematics, gravity and optics.

Three successive disasters marked the first decade of Charles's reign: the Great Plague, the Great Fire of London and a Dutch attack on Thames shipping. The Puritans, shocked at the moral laxity of the king and court, attributed the run of bad luck to divine retribution. Others blamed a papist plot. In fact, Charles *was* a closet Catholic, but he waited until he was on his deathbed to embrace the faith.

His brother James wasn't as sensible. Declaring his Roman faith and French sympathies, James II attacked the Church of England and disregarded the law of the land. Parliament forced him to abdicate and flee the country after only three years. The Glorious Revolution of 1688 brought the Protestant William of Orange (a grandson of Charles I) and his wife Mary Stuart (daughter of James II) jointly to the throne and gave England a stable constitutional monarchy at last. The Bill of Rights finally and officially abolished absolutism and established the supremacy of Parliament.

There was no open opposition to him in England, though William had to put down a rising of James II's Catholic supporters in Scotland. In 1690 James sailed to Ireland from exile in France for a showdown with his son-in-law at the Battle of the Boyne near Dublin. William and the Orangemen, aided by troops from other Protestant nations, came out the clear winners. To this day the anniversary (12 July) is celebrated by the Protestants of Northern Ireland.

Fighting broke out again when William's old enemy, Louis XIV, put his grandson on the throne of Spain (1701). William died and his successor and sister-in-law, Queen Anne (1702–14), appointed John Churchill, Duke of Marlborough, as commander-in-chief. A brilliant tactician, the duke led the Grand Alliance of several Protestant countries to an upset victory over the French in the War of the Spanish Succession (1701–13). Marlborough's reward, Blenheim Palace, was named after the place in the Netherlands where the first great victory of the war took place.

The 1707 Act of Union formalized the merger of England and Scotland accomplished a century before. Henceforth there would be one flag and one parliament, with the Scots represented as a minority in the two houses in Westminster. The Scots accepted the Hanoverian succession, but kept their own courts and legal system, and their national Presbyterian Church.

Georgian Period

The first King George (1714–27) gained the throne by virtue of his Stuart blood and Protestant faith, but the German from Hanover never bothered to learn English. Parliament was firmly in the driver's seat now, and party rivalries (Tory vs Whig) dominated the political scene. Some of the conservative Tories favoured the "Old Pretender", James II's son, and fell into permanent disfavour with George. The radical Whigs filled all the jobs in the evolving cabinet and ministries.

A Whig, Sir Robert Walpole, served as Britain's first prime minister (1721–42). He presided over an era of peace, prosperity—and corruption. Whig politicians were not averse to a bit of bribery or worse, if that was what it took to stay in office. Even the king was implicated in the South Sea Bubble scandal, but Walpole managed to cover for the monarch, while keeping his own reputation untarnished.

Even after George II was crowned in 1727 the Jacobites were still working for the return to the British throne of James II's line. But the defeat of James's grandson, Prince Charles Edward Stuart, better known as "Bonnie Prince Charlie", in the 1745 Rebellion dashed Jacobite hopes of power.

The Georgian period was one of genteel pleasures. The British began drinking tea and taking the waters at Bath, Tunbridge Wells and Cheltenham. Sea resorts like Weymouth were all the rage, too. New wealth competed with old to build great houses in the country, complete with Adam fireplaces and Chippendale furniture. But there was a darker side: the urban poor took to drink, and the crime rate soared.

Overseas, an empire was growing fast—the Seven Years' War with France (1756–63) brought huge conquests in Canada and India. The American colonies were another going concern, and important consumers of British manufactures. Unfortunately, a tax dispute caused a rift with the mother country that escalated into full-scale revolutionary war. To the astonishment of George III, the colonists won. In 1783 Britain formally recognized the independence of the new United States of America. Six years later the French Revolution evoked the sympathies of the British masses.

Another sort of revolution was brewing at home: 18th-century inventions like Watt's steam engine, Arkwright's water-powered frame for spinning and Cartwright's power loom laid the foundations for the world's first mass industrial society. Thousands of miles of turnpikes and canals were constructed, linking town and country, seaport and factory. Agriculture geared up to feed an exploding population— nearly 8 million in 1790, against 5½ million in 1700. By now one Briton in three lived in towns—and one town-dweller in three lived in London—the modern world's first city of a million in 1800.

Rule Britannia

Britain entered the 19th century preoccupied by the Irish problem. Irish agitation resulted not in greater independence, but in the 1801 Act of Union establishing the United Kingdom of Great Britain and Ireland. The idea was that the economic and political destinies of the two islands would become inseparable. But Irish nationalism never faded away.

Nor did French imperialism. This time the challenge came from Napoleon. Lord Nelson disposed of the French fleet at Trafalgar in 1805, assuring that Britannia would continue to rule the waves. Wellington, the Iron Duke, triumphed finally over Napoleon at Waterloo in 1815. After two decades of preparations against invasion, the country could relax and celebrate a little. The territorial gains alone were cause for jubilation. They spanned the globe, from Trinidad to Ceylon to the Cape (present-day South Africa).

Oblivious of the great empire he commanded, King George III lapsed into permanent insanity by 1811. His oldest son ruled until 1830, first as Prince Regent and then in his own right as King George IV. He was not a popular figure. The decadence and conspicuous consumption of court life contrasted all too sharply with the miserable existence of the poor—perhaps a third of the population. Their lot deteriorated further when the post-war economy took a temporary nose-dive.

Unemployment and soaring food prices led to rioting in the cities. Protesters called for repeal of the Corn Laws which taxed imported grain in support of high domestic prices—benefiting landowners at the expense of urban workers. Other voices joined in, demanding liberalization of the vote and parliamentary representation.

The era of Victoria—the queen reigned from 1837 to 1901—was the great age of steam and iron, of transport, communications and commerce, of empire and reform. British engineers pioneered the steamship and railway, consuming millions of tons of coal and iron in the process. There was plenty to go round. Britain was the world's biggest producer and exporter of both commodities—until the Germans and Americans began catching up at the end of the century.

It was a hard life for workers underground and on the factory floor. From the mill towns of Yorkshire and Lancashire to the mining towns of South Wales, long hours, bad conditions, low pay and poor housing blighted the health of men, women and children. Even six and seven year olds were hauling coal. A subversive British resident named Karl Marx took note and predicted revolution in the 1848 Communist Manifesto. Instead, things looked up for the workers. They won the vote before the century was out, as well as the right to form unions and to strike. Legislation put limits on working hours and child labour.

People in the countryside had fared badly too, especially in the "hungry Forties", a decade of poor harvests known in Ireland as the potato famine. The move to the cities—and colonies—accelerated. Many people went into "service" (domestic employment).

Respectability, commitment to duty and hard work were the great 19th-century virtues. Family values and a strict moral code paid dividends in a falling crime rate, but appearances

could be deceptive. Public morality went hand in hand with private vice, prostitution mainly, and the thriving underworld Charles Dickens depicted in *Oliver Twist* and other novels. But the Victorians were incurable optimists. Taking their cue from Darwin (his *Origin of Species* came out in 1859), people believed that progress, like evolution, would go on and on. The poor were expected to pull themselves up by their own bootstraps.

After nearly half a century of peace, Britain took up arms to defend Turkey (and its own imperial interests) against Russian aggression in the Crimean War (1854–56). Britain and allied France barely managed to win through. The only real victory belonged to Florence Nightingale and the nursing profession.

The empire burgeoned with the addition of many new colonies in Africa, Asia and the Pacific, though there was mutiny in India, the "jewel in the crown", and trouble over the strategic Suez Canal, opened in 1869. Britain subsequently occupied Egypt to protect the canal and the route to India.

South Africa was another trouble spot. The original Dutch (Boer) settlers flouted British interests in the diamond- and gold-rich Transvaal and Orange Free State. In 1899, after years of friction, they attacked Natal and the Cape, Britain's colonies. Winston Churchill, who saw action in the Boer War, commented that it was "very sporting of the Boers to take on the whole British Empire". In fact, the Boers had the backing of a formidable power—the newly unified German state—and Britain's victory, after a costly three-year engagement, was hard won.

Modern Times

The death of Queen Victoria in 1901 marked the end of an era. The Industrial Revolution was running out of steam, along with belief in self-help and perpetual progress. Socialism posed new solutions to old problems and the new Labour Party won 29 seats in the 1906 General Election.

Parliament laid the foundations of the modern welfare state before World War I, approving old age pensions, health and unemployment insurance and a supertax on the rich. Two-thirds of the national wealth was still concentrated in the hands of one per cent of the population. The Edwardian Age—King Edward VII ruled for nine years from 1901—was the last, brief golden age of that one per cent.

Britain plunged into war with remarkable abandon in August 1914, but the conflict that was supposed to be over before Christmas dragged on for four years and took an unprecedented toll of lives: 750,000 dead and over a million and a half injured. A generation of young men was wiped out by the "monstrous anger of the guns". The phrase comes from *Anthem for Doomed Youth* by the war poet Wilfred Owen, who was still in his twenties when he died on the battlefield in 1918.

Life would never be the same again. Women entered the workplace during the war—and stayed there, winning the

*B*y the time of her diamond jubilee in 1897, Queen Victoria reigned over an empire that covered a quarter of the globe.

right to vote when hostilities ended. The Irish took advantage of the war to press for independence. In the Easter Rising of 1916, radical nationalists proclaimed an Irish Republic. The British government quelled the rebellion and sent the leaders to the firing squad—shocking the Irish people and many in Britain. In 1922 the Irish Free State was created, comprising the 26 Catholic counties of southern Ireland. The six largely Protestant counties of Ulster in the north-east remained part of the United Kingdom.

Industrial decline and unemployment came to plague Britain. While the Left (Labour and disaffected Liberals) advocated nationalization of the depressed mining industry—Britain's biggest—the Conservative government curtailed subsidies, instigating wage cuts and dismissals. The miners walked out in May 1926, and the National Trades Union Congress (TUC) called a general strike in sympathy. After nine days, the TUC gave in to government pressure and ordered members back to work, though the miners stayed out for several more months. Bitterness and class hatred were the legacy of 1926 and the Great Depression made a bad situation worse.

For a while in 1936, crisis in the monarchy diverted public attention from the bad economic news. Edward VIII was forced to choose between the throne and the woman he loved, the twice-divorced American Mrs Simpson. Edward stepped down and his brother was crowned King George VI. He would lead the country through another war.

At first, Prime Minister Neville Chamberlain's government avoided conflict through the appeasement of Germany and Italy. At the Munich Conference in 1938, Chamberlain and the French president Daladier accepted Hitler's annexation of the Sudetenland of Czechoslovakia, if Germany would respect the independence of the rest of Czechoslovakia. Chamberlain returned to Britain claiming he had won "peace for our time". Six months later the Nazis invaded Czechoslovakia. An attack on Poland followed, and Britain went to war.

There was no militaristic fervour this time. By summer of 1940 the war had begun in earnest as Hitler's bombs rained down on London. The Battle of Britain was fought in the air by "the few", the legendary pilots in Spitfires and Hurricanes. They deprived the Luftwaffe of mastery of the skies and postponed the threat of German invasion. The spirit of wartime Britain was personified by Winston Churchill, cigar in hand, exploring the morning-after wreckage—exhorting the people to fight on. The Blitz and the flying bomb attacks of 1944 claimed 60,000 civilian lives. In all, 270,000 servicemen died in action on the Continent, in North Africa, the Eastern Mediterranean and Far East.

The war blurred class distinctions and stirred a new social consciousness which brought the Labour Party and Prime Minister Clement Attlee to power in the 1945 election. The welfare state was created to provide cradle-to-grave care for the population. Key industries were nationalized, and the dismantling of Britain's empire began. India, Pakistan, Burma and Ceylon (Sri Lanka) achieved independence in the late 1940s, followed by a host of other

---

Hard Facts

Geography: The United Kingdom covers 244,100km² (94,250 square miles), including 31,000km² (12,000 square miles) of inland waters. Mainland Britain extends 965km (600 miles) from north to south and 483km (300 miles) from east to west at the widest part. The island divides into a highland and a lowland zone along a line that runs from the mouth of the River Tees in the north-east to the mouth of the Exe in the south-west. Chief mountain ranges include the Pennines, England's "spine", the Cumbrian Mountains in north-west England, the Snowdon and Cambrian ranges of Wales, and Scotland's Grampians. Scotland claims Britain's highest peak: Ben Nevis, 1,342m (4,406ft).

Population: About 55 million (some 47 million in England, nearly 3 million in Wales, 5 million in Scotland).

Capital: London (pop. 3.5 million, metropolitan area 6.7 million).

Major Cities: Birmingham (1 million), Glasgow (730,000), Leeds (710,000), Sheffield (530,000), Liverpool (490,000), Bradford (460,000), Manchester (450,000), Edinburgh (430,000), Bristol (390,000), Coventry (312,000), Cardiff (270,000).

Climate: Cool summers and mild winters. Annual variations in temperature are relatively modest. Rainfall is heaviest in the west and north, and between October and January.

Government: Constitutional monarchy. Parliament, Britain's legislative body, is made up of the elected House of Commons and the subordinate and largely hereditary, partly nominated, House of Lords. The sovereign opens sessions of Parliament and nominally approves all legislation.

The executive branch of government consists of the Prime Minister, leader of the majority party in the Commons, and the Cabinet, chosen by the Prime Minister from the Commons and Lords.

Religion: The two state churches, the Anglican Church of England and the Presbyterian Church of Scotland, are Protestant, but attendance is sparse and falling. The Roman Catholic Church has a sizeable membership, followed by the Methodist and other reformed churches. There are well over 1 million Muslims, 350,000 Jews, and smaller numbers of Hindus and Buddhists.

---

colonies from Ghana (1957) and Malaya (1963) to the Bahamas (1973) and Belize (1981). For most, membership in the Commonwealth—a largely ceremonial organization with the British sovereign as its head—perpetuated a link with the mother country. A few outposts still fly the Union Jack, including Gibraltar, Hong Kong and the Falkland Islands.

As decolonization stepped up, so did the influx from the former colonies (1 million by 1963). The presence of so many Indians, Pakistanis, Jamaicans and other immigrants added a new dimension to British life, though not without some racial friction.

The development of North Sea oil in the 1970s started a stampede for Aberdeen, the centre for the off-shore activities that have made Britain self-sufficient in energy. The oil industry was a bright spot in an economy that had been stagnating, combining high unemployment with double-digit inflation. Miners in the declining coal industry repeatedly went on strike in protest, wringing some concessions from the government. Other workers followed suit, not always successfully.

A referendum in 1975 affirmed Britain's controversial 1973 entry into the European Community. After heated debate, two-thirds of the voters gave the green light to participation in Europe in a reversal of traditional British suspicion of Continental entanglements.

Elected in 1979, Margaret Thatcher was Britain's first woman prime minister. She stood up to the unions, dominated her cabinet and sent a task force to recapture the Falklands when others counselled caution. Privatization of state-owned industries and a new emphasis on entrepreneurial skills were hallmarks of the Thatcher Revolution. The boom in the late '80s gave way to recession and high levels of unemployment. A new system of local taxation (the "poll tax") was resented. Fearing electoral defeat, the Conservative party ousted Mrs Thatcher. Against most predictions, they won the next election under John Major, but the new government faced growing economic and other problems. In today's harsher world climate, the British need to call on all their old resilience.

Historical Landmarks

Prehistoric Beginnings

20,000 BC	Stone Age hunters well established in Britain.
4000	Agriculture develops.
3000	Megalithic period begins.
2000	Bronze Age dawns in Britain.
8th–1st C	Celtic incursions. Iron technology introduced.

Roman Era

55/54 BC	Julius Caesar's expeditions to Britain.
AD 43	Romans return to stay, build roads, found cities.
78–80	Wales and Scotland subdued.
128	Hadrian's Wall completed.
4th C	Christianity takes root.
367	Picts and Scots attack Roman Britain. Saxons, Angles and Jutes help to defeat them, but invade in turn.

Anglo-Saxon

597	St Augustine converts people of Kent.

Kingdoms

8th–9th C	Vikings attack British coasts. "Danelaw" established.
878	Alfred the Great of Wessex defeats Danes at Edington.
924–939	Athelstan first king of all England.
1016–35	Canute rules.
1066	Norman Conquest.

Middle Ages

1170	Thomas Becket murdered in Canterbury Cathedral.
1172	Henry II conquers Ireland.
1215	King John seals Magna Carta.
1281	Edward I subdues Wales.
1314	Robert Bruce triumphs over English at Bannockburn.

1337	Hundred Years' War with France begins.
1348	Black Death epidemic spreads.
1381	Wat Tyler leads Peasant Revolt.
1399	Henry IV deposes Richard II.
1455–85	Wars of the Roses.

House of Tudor

1533	Henry VIII divorces Catherine of Aragon.
1534	England breaks with Rome.
1558–1603	Elizabeth I rules.
1588	English defeat Spain's Invincible Armada.

House of Stuart

1603	James I king of England and Scotland. Union of Crowns.
1620	Pilgrims sail to America.
1642	Civil War breaks out.
1649	Charles I beheaded.
1660	Monarchy restored under Charles II.
1665	Great Plague.
1666	Great Fire of London.
1688	Glorious Revolution brings William and Mary to throne.
1701–13	War of the Spanish Succession against Catholic France.
1707	English and Scottish parliaments merge.

Georgian Period

1714	King George I accedes to throne.
1721–42	Sir Robert Walpole serves as first prime minister.
1745	Bonnie Prince Charlie leads Jacobite Rebellion.
1756–63	Seven Years' War with France.
1783	Britain formally recognizes independence of the United States of America.
1801	United Kingdom of Great Britain and Ireland established.
1805	Lord Nelson defeats French fleet at Trafalgar.
1815	Wellington triumphs at Waterloo.

Victorian Britain

1837	Queen Victoria ascends the throne.
1854–56	Crimean War.
1869	Suez Canal opened.
1899–1902	Boer War.

Modern Times

1901–10	Edward VII reigns.
1914–18	World War I.
1922	Irish Free State created. (Six mainly Protestant counties excluded.)
1936	Edward VIII abdicates, George VI takes over.
1939–45	World War II.
1947–48	India, Pakistan, Burma and Ceylon (Sri Lanka) independent.
1973	United Kingdom joins European Community ("Common Market").
1979–90	Margaret Thatcher prime minister.
1982	Falklands War.
1994	Channel Tunnel opens.

Just the Essentials

Britain's wealth of sights to see will continually force you to make choices and set priorities. So what's most important, what should you see in each region? Especially if it's your first visit, it would be a shame to miss out on these suggestions, as you travel round the relevant area.

London and Environs

Buckingham Palace: Changing of the Guard
Houses of Parliament: where the Lords and Commons convene
Westminster Abbey: Britain's coronation church
St Paul's Cathedral: Wren masterpiece
Tower of London: Crown Jewels on display in Norman fortification
British Museum: Elgin marbles; Egyptian mummies
National Gallery: painting collection
Hampton Court Palace: royal retreat of King Henry VIII
Windsor Castle: home of Queen

The South-East

Canterbury Cathedral: focus of medieval pilgrimage
Battle: 1066 site
Brighton: old seaside resort with Royal Pavilion

The South

Portsmouth: historic ships on view
Winchester Cathedral: England's longest
Salisbury: market town and great Early English cathedral
Stonehenge: prehistoric stone circle
Longleat: stately home and safari park
Stourhead: the last word in gardens

The South-West

Bath: Georgian spa town
Bristol harbour: once port for America
Wells: the town and the cathedral
Glastonbury Abbey: evocative ruin
Plymouth: from where the *Mayflower* sailed
Fowey: Cornish fishing port
North coast of Cornwall

East Anglia and the Fens

Cambridge: university town on River Cam
Ely Cathedral: of Norman foundation
Constable Country: immortalized in John Constable's paintings
Lincoln and cathedral: dominant feature of historic centre

Central England

Oxford: England's oldest university town
Stratford-upon-Avon: where Shakespeare was born
Cotswolds: showpiece villages in the hills
Peak District: spas and dramatic scenery

Wales

The Wye Valley: Tintern Abbey
Pembrokeshire coast: holiday area
Caernarfon Castle: coastal stronghold
Snowdonia: mountainous national park

The North of England

Yorkshire Dales: national park
Fountains Abbey: imposing remains
York and York Minster: with superb stained glass
North York Moors: heather-covered uplands
Lake District: haunt of Wordsworth and friends
Hadrian's Wall: built by the Romans

Scotland

Edinburgh: capital city
Glasgow: city of culture and commerce
Loch Lomond: beautiful inland lake
The Trossachs: scenic hills and lakes
Glen Coe: brooding pass
Loch Ness and the Great Glen

Going Places with Something Special in Mind

Britain's cultural riches are enough to overwhelm the most determined sightseer. Rather than trying vainly to see all the stately homes, cathedrals, museums and archaeological sites in an area, you may want to pursue special interests of your own, or to use a theme to structure your trip. Here are a few suggestions, some concentrated in one part of the country, some spread widely.

Prehistory in Wiltshire

The most important monuments of ancient Britain are found in Wiltshire. Here, in the 3rd millennium BC, powerful chieftains began burying their dead in stone tombs. They also raised ceremonial earthworks, later amplified by huge standing stones.

1 AVEBURY
Neolithic stone circle surrounded by earth-works and ditch, linked by avenue of standing stones.

*M*agnificent stained glass windows like this one at Winchelsea are well worth a visit.

2 WEST KENNET LONG BARROW
Well-preserved Stone Age tomb.

3 SILBURY HILL
Largest artificial mound in Europe, dating from the Stone Age.

4 STONEHENGE
Most famous of Britain's prehistoric monuments, circles of giant stones erected between 2200 and 1300 BC.

5 OLD SARUM
Earthworks of Iron Age hill fort and medieval town.

6 SALISBURY
Finds from Stonehenge and Old Sarum in South Wiltshire Museum

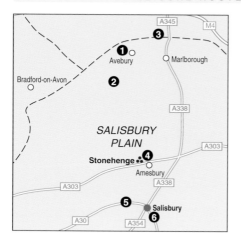

Explore ancient Britain around Wiltshire.

Roman Britain

The Romans first invaded Britain in 55 BC and came to stay in AD 43. Traces of their 400-year rule include the arrow-straight roads, defensive walls and forts, as well as the remains of baths and villas.

1 LONDON
Sections of city wall at Cripplegate and Tower of London. Bathhouse in Lower Thames Street. Temple of Mithras, Queen Victoria Street. British Museum: Mildenhall Treasure and other relics.

2 ST ALBANS, Hertfordshire
Ancient Verulamium. Remains of town walls and theatre. Roman collection in Verulamium Museum.

3 FISHBOURNE PALACE
Immense complex built for 1st-century king. Mosaic flooring and restored formal gardens. On-site museum.

4 PEVENSEY
Roman fort near where William the Conqueror landed centuries later. Norman castle stands within its walls.

5 LULLINGSTONE VILLA
Roman villa with mosaics and early Christian chapel.

6 BATH
Roman baths, temple complex and adjoining museum.

7 CAERLEON
Roman Isca Silurum. Ruins of Roman barracks and amphitheatre.

8 CIRENCESTER
City walls, amphitheatre, collection of finds in Corinium Museum.

9 CHEDWORTH VILLA
2nd-century villa with well-preserved mosaic pavements and bathhouse.

10 LEICESTER
Section of Roman masonry known as Jewry Wall.

11 LINCOLN
Part of Roman gate preserved in Newport Arch.

12 WROXETER ROMAN CITY
Remains of baths and exercise halls. Museum of finds.

13 CAERNARFON, Gwynedd, Wales
Excavations of Roman fort.

14 CHESTER
Roman amphitheatre and ramparts. Grosvenor Museum.

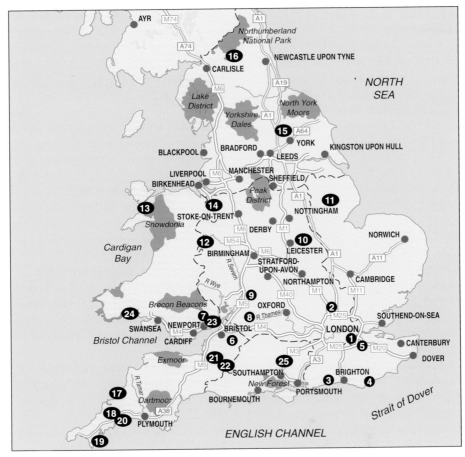

*E*vidence of Roman rule in Britain (1–16), and the mystery of King Arthur (7–25).

In Search of King Arthur

The legendary King Arthur may have been a 6th century Romano-British chief who held off the Saxons for a while. Here are some of the sites claiming links with the hero (often with no evidence at all).

15 YORK
Roman fort of Eboracum. Large collection of finds in Yorkshire Museum. Part Roman Multiangular Tower in museum gardens.

16 HADRIAN'S WALL
Roman frontier defence, built around AD 122, running from Solway Firth to Wallsend-on-Tyne. Museums at Carlisle and Newcastle.

17 TINTAGEL, Cornwall
Ruins claimed to be of Arthur's castle, where king was born and lived with Queen Guinevere. Cave of magician Merlin. King Arthur's Hall, built in

1933, with stained-glass windows of knights.

18 BODMIN MOOR, Cornwall
Site of King Arthur's last battle against his evil nephew Prince Mordred at Camlann on river Camel. Magic sword Excalibur was flung into Dozmary Pool on moor.

19 MOUSEHOLE, Cornwall
The wizard Merlin lived on rock below village.

20 FOWEY, Cornwall
2.5m (8ft) Tristan Stone, a mile to north, commemorates one of Arthur's knights; Castle Dore, overgrown Iron Age mound a couple of miles further on, once held castle of Tristan's uncle, King Mark.

21 GLASTONBURY, Somerset
Glastonbury Tor is held to be the Isle of Avalon, where the dying king was brought. He is said to have been buried at Glastonbury Abbey.

22 SOUTH CADBURY, Somerset
A hill-fort where archaeologists found traces of a large building. Often claimed to be the site of "Camelot".

23 CAERLEON, South Wales
Roman camp which may have been Arthur's base.

24 CARMARTHEN, South Wales
The name means "Merlin's city", and an ancient tree stump is known as "Merlin's oak".

25 WINCHESTER, Hampshire
Claims to have been Arthur's capital.

Castle Hall's Round Table dates only from Tudor times.

London's Historic Palaces

A tour of London's royal palaces spans England's history from William the Conqueror's time to the present day.

1 TOWER OF LONDON
Begun in 1087 by William the Conqueror, it has served as palace, fortress, prison and place of execution.

2 PALACE OF WESTMINSTER
Principal royal palace until 15th century. Only Jewel Tower and Westminster Hall (1099) remain, incorporated into Houses of Parliament.

3 ELTHAM PALACE, Woolwich
Fifteenth-century palace of Plantagenet kings. Great Hall and moat bridge survive.

4 HAMPTON COURT PALACE,
Kingston-upon-Thames
Favourite residence of Henry VIII.

5 ST JAMES'S PALACE,
St James's Street
Tudor and Stuart palace. Charles I slept here the night before going to scaffold.

6 BANQUETING HOUSE,
Whitehall
Where Charles I was executed; originally part of Whitehall Palace.

7 MARLBOROUGH HOUSE,
Pall Mall
Former royal residence designed by

Christopher Wren. Now Commonwealth conference centre.

8 SOMERSET HOUSE, The Strand
Built in 18th century on site of Elizabeth I's palace. Royal residence until George III bought Buckingham Palace. Grand setting for Courtauld Institute art galleries.

9 KEW PALACE, Kew Gardens
Small, Dutch-style residence of George III.

10 KENSINGTON PALACE,
Kensington Gardens
Queen Victoria learned here of her accession to throne.

11 BUCKINGHAM PALACE
Home of sovereign and royal family.

The Royal Parks

The Royal Parks, owned by the Crown but open to the public, are one of the delights of London. Cross the first four listed, a distance of 5km (3 miles), and you'll negotiate the busiest part of the metropolis from Bayswater to Whitehall, with only two brief encounters with traffic.

12 KENSINGTON GARDENS
Former grounds of William III's Kensington Palace. A children's favourite for sailing model boats on Round Pond, and the statue of Peter Pan.

13 HYDE PARK
One-time hunting preserve of Henry VIII. Bathers and boaters crowd Serpentine lake in summer.

14 GREEN PARK
Open parkland with massive trees, favourite of Charles II.

15 ST JAMES'S PARK
Long lake and rampant shrubberies attract wild birds and relaxing civil servants.

16 REGENT'S PARK
Named after Prince Regent, later George IV. Vast park includes London Zoo, formal flower gardens and Open Air Theatre.

17 GREENWICH PARK
Former hunting grounds, site of Old Royal Observatory. Brass strip marks Meridian from which world measurements are taken.

18 RICHMOND PARK
Largest and wildest of royal parks. Deer still roam this one-time hunting preserve of Charles I.

Wren's City

The Great Fire of 1666 gave London the chance to build anew in stone, embellished by the genius of Sir Christopher Wren (1632–1723). Many of his churches were bombed in World War II, but they have been meticulously restored. A short walk will take you past some of Wren's best.

A tour of London (following pages).

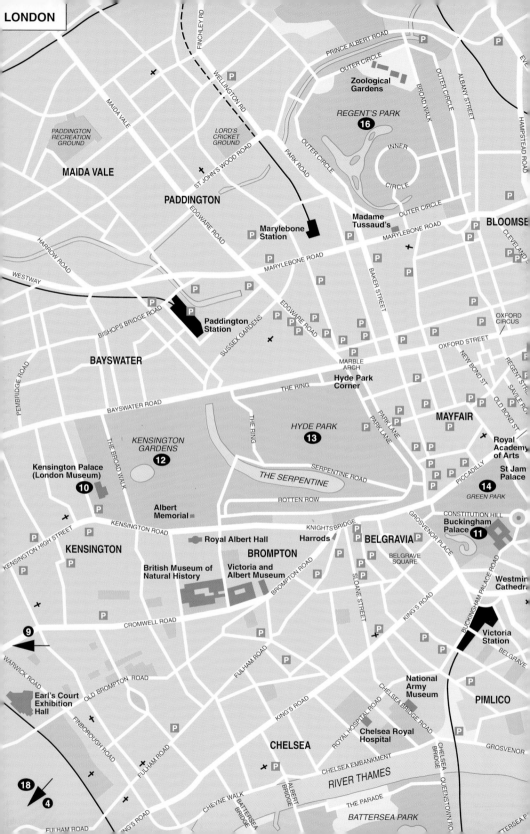

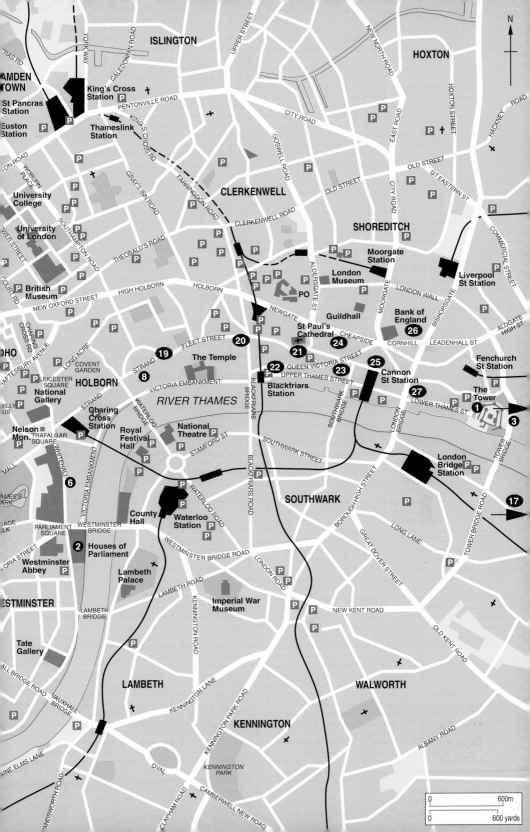

19 ST CLEMENT DANES,
The Strand
Isolated between streams of traffic at entrance to City of London. On site of 9th-century church built for the Danes.

20 ST BRIDE, Fleet Street
The printers' church with "wedding cake" tower. Burned out in World War II but rebuilt. Museum in crypt.

21 ST PAUL'S CATHEDRAL,
Ludgate Hill
Wren's masterpiece topped by famous dome. Place of royal ceremonial containing tombs of the great.

22 ST ANDREW-BY-THE-WARDROBE, Queen Victoria Street
Fine church with square tower.

23 ST JAMES GARLICKHYTHE,
Garlick Hill
Has typical, elegant Wren steeple.

24 ST MARY-LE-BOW, Cheapside
The Bow Bells of Cockney fame ring out from its superb steeple. Restored after World War II.

25 ST STEPHEN WALBROOK,
Walbrook
One of Wren's best. Forerunner of St Paul's, with dome, steeple and Corinthian columns.

26 ST PETER-UPON-CORNHILL,
Gracechurch Street Corner
A Wren church on ancient sacred site.

27 THE MONUMENT,
Monument Street
Begun by Wren in 1671 to commemorate the Great Fire.

Stately Homes

Britain's great houses count among the country's finest assets. Here are some of the best that are open to the public, grouped by region. Confirm dates and times with tourist authorities or the National Trust before visiting.

In the London Area
KENWOOD HOUSE, Hampstead, London
Elegant mansion surrounded by parkland. Remodelled by Adam in 18th century. Fine art collection.

SIR JOHN SOANE'S MUSEUM,
Lincoln's Inn Fields, London
House and collections of great architect, as he lived in it until his death in 1837.

APSLEY HOUSE, Hyde Park Corner, London
Adam house remodelled by Benjamin Wyatt for first Duke of Wellington. Old Masters, silver and porcelain.

CHISWICK HOUSE, Chiswick, London
Beautiful Neoclassical building inspired by Palladio. Built to Lord Burlington's design in 1729. Striking William Kent interior.

OSTERLEY PARK HOUSE,
Isleworth, Middlesex
Elizabethan mansion, charmingly remodelled by Adam. Superb interior decoration.

HAM HOUSE, Richmond, Surrey
Imposing 17th-century house with extremely rare original Restoration furnishings.

MARBLE HILL HOUSE,
Twickenham, Surrey
English Palladian villa. Lovely interior.

SYON HOUSE, Brentford,
Middlesex
Old monastery modernized with characteristic style by Adam. Lavish decor.

North of London
HATFIELD HOUSE, Hatfield,
Hertfordshire
Jacobean building with state apartments for royalty.

ASHRIDGE, Berkhamsted,
Hertfordshire
Monastic building transformed into residence by Henry VIII. Largely rebuilt in neo-Gothic style in early 19th century.

WOBURN ABBEY, near Leighton
Buzzard, Bedfordshire
Outstanding collection of paintings. Wild animal park in extensive grounds.

AUDLEY END, Saffron Walden
Essex
Jacobean house on site of Benedictine abbey. Renovated in 18th century.

South-East of London
CHARTWELL, Westerham, Kent
Winston Churchill's country retreat. Renovated farmhouse in attractive grounds.

KNOLE PARK, Sevenoaks, Kent
Vast home of the Sackvilles. Unique collection of Jacobean furniture with some rare silver pieces.

IGHTHAM MOTE, Ivy Hatch,
Sevenoaks, Kent
Well-preserved 14th-century moated manor house and meeting place (mote).

PENSHURST PLACE, Penshurst,
Kent
Battlemented 14th-century house with fine Great Hall.

HEVER CASTLE, near Edenbridge,
Kent
Childhood home of Anne Boleyn. Thirteenth-century moated castle, converted into 20th-century residence for Lord Astor.

LEEDS CASTLE, near Maidstone,
Kent
Fairy-tale castle built on two islands in lake.

Around Oxford
BLENHEIM PALACE
Stateliest of them all. Duke of Marlborough's mansion, where Winston Churchill was born.

ROUSHAM HOUSE, Steeple Aston
Tudor house, battlemented in 18th century. Landscaped garden.

COMPTON WYNYATES, Tysoe,
west of Banbury
Delightful Tudor house in garden of yews.

STONOR PARK, Henley-on-
Thames
Medieval house surrounded by parkland, refuge of Catholic priests during persecution.

MILTON MANOR, near Abingdon
Built to design of Inigo Jones, with addition of two Georgian wings.

In the South and South-West

COTEHELE HOUSE, St. Dominick, near Saltash, Cornwall
Romantic grey granite manor house, little changed since medieval times. Period furniture.

PENCARROW, Washaway, Bodmin, Cornwall
Stuccoed Palladian house with charming Georgian decor and furniture.

BUCKLAND ABBEY, near Yelverton, Devon
Converted Cistercian monastery, former home and museum of Sir Francis Drake.

SALTRAM HOUSE, Plymouth, Devon
Elegant Georgian mansion with Adam interior.

FORDE ABBEY, Chard, Dorset
Long, low house incorporating monastic building. Notable tapestries based on Raphael cartoons.

KINGSTON LACY HOUSE, near Wimborne, Dorset
One of earliest classical houses in England. Fine collection of paintings.

MONTACUTE HOUSE, near Yeovil, Somerset
Imposing Elizabethan mansion, scarcely changed since completed in 1600.

LITTLECOTE HOUSE, near Hungerford, Wiltshire
Tudor manor. Weaponry museum in great hall. Haunted bedroom, scene of gruesome child murder in 1575.

LONGLEAT HOUSE, Warminster, Wiltshire
Massive Renaissance mansion lit by ranks of mullioned windows. Visited by Queen Elizabeth I. Safari park with lions.

STOURHEAD, Stourton, Warminster, Wiltshire
Palladian house with Regency interior in Italianate grounds.

WILTON HOUSE, Wilton, Wiltshire
Built under supervision of Inigo Jones. Outstanding paintings include family portraits by Van Dyck. Furniture by Chippendale and William Kent.

In Yorkshire and Humberside

HAREWOOD HOUSE, north of Leeds
Stately home in Palladian style, with Adam interiors and Chippendale furniture.

NEWBY HALL, Newby, south-west of Ripon
Graceful brick mansion with fine sculpture gallery by Robert Adam and collection of rare chamber pots.

CASTLE HOWARD, west of Malton
Grandiose house designed by Sir John Vanbrugh.

BURTON AGNES HALL, near Driffield
Jacobean red-brick house, with magnificent woodwork, mullioned windows and original staircase.

BURTON CONSTABLE, Sproatley, near Hull
Tudor house, with battlemented towers in extensive park.

Castles of Wales

A tour of castles from Cardiff in the south to Beaumaris and Conwy in the north-west combines history with coastal scenery. Don't call them Welsh castles, by the way. Most were built by the Normans or by Edward I of England to subjugate the Welsh.

1 CARDIFF CASTLE
Norman castle on site of Roman fort, rebuilt in 19th century.

2 CASTELL COCH
Neo-Gothic remake of 13th-century structure. A William Burges fantasy.

3 CAERPHILLY CASTLE
One of greatest surviving medieval castles, ringed by towers and water defences.

*H*istoric castles and scenic coastlines in Wales.

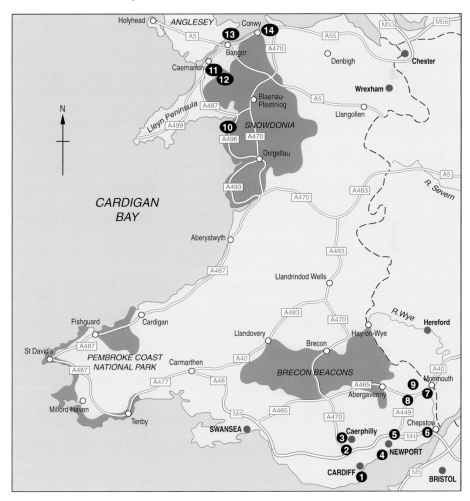

4 NEWPORT CASTLE

Ruins of 15th-century fortress guarding river crossing.

5 CAERLEON ROMAN FORTRESS

Remains of barracks, baths and amphitheatre.

6 CHEPSTOW CASTLE

Britain's first stone-built fortress, guarding strategic route from England to Wales.

7 MONMOUTH CASTLE

Birthplace of King Henry V of Agincourt fame.

8 RAGLAN CASTLE

Impressive ruins of 15th-century castle. Tall "Yellow Tower" outside walls was destroyed by Cromwell in Civil War.

9 WHITE CASTLE

Norman fortification surrounded by steep moat.

10 HARLECH CASTLE

One of Edward's forts. Here Henry V besieged Welsh hero Owain Glyndwr.

11 CAERNARFON CASTLE

Edward I's spectacular fortress and palace, scene of investiture of Princes of Wales.

12 DOLBADARN CASTLE

Ruined 13th-century castle of Welsh princes guards Llanberis pass.

13 BEAUMARIS, Isle of Anglesey

Castle noted for its concentric walls, turrets and moat. Built by Edward I to guard Menai Strait.

14 CONWY CASTLE

Built by Edward I. A formidable fortress with eight massive towers.

Great Cathedrals

The great cathedrals of England and Wales illustrate among them the whole development of medieval architectural style, from Norman (1066–1180) to the three subdivisions of Gothic: Early English (1189–1307), Decorated (1307–77) and Perpendicular (1377–1485). Here are some of the finest examples.

1 WINCHESTER

Norman transepts and crypt date from 1079, when Winchester was capital of England. Striking Perpendicular nave is Europe's longest.

2 SALISBURY

Early English style throughout. Only English cathedral designed to a single concept. Begun in 1220, completed 1280. Tower and soaring spire added in 14th century.

3 WELLS

First English cathedral to be constructed in Gothic style (1175-1260). Superbly carved west front.

4 EXETER

Retains Norman transept towers. Remainder rebuilt in Decorated style in 13th and 14th centuries.

5 CANTERBURY

Founded 1070. Eastern end magnificently rebuilt in Early English style after a disastrous fire in 1174. Perpendicular nave and Bell Harry Tower.

A feast of medieval architectural styles.

10 DURHAM

Finest example of Norman architecture in Britain (1093). Beautifully proportioned nave with massive incised columns.

Great Scottish Houses and Castles

Several of Scotland's most famous castles and historic houses lie within easy reach of Edinburgh.

1 EDINBURGH CASTLE

Imposing fortress on rocky summit, stronghold for more than 1,000 years.

2 PALACE OF HOLYROOD HOUSE, Edinburgh

Home of Mary Queen of Scots. Official residence in Scotland of British sovereign.

3 HOPETOUN HOUSE, near Queensferry

Eighteenth-century mansion with Adam interior, set in beautiful park on south shore of Firth of Forth.

4 FALKLAND PALACE

Stuart castle with French-style façade.

5 SCONE PALACE, near Perth

Neo-Gothic house built on site where early Scottish kings were crowned. Collection of furniture and china.

6 STIRLING CASTLE

Guardian of the route between the lowlands and highlands.

7 GLAMIS CASTLE, near Forfar

A pinnacled tower, home of the earls of

6 ELY

Norman nave and tower (1083). Early English and Decorated additions. Octagonal lantern in Decorated style.

7 GLOUCESTER

Norman core (1089), rebuilt in Perpendicular style. Holds alabaster tomb of Edward II.

8 LINCOLN

Supreme example of Early English style, with Norman west front preserved. Some Decorated and Perpendicular elements.

9 YORK MINSTER

Britain's largest cathedral, with massive central tower and fine stained glass.

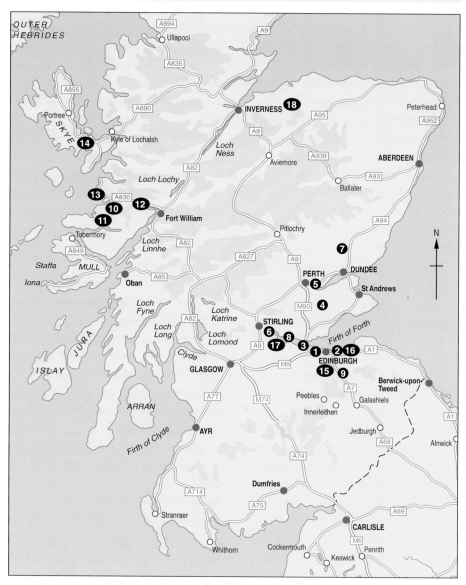

*F*amous Scottish castles (1–9) and the trail of Bonnie Prince Charlie (10–18).

Strathmore since 1372, birthplace of Queen Elizabeth the Queen Mother. Fine collections.

8 CULROSS PALACE, south-east of Stirling
Royal palace where Charles I was born.

9 MELLERSTAIN, near Gordon, south-east of Edinburgh
Finest Adam mansion in Scotland, home of the earls of Haddington.

In the Steps of Bonnie Prince Charlie

The 25-year-old Prince Charles Edward Stuart (1720–88), sailed on a French ship to the Hebridean island of Eriskay in 1745 to try to win back the British throne for his father. You can trace his odyssey from his landing on the mainland to his final defeat and abandonment of Scottish soil.

10 LOCH NAN UAMH, north of Lochailort
Where Bonnie Prince Charlie landed in June 1745. Footpath leads to cave where he spent first night. And in September 1746 a French boat took the defeated prince from here to France, after five months in hiding in the Highlands and islands.

11 KINLOCHMOIDART
Row of seven beech trees commemorates seven followers who landed with prince. Ruined castle of Tioram belonging to Clanranald, one of the seven, lies on island in Loch Moidart.

12 GLENFINNAN
Where prince raised his standard at gathering of clans on 19 August 1745, and proclaimed his father king. Memorial tower surmounted by kilted Highlander stands at head of Loch Shiel.

13 ARISAIG, north of Lochailort
Where hunted prince lay hidden in hut on 18 July 1746, with price of £30,000 on his head.

14 SKYE
On the run in islands of Outer Hebrides, prince crossed to Isle of Skye. He was disguised as maid of young woman supporter, Flora Macdonald. From Skye he returned to mainland.

15 EDINBURGH
Captured by prince, who held court in Holyrood House.

16 PRESTONPANS, east of Edinburgh
Where prince's forces decisively defeated government troops on 21 September in 10-minute battle. Southward push into England followed.

17 FALKIRK
On the retreat, prince's generals gained one last victory over government army here on 17 January 1746.

18 CULLODEN MOOR, east of Inverness
Where prince's Highlanders, pursued by Duke of Cumberland and his men, gave battle on 16 April 1746. Highlanders were annihilated in less than an hour. Battlefield museum in old farmhouse.

Peaks and Dales of Derbyshire

Derbyshire's Peak District, easily reached from Manchester, Sheffield or Derby, offers rugged scenery of high moors and deep gorges. To the south, the landscape is gentler, with spa towns and stately homes.

1 MATLOCK BATH
Former spa in beautiful Derwent Valley. Grottoes and caves. The wooded Heights of Abraham are accessible by cable car.

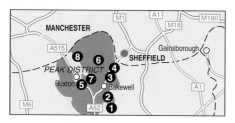

*T*he Peak District area
of Derbyshire.

2 HADDON HALL, between
Matlock and Bakewell
Medieval house with priceless tapes-
tries.

3 BAKEWELL
Charming old spa town, with a 700 year
old bridge.

4 CHATSWORTH HOUSE, north-
east of Bakewell
Immense Baroque mansion, home of
the Dukes of Devonshire.

5 BUXTON
Spa since Roman times. Mary Queen of
Scots, as a prisoner, was treated for
rheumatism here.

6 CASTLETON
Peveril Castle, setting for Sir Walter
Scott's *Peveril of the Peak*. Under-
ground caverns.

7 TIDESWELL
Notable 14th-century church of St
John. Annual "well-dressing" cere-
mony.

8 DOVEDALE GORGE
Twisted rocks along peaceful river valley. Caves at Dove Holes.

Dartmoor

Dartmoor National Park covers
945km^2 (365 square miles) of open
moorland and wooded valleys. A
80km (50-mile) tour starting from
Buckfastleigh will take you through a
variety of Devon landscapes.

BUCKFASTLEIGH
Terminus of picturesque Dart Valley
Railway from Totnes.

BUCKFAST ABBEY
Modern abbey built by Benedictine
monks.

ASHBURTON
Former wool town and slate-mining
centre.

BUCKLAND-IN-THE-MOOR
Romantic Devon village of thatched
stone houses.

WIDECOMBE-IN-THE-MOOR
Famous for the fair immortalized in
song; held on second Tuesday in
September.

MANATON
Fifteenth-century moorland church.

CHAGFORD
Pretty town, a centre for touring and
walking.

POSTBRIDGE
Granite "clapper bridge" over East
Dart River.

TWO BRIDGES
Medieval "clapper bridge" over West
Dart.

PRINCETOWN

The high, bleak location of the famous Dartmoor Prison, home to many of Britain's most dangerous criminals.

Shakespeare Country

The memory of William Shakespeare (1564–1616), Britain's most famous bard, lives on in his home town of Stratford-upon-Avon and the villages around it. See the sights that launched a tourist industry more than two centuries ago:

1 STRATFORD-UPON-AVON
Shakespeare's birthplace. Holy Trinity Church, burial place of the bard.

2 SHOTTERY, west of Stratford
Anne Hathaway's Cottage, childhood home of Shakespeare's wife.

3 WILMCOTE, north-west of Stratford
Mary Arden's House. Sixteenth-century farmhouse where Shakespeare's mother grew up.

4 ASTON CANTLOW, north-west of Stratford
Church where Shakespeare's parents are said to have been married.

5 CHARLECOTE PARK, Wellesbourne
Elizabethan house typical of Shakespeare's time, that has been extensively restored. According to local tradition, Shakespeare was caught poaching a deer in the park and was brought before the owner, Sir Thomas Lucy, to be fined.

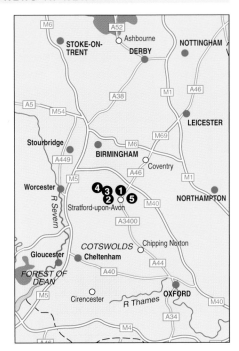

*M*emories of one of Britain's more famous bards.

Charles Dickens in Kent

From the age of five to ten, Charles Dickens (1812–1870) lived with his family in Chatham. These were the happiest years of a rather difficult childhood. Later, as a famous novelist, he bought Gad's Hill Place near Rochester, a house he had admired since he was a boy. This part of Kent inspired scenes in many of his books.

1 CHATHAM
The Dickens' family house was at No. 2 (now No. 11) Ordnance Terrace.

*D*ickensian Kent, inspiration for many of the author's novels.

2 ROCHESTER

Cathedral appears in *The Mystery of Edwin Drood* and Jasper's Gate was home of drug addict John Jasper in that novel. Restoration House was model for Miss Havisham's home in *Great Expectations*. Royal Victoria and Bull Inn was scene of meetings of fictitious Pickwick Club. Charles Dickens Centre (Eastgate House, High Street) contains wax-work displays and mementoes. Also in Centre's grounds Swiss chalet, removed from Gad's Hill Place, in which Dickens wrote *A Tale of Two Cities*.

3 COBHAM, west of Rochester

Leather Bottle Inn, described in *The Pickwick Papers*.

4 COOLING (7 miles/11km from Rochester)

Children's graves, which Pip in *Great Expectations* claims are of his family.

5 CHALK (5 miles/8km from Rochester)

House where Dickens and wife Catherine spent honeymoon. Forge on which Dickens modelled Pip's childhood home.

6 GAD'S HILL PLACE

Bought by Dickens in 1856 and where he died, now girls' school.

7 BROADSTAIRS

Dickens's favourite seaside resort. Annual Dickens Festival. Bleak House, where he wrote part of *David Copperfield*, contains personal mementoes. Dickens House Museum was original of Miss Betsey Trotwood's house in *David Copperfield*. Royal Albion Hotel, where Dickens wrote part of *Nicholas Nickleby*. At Lawn House (now Archway House) he wrote some of his most famous novels.

8 SARRE, near Canterbury

Crown Inn, frequented by Dickens.

Hardy's Dorset

Thomas Hardy (1840–1928) lived most of his life in the county of Dorset, the heart of the "Wessex" where his novels are set. A tour of places associated with the writer takes you through some lovely countryside. Names in parentheses are those used by Hardy in the novels.

1 DORCHESTER (Casterbridge)

Featured prominently in Hardy novels. Thomas Hardy statue at Top o' Town. Hardy's study in County Museum. Max Gate, house on Dorchester outskirts, where writer lived for 43 years till his death. Maiden Castle and Maumbury Rings, featured in *The Mayor of Casterbridge*.

2 STINSFORD (Mellstock)
Hardy's heart buried in churchyard (but his ashes are in Westminster Abbey).

3 PUDDLETOWN (Weatherbury)
Waterston Manor was model for Bathsheba's Weatherbury Farm in *Far from the Madding Crowd*.

4 HIGHER BOCKHAMPTON (Upper Mellstock)
Hardy's Cottage, his birthplace and early home, where he wrote *Under the*

*T*he Dorset that Hardy knew so well.

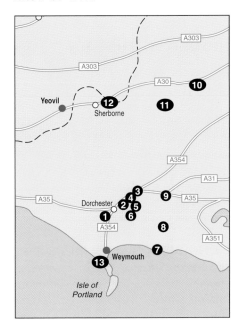

Greenwood Tree and *Far from the Madding Crowd*.

5 PUDDLETOWN HEATH (Egdon Heath)
Featured in *The Return of the Native*.

6 WEST STAFFORD
Church in *Tess of the D'Urbervilles*, where Tess and Angel Clare were married.

7 LULWORTH COVE (Lulstead Cove)
Troy swam out from here and was believed drowned in *Far from the Madding Crowd*.

8 WOOL
Woolbridge Manor (Wellbridge Manor), where Tess and Angel Clare spent blighted honeymoon.

9 BERE REGIS (King's Bere)
In *Tess of the D'Urbervilles*, Tess and her family camped out on a four-poster bed outside church, under stained-glass Turberville window in south wall.

10 SHAFTESBURY (Shaston)
Background to *Jude the Obscure*.

11 MARNHULL (Marlott)
Tess Cottage, believed original of Durbeyfields' home.

12 SHERBORNE (Sherton Abbas)
Old town little changed since it figured in *The Woodlanders*.

13 WEYMOUTH (Budmouth)
Hardy worked for a Weymouth architect and stayed here again while writing *The Trumpet Major*.

Pilgrims' Roots

American roots lie deep in English history, and many places have strong American associations. Nowhere more than East Anglia and the Fens: so many of the Founding Fathers of the United States came from there, it has sometimes been called "Pilgrim Country".

GAINSBOROUGH, Lincolnshire

Medieval Old Hall, where the Puritans (then called Separatists) met towards end of 16th century. John Robinson Memorial Church, built in 1896, commemorates the Separatist pastor who intended to sail on *Mayflower*, but died before it left.

SCROOBY, Nottinghamshire

Reverend Richard Clyfton brought his followers here after a split in Gainsborough Puritan congregation. They met in William Brewster's Manor House. Under persecution, the Puritans tried to flee to the Netherlands in 1607, but were seized on board boat in Boston. They eventually went to Leyden in 1609 and sailed on *Mayflower* in 1620.

AUSTERFIELD, South Yorkshire

William Bradford, leader of the Pilgrims and second governor of Plymouth Colony was born here. His *History of Plimouth Plantation* recorded Pilgrim Fathers' odyssey. North aisle of church was restored in Bradford's memory by Society of Mayflower Descendants.

BOSTON, Lincolnshire

Pilgrim Fathers were arrested here when they first tried to flee in 1607. Cells in Guildhall where they were imprisoned were restored by Bostonian Society of Massachusetts. Column at Scotia Creek marks spot where group of Puritans led by John Winthrop sailed for New World in 1630. St. Botolph's Church was restored by American Bostonians in 1857 in memory of John Cotton, who sailed for Massachusetts in 1633 after being ousted as vicar because of his beliefs. Church tower, known as the Boston Stump, was rebuilt by Americans after World War II. Fydell House contains an American Room.

LINCOLN

Stained-glass window in cathedral honours Captain John Smith, leader of colony at Jamestown, Virginia, who was released from Indian captivity by the chief's daughter, Pocahontas. Another window commemorates pilgrim ship *Arbella* on which John Winthrop, first governor of Plymouth colony, sailed in 1630.

Industrial History

The Industrial Revolution began in Britain, transforming it from a rural to an urban society in less than a century. Historic mills, mines, factories and other installations across the country have been preserved as monuments to the early days of the machine age. A number of museums also highlight Britain's great industrial heritage.

BATH

Camden Museum, displays of Victorian engineering tools.

BIRMINGHAM

Museum of Science and Industry in one

of the world's first industrial cities.

BLAENAVON, Wales
Big Pit Mining Museum, until recently a working coalmine.

BRADFORD
Industrial Museum at Moorside Mills.

BURTON-ON-TRENT
Bass Museum of 200 years of brewing.

CORNWALL
Geevor Museum of tin mining at Penzance. Poldark mine at Wendron.

GLASGOW
Summerlee Heritage Park at Coatbridge Sunnyside, with displays of engineering equipment from Victorian times.

IRON-BRIDGE, Shropshire
World's first cast-iron bridge, spanning River Severn; Iron-Bridge Gorge Museum, open-air site includes blast furnaces, beam engines, tile and china works, mine and printing works.

MANCHESTER
Greater Manchester Museum of Science and Technology, including 1830 Liverpool Road Station, oldest railway passenger station in world. Castlefield Visitor Centre, Deansgate, an urban heritage park with displays on area's industrial past.

NEWCASTLE-UPON-TYNE
Museum of Science and Technology features Tyneside shipbuilding, mining and engineering.

NOTTINGHAM
Industrial Museum at Wollaton Hall has displays on local printing and lace works. Canal Museum in warehouse on Beeston Canal. Lace Hall, depicting history of lace-making from 1850 to today.

STANLEY, near Durham
Beamish North of England Open Air Museum, featuring coal miners' cottages and pit machinery.

SWANSEA, Wales
Industrial Maritime Museum. Trostre Tinplate Works at Llanelli, still functioning.

STOURBRIDGE, West Midlands
Glassworks, exhibits and demonstrations.

WOLVERHAMPTON
Bilston Museum of copper work, displaying decorative, machine-made boxes, candleholders and plaques.

Capital City

London has more of everything—more traffic, more people, more litter, more contrasts, more excitement. Londoners revel in the cosmopolitanism, the diversity and the pace. For an Englishman "up" from the country, the capital is the place for shopping, going to the theatre and eating out. Tourists enthuse about London's Englishness, the historic aura, the quiet charm of garden squares and terraces. You will probably start your trip in London, and gain valuable insights into Britain's past and present that will help you put your travels into perspective. There are good logistical reasons for starting here: road, rail and air routes all radiate from the capital.

It is perfectly possible to visit attractions in the South-East and parts of the South, East Anglia, Central England and the South-West from a base in London—Winchester, Cambridge and Bath, for example. But don't do too many of these long day-trips. Distances may look short on the map, but crowded roads and inconvenient train schedules mean that you will find it more pleasant and less tiring to lodge locally and get to know an area.

Big Ben is not the tower, but the bell heard round the world, marking the hours in Greenwich Mean Time (or British Summer Time, in season).

London

Developing from a Celtic outpost into the largest town in Roman Britain, London became England's capital with the Norman Conquest in 1066. The union of England and Scotland in 1707 made it capital of Britain. Today, London retains a commercial, financial and cultural prominence out of all proportion to Britain's diminished post-imperial status.

The sheer size of London, the irregular street pattern and the way so many sights are hidden from view make the city a difficult place to get to know. Try to find time early in your stay for an introductory bus tour. Once you have taken in the larger picture, you can set out to explore on foot.

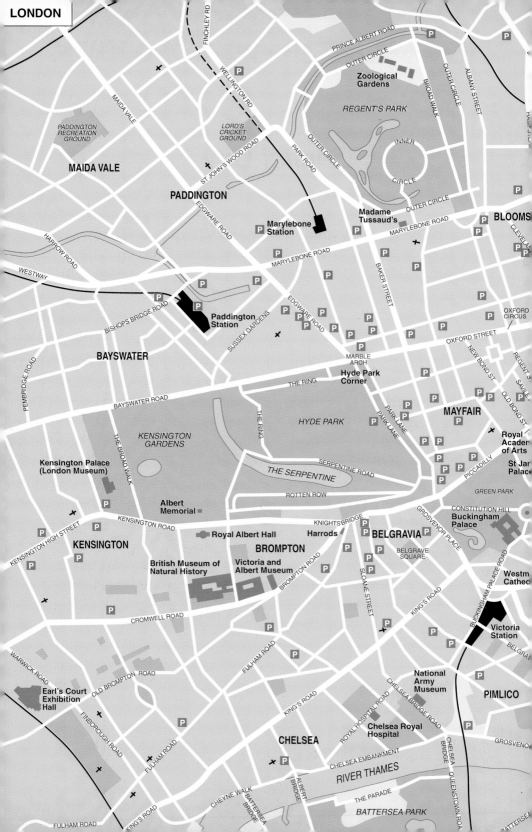

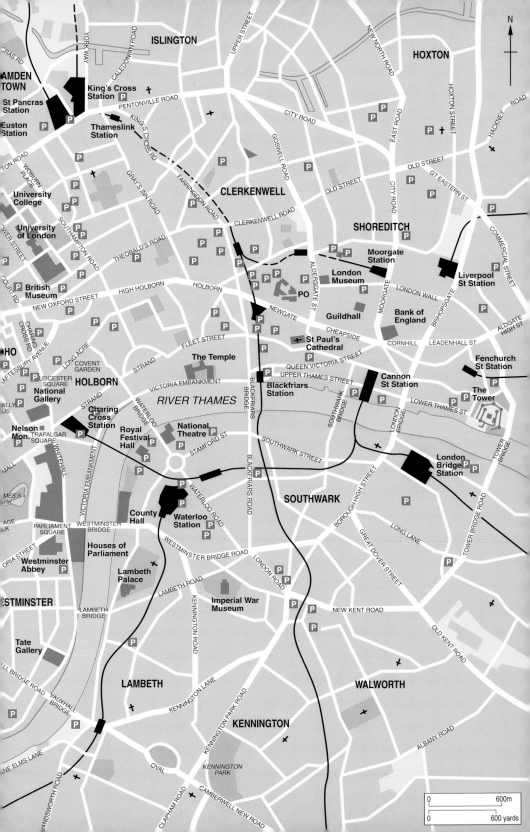

Expansive in every way, London has not one but three distinct "centres". Westminster claims the Houses of Parliament and the Abbey. The West End embraces theatreland, the shops of Mayfair and St James's, Chinatown and Soho. And the historic City, the business and financial district, also contains St Paul's Cathedral and the Tower of London.

Westminster

One of London's chief hubs, **Trafalgar Square**, is a focus for demonstrations and a vast gathering place for visitors and pigeons. The name recalls the 1805 battle in which Lord Nelson defeated Napoleon's fleet off the Spanish coast. Nelson's statue tops the tall Corinthian column in the centre of the square, his tricorn hat a perch for the birds.

City plan of London (previous page).

Map of the London Underground system.

Grand public buildings face the square. On the north side stands the **National Gallery**, Britain's great collection of European art (*see* pages 117–18), with the fine baroque Church of St Martin-in-the-Fields to the east (with a brass-rubbing centre). On the south side, Admiralty Arch frames a magnificent view of **The Mall** (pronounced to rhyme with "pal"), the sweeping boulevard that edges **St James's Park**. On a sunny day this patch of green lures civil servants from the neighbouring ministries of Whitehall.

Overlooking the park is a series of elegant houses: Carlton House Terrace, incorporating the Institute of Contemporary Arts; Marlborough House, where Commonwealth officials meet in conference; Clarence House, home for many years of Queen Elizabeth the Queen Mother; and the much older **St James's Palace**, a maze of passages and courtyards reconstructed many times. From 1698 to 1837 this was a royal residence. Queen Victoria preferred Buckingham Palace, but even today foreign ambassadors are officially accredited to the Court of St James's.

Buckingham Palace, behind high iron railings, is solid, columned, porticoed and impressive, with sentries at the gate. Constructed in 1703 for the Duke of Buckingham, the palace was remodelled by John Nash in 1825. The imposing façade of white Portland stone dates from 1913. When the sovereign is in residence, the royal standard flies overhead.

Changing of the Guard

Everyone should see London's finest free show at least once. The guard changes year-round, weather permitting, in two different locations:

At Buckingham Palace, in front of the main entrance, at 11.30 a.m. daily, from May to July (alternate days from August to April). The 30-minute ceremony features a military band which marches from St James's Palace down the Mall. In Whitehall, at Horse Guards. The Household Cavalry, astride sleek black mounts, changes guard at 11 a.m. weekdays and 10 a.m. Sundays.

The palace proper is out of bounds, but you can visit the **Queen's Gallery**, where changing exhibitions highlight works of art from the fabulous royal collections. Enter from Buckingham Palace Road. Further up the street, the **Royal Mews** provides opulent stabling for the queen's horses. The ceremonial carriages are on display in the Coach House (Wednesday and Thursday afternoons, April to mid-July).

Cromwell fought for Parliament—and then contemptuously dismissed it—but his statue still stands outside the Palace of Westminster.

Palace of Westminster

The Houses of Parliament occupy the building known as the Palace of Westminster, after the medieval royal residence that stood on this site. The original palace went up in flames in 1834, making way for the neo-Gothic extravaganza you see today. Sir Charles Barry (knighted for his efforts) provided the bold rectangular plan, while the medieval detail inside and out is the inspired work of AWN Pugin, the Victorian apostle of the Gothic.

In the interests of security, access is strictly controlled, but the public may attend debates in the Commons and Lords. Join the queue after 5.30 p.m. Monday to Thursday and from 9.30 a.m. to 3 p.m. Friday.

Parliament meets from November to July, recessing at Christmas and Easter. The House of Commons sits from early afternoon to late evening Monday to Thursday (late morning to early afternoon Friday). The prime minister is on hand to answer members' questions on Tuesday and Thursday afternoons.

The House of Lords sits every afternoon, winding up earlier than the Commons. The Royal Gallery is reserved for the queen when she visits the Lords; the sovereign does not have the right to enter the Commons.

Mother of Parliaments

England had a parliament as early as the 13th century (Iceland claims an even older one), when representatives of the whole country—nobles and burghers alike—came together to consult with the king, either at the Palace of Westminster or in the abbey opposite. By 1529, when Parliament took up permanent quarters at Westminster, the body had already divided into the Commons (spokesmen for the communes or shires) and Lords. Today there are 650 Members of Parliament, elected to the Commons by universal suffrage. The House of Lords consists of about 1,100 members, both hereditary and life peers. The chamber reviews, and sometimes revises, bills sent from the Commons. Peers have only limited powers to delay a bill. Occasional campaigns call for the abolition of the House of Lords, or reform to make it more representative.

From Parliament Square you have a good view of **Westminster Hall**, a surviving element of the old Palace of Westminster masterfully incorporated with the new. (In this hall, the former seat of the Law Courts, Guy Fawkes and Charles I stood trial.) Even more impressive is the river elevation, a counterpoint of pinnacles and spires, the square bulk of Victoria Tower balanced by the belfry that houses **Big Ben**. This 13½-tonne bell strikes the hours with a chime known around the world. Strictly speaking, only the bell, and not the clock or the tower, is referred to as "Big Ben". The name recalls the rotund Sir Benjamin Hall, Commissioner of Works when the bell was cast in 1859.

Westminster Abbey

The abbey is Britain's coronation church—the high altar has been the scene of every coronation for the last 900 years—a royal mausoleum and a national shrine. Kings and queens lie buried here alongside eminent statesmen, soldiers and scientists, musicians and writers. Westminster Abbey also remains a house of worship: regular

*T*he Lady Chapel of
Westminster Cathedral, the
most important Roman
Catholic church in England,
finished in 1910.

services take place on Sundays, when the highly regarded boys' choir sings.

There may have been an abbey at Westminster as early as the 7th century, but it was Edward the Confessor who laid the foundations for the church as we know it. In 1245, Henry III took Edward's creation and built it anew in grander Gothic style. Henry VII contributed the chapel that bears his name.

The West Door leads directly into the soaring stone vault of the **nave**. Moving down the aisle, you pass the tomb of that nameless World War I hero, the Unknown Warrior. Memorials to men of science—Faraday, Darwin and others—cluster round the tomb of Isaac Newton, nearby. **Statesmen's Aisle** in the north transept is the province of Disraeli, Peel and Gladstone, while across the way in **Poet's Corner** lie Chaucer and Spencer, Dickens, Hardy and Browning.

The royal tombs lie apart in the area beyond the high altar. The **Chapel of Edward the Confessor** contains the shrine of the king-saint, canonized in 1161. Until the Reformation, pilgrims came here to meditate and confess their sins. On view in the chapel between enthronement ceremonies, the **Coronation Chair** gathers dust as casually as a family heirloom in an attic. Since 1308, every monarch has been crowned on this battered oak throne. Beneath the seat is the ancient Stone of Scone, a block of Scottish sandstone identified by romantics with Jacob's pillow. Edward I filched it from the Scots, whose coronation stone it was.

Further along, the **Chapel of Henry VII** is simply magnificent. Henry, the first Tudor king, commissioned this last great masterpiece of the Gothic as his final resting place. The uniquely English "Perpendicular" style of the architecture stresses the vertical, as the name suggests. At the head of the chapel repose Henry and his queen, Elizabeth of York. A constellation of royalty surrounds them: Elizabeth I, James I and his mother, Mary Queen of Scots, Charles II, William and Mary, Queen Anne.

While in this area you could take in the **Tate Gallery**, showcase of British and modern art (*see* page 118). It is only a short walk along the Thames, up-river from the Houses of Parliament.

Whitehall

This area of government buildings extends from Parliament Square to Trafalgar Square. The name derives from Henry VIII's defunct Palace of Whitehall and applies equally to the neighbourhood, its main thoroughfare, the civil servants who work here and the bureaucracy to which they belong.

Heading up Parliament Street from Parliament Square, you pass the imposing late 19th-century headquarters of the Treasury. Here, some 3m (10ft) below ground, the **Cabinet War Rooms** were Churchill's command post from 1940 (entrance at Clive Steps in King Charles Street). With the surrender of Japan, the door was literally closed on this chapter of British history, leaving the labyrinth of blast-proof rooms intact. You can see the Transatlantic Telephone Room, where scramblers coded Churchill's calls to Roosevelt, and the Map Room, with charts plotting the troop movements on the Russian front and any developments in the Pacific theatre.

A few steps away is an address known around the world: **10 Downing Street**, which has been the office and residence of Britain's prime ministers since 1735. Only visitors on official business may approach the unassuming doorway of No. 10.

Beyond this point, Parliament Street continues as Whitehall. Outstanding on this stretch, the **Banqueting House** of 1619 provides a gilded setting for court ceremony. The **Horse Guards**, opposite, maintain their traditional sentry posts at the entrance to the royal domain of St James's. Housed in 18th-century elegance next door, the **Admiralty** commanded the world's greatest fleet.

The Lord Mayor's Show

The Lord Mayor of London is the First Citizen of The City, but not of the rest of London. He wields power only in the Square Mile which is administered by the thousand-year-old Corporation of London. The City jealously guards its independence, maintaining a separate police force and its own small court and prison. The developers of the skyscrapers that are mushrooming all over the business district look no further than the Guildhall, the seat of City government, for the planning permission often denied them elsewhere in London.

Liverymen—members of the City trade guilds—choose the aldermen and sheriffs from whom the Lord Mayor is selected for a 12-month term of office. Every year in November, the new Lord Mayor rides to his investiture in an ornate gilded carriage, followed by his retinue and decorated floats. Now, as in the Middle Ages, crowds line the route to watch the Lord Mayor's Show pass.

East of Trafalgar Square, the **Strand** links Westminster to The City along a route opened in Edward the Confessor's time. This is a busy street of hotels, theatres and commercial premises, not a place for strolling. Watch the sights go by from the window of a bus: the Savoy Hotel, a monument to Art Deco, and 18th-century Somerset House, home of the **Courtauld Institute Galleries,** the small but select study collections of London University's school of art history.

Down on the Thames embankment, raised benches offer unimpeded views of the river, which is muddy and sluggish here. The obelisk by the water's edge is a 3,000-year-old Egyptian original from Heliopolis, dubbed **Cleopatra's Needle**.

The "City", London's financial district. Look carefully and you can still see some of Wren's churches half-hidden among the modern towers.

Hungerford Footbridge takes you across the Thames to the **South Bank** complex, a forbidding fortress of the arts. Don't let the grim exterior deter you from the exhibitions at the Hayward Gallery or the Museum of the Moving Image, the National Film Theatre's retrospectives, the concerts at Festival Hall or the best of British theatre at the National Theatre.

The City of London

The City takes care of business—insurance, banking, the stock market, commodities trading. Every working day, half a million commuters descend on London's compact commercial centre, an overnight ghost town of 5,000. The "Square Mile" extends from the boundary stone of Temple Bar in the Strand to the Tower of London, and from the Thames to the Barbican—the area originally within the Roman wall. Beyond Temple Bar, begins Fleet Street, an extension of the Strand.

Make your way back to **Fleet Street**, a name that lives on as a metaphor for British journalism. None of the big national newspapers has offices here

Legal London

Hidden from view on either side of Fleet Street are the Inns of Court: the Temple, Lincoln's Inn and Gray's Inn. For members of the bar these venerable societies are a professional home for life.

Access to the **Temple** is through two narrow gatehouses near Temple Bar, one leading to Middle Temple and the other to Inner Temple. Originally the headquarters of the crusading Knights Templar (hence the name), the Temple has been associated with the legal profession since the 14th century, first as a school of law and then as a professional society. Like the other Inns of Court, the complex comprises dining hall, chapel, gardens, offices and judges' lodgings.

Anyone may enter the Temple precinct, but most of the buildings are closed to sightseers. One exception is the round Norman Templar church, put up in 1185. In the old days, lawyers met their clients in the crypt.

Chancery Lane takes you past the Public Records Office to the gatehouse of **Lincoln's Inn**. Notice the medieval diamond-patterned brickwork of the late 15th-century Old Hall, the oldest surviving structure in the compound. If you look into the windows of the New Buildings (a mere three centuries old), you can see stacks of legal documents on the ledges, bound with the "red tape" that has become a synonym for bureaucracy in the English language.

At the bottom of Chancery Lane, across High Holborn, **Gray's Inn** is famous mainly for its gardens.

now—most have transferred to new premises east of The City in Wapping. Not that the historical associations have gone away. You can visit **Dr Johnson's House** in Gough Square, and climb up to the attic room where the original Fleet Street hack compiled the first

Dictionary. A museum in the crypt of **St Bride's**, the old printers' church, chronicles the rise—and fall—of the industry in Fleet Street. Famous in its own right is the Wren sanctuary and wedding-cake steeple of St Bride's.

Fleet Street comes to an end at Ludgate Circus. Ahead lies St Paul's, a very visible landmark on top of Ludgate Hill.

St Paul's Cathedral

Christopher Wren had the privilege rarely granted a cathedral builder: after more than three decades of work on St Paul's, he saw his design realized in 1708. The architect, then 75, lived on till the age of 90, to be buried at last inside the walls of the cathedral. The Latin epitaph on his tomb translates: "Reader, if you seek his monument, look around you."

Wren's cathedral is the third or fourth on this site. The even larger Gothic "Old St Paul's", destroyed in the 1666 Great Fire, was preceded by a Romanesque church which had grown from Bishop Mellitus' foundation of 604. Balance and clarity distinguish Wren's design for St Paul's, a Latin cross in plan, a Classical dome and baroque west towers. Outstanding features of the interior include Grinling Gibbons' beautifully carved choir stalls, Jean Tijou's wrought-iron choir

*F*ire destroyed Old St Paul's, and Wren's masterpiece would have burned, too, but for the volunteers who kept a nightly vigil during the World War II Blitz.

screen and gates, and the scenes from the life of St Paul that cover the dome, painted by Sir James Thornhill.

St Paul's has its quota of monuments and famous tombs: the outsize **Wellington memorial**, in the aisle to your left as you go in; the **effigy of John Donne**, in the choir aisle; and **Nelson's monument**, in the south transept. You'll see the stairs to the soaring dome nearby. An easy climb leads to the **Whispering Gallery** at the base of the drum. Put one ear close to the wall and

Victoria as Queen-Empress stands before the west front of Sir Christopher Wren's masterpiece, St Paul's Cathedral, finished in 1708.

you can hear a whisper as it travels from the other side of the gallery, more than 30m (100ft) away.

North of St Paul's stands that concrete and brick colossus, the **Barbican Arts and Conference Centre**. The complex houses concert and exhibition halls, theatres, cinemas, a library and art gallery on eight levels—half of them underground. Not everyone raves about the architecture, but the standard of cultural offerings is high. Try to get tickets for a performance of the resident London Symphony Orchestra or Royal Shakespeare Company, or a free lunchtime concert.

Approaching from St Martin's le Grand, you enter the Barbican via the striking modern **Museum of London**. One of the largest exhibits stands outside in the grounds: a section of the medieval town wall, which was built on Roman foundations.

The Bank

The heart of London's financial district centres on the complex of eight streets that converge outside the **Bank of England**, impregnable behind high, windowless walls. Security is of the essence: vaults within hold the nation's gold reserves. Needless to say, tourists are barred from the bank, but they are welcome in the museum adjacent, with historical exhibits and video displays (enter from Bartholomew Lane).

The Lord Mayor's official residence is **Mansion House**, the Renaissance-style palace across the way. A law court and prison cells are part of the original fixtures and fittings. North-west of the Bank, off Gresham Street, **Guildhall** is the town hall of The City. This resilient building, dating from 1411, has

withstood every disaster from the Great Fire to the Blitz. Step inside (during office hours) for a look at the ancient Great Hall with its minstrel's gallery and Gothic stonework.

Computer screens scattered about the City and beyond replaced the trading floor of the Stock Exchange, revolutionizing a business that had scarcely changed its methods since the early 18th century. **Lloyd's of London**, the international insurance underwriters, originated even earlier, in Edward Lloyd's coffee house near the Tower of London. Three centuries on, they can be found in a controversially high-tech high-rise in Leadenhall Street, designed by Richard Rogers. Any working day, groups who book in advance are welcome to observe members at work in the Underwriting Room.

The Tower of London

The castle begun by William the Conqueror has been a fortress, a palace, a prison and a place of execution for more than a thousand years. Among the celebrated victims: the sons of Edward IV (the "Little Princes in the Tower"), Henry VI, Anne Boleyn, Catherine Howard, Sir Thomas More and Sir Walter Raleigh. Now it is amiably defended by Yeomen Warders—about 40 men in Tudor costume, halberds (a combined spear and battleaxe) at the ready. Also known as Beefeaters, these royal bodyguards conduct free guided tours (weather permitting).

Crossing the moat, grassed over in the last century, you pass into the outer enclosure with its display of cannon. The gloomy river entrance is known as **Traitors' Gate**. In the **Bloody Tower** opposite, the Little Princes died and

Begun in William the Conqueror's time, the Tower of London has been palace, fortress and prison and is now one of the world's most visited sights.

Raleigh languished. A passageway through the Bloody Tower opens onto the inner enclosure. Look for the **scaffold site** on the emerald lawn of Tower Green. The ravens you see flapping about have always nested within the walls. According to legend, the tower will collapse if they ever fly away.

Straight ahead is the queue for the **Jewel House**. The line may seem dauntingly long, but it usually moves fairly quickly. Railings channel sightseers past ceremonial silver and vestments—notice the splendid coronation robe—to the vault containing the **Crown Jewels**. Look out for the crown of St Edward; the Imperial State Crown, set with diamonds and precious stones; and the royal sceptre, with the largest cut diamond in the world, the 530-carat *Star of Africa*.

Across the yard, the **White Tower** is the oldest part of the fortification, now housing the **Royal Armouries**, one of the world's definitive collections of arms and armour. On an upper floor, the Norman **St John's Chapel** has the distinction of being London's oldest church (1080).

East of the Tower is one of London's trademarks, **Tower Bridge**, a marvel of Victorian engineering in mock Gothic style. Until the 1970s, the original hydraulic engines powered the control gear. You may want to have a look at the machinery in the **Engine Room Museum**, but the outstanding attraction is the **panorama** from the walkways—a vast view of the wide, smooth river and the high-rise City beside it.

East again, **St Katherine's Dock**, so hard hit by the Blitz, has reopened as a marina. The complex is part of the reviving **Docklands** area, a 22km² (8½-square-mile) enterprise zone that extends along both banks of the Thames from the Tower of London to Greenwich. Once largely derelict, Docklands now offers places to work, shop and live—in a converted warehouse, perhaps, or a futuristic tower block. New developments include Tobacco Dock and Butler's Wharf with shops, restaurants, offices and flats; the London Arena sports and entertainment centre; and London City Airport. Get there via a Thames riverbus or the Docklands Light Railway.

*E*very April, tens of thousands of runners cross Tower Bridge on their way from Greenwich to Westminster in the London Marathon.

West End

For suburbanites, visiting the West End is "going up to town". The focus for theatre, shopping and entertainment, this somewhat diffuse district claims the smart hotels, restaurants and clubs, with Piccadilly and Oxford Street for its main thoroughfares.

West End sightseeing begins in **Piccadilly Circus**, where the city lights shine brightest. The celebrated traffic circle has been abolished to ease circulation into Shaftesbury Avenue and on to The City, and a pedestrian zone surrounds the Shaftesbury Memorial, improving access to the famous statue of **Eros** (1893) on its fountain pedestal.

Piccadilly Circus has always been a great gathering place. Now all the people have somewhere to go: the **London Pavilion**, a shopping and leisure centre on the north side of the Circus (home of the waxwork Rock Circus attraction); and the neighbouring **Trocadero**, incorporating the Guinness World of Records exhibition. A few steps away in **Leicester Square** (pronounced "lester"), the big West End cinemas screen first-run hits, competing for business with 40 or more theatres scattered throughout the neighbourhood.

Busy **Piccadilly** links the Circus to Hyde Park Corner, exactly one mile (1.6km) away. Among all the airline offices, restaurants, shops and hotels, the square brick tower of **St James's, Piccadilly** stands out. Yet another Wren church—some would say it is his best—St James's puts on concerts and craft

markets, and is the parish church of the **Royal Academy of Arts** in Burlington House just across the street. The avant-garde may regret the conservative stance of this august body, but everybody agrees that the Royal Academy stages some of the best exhibitions to be seen in town.

Shopping is a consuming activity in Piccadilly's elegant arcades and department stores. Beadles in livery guard the entrance to **Burlington Arcade**, among the oldest (1819) and most exclusive of the capital's covered shopping promenades. Over the road at **Fortnum & Mason**, shop assistants in tail coats preside over purchases of caviar and quail's

T he multinational advertising could be anywhere, but at ground level Piccadilly Circus is a focal point of London's theatreland.

eggs in what must be the grandest grocery department anywhere in the world.

Beyond the arcades of the Ritz Hotel, **Green Park** parallels the south side of Piccadilly. On a Sunday, London's street artists make this stretch of open land their pitch.

Piccadilly ends in style at Hyde Park Corner. **Apsley House**, the lone town house by the park, was once the westernmost residence in the city, known simply as No. 1, London. The Duke of Wellington moved in two years after Waterloo, and his descendants still keep a *pied-à-terre* here. The lower floors house the **Wellington Museum** of Napoleonic memorabilia, with some Old Masters from the Wellesley family collections on view.

Across the way lie the crescents and squares of **Belgravia**. Not everyone can afford the property taxes in this stately district, and many of the cream stucco houses now belong to foreign embassies.

Mayfair

Expensive apartments, elegant shops, exclusive clubs and casinos make up Mayfair, the area north of Piccadilly, between Park Lane and Regent Street. **Bond Street**, Old and New, specializes in furs, jewellery and Old Masters and leads London's art and antiques trade, bolstered by the presence of **Sotheby's** auction house. Galleries spill over into the surrounding streets—Cork, Albemarle, Grafton, Dover. The ethnographic **Museum of Mankind** is near at hand in Burlington Gardens. Running north from here, **Savile Row** traditionally outfits Britain's best-dressed men.

Of course, Mayfair also has its secluded residential streets—and a Mayfair address has an undeniable

Many of London's old-established specialist shops still survive amid the giants of retailing.

cachet—but the squares are not the patrician compounds they were. Most of the buildings that surround Berkeley (pronounced "barkly") Square are modern, and it was here that the cream of London society lived. Grosvenor (pronounced "grovener") Square is the site of the 1960s-style US Embassy.

Large luxury hotels line **Park Lane**, no longer a lane but a very busy boulevard. West-facing rooms have a million-pound view of **Hyde Park** across the road, accessible by subway (pedestrian underpass). A path leads diagonally across the park to the Serpentine, an artificial lake, and Lido bathing beach. Another path parallel to Park Lane takes you to **Speaker's Corner**. This open space near Marble Arch echoes to unbounded eloquence on Sunday afternoons. Any orator who has a message—philosophical, religious, ideological, but rarely dull—can face the hecklers here.

Just behind Park Lane, an enclave of 18th-century Mayfair survives in **Shepherd Market**, an area of outdoor cafés, antique shops and boutiques. **Marble Arch**, at the north end of Park Lane, is the gateway to Oxford Street. John Nash designed the neoclassical portal for Buckingham Palace in 1828, but unfortunately, he got his measurements wrong. Too narrow to admit the royal coach of state, Marble Arch had to be scrapped. Eventually it was set up here, on the site of Tyburn Tree, a place of public execution from the 12th to the 18th centuries.

Brash **Oxford Street** mixes big stores, chain outlets and fly-by-night fast-buck operators on the way to Oxford Circus and the smarter shopping of **Regent Street**, with Garrard's,

the crown jewellers, Hamley's giant toy emporium and Liberty's, renowned for its floral fabrics and half-timbered façade, a charming 1920s pastiche of the Tudor style. North of Oxford Circus, Regent Street leads to Portland Place (home of the BBC) and **Regent's Park**, with its lake, canal and open-air theatre. **London Zoo**, threatened with closure, through lack of funds (*see* page 119) occupies a triangle of land in the park.

The lower end of Regent Street curves east to Piccadilly Circus, following John Nash's elegant plan.

St James's

Officers and gentlemen frequent St James's, south of Piccadilly. Here in the heart of London's clubland you will find the centuries-old wine merchants, barbers, hatters, shirtmakers and cobblers that cater to the most discerning masculine tastes. Famous **clubs** line St James's Street and Pall Mall. Don't look for a placard on the door— White's, Boodles, Brooks's and others turn an anonymous face to the world. The concept of an exclusive male meeting place evolved from the coffee house of the 18th century. Once there were as many as 150 clubs in St James's, but the number has declined this century. An anachronism in a modern world, the majority of the clubs still ban women.

Even the art and antique dealers put the accent on the masculine, featuring sporting pictures, outsize leather armchairs and old meerschaum pipes. Focus for the art trade is Christie's, the auctioneers in King Street.

Soho

Hard-drinking, hard-living, hard-core Soho is famous for its bohemian pubs, jazz clubs, ethnic restaurants, food shops and sex shops. You are generally safe here, except from rip-offs, so use discretion in choosing the establishments you enter.

Cosmopolitan Soho developed in the 17th century, when Huguenot and Greek refugees flooded into London. A contingent of French followed after the Revolution, then the Italians, Spanish and Chinese. The name "Soho" is an old hunting cry that goes back to the days when Londoners rode to hounds across the fields of Leicester. Now Leicester Square marks the southern boundary of the district.

Adjacent to the square is **Chinatown**, recently furnished with bilingual street signs, oriental gateways and pagoda-style phone boxes. Oblivious to the tourist trappings, the local community goes about its business—queuing up at the Hong Kong Cinema, dining out at the local restaurants. Join them at one of the busy establishments in Gerrard or Wardour Streets.

Following Wardour Street across theatre-lined Shaftesbury Avenue into the heart of Soho, you pass the moody ruin of **St Anne's Church** (1680), which was bombed in the Blitz and never restored. Continental bakeries, food shops and restaurants are scattered along Brewer, Old Compton, Frith and Greek Streets.

Not far from Oxford Street and the bookshops of Charing Cross Road, peaceful **Soho Square** isolates itself from the excitement, while **Carnaby Street**—that faded sixties mecca where a new world of clothing styles began—runs behind Regent Street. Fashion moved on a long time ago, but the tourists still keep coming.

Covent Garden

Today's Covent Garden offers buskers (street entertainers) and bustle around the old market buildings vacated by London's fruit and vegetable traders. Trendy shops have invaded the **Central Market** and surrounding streets, with stalls for crafts and clothing under cover and out on the Piazza. This is one area where you can browse and buy in the evenings and on Sundays. The wine bars and restaurants keep late hours, too, making Covent Garden a popular after-theatre rendezvous. The name is a corruption of "convent" garden, and serves as a reminder that the land was once cultivated by the monks of Westminster Abbey.

Inigo Jones's striking **St Paul's Church** holds down the east side of the Piazza, the forecourt of the church an arena for street theatre. To the west, the former Flower Market accommodates the vintage tube trains and buses of the **London Transport Museum**, with room to spare for the exhibits of the **Theatre Museum**. Of course, the great cultural institution here is the **Royal Opera House**, showcase for the Royal Opera and Ballet companies (box office in Floral Street).

Bloomsbury

This district evokes memories of London's early 20th-century literary life. Between the wars, the novelist Virginia Woolf, historian Lytton Strachey and art critic Roger Fry all lived and worked here. There are many pleasant squares and two internationally renowned institutions—the **British Museum** (*see* page 117) and the administrative centre of the scattered University of London.

Covent Garden, off the Strand, once London's wholesale fruit and vegetable market, is now a food, shopping and entertainment centre.

London's Villages

Hundreds of villages have been woven into the urban fabric of London, each with its own high street and village green, its shops, pubs and local characters. We concentrate on three of these that every visitor will want to explore.

Knightsbridge

Shoppers waiting for the bus by Knightsbridge Green, near Harrods, may not take that triangle of grass for the old common of Brompton village. The humble hamlet of 150 years ago has become one of London's most desirable residential neighbourhoods and a leading shopping centre.

Harrods, biggest of the big stores, grew up with Knightsbridge. Henry Charles Harrod opened his Brompton Road grocery business in 1849, building the present terracotta palace at the turn of the century. Much more than a store, Harrods is a national institution. The range of services is simply phenomenal: pharmacy, kennels, bank, pub, undertakers—Harrods has them all.

Beyond Harrods and its several fashion floors is diminutive **Beauchamp Place** (pronounced "beechum"), the former village high street—now a street of high-fashion shops. Brompton Road and Sloane Street, the main shopping arteries, converge beyond the green with Knightsbridge, the wide avenue that parallels Hyde Park.

Kensington

The "Royal Borough of Kensington and Chelsea" skirts the rambling red brick **Kensington Palace**, one royal

*F*ood halls in the big
department stores go in for
artistic displays, like this
one at Harrods.

home open—in part at least—to the public. You can tour the historic State Apartments, occupied by kings and queens from William and Mary to Victoria, and then take a walk around the grounds, a pleasant expanse of public parkland better known as **Kensington Gardens**.

The tumult of **Kensington High Street** begins beyond the palace gates.

Chain stores dominate the high street, with white stucco terraces and gardens of tangled greenery behind. Branching off to the north, **Kensington Church Street** is an address known to antique collectors the world over.

Down in South Kensington—"South Ken" for short—a complex of four major **museums** draws the crowds to the busy junction of Exhibition, Brompton and Cromwell roads. The decorative arts collections of the **Victoria and Albert Museum** occupy the Renaissance-style brick building, with the **Natural History Museum** in all its neo-Romanesque splendour opposite, adjacent to the more functional premises of the science and geological museums. These temples to the Victorian gods of Art and Science are larger than any cathedral. Even in a less reverent age, they still inspire awe.

Chelsea

The mod look, the punk craze, the romantic revival—whatever's next, you may well see it first in the **King's Road**, Chelsea's main street. Chelsea has often set the trends for the world to follow. Stroll from Sloane Square to the river by way of Christopher Wren's sprawling **Royal Hospital**, which has been a Chelsea landmark since 1682. Charles II founded this retirement home for old and disabled soldiers, with veterans of the Civil War in mind. Some 420 pensioners live here today. The hospital's vaulted chapel and Great Hall (the pensioners' mess hall) are open to visitors most mornings and afternoons. A small museum in the grounds traces the history of the institution.

Between the hospital and Chelsea Embankment, the well-tended lawns of

Ranelagh Gardens provide the setting for Britain's most fashionable flower show every spring, while the modern building on the far side of the hospital houses the **National Army Museum**.

Major Museums and Galleries

British Museum
(*Great Russell Street, WCI*).
This vast storehouse of culture originated in Sir Hans Sloane's 18th-century "Cabinet of Curiosities", with its fossils,

A monument to the Victorian mission to educate, the Neo-Romanesque Natural History Museum in South Kensington.

coins and classical antiquities. The collection divides into eight sections: the art of classical Greece, ancient Egypt and Western Asia, treasures from Roman Britain and medieval Europe, oriental objects, coins and medals, prints and drawings. Don't even attempt to cover every area; concentrate on two or three—or simply seek out some of the highlights:

Elgin Marbles 5th century BC. Friezes and figures from the Parthenon in Athens.

Portland Vase 1st century BC. Roman cameo glass.

Khorsabad Entrance Colossal gateway of 710 BC from the citadel of the Assyrian King Sargon II.

Rosetta Stone Key to the deciphering of Egyptian hieroglyphics.

Mummies Humans, *and* animals from crocodiles to cats.

Sutton Hoo Treasure 7th century. Treasures from the burial ship of King Raedwald of the Angles.

Prints and Drawings The complete engraved and etched works of Schongauer, Dürer, Rembrandt. Drawings by Michelangelo, Rubens, Watteau.

Manuscripts and Printed Books Magna Carta, Gütenberg Bible, Shakespeare's First Folio.

Reading Room Where Karl Marx wrote *Das Kapital*.

National Gallery
(*Trafalgar Square*)

From a group of 38 paintings purchased for the nation from the estate of the banker John Julius Angerstein in 1824, the collection has grown to more than 2,000, including many landmarks in the history of Western European art. Some highlights:

Masaccio His very human *Virgin and Child* of 1426.

Piero della Francesca The timeless *Baptism of Christ* and joyous *Nativity*, an unfinished late work.

Botticelli The *Mystic Nativity* of 1500, so full of grace and movement.

Leonardo da Vinci *Virgin of the Rocks* and cartoon of the *Virgin and Child with St Anne and St John the Baptist*—shot at by a madman and expertly restored.

Bellini A striking portrait of *Doge Leonardo Loredano.*

Titian *Noli Me Tangere, Portrait of a Man* and the wonderfully stagey *Bacchus and Ariadne.*

Rubens The *Judgement of Paris*, all rosy, rippling, opalescent flesh.

Jan van Eyck That minutely observed portrait of a marriage, *Giovanni Arnolfini and his Wife.*

Hans Holbein the Younger *The Ambassadors*, a complex allegorical work.

Rembrandt Two self-portraits, painted three decades apart, and a loving portrayal of Hendrickje Stoffels as the *Woman Bathing in a Stream.*

Velázquez *Rokeby Venus*, the artist's only nude.

Gainsborough *Mr and Mrs Andrews*, a masterpiece of 18th-century portraiture, and *Morning Walk.*

Constable His *Haywain, Cornfield* and *Salisbury Cathedral* capture the very essence of the countryside.

Turner The great *Rain, Steam and Speed.*

Tate Gallery
(Millbank, SW1)

The Tate is several museums in one: a collection of British art, a Turner gallery, a gallery of modern painting and sculpture, and a showcase for "new art".

Some **British** highlights: the Hogarths, especially *Painter and His Pug*; the sporting pictures of George Stubbs; Blake's colour prints for the *Divine Comedy* and *Job*; Constable's virtuoso landscape prints; the Pre-Raphaelites.

The **Turners** (on show in the Clore Gallery designed by James Stirling): *Snow Storm: Hannibal and his Army Crossing the Alps*; *Venice with Salute*; *Norham Castle.*

The **moderns**, from Picasso's *Three Dancers* of 1925 to Carl Andre's *Equivalent VIII* (1966).

Diversions

Madame Tussaud's
(Marylebone Road, NW1)

A London tradition since 1835, the ever-popular waxworks offers some enjoyable moments of high kitsch. See the diarist Samuel Pepys at his desk, Mary Queen of Scots preparing for her execution, and today's politicians and pop stars. Photo opportunities abound in the Gallery of the Famous, where you are invited to "picture yourself" with celebrities from Picasso to Gaddafi. The famous Chamber of Horrors is very dark and very crowded. Hang on to your money in the mob.

Contrasts

It would be hard to imagine two more different collections—or ways to display them—than the wonderfully eclectic **Wallace Collection** (*Manchester Square, W1*) of fine and decorative art housed in an 18th-century mansion, and the Saatchi Collection, the cutting edge of modern art shown in a vast new exhibition space (*98A Boundary Road, NW8*).

Highgate Cemetery
(*Swain's Lane. Tube to Archway, then bus 271 or 210*)

To visit the historic western section, the "Valhalla of the Victorians", you have to join one of the free, hour-long daily tours. Guides lead the way to the graves of personalities as diverse as George Cruft, founder of London's annual dog show, and Robert Addis, the toothbrush tycoon. The most famous grave, that of Karl Marx, lies across the road in the modern eastern part, open all day long. Inevitably, his monument urges: "Workers of all Lands Unite".

London Zoo
(*Regent's Park, NW1*)

About 8,000 animals live and breed here. Deer and antelope roam in an open paddock, and lions stalk modern moated terraces, while rhinos and elephants have a spacious free-form brick pavilion. Have a look, too, at some of the historic installations: the original Regency camel house, now an information centre, and the 1930s penguin pool.

Environs of London

Greenwich
(*London SE10*)

Approaching from the water you see Greenwich at its best, the twin domes of the Royal Naval College framing the white cube of Queen's House. Hard by the pier rise the spindly masts of the clipper *Cutty Sark* (1869). Nearby is *Gypsy Moth IV,* the ketch that took Sir Francis Chichester on his solo journey around the world in the 1960s.

An uphill climb leads from the pier to the **Old Royal Observatory**. Established in 1675, the observatory functioned here until smog and city lights forced the scientists out into the countryside in the 1930s. They left behind a historic collection of instruments, including the telescope used by Edmund Halley to sight his comet. A strip of brass in the courtyard marks 0° Longitude, the Greenwich Meridian officially adopted in 1884 as the prime meridian.

Downhill, the **National Maritime Museum** presents the history of British seafaring from sail to steam. The West

M orris dancers and the Cutty Sark, one of the clipper ships which raced to bring the first tea of the season from China in the 1870s.

Wing has the most interesting exhibits, including a flotilla of **royal barges** (the boats that slipped down the Thames to the strains of Handel's *Water Music*) and the **Nelson relics**, above all the bloodstained uniform from Trafalgar.

An arcade runs from the West Wing past **Queen's House** (notable for its Palladian architecture) to the East Wing, where there are exhibits on Britain's navy and life at sea.

The **Royal Naval College** occupies the historic baroque buildings of the Royal Naval Hospital, set dramatically at the water's edge.

Round the next big bend down-river, the giant clamshells of the **Thames Barrier** stand ready to repel any tidal surges which might threaten London with flooding.

Kew Gardens

(*Kew, Surrey*)
Officially the Royal Botanic Gardens, with 50,000 species of plants from all

Springtime in Kew Gardens, but it could be anywhere in England as flowers explode in succession to signal the end of dreary winter.

over the world, Kew fulfils its scientific purpose in a setting of sheer beauty. It was thanks to the pioneering botanists of Kew that breadfruit took root in the West Indies, and rubber trees in Malaysia. Today Kew remains one of the world's major experimental centres. Whatever your botanical interests, take a look at the period glasshouses: John Nash's classical **Aroid House**, enclosing a mini tropical rainforest, and Decimus Burton's mid-19th-century **Palm House**, restored after a freak 1987 hurricane. That storm toppled some of Kew's rarest hardwood trees, including specimens dating back to the gardens' early 18th-century beginnings. But the scars are healing, and the rhododendron dell, bamboo and azalea gardens are as lovely as ever.

Hampton Court Palace

(*Hampton Court, Middlesex*)
This red-brick Tudor mansion lies 20km (12 miles) upstream from London. Built in 1515 by Cardinal Wolsey, it was appropriated by Henry VIII 15 years later when Wolsey fell from favour. Henry liked Hampton Court so much that he spent all his honeymoons here but one—the first. Catherine of Aragon got a look in all the same. She and Henry were Wolsey's first guests.

Of later monarchs, only William and Mary shared Henry's enthusiasm for the place—they asked Wren to build a new suite of rooms. Queen Victoria finally opened Hampton Court to the public in 1838. In the meantime, crown pensioners had begun to occupy "grace and favour" accommodation on the premises. It was one such lodger who started the 1985 fire that devastated the Wren wing, including the King's Audience Chamber and Cartoon Gallery, now happily restored.

You enter the palace through the Great Gatehouse, leading to Base Court and Anne Boleyn's Gateway. Continue into Clock Court, where the sun revolves briskly around the earth in Nicolas Oursin's astronomical clock of 1540—utterly oblivious to the Copernican revolution.

The interior offers the contrast of William and Mary's carved, gilded and upholstered **State Apartments** (separate but equal), with the timber-and-plaster Tudor rooms: **Wolsey's Closet**, a study faced with fine linenfold panelling;

Henry VIII's Haunted Gallery (haunted by the ghost of Catherine Howard); and the **Great Hall**, where king and court ate, drank and made merry.

Windsor Castle

(*Windsor, Berkshire*)
Picturesque in the extreme, the world's largest occupied castle sprawls atop a bluff beside the Thames. The walled precinct divides into a lower, middle and upper ward, dominated by the Round Tower of 1170. Additions were made piecemeal through the centuries, notably St George's Chapel (1478–1511) and the luxurious State Apartments, begun by Charles II.

As you enter through the main gateway, **St George's Chapel** lies straight ahead. This triumphant example of the Perpendicular style ranks with Henry VII's Chapel in Westminster Abbey. The West Window (1509) portrays kings and queens of England in a blaze of stained glass, including the reigning monarch at that time, King Henry VIII. On his death in 1547, Henry was buried in a vault below the floor of the chapel. Edward IV and Charles I are also entombed here, as well as more recent kings and queens, beginning with George III.

A garden grows in the moat encircling the Round Tower. A passage leads to the **State Apartments** in the upper ward, St George's Hall, the Waterloo Chamber and adjoining rooms—destroyed in the disastrous fire of 1992, though their contents were saved.

While this section of the palace is closed for restoration, there is much else to see at Windsor—**Queen Mary's Dolls' House**, to start with. Don't dismiss this charming period piece as a

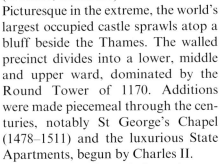

mere toy. Conceived specifically to raise money for a children's charity, the house was commissioned by the queen from the outstanding architect of her day, Sir Edwin Lutyens, and its contents from leading manufacturers, artists and designers, including the Wedgwood china and a tiny working Hoover. The **Exhibition of Drawings** next door features art from the queen's comprehensive collection of Old Masters—Michelangelos, Leonardos and Holbeins.

The small shops near Castle Hill are worth a wander, as is the neighbouring township of Eton. A footbridge leads from Thames Street across the river to the quadrangles of **Eton College**, the most private of England's public schools, whose "old-boy network" is still famously influential.

Whipsnade Wild Animal Park
(*near Dunstable, Bedfordshire*)
A pioneering institution run by London Zoo, Whipsnade was one of the first zoos to dispense with cages. The 200 species of animals—wild horses, white rhinos, deer, gazelle—have the freedom of expansive enclosures. Ride through the African section on the narrow-gauge Whipsnade and Umfolozi Steam Railway, a vintage train that originally operated in Zululand.

Woburn Abbey
(*Woburn, Bedfordshire*)
Commercialization detracts only a little from Woburn's stately appeal. The 18th-century house occupies the site of a Cistercian monastery, three wings around a central courtyard echoing the layout of the old cloisters. A fourth

wing of the building was lost to dry rot in 1950, an event that inspired the Duke of Bedford's entry into the stately home business. A tour of the house is only the beginning of a visit to Woburn, a vast leisure complex incorporating a safari park, the **Wild Animal Kingdom**. Various restaurants, gift shops and an antiques centre (nominal admission fee) generate the additional revenue needed to keep Woburn in trim.

The **Private Apartments** in the north wing are closed to the public when the family is in residence. The **Canaletto Room** takes its name from no fewer than 21 views of Venice by the artist. The Sèvres was a gift to a ducal ancestor from Louis XVI. The **State Rooms** (west wing) have gilded rococo ceilings, silk wall coverings and, in the Chinese Room, wallpaper imported from China some 250 years ago. Reserved for royal visits—Queen Victoria and Prince Albert came to stay in 1841—these rooms were hardly ever used, which explains the superb condition of the upholstery and decoration.

The focal point of the remaining wing is Henry Holland's sumptuous **library** of 1790. Above the bookcases hang portraits by Rembrandt and Van Dyck.

Luton Hoo
(*Luton, Bedfordshire*)
A succession of distinguished architects worked on this house, beginning with Robert Adam. The park bears the

*W*indsor Castle, one of the many royal retreats and an impressive feature of the landscape for miles around.

stamp of the ubiquitous Capability Brown. But the contents of the house steal the show. The South African diamond magnate Sir Julius Wernher and his son, Sir Harold, assembled most of the art objects on display: medieval ivories, Limoges enamels and some exceptional paintings by Franz Hals, Hobbema, Memling and Bartolomé Bermejo (an earthy *St Michael*). Among many impressive Italian Renaissance bronze statuettes, a *St John the Baptist* by Sansovino stands out. The superb Fabergé jewellery came to Luton Hoo through Sir Julius's marriage to a Russian aristocrat, the granddaughter of Alexander Pushkin.

Hatfield House
(*Hatfield, Hertfordshire*)
Queen Elizabeth I was reading under an oak tree in the park at Hatfield when she received the news of her accession to the throne. Only a section of Old Palace, her childhood home, survives. Robert Cecil, 1st Earl of Salisbury and prime minister to King James I, demolished most of the building in 1608 to make way for a new house in the fashionable Jacobean style. A visit to Hatfield concentrates on the imposing residence of the Cecils, with its woodpanelled **Great Hall**, grand Renaissance **staircase** and separate **state apartments** for the king and queen. Mementoes of Elizabeth I range from two famous portraits to the queen's silk stockings and her gardening hat.

The remaining wing of the Elizabethan Old Palace, situated in what are now known as the West Gardens, provides a suitably historic venue for **medieval banquets**, complete with minstrels, serving wenches and mead.

British Art

Art at the time of the Tudors was an international affair, with European painters travelling from one country to work for the kings and courts of others. A number of foreign artists came to England, among them **Hans Holbein the Younger** (1407–1543). Holbein's art had its roots in the German realist tradition. More distinctively English was the work of miniaturist **Nicholas Hilliard** (1547–1619), who painted tiny, jewel-like portraits of courtiers in a country setting.

Little more than a hundred years later, England in the period of *The Beggar's Opera* combined an elegance and squalor that **William Hogarth** (1697–1764) catches perfectly. Genuine moral outrage informs the grisly black humour of *Gin Lane, Marriage à la Mode* (National Gallery, London) and other Hogarth works, including his masterpiece, *The Rake's Progress* (Sir John Soane's Museum, London). Designed to be engraved, Hogarth's incisive Neoclassical pictures belong to a tradition of English satirical graphics that continues through the florid lampoons of **James Gillray** (1757–1815) and the Dickensian quirkiness of **George Cruikshank** (1792–1879).

Millais' An Enemy Sowing Tares.

After the cynical polish of the 18th century, the years around 1800 saw the rise of Romanticism. The poetry of Wordsworth and Coleridge exemplifies the more spiritual and rural tendencies of the movement, which found artistic expression in the landscape paintings of lakes, cliffs and mountains by James Ward, John Martin and others. But perhaps the greatest Romantic artist was the highly individual visionary, **William Blake** (1757–1827). As much a poet as a painter, Blake used his mastery of dynamic line and colour to illustrate his own handmade books of poetry (of which the Tate Gallery, London, has a beautifully displayed collection). His art features such subjects as roses, fruit trees, lambs and angels in a pastoral setting. Yet despite this typical Romanticism—for Romanticism was in part a reaction against the increasingly ugly and prosaic world of the Industrial Revolution—Blake himself was a confirmed Londoner who lived in Soho and rarely travelled outside the city.

John Constable (1776–1837) and the idea of the English countryside are inextricably

Turner's Music Party.

linked. Constable's pictures of Suffolk were boldly revolutionary in their attempt to show the natural world as it actually looks—a celebrated example is *The Haywain* of 1821 (National Gallery, London)—capturing the light and feel of the English countryside, just as the French Impressionists would do for their own landscape several decades later.

The work of **JMW Turner** (1775–1851), on the other hand, is much more Romantic than Constable's, and his magnificent symphonies of colour and light, sometimes only loosely and inspirationally based on a recognizable scene, have something of the grandeur of Beethoven. The *Fighting Téméraire 1838* (National Gallery, London) conveys an airy and dramatic nostalgia as the sun sets on a great wooden ship, symbol of an earlier age, brought to her last berth by a stocky little steam tug.

Later in the 19th century a continuing idealism prevailed among the painters of the Pre-Raphaelite Brotherhood, most notably **John Everett Millais** (1829–96), **Dante Gabriel Rossetti** (1828–82) and **William Holman Hunt** (1827–1910). These painters sought to counter the harsh and often shoddy aspects of the age of Dickens with a purity, beauty and fidelity to nature that they chose to believe existed in the Middle Ages and the early Renaissance before Raphael (before the 16th century), from which they took their inspiration and their name. The hyper-real and finely detailed pictures, such as Millais' *Ophelia* of 1852 and Holman Hunt's *Our English Coasts* of the same year (both Tate Gallery, London), typically focusing on women and nature, show the same arduous attention to detail which characterized Britain in the reign of Victoria—here turned to the pursuit of aesthetic excellence.

Unlike the French, the British are not by temperament theoretical or intellectual. Thus, 20th-century British art has stayed slightly outside such prevailing movements as Cubism or international abstraction, concentrating rather, as it always has, on the human body and the real world, especially the countryside.

Henry Moore (1898–1986), a Yorkshire miner's son, united both preoccupations in his monolithic sculptures of the female nude, which may go some way towards accounting for his phenomenal success. The harsh and unruly landscapes of his childhood gave him a deep respect for the integrity of his materials, and he even verges on abstraction in his relentless pursuit of their true nature.

The 20th-century painter with the most uncompromising vision of the body must be **Francis Bacon** (1909–1992), leading member of the figurative and physical School of London, whose work lives up to the meatiness of his name. His awesomely raw and howling pictures (*Three Figures and a Portrait*, 1975, Tate Gallery, London), like the plays of Samuel Beckett, express all the despair of the human condition.

In contrast to Bacon, **David Hockney** (born 1937) has been accused by some critics of blandness. After the Pop-Art irony of his early output, the more recent work of this flamboyant and colourful character seems highly civilized in a distinctly contemporary way (*A Bigger Splash*, 1967, Tate Gallery, London). Hockney wears his considerable technical skill and knowledge of art history lightly to create a vision of a modern good life without national boundaries.

Figure I *by Francis Bacon.*

Gateway and Garden

The South-East has always been Britain's front door. The English Channel is at its narrowest, tempting swimmers—and invaders—across. Celts and Romans, Angles, Saxons and Normans all made it to shore, but Napoleon and Hitler only dreamed about storming this island fortress. The road and rail lines linking London to the coast extend out from the capital. Head out of the city to discover peaceful countryside and the rolling beauty of the Downs. The hills end abruptly at the Kent and Sussex shorelines, where high chalk cliffs drop down to the sea. The white cliffs are a symbol, not only of the South-East, but of all England. Sighting them, visitors know they have arrived, and locals feel they are nearly home.

Kent

The county takes its name and boundaries from the 6th-century Saxon kingdom. This is the "Garden of England", an area of orchards and the fields of climbing hops essential to beer-making. Along Kent's historic coastline, resorts and ports alternate with castles and forts.

Canterbury

In the Middle Ages, all roads led to Canterbury and its cathedral, the site of

A lighthouse warns shipping away from the towering chalk cliffs of Beachy Head, Sussex.

St Thomas Becket's shrine. Chaucer's pilgrims made the journey from Southwark, now a borough of London, nearly 100km (60 miles) away. Other penitents followed the Pilgrim's Way along the North Downs from Winchester.

The cathedral is the centrepiece of the old town, still partially enclosed by medieval walls. Although wartime bombs tore the heart out of the city, many ancient buildings survive. Were the Wife of Bath to return today she would be able to find her way from **West Gate** along the cobblestones of St Peter's and High Streets to narrow **Mercery Lane**, the traditional approach to the cathedral precinct. Modern pilgrims enter through the archway of **Christ Church Gate**, built of the same buff-coloured stone as the cathedral.

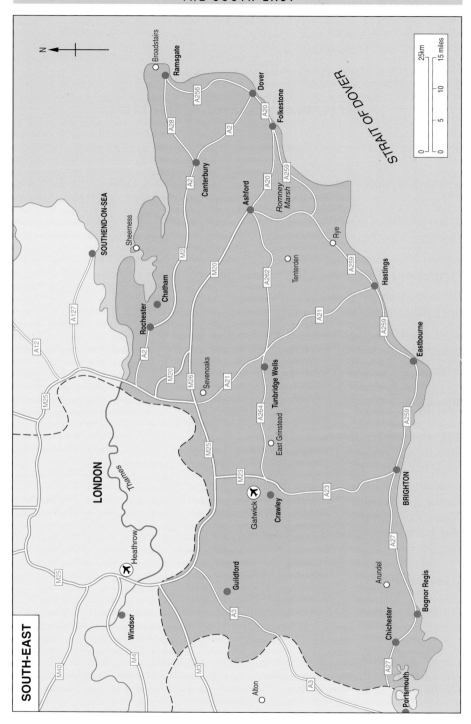

SOUTH-EAST

STRAIT OF DOVER

25km
15 miles

N

Broadstairs
Ramsgate
Dover
Folkestone
A256
A28
A2
A20
A259
Canterbury
A2
Ashford
A20
Romney Marsh
SOUTHEND-ON-SEA
Sheerness
Chatham
M2
M20
A262
Tenterden
Rye
A259
Hastings
Rochester
A2
A12
A127
M20
M26
Sevenoaks
A21
Tunbridge Wells
A21
A259
Eastbourne
M25
M25
A264
East Grinstead
A259
BRIGHTON
LONDON
Thames
M23
A23
Gatwick
Crawley
Heathrow
A27
Guildford
Arundel
Bognor Regis
M25
A3
Windsor
Chichester
Portsmouth
M40
M4
M3
A3
Alton
A27

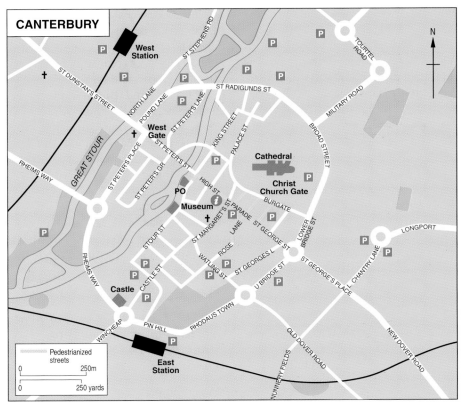

City plan of Canterbury.

Canterbury (*Durovernum Cantia-corum* to the Romans) looks back on at least 2,000 years of history. This was a Saxon royal capital long before Thomas the Martyr brought it fame and wealth (*see* page 58). Even had Becket never lived, Canterbury would have been revered as the cradle of English Christianity. In 597 a monk called Augustine arrived here from Rome to convert the people. He established his see and founded **Canterbury Cathedral**.

South-east England.

This great example of Gothic architecture illustrates the evolution of the style, from the earthbound magnificence of the Early English choir to the lofty grace of the Perpendicular nave and Bell Harry tower and the outstanding stained-glass windows. Directly across from the cathedral entrance in the north-west transept, a stone slab marks the place where Becket was murdered. His shrine at the cathedral's east end was destroyed on Henry VIII's orders in 1538. Now a lighted candle in Trinity Chapel keeps the memory of St Thomas alive.

The old houses and inns around the cathedral recall the heyday of the pilgrimage circuit, when Chaucer's band set out. This is the theme of the

Pilgrim's Way tourist "experience" (St Margaret's Street).

A short drive east takes you to **Whitstable** and the sea. Try to visit this old fishing town in a month with an "r": Whitstable means oysters and the harbourfront pubs that serve them. Canterbury's historic port, Whitstable occupied a strategic site on the stretch of coast called the Saxon Shore at the time of Rome's decline. The ruined Roman fort at nearby **Reculver** is a landmark on Kent's coastal footpath, the Saxon Shore Way.

Margate doesn't make the best introduction to the British seaside. The wide sand beach, guesthouses and "prom" (promenade) are all here, along with the traditional fun fair on the "front". But the crowds have been diverted—by package flights to Greece and Spain. Language schools have taken over some of the old hotels.

Charles Dickens' **Bleak House** puts neighbouring **Broadstairs** on the tourist map. The cliff-top house, one of several holiday residences rented by the writer, was named after the book and not the other way around. But the name is apt all the same, since the house inspired the novel. A competing attraction, the **Dickens House Museum** on the seafront displays a small collection of Dickensiana.

Cinque Ports

Attractive **Sandwich** has enough old-world charm for two towns. The streets are narrow and medieval and the

*T*he oast-houses of Kent *were used for drying hops to flavour beer. These are at the Whitbread Centre.*

houses suitably half-timbered. Sandwich's designation as a Cinque (pronounced "sink") Port dates back to the 13th-century reign of Edward I, when five towns on the south-east coast received special privileges from the Crown in exchange for "ship service"—the provision of warships and men. Sandwich's harbour later silted up, and 3km (2 miles) now intervene between the sea and the town's riverside quay.

Inland, too, is **Richborough**, the place where the invading Romans probably landed in AD 43. The conquerors knew the importance of fortifying the site: **Richborough Castle** incorporates the remains of formidable Roman defences.

By the 14th century, most of the towns between Sandwich and Hastings had joined the Cinque Ports confederation. Waterfront **Deal** was no exception. Once famous for its dockyard, Deal has a strip of steeply shelving pebble beach but no harbour: ships drop anchor in the sheltered Downs offshore. It was near here that Julius Caesar's raiding party waded ashore in 55 BC.

An easy walk leads to **Walmer Castle**, a couple of miles south along the Saxon Shore Way. The Tudor fort is the official residence of the Lord Warden of the Cinque Ports, an honorary post held by among others, Sir Winston Churchill and Queen Elizabeth, the Queen Mother, who once remarked that she had never received the spoils of shipwreck that traditionally accompanied the title. In the old days the Lords Warden grew rich on booty, so many ships broke up on the treacherous Goodwin Sands, 6km (4 miles) out.

Have you been wondering where swimmers start their cross-Channel marathons? **St Margaret's Bay**, off the Dover Road at the end of the B2058, is the time-honoured spot. Here, at the Strait of Dover, the English Channel narrows to a mere 27km (17 miles), bringing England and France within firing range. The port of **Dover** suffered extensive damage during World War II from bombing raids and V-1 buzz bombs launched from the Boulogne coast, but the Norman castle, adjacent Saxon church and Roman lighthouse still stand. Not far away a granite outline of Bleriot's aircraft commemorates his flight across the Channel in 1909. At low tide you can walk west along the beach to **Shakespeare Cliff**, a 107m (350ft) wall of chalk identified with a scene from *King Lear*.

The main business of Dover is ferrying passengers and freight across the Channel by boat: neighbouring **Folkestone** is close to the terminal for the train through the Channel Tunnel.

Ten kilometres (6 miles) from Folkestone, **Hythe** is another old Cinque Port with charm. Go for a ride on the

The Great Bore

Bridge, causeway, tunnel and permutations of the three—over the centuries all were proposed as ways to cross the English Channel between Britain and France. So many projects were abandoned over the years that it seemed unlikely that anything would ever be done. At last the Eurotunnel was started in 1988 and three years later, French and British diggers met. The system is designed to carry cars and passengers on shuttle trains in dual tunnels, one for east- and the other for west-bound traffic. Travel time between Folkestone, England, and Sangatte, France, is about 35 minutes. Claustrophobes will continue to use one of the ferries.

pint-sized Romney, Hythe and Dymchurch Railway—one-third the size of a normal train. The miniature line skirts the moody, misty (but no longer marshy) **Romney Marsh**. Sheep by the thousands graze the flatlands, planted with a dozen villages and as many stone churches. New Romney's Norman and Early English **St Nicholas** is just one of them.

A 14th-century latecomer to the Cinque Ports confederation, **Rye** is landlocked now. Three kilometres (2 miles) separate the forest of masts in Rye Harbour from the steep, cobbled streets of the town. Walk uphill past the tea shops and antique shops to the parish church and **Ypres Tower**, the remnant of a 13th-century fort. The museum within highlights Rye's Cinque Ports connection. The writer Henry James spent the last two decades of his life in the Georgian elegance of **Lamb House** (West Street), a National Trust property open to the public a couple of days a week.

James rated **Winchelsea** as highly as Rye, commenting, "The great thing is if you live at Rye you have Winchelsea to show." Chief sight today: the 14th-century **parish church**, dedicated to St Thomas Becket.

Orchard Country

Inland from Rye, a network of small country roads penetrates a fertile plain known as the Weald of Kent. Apples, pears and cherries are the big crops, followed by grapes and hops. Fields and

A pint-sized but perfect scale model railway at New Romney offers nostalgics a ride back into the Age of Steam.

Fishing boats and yachts share Rye Harbour: the Cinque Port of Rye itself has long been silted up and left well inland.

farmland surround a clutch of appealing villages: tile-hung **Goudhurst** on its hill; half-timbered **Biddenden**, a medieval centre of the cloth trade; and little **Smarden** (pop. 1,000), a charming collection of black-and-white timberwork and weather-board (clapboard) cottages. Half-way between Goudhurst and Biddenden, stop off at **Sissinghurst Castle** to see the great garden created by the writer Vita Sackville-West and her husband, diplomat Sir Harold Nicolson. Enthusiasts rave about the walled White Garden.

The "Jewel of the Weald", **Tenterden**, south-east of Biddenden, is the terminus of the nostalgic steam-powered **Kent & East Sussex Railway**. The line ends just over the Sussex county line at **Bodiam**, noted for its moated 14th-century castle, which is roofless but entire.

Scotney Castle, near Lamberhurst, is another romantic ruin in landscaped grounds. A third variation on the theme, **Leeds Castle** (north of Biddenden) stands astride two islands in a mirror lake. You could easily spend a couple of days exploring this small area of Kent, basing yourself at a farmhouse (look for the roadside signs advertising vacancies) or village inn.

Royal Tunbridge Wells also makes a good touring centre. Kent's answer to Bath, the town developed as a spa in the 17th century. Don't miss the arcaded pedestrian street called the **Pantiles** (south-west of the modern centre). The Georgian shopfronts—displaying jewellery, clothes and bibelots—have an unself-conscious period charm.

Scotney Castle's moated 14th-century tower and Tudor manor house.

Sussex

Bucket-and-spade holiday-makers and, increasingly, conference-goers patronize the traditional resorts along the coast, from Hastings to Brighton. Another Sussex lies inland, however, in the rural Weald and downland villages. This has been corn and sheep country since the Romans first developed the agricultural potential of the area. Nowadays there are fewer sheep and more commuters, but a county identity still holds.

Hastings

Some way from the old town and ruined castle (William the Conqueror's first English fort) the site of the Battle of Hastings lies in open country 10km (6 miles) to the north-west.

The town of **Battle** grew up beside the field where King Harold's English army met Duke William's Norman knights in 1066. The ruins of **Battle Abbey**, destroyed in the Dissolution, mark the site. Walk through the massive entrance gate, past the crumbling monastic buildings and out on to the ridge held by the axe-wielding English infantrymen. Signs posted around the battlefield explain the events of 14 October as they unfolded: the Norman cavalry attacked repeatedly and were repeatedly repulsed—until William feigned retreat. Drawing

Harold's soldiers to lower ground, he rounded on them, decimating the Anglo-Saxons. Symbolically enough, Harold died at dusk, shot through the eye with an arrow. A modern stone slab marks the place where the king was slain. Here, for five centuries, stood the high altar of the abbey church founded by William to commemorate the conquest.

Eastbourne

Like the crowds on the pier and Grand Parade, Eastbourne is somewhat past its prime, but there is some superb scenery in the surrounding area. A cliff-top path takes walkers out around **Beachy Head** (keep away from the edge!) and the **Seven Sisters**, a rippling wall of chalk with seven distinct summits. Seabirds nest on the heights and there are vertiginous views of the coast and countryside. Look east beyond

Battle Abbey was founded to mark the first victory of William the Conqueror's campaign to capture England.

Eastbourne to William the Conqueror's 1066 landing place at **Pevensey Bay**—and west past the Seven Sisters towards Brighton. Completely built up now, the coastline developed during Rudyard Kipling's lifetime, and the writer found it "of great horror". Turn away from the sea for a while and set your sights inland, where the South Downs villages offer appealing rural contrasts.

Brighton

Its antiquated charm may not be to everyone's taste, but Brighton's Regency architecture is unique. It was the future George IV who catapulted the developing resort of Brighthelm-stone to fame and fashion in the 1780s. He leased a farmhouse in Brighton, as he called the place, and elegant society followed. An adventurous few had paved the way 30 years earlier. Taking the advice of a local doctor, they came here to breathe sea air and bathe in—even drink—sea water. Thus was born the notion of a holiday by the sea, but that is all history now as Brighton turns its attention to the conference, language school and tourist trade.

South Downs Detour

The South Downs Way—footpath, bridle path and cycleway—follows the line of hills west to the Hampshire border. Walkers prepared to go the distance should allow about a week to cover the full 129km (80 miles), but there is a lot to see near the starting point of Eastbourne.

The first landmark on the Way is the 69m (226ft) **Wilmington Long Man**, near Wilmington village. This ancient outline figure carved into the chalk flank of Windover Hill holds what looks like a staff in each hand. He may represent a medieval pilgrim, Saxon cult figure or Roman god—no one can say for sure.

In neighbouring **Alfriston** village, directly on the South Downs Way, you will see large boulders which may have marked the original prehistoric footpath. Some of the stones lie on the Tye, the picturesque village green. Here, too, stands St Andrews, "Cathedral of the Downs", and the church's thatched medieval **Clergy House**, home of the priest and, latterly, the parson. It was the first building to be acquired by the National Trust in 1896.

This corner of Sussex found favour with artist Duncan Grant (1885–1978), who lived at **Charleston Farmhouse**, near Firle village, for 60 years. A breath of Bohemia survives at Charleston (open to the public several afternoons a week), decorated by Grant and the painter and designer Vanessa Bell in idiosyncratic "Bloomsbury" style.

Vanessa Bell's sister, the novelist Virginia Woolf, summered close by at **Monk's House** in Rodmell, on the River Ouse, and it was in the Ouse that Virginia Woolf drowned herself in 1941. The National Trust opens Monk's House as a shrine to the author of *Orlando* and *The Years*.

Yet another reason to linger in the area is the opera house at **Glyndebourne**, famous for its summer productions. Performances begin in the late afternoon, allowing time for a leisurely champagne supper (weather permitting) on the lawn during the interval. You have to book tickets—and accommodation—well ahead: hotels and inns for miles around are full up during the Glyndebourne season.

The first stop is the ultimate in holiday houses, the Prince Regent's **Royal Pavilion**, bordering on The Lanes, the area of pedestrian streets and antique shops near the seafront. John Nash designed this domed and turreted "Hindoo" fantasy in 1815, transforming an earlier palace that had incorporated the original farmhouse leased by the prince in the 1780s. No expense was spared in the construction of the Pavilion or the extravagant exoticism of the interior, featuring Chinese motifs—flying dragons, writhing serpents and costumed oriental figures. Follow the arrows to view the drawing rooms, Banqueting Room, library and bedrooms in sequence. Even the kitchen has an eastern look, with rows of cast-iron palm-tree columns.

The former royal stables house the **Brighton Museum and Art Gallery** in Church Street, noted for modern British paintings and 20th-century decorative arts.

*T*he Prince Regent *entertained his mistresses under the pleasure domes of his Royal Pavilion at Brighton. He kept up a lifetime love affair with the resort.*

A rundel Castle's almost toy-like appearance belies a choppy history, with a cast of characters often on the wrong side of the powers that be.

Down by the water, the Victorian **Palace Pier** echoes the architecture of the Pavilion in wood and cast iron.

Some other classic Brighton-area sights lie inland. The **Devil's Dyke**, a beauty spot several miles to the northwest, has long attracted excursionists. As the story goes, the devil made this gash in the Downs to flood the churches of Sussex. But, confusing the light of a candle for daybreak, he stopped work before he had finished the job. Legend aside, the view from the crest of the dyke is memorable. Inland lies the Sussex Weald, the undulating continuation of Kent's fertile agricultural land.

The popular **House of Pipes** in the nearby village of Bramber displays one man's collection of smoking equipment, from meerschaum pipes to tobacco tins, recalling that innocent period in the history of tobacco, before government health warnings.

Arundel

The town rises from the peaceful river Arun to hilltop **Arundel Castle**, a picturesque jumble of battlements and towers. Its present incarnation dates from the late 19th century, though the keep and drawbridge go back to the castle's 11th-century beginnings. Fine furniture, tapestries and Old Masters by Holbein the Younger, Van Dyck, Gainsborough and Reynolds enhance the neo-Gothic interior.

This has always been the home of the Earls of Arundel, a title that passed to the Howard family in 1580. The Howards, like the Fitzalans before them, are staunch Roman Catholics. They had their family chapel partitioned off from the Anglican parish church after the Reformation, and financed Arundel's Gothic-style Catholic **cathedral** some 300 years later. It is dedicated to a 16th-century forebear, St

138

Philip Howard, who died a martyr's death in the Tower of London, where he was imprisoned for allegedly having had a mass said for the success of the Spanish Armada.

Five kilometres (3 miles) to the north, the village of **Amberley** on the banks of the Arun attracts artists and anglers in droves. At the nearby Amberley Chalk Pits, an award-winning open-air **museum** highlights the industrial heritage of the Downs. Local craftsmen demonstrate bygone trades (from boat-building to brickmaking), and there are collections of vintage tools and vehicles on display.

Petworth

Imposing 17th-century **Petworth House** inspired Turner to paint the luminous landscapes on display in Petworth's Turner Room and other Turner works hang in the North Gallery, a private museum created by the 2nd Earl of Egremont in 1824. However, Turner isn't the whole story here. Take in the state rooms, with an impressive collection of Old Masters, the Carved Room (by Grinling Gibbons), painted Staircase Hall and artfully contrived gardens designed by Capability Brown.

Dominated by the house, pretty **Petworth village** has some well-stocked antique shops.

Chichester

An inland town strictly speaking, Chichester adjoins its **harbour**, 80 superb kilometres (50 miles) of indented shoreline, with 27km (17 miles) of navigable channels. Harbour **cruises** start from Itchenor, and sailing boats and sailboards can be rented there and at several other towns in the area. Harbourside **Bosham** (pronounced "bozzem"), a picturesque huddle of wood and brick cottages, is another likely place.

Chichester proper retains its grid-like Roman street plan. The Gothic **Market Cross** stands at the junction of the four main streets, named after the cardinal points. Off West Street rises the **cathedral**, whose spire is visible out to sea. Two fires in the 12th century damaged the original Norman structure, but many Norman features survive, along with Early English additions—and some contemporary pieces: a Graham Sutherland altarpiece (1962), a John Piper tapestry (1966) and a Chagall window (1980).

In the south-east quadrant of the city, an area called the Pallants preserves some exceptional 18th- and 19th-century houses. The **Queen Anne**

*F*ourth century mosaic at the Bignor Roman villa in Sussex, clearly the home of an important Romano-British leader.

Pallant House Gallery contains a selection furniture, porcelain and glass from that gracious era.

An easy walk or bus ride will bring you to **Fishbourne Roman Villa** (west of the city), one of the largest buildings of the period discovered outside Italy. A British chieftain called Cogidubnus lived in luxury here. There are many fine mosaics to see and also a "Roman" garden, replanted according to archaeological information.

Nearby **Goodwood House** contains the French furniture, Gobelins tapestries and Sèvres porcelain acquired by the 3rd Duke of Richmond, who was an ambassador to the court of Louis XV. The architect James Wyatt designed the house specifically to complement the collection, which it does with appropriate neoclassical restraint. Wyatt's Tapestry Room, hung with scenes from *Don Quixote*, holds some of the best pieces.

Goodwood Park, the racecourse in the grounds, is the scene of "meetings" from May to the end of September.

The **Weald and Downland Open-air Museum** at Singleton resembles a real little village, with its farmhouses, barns, market hall, artisans' workshops and village school. Of timber, flint or brick, the buildings exemplify the rural architectural traditions of the southeast. All were rescued from demolition and set up on this wooded 24-hectare (60-acre) South Downs site.

Surrey

Greater London long ago engulfed the northern fringes of the county, but the green belt of protected fields and woods around the metropolis has kept further urbanization in check. Pockets of ancient heath and downland grazed by sheep survive, but the chief impression is of prosperous "dormitory" (commuter) towns and villages, substantial houses and well-kept gardens.

Guildford

Londoners are deserting the capital for cities like Guildford (pop. 60,000)—old enough and small enough to have a sense of history and community, situated in the heart of the countryside, yet within easy commuting range of the West End and City. The attractive high street climbs a hill past the 17th-century **Guildhall**, or town hall (the building with the projecting clock), to the **Grammar School**, Guildford's upper school since 1557. The red-brick cathedral of 1936, in a spare Gothic style, stands high on Stag Hill, north-west of the centre, near the modern buildings of the University of Surrey.

Loseley Park (near Guildford)

The popular dairy and cereal products made here carry the logo of Loseley's many-gabled façade. The house was built during Elizabeth I's reign, and the queen herself was a guest at Loseley on several occasions. Stones for its construction were plundered from nearby Waverley Abbey. The More-Molyneux family (descendants of Sir Thomas) open the house and grounds to visitors. Guides show you around the Great Hall, Library, Drawing Room and bedrooms. There are some important pictures, mainly portraits, and fine period furniture, but the overall impression is of a (quite grand) family home, rather than a museum. The farm, in 567 hectares (1,400 acres), very nearly upstages the house. To join a guided farm walk you have to book in advance. Call (0483) 571881 for details.

Ripley

Gardeners amateur and professional consider a visit to the Royal Horticultural Society's **Wisley Garden** on the order of a pilgrimage. The display of azaleas and rhododendrons is justly famous, but also have a look at the laboratories, glasshouses, rock garden and pinetum included in Wisley's 122 hectares (300 acres).

Ancient and Modern

The seafaring South takes in Portsmouth's naval history and Southampton's docks as well as the exhilarating yachting waters of the Solent and Channel. Bays, coves, harbours and headlands punctuate a long and eventful coast, backed by Dorset's downland cliffs and Hampshire's oak and beech woods whose timber built Nelson's fleet. His flagship, *Victory,* is Portsmouth's unique attraction. But Trafalgar counts as recent history on the time-scale of the South. The cathedrals of Salisbury and Winchester take you back six to eight centuries before that, and another four to five millennia separate them from the oldest megaliths at Stonehenge.

Hampshire

The county is still richly agricultural—if you discount the urban sprawl around Portsmouth and Southampton, and the New Forest (which, confusingly, is old, and mostly open heathland). Cattle graze the low-lying meadows, but wheat has displaced sheep from the slopes of the downs. The soft climate suits strawberries and asparagus, and there are a growing number of vineyards. Listen for the soft, rolling local accent, to match the gently rounded landscape.

*N*elson's flagship was preserved after the 1805 Battle of Trafalgar. The old ship of the line has 104 cannon ranged on three decks.

Portsmouth

This is the Royal Navy's town. Lord Nelson sailed from Portsmouth to victory—and death—at Trafalgar in 1805. The D-Day invasion force assembled here in 1944, and the Falklands Task Force in 1982. There's a lot to see in the harbour-front **Royal Dockyard**, focus for a visit. Start with the most visible landmark around, the three-masted **HMS Victory**, Lord Nelson's ship, in dry dock near the entrance. To go on board you have to join one of the guided tours which are run at frequent intervals throughout the day, every day except Christmas.

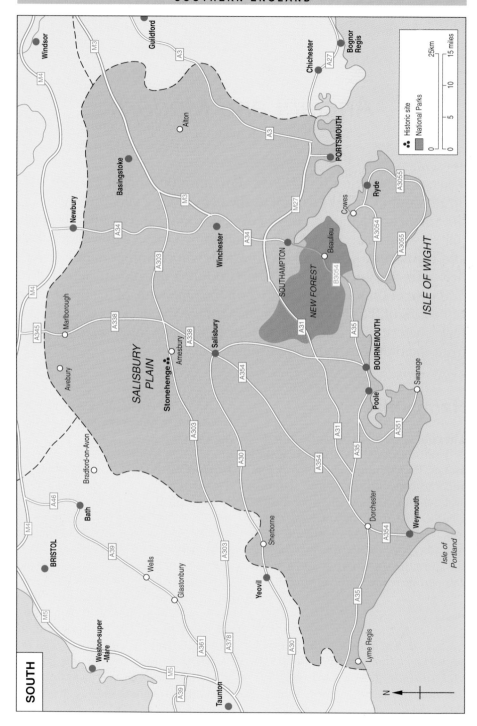

SOUTH

SALISBURY PLAIN

Stonehenge

NEW FOREST

ISLE OF WIGHT

Isle of Portland

Historic site
National Parks

25km
15 miles
10
5
0

Windsor
Guildford
Chichester
Bognor Regis
Portsmouth
Alton
Basingstoke
Ryde
Cowes
Beaulieu
Newbury
Winchester
Southampton
Marlborough
Salisbury
Amesbury
Avebury
Bournemouth
Poole
Swanage
Bradford-on-Avon
Bath
Dorchester
Weymouth
Bristol
Wells
Sherborne
Glastonbury
Yeovil
Lyme Regis
Weston-super-Mare
Taunton

M3
M4
A3
A27
A3
M3
A3055
A34
A34
M27
A3054
A3055
A303
B3054
A31
A35
A338
A345
A338
A354
A31
A35
A351
A35
A30
A46
A354
A39
A303
A30
M4
M5
A361
A378
A90
M5
A39

N

Black rigging and red-and-black painted trim give the *Victory* a suitably martial look. The 2,100-tonne man-of-war carried 104 guns and 850 men—300 officers, 550 crew. The young sailors from today's navy who serve as guides take evident satisfaction in describing conditions on board 200 years ago, when leg irons and flogging kept the men in line, and a daily ration of rum kept them quiet. While the crew endured squalor and privations below decks, the admiral lived in considerable style above. His sleeping cabin (with a silk upholstered cot) and wood-panelled day and dining cabins have all the elegance of a Georgian town house. The furniture also bears comparison with the period's best—except that these pieces could be folded and stowed away to clear the decks for action.

The fateful encounter at Trafalgar began at about 12.40 in the afternoon of 21 October. Less than an hour later, Nelson was mortally wounded by a French sniper. A plaque marks the place on the quarter deck where the admiral fell. He was taken below to the cockpit, where he learned the outcome of the battle before he died. (The Trafalgar diorama in the **Royal Naval Museum** adjacent to the *Victory* puts you in the thick of the action.)

Only a part of the hull survives of Henry VIII's **Mary Rose**, salvaged from the seabed in 1982. In the ship hall (a few steps from the *Victory*), you may see restorers at work in a special temperature- and humidity-controlled environment. On display in the neighbouring exhibition hall are objects

*S*outhern England.

*N*o power steering in *the days of the men o'war; it was all hands to the wheel(s).*

recovered with the ship, from cutlery, tools and clothing to pocket sundials.

Two other vessels to visit: the ironclad **HMS Warrior** (1860), berthed at a pier near the dockyard gate, and the submarine **Alliance**, across the harbour at the Royal Naval Submarine Museum in Gosport. Get there via the Portsmouth Harbour Ferry. Or board a launch for a spin around the **harbour,** an expansive 6km (4 miles) long and 3km (2 miles) across, narrowing to 274m (300yds) at the mouth.

Old Portsmouth, the area bordering on the dockyard, is more new than old, thanks to wartime air raids.

The Isle of Wight

The trip across Spithead to Ryde takes just seven minutes by hovercraft from Southsea (the fastest way to go), twice as long by catamaran from Portsmouth, longer still by ferry. A chip off the "old block" of the mainland, this holiday isle has miniature downs and chalk cliffs, beaches, resorts and piers, and a relatively mild climate. If the Victorians had colonized California, it would probably look like the Isle of Wight—full of flower beds, promenades and parish churches.

The sheltered east coast has the popular **resorts**: Ryde, Bembridge, Sandown, Shanklin and Ventnor. Yarmouth, in the west, and Cowes are famous yachting centres. One of Queen Victoria's favourite palaces, **Osborne House**, epitomizes the spirit of the Victorian era. Less happily, Charles I sought refuge in **Carisbrooke Castle** in 1647, but his stay soon turned into imprisonment and led eventually to his execution.

Southampton

Post-war reconstruction has given the city a deceptively modern appearance, and the old docks have become a big container port. Few liners use the Ocean Terminal these days, apart from *Queen Elizabeth 2* making her transatlantic crossings. Other overseas visitors arrive by car-ferry from France. If you are passing through, you can spend some time around the waterfront area, cruising the harbour and docks, and having a drink at a pub or wine bar in Town Quay or the Ocean Village leisure complex.

The **Southampton Art Gallery** in the Civic Centre ranks among the best of Britain's provincial museums, with exceptional displays of historic and contemporary British works.

New Forest

New in William the Conqueror's day, and a forest in the old sense of "hunting ground", this National Park embraces 375km^2 (145 square miles) of woods, heath and farmland between Southampton Water and Hampshire's River Avon. Of a scattering of villages, **Lyndhurst**, the largest (pop. 3,000), has the most shops and the biggest traffic jams, as well as the museum and **Visitor Centre**. Pick up their map of suggested itineraries, and ask about guided walks and other activities.

Walking is the best way to see the flora and fauna—from red deer and the ubiquitous semi-wild ponies to rare wild orchids and gladioli. You can, however, get a general impression by car, especially via the **Rhinefeld** and **Bolderwood ornamental drives** (signposted off the A35, Lyndhurst–Bournemouth road). Banks of fern colour the roadside deep green in high summer, russet and gold in autumn, and there are ancient stands of oak and beech trees. The sky opens over the heathland of heather and gorse, where the cream, grey and brown New Forest ponies run. The **Rufus Stone**, nearby, marks the spot where William Rufus (King William II) met his death, out hunting in 1100. The arrow that killed him allegedly rebounded off a tree. There is no longer any hunting in the forest, but camping, picnicking, horse riding and fishing are all permitted in designated areas. This makes it very popular with local holiday-makers, and a great place to observe the British at ease.

Beaulieu

The theme attractions at Beaulieu (pronounced "bewlee") in the heart of the

*H*ampshire's New
Forest was new in William the
Conqueror's time when it was set
aside as a royal hunting reserve.

New Forest keep Lord Montagu's bank balance in the black. Not every peer of the realm has a monorail at his doorstep; and his **Motor Museum** is perhaps the world's finest collection of historic cars. **Palace House**, the Montagu family home (13th-century core with Victorian additions), is open to the public—along with the rides, amusements and theme exhibits—364 days a year. By way of added attractions, there are the ruins of a Cistercian abbey to visit in the grounds.

Entrepreneurship must run in the Montagu family. An 18th-century ancestor set up the shipyard at **Buckler's Hard**, a couple of miles away, and proceeded to build the "wooden walls" of England with New Forest timber. The Maritime Museum here documents that erstwhile industry.

Romsey

This market town grew up around the Norman **Abbey Church**, a particularly pure example of the style. Now, the church is the burial place of Earl Mountbatten, who was killed by IRA terrorists in 1979. Exiting the A31 at Romsey, you see the main entrance to **Broadlands**, Mountbatten's Hampshire home. His grandson, Lord Romsey, lives here now. A tour of the property includes the Mountbatten Exhibition in the old stables, where a film show recaps Lord Mountbatten's 60-year career as sailor, wartime supremo and royal adviser. The neoclassical house is interesting in its own right. The furnishings and fittings commissioned by Lord Palmerston, the 19th-century statesman, were augmented by the family collections of Lord Mountbatten, who inherited Broadlands in his youth.

Winchester

One of England's most historic cities, Winchester predates even the Romans. Later, it was the capital of King Alfred's Wessex and, for a time after the Norman conquest, co-capital (with London) of England. Centuries of prosperity have given Winchester the attractive medieval, Georgian and Victorian buildings that make the compact city centre such a pleasant place to visit. Notice especially the charming bow-windowed facade of the *Hampshire Chronicle* in the High Street and, further along, the slender Perpendicular Civic Cross of 1450.

A passageway beside the cross leads to Winchester's **cathedral** in its peaceful close. On this site, in earlier times, stood the Roman forum. The original Saxon Old Minster was dedicated to a trio of saints that included the 9th-century Bishop of Winchester, St Swithin. The present cathedral—England's longest—is mainly Gothic, though the original Norman style prevails in the transepts and crypt. Tour the crypt (during the summer months only) and hear the story of William Walker, the diver who a century ago shored up the cathedral's flooded foundations, thus saving it from collapse.

The high, wide Perpendicular nave makes a tremendous impact, the bays repeating themselves into a seeming

*T*he quiet cathedral precinct at Winchester, where Jane Austen used to stroll.

Rain Man

St Swithin was buried, at his own request, in the churchyard of Winchester Cathedral. He wanted to lie outdoors, where the rain would fall on his grave. But in 971, as his cult grew, it was decided to move the saint's body to a shrine of gold inside the church. An attempt was made to open the grave on 15 July, but rain halted the work. It continued to rain for 40 days—a sign of St Swithin's holy displeasure. This effect on the elements made Swithin patron saint of weather and, even today, rain on St Swithin's Day (15 July) is said to mean 40 consecutive wet days—not an unlikely prediction in Britain.

infinity. Look for the graves of Jane Austen (north aisle), marked by an inscribed stone slab, and Compleat Angler Izaak Walton, who lies in Silkstede Chapel. A marble tomb under the central tower holds the remains of William Rufus (King William II). No religious ceremony accompanied his interment, a hurried affair that took place within a day of his death. Rumours, barely voiced, that the king was a heretic and a practitioner of the occult arts could explain his "accidental" demise and unceremonious burial.

Cathedral guides will be happy to point out these and other monuments, including St Swithin's shrine (a modern replacement), Mary Tudor's chair (left behind after her ill-starred wedding to Philip II of Spain) and the wooden mortuary chests that contain the bones of England's early kings (Egbert, Egwyn and the Dane Canute). Visit the library before you leave, if only to see the 12th-century **Winchester Bible**, a masterpiece of the medieval illuminator's art.

South of the cathedral, through King's Gate, is **Winchester College**, one of the oldest (1382) and most intellectually demanding of England's public schools. South again, via the riverside footpath, you will come to the **Hospital of St Cross**, an almshouse of 12th-century foundation. Ask for the Wayfarer's Dole and you will be given age-old sustenance—a horn of ale and some bread.

Chawton

Anyone who has read *Mansfield Park*, *Emma* or *Persuasion* will want to visit **Chawton Cottage**, the red-brick house

Jane Austen

Ordinary people living comfortable lives were the subject of Jane Austen's novels. The daughter of a country clergyman, Jane opposed a healthy realism to the melodrama that was the stock-in-trade of novelists of her day.

Trips to Bath and London, and frequent visits to friends and relatives in the neighbourhood of Steventon, the Hampshire village where Jane grew up, informed her writing. Although she returned time and again to the themes of courtship and marriage in her novels, Jane herself remained single. Evidence suggests that her great love—probably a military officer or clergyman—died.

In keeping with the convention of the times, Jane Austen did not sign her books. *Sense and Sensibility* came out anonymously in 1811, followed rapidly by *Pride and Prejudice* and *Mansfield Park*. When *Emma* appeared in 1815, the novel carried a dedication to the Prince Regent, a great fan, from the still nameless author. Only after her death, with the posthumous publication of *Northanger Abbey* and *Persuasion*, was Jane Austen's identity revealed.

where Jane Austen (1775–1817) wrote her most accomplished novels. She must have had, in addition to her other gifts, an incredible power of concentration. Jane did all of her writing in the busy sitting room of the house which she shared with her mother, sister and a family friend.

Wiltshire

There is something eternal about the Wiltshire landscape—the undulating open spaces of Salisbury Plain, the oblique light and the silence. Not even the tour buses can disturb the rural peace of the countryside, scattered with villages, sheep, cows and scores of prehistoric sites.

Salisbury

This archetypal market town has substantial houses of timber and brick, historic inns with names like "The Pheasant" and "Haunch of Venison", and a tree-lined central market square where traders have been setting up their stalls for close to 800 years. (Tuesdays and Saturdays are market days.)

On the south side of the city, the cathedral distances itself from commerce behind the walls of the close. There is nothing haphazard about the arrangement: purpose-built during a few short years of the 13th century. New Sarum, as Salisbury was then known, replaced the ancient hilltop town of **Old Sarum**, a couple of miles away. The abandoned site was quarried for its stone, and all trace of habitation there has vanished, though the impressive earthworks retain the imprint of the citadel and original cathedral.

The foundations of the new riverside **cathedral** were laid in 1220. The choir, transepts and nave went up in record time—38 years—and by 1265 the magnificent west front was completed. A splendid afterthought, the soaring spire was added a century later. This is very tall (over 120m/400ft) and very heavy (more than 6,000 tonnes)—so heavy that the cathedral staggers under the weight. The columns carrying the tower have

actually buckled, causing the spire to lean. A brass pin in the floor of the crossing documents the tilt: 75cm (2ft 6in) from the vertical. Beautifully proportioned, in Early English style throughout, Salisbury is the most harmonious of England's medieval cathedrals. And although the strength of line and interplay of form impresses, remember that what is now cold grey stone was originally all painted in a riot of colour.

*T*hey've been farming *Salisbury Plain since the Stone Age. There are no big towns, but the military presence is all-pervasive: the plain is great for manoeuvres, whether it be on foot, or in a tank or helicopter.*

The old Wiltshire market town of Salisbury and its cathedral, with the tallest spire in England.

By way of curiosities, the cathedral displays one of the four surviving copies of Magna Carta (on view in the Chapter House) and, in the north aisle, what is said to be the world's oldest working clock (1386). Designed to be heard, rather than seen, it has no face but sounds the hours.

Wilton

If you have seen one stately home, you *haven't* seen them all. **Wilton House** (4km/2½ miles west of Salisbury) is another of the really great ones. The property fell to the Herbert family through old-fashioned, 16th-century nepotism: William Herbert, first Earl of Pembroke, just happened to be the brother-in-law of Henry VIII's sixth wife, Catherine Parr. The original Tudor house (incorporating a medieval monastery) was remodelled along classical lines by Inigo Jones after a devastating 1647 fire.

An architectural tour de force, the eight state rooms created by Jones culminate in the **Double Cube Room** (18 by 9 by 9m/60 by 30 by 30ft). Apart from John Webb's opulent carved and gilded decoration, there are choice pictures by Van Dyck, and the bold furniture designed by William Kent a century later specifically for this setting.

Herbert family tradition maintains that Shakespeare acted here in *As You Like It*, but the visits of Marlowe, Spenser and Ben Jonson are better documented.

Stonehenge

From afar, the grey-green monoliths look deceptively small in the immensity of Salisbury Plain. Half-toppled now, they lie in partial disarray, like abandoned pieces from an outsize game of building blocks.

On average, 7,000 people a day visit Britain's most famous prehistoric monument. Pay the entrance fee at the turnstile in the car park opposite, and join the inevitable queue that snakes its way through the passage under the roadway. The pressure of tourism is such that visitors can no longer wander among the stones at will but circle them instead, at a distance.

Stonehenge evolved over a period of more than a thousand years, in three distinct phases. Starting in about 2800 BC, Neolithic people created the circular earthworks (very apparent still) and positioned what are now known as the Station Stones, Heel Stone and Aubrey Holes. Around 2100 BC, concentric rings of bluestones went up and a stone entrance avenue began to take shape. However, this scheme was completely transformed a hundred years later by a Bronze Age people who are regarded as the real builders of Stonehenge. They exchanged the outer circle of bluestones for the now incomplete ring of tall sarsen stones. Inside it they erected five huge trilithons—pairs of giant stones topped with a lintel, of which three remain in place—and 19 smaller bluestones (now 11), both arranged in a U-formation opening towards the entrance.

What actually went on here remains the subject of speculation. The alignment of the Heel Stone and sarsens to the sun points to Stonehenge's function as a solar temple, a theory that has gained almost universal acceptance. Other orientations to the moon and heavenly bodies would indicate that

> **Secular Order of Druids**
> Larger than you might think, membership in Britain's twelve Druid orders numbers over 100,000. There is no direct connection with the original priestly caste. That died out a couple of millennia ago, along with an insistence on human sacrifice. Modern Druids are not even all Celts. They merely practise the rituals of the old Celtic nature religion, with its New Age emphasis on harmony between man and the universe.
>
> The midsummer gatherings at Stonehenge used to be the culmination of the Druid ritual year. However, the number of people attending got out of hand. The wear and tear on the site was considered too great, and the stones have been closed to celebrants.

Stonehenge also served as an astronomical observatory or calendar, but these orientations may be coincidental—controversy rages. A strong case can however be made for the funerary or ritual significance of the site. The Aubrey Holes, from the earliest phase of occupation, were found to contain cremated human remains.

As for the Druids, they were mere upstarts, appropriating Stonehenge for their shrine in the 3rd century BC, hundreds of years after it had fallen into disuse.

Longleat House

(*Warminster*)

A series of startling innovations sets Longleat apart from the rank and file of country houses. England's first significant Renaissance building (completed in 1580), it was the first house to open its doors commercially to the public (1949) and the first to add an unrelated attraction: Longleat's famous lions, installed in the Capability Brown designed park in 1966. Single and combined tickets are available for admission to the house, safari park, VIP Vehicles display, Dr Who Exhibition, miniature railway and so on. The profits from these sidelines go to the upkeep of the house itself.

Longleat is open daily, year-round except for Christmas. It is still very much a family home, though the Thynne family no longer occupies the area on show to the public. An era ended when Longleat's Bath Bedroom, the original bedroom with adjoining bath, went into retirement in 1946—after more than a century of use by three generations of Thynne men, coincidentally marquesses of Bath.

Apart from the Elizabethan Great Hall, most of the rooms on view have a 19th-century Italianate look. However, some earlier features survive, like the 17th-century Cordoba leather wall covering in the State Dining Room and the Flemish tapestries and Boulle furniture in the Saloon.

Stourhead
(*near Mere*)
Banking money built Stourhead in the 18th century. Henry Hoare I ("Henry the Good") put up the Palladian house in the 1720s, and the second Henry ("the Magnificent") laid the groundwork for the extraordinary landscape garden in the 1740s. See the house first or you risk a disappointing anticlimax after a tour of the grounds.

Fire destroyed the central part of the building in 1902, but the contents were salvaged and the impressive Regency library was spared. The scholar and antiquarian Richard Colt Hoare, grandson of Henry Hoare II, wrote his 13-part *History of Modern Wiltshire* in this quiet, carpeted retreat. Thomas Chippendale supplied the furniture—including the massive "Egyptian" desk and library steps. More Chippendale pieces decorate the Picture Gallery in the opposite wing, displaying the kind of classical landscapes that inspired the garden.

It may look natural, but every detail at Stourhead is contrived, from the undulating shoreline of the lake to the distant vistas of massed trees. An amateur of genius, Henry Hoare II collaborated with Henry Flitcroft on the architectural focal points of his scheme: the Temple of Flora, grotto, dominant Pantheon (a replica of Rome's), Temple of Apollo and other follies. Even the church of Stourton village, on the estate, has been drawn into the design by the careful positioning of the Gothic high cross that stands on lower ground, closer to the water.

"Village" is a big word for Stourton's handful of buildings: the church, the National Trust shop and the Spread Eagle Inn, which was originally Stourhead's guest annexe.

Dorset

The pastoral spirit of Thomas Hardy's novels lives on in the thatched cottages, lanes and fields of Dorset. The region formed part of Alfred the Great's kingdom of Wessex, a name that Hardy revived in his writing. To his admirers, Dorset is 'Hardy Country'.

Bournemouth
Untypical of the rest of Dorset, this sprawling resort only joined the county

in a 1970s boundary change. Thomas Hardy's name for it was Sandbourne, and as such it figures in several of the novels, including *The Hand of Ethelberta* and *Tess of the D'Urbevilles*, as 'a fashionable watering place'. Today, little remains of the Victorian atmosphere that Hardy knew: holiday flats have replaced many of the grand hotels, and the streamlined Bournemouth International Centre signals a commitment to the developing conference trade. The "Mediterranean-look" pine trees, incidentally, were imported in the 1840s. The heart of the poet Shelley, rescued from his funeral pyre in Italy, is buried at St Peters' Church.

Two museums attract sightseers to the East Cliff area: the **Rothesay Museum**, an astonishing miscellany of ceramics, typewriters, hand-guns and more; and the **Russell-Cotes Art Gallery and Museum**, the former home of Sir Merton Russell-Cotes, an Edwardian hotelier with a taste for exotic art with erotic overtones (a Rossetti *Venus,* nudes by William Etty).

Poole and the Purbecks

Five kilometres (3 miles) of sandy beaches link Bournemouth to the historic port of **Poole**, Dorset's yachting centre. For local colour, make for **The Quay**, a busy marine scene of sailing boats and fishing boats, ships' chandlers and pubs. The handsome buildings on the waterfront and in the **Old Town** just behind it date mainly from the Georgian period, when Poole's lucrative fishing industry was at its peak. Prior to

When seaside holidays became all the rage in Edwardian times, rented beach huts gave shelter from the unpredictable weather. They still do.

Old Harry Rocks off the Dorset coast, where chalk hills make a last stand against the power of the sea.

that, wool brought Poole prosperity. **Scaplen's Court**, a medieval merchant's house in the High Street, recalls the good old days of the cloth trade.

Pooles' great natural **harbour** is one of the world's largest, with countless coves, creeks and inlets around its 100km (60-mile) rim. Ferries connect Poole Quay to the harbourside towns and (April to October) to **Brownsea Island**, a National Trust nature reserve at the mouth of the harbour, where you can swim, picnic, or walk. Waterfowl, peacocks, red squirrels and sika deer are the protected species here. On the south-west side, Baden-Powell Stone offers a panorama of the Purbecks, with Corfe Castle on its high hill.

Wareham, across the harbour from Poole, dominated Dorset trade between the 9th and 13th centuries— Poole gradually taking over as Wareham's port silted up. In the Saxon **Church of St Martin**, Dorset's oldest, there is a fine effigy of T E Lawrence. The church was one of the few buildings to survive a devastating 1762 fire. But Wareham (Hardy's Anglebury) was charmingly rebuilt in harmonious Georgian style.

There's good swimming at several beaches along the Dorset coast. Fossil hunters search the cliffs for traces of prehistoric life trapped in the rock.

To the south-east lies the **Isle of Purbeck**, a peninsula that encompasses hills, moors and a rugged coastline. **Corfe Castle**, or what is left of it, commands the only break in the smoothly contoured, 19km (12-mile) Purbeck range. The Norman fortifications were blown apart by Parliamentary forces during the Civil War. With the Restoration, the royalist Bankes family recovered the title to the property, but rather than rebuild, they decided to construct a new house, Kingston Lacy, near Wimborne Minster. The key to the castle hangs there still. (A descendant bequeathed first the castle, then the house to the National Trust.) The village of Corfe Castle—an attractive cluster of shops and houses at the foot of the castle hill—survived the war intact. Buildings are of the local limestone, a hard, fine-grained variety known as Purbeck marble.

Swanage, the quarry town, was a quiet backwater when Thomas Hardy lived here (1875–76), but by the end of the century it had developed into a popular resort. Some of the most prominent civic monuments arrived as ballast on the sailing ships that carried Purbeck stone from Swanage to London: two of these are the Wellington Clock Tower (from Waterloo Bridge) and Town Hall façade (originally the front of a City guildhall).

The **Dorset Coastal Path** follows the Purbeck peninsula from Studland, where there is a long-established nudist beach, to Swanage and on to Kimmeridge and **Lulworth Cove**, a cliff-fringed circle of blue. (Most weekdays, a short section west of Kimmeridge is closed to walkers for military manoeuvres.) The path then passes the natural rock bridge **Durdle Door** on the way to Weymouth and Lyme Regis before continuing into Devon.

Dorchester

The town is as venerable as they come, with an important Neolithic site and the odd Roman relic (a section of wall, the remains of an amphitheatre). However, it was Thomas Hardy who really brought Dorchester fame. The writer studied, worked and eventually lived here, from 1883 until his death in 1928. The local Tourist Information Centre at 1 Acland Road stocks an impressive range of literature on Hardy Country, and the staff there can advise you about special tours and activities (tel. [0305] 267992). For readers of Hardy who want to visit some of the places identified with scenes in the novels, we propose an itinerary in the LEISURE ROUTES (*see* pages 92–3).

Red-brick **Max Gate**, the house Hardy designed for himself in Dorchester proper, is closed to the public, but you can see a reconstruction of his

---

Lawrence of Arabia

During one of his attempts to retreat from celebrity status by changing his name and enlisting in the ranks, the former Colonel Lawrence bought a tiny gamekeeper's cottage at Cloud's Hill, near Bovington in Dorset in 1925. Ten years later, he was killed when his motorbike crashed on the road between the cottage and the nearby army camp. The cottage is now a National Trust property and furnished with Lawrence memorabilia. He was buried at Moreton, a few kilometres away. As he himself had specified, the gravestone records only one of his distinctions: "Fellow of All Souls College, Oxford".

Thomas Hardy

Britain's greatest regional novelist, Hardy (1840–1928) maintained strong links with his native Dorset in his art as in his life. Hardy was born in Higher Bockhampton village to a stonemason and his wife, a former serving maid. He was educated there and in neighbouring Dorchester, where he served a five-year architectural apprenticeship. Work and travel subsequently took him to London and the Continent, but Hardy always returned to Dorset, the inspiration of *Under the Greenwood Tree* (1872), the first of the Wessex novels, and *Far From the Madding Crowd*, his first success, published serially in 1874. A decade later, he settled permanently in Dorchester. The powerful late novels followed: *Tess of the D'Urbervilles* and *Jude the Obscure* (1895), as well as numerous volumes of poetry.

Hardy wrote about what he knew best; the people and rural scenes he saw around him, but his work transcends time and place to deal with the human condition. He treated the themes of adultery, immorality, and even murder in a non-judgemental manner that shocked Victorian morality. Hardy neither condemns nor condones, but understands, a point of view that makes him seem such a modern writer today.

The archaic name for **Maiden Castle**, Mai-Dun ("Strong Fort") is one you will understand once you have climbed its steep grass-covered ramparts. The hilltop was first occupied some 5,000 years ago, and the huge concentric defences you see today were constructed around the middle of the 4th century BC. Iron Age chiefs lived with their dependents on the heights, surrounded by a buffer zone of farms and tribal settlements. They were kings of the castle until AD 43 when it fell to the Roman legionaries, commanded by a future emperor, Vespasian. A footpath climbs up through the succession of ramparts to the top, where there is a great view back towards Dorchester.

Cerne Abbas

The thatched village preserves the remnants of a 10th-century Benedictine Abbey and, on the hillside above the abbey, the startlingly nude image of a fertility god, the **Cerne Giant,** cut into the chalk between 1,500 and 2,000 years ago. Archaeologists speculate that the 55m (180ft) outline figure represents Hercules, complete with signature club.

study at the **Dorset County Museum** (High West Street). Apart from extensive Hardy material (manuscripts, notebooks and the like), the museum exhibits a collection of fossils and fascinating artefacts from Maiden Castle, only a couple of miles away on Dorchester's southern outskirts. The statue outside the museum is of one of its founders, William Barnes, "The Dorset Poet" who wrote in the local dialect which retains strong echoes of Anglo-Saxon.

Sherborne

This is Dorset's most beautiful country town, with an abbey, two castles and a medieval centre. The magnificent **Abbey Church** incorporates Saxon, Norman, and Early English features, but it is the fan vaulting of the Perpendicular choir and nave that stands out. Horizontal mirrors allow you to inspect the carved stone in detail, especially the decorated bosses at the intersections of the ribs. The old monastery school survives as Sherborne, one of the élite public schools. According to tradition, King Alfred the Great was educated by the monks of Sherborne.

As for the castles, they occupy a Capability Brown park: Old Castle, a Norman ruin, and Sir Walter Raleigh's **Sherborne Castle** (1594). Elizabeth I "gave" Raleigh the property when he presented her with a hint and a jewel of equivalent value. The explorer initially attempted to restore the Old Castle, but he ended up by building the new. It was not his to enjoy for long. Raleigh ended up in the Tower of London, and his house reverted to the Crown. A diplomat, Sir John Digby, subsequently bought it, and Digbys live here still, although most of the castle is open to visitors.

Sherborne Abbey's fan-vaulted roof of honey-coloured stone is one of the most graceful in England. The town centre is rich in fine old houses.

The Cerne Abbas Giant's creators have left no clue to their identity, nor who the potent chalk figure was meant to represent.

Weymouth

The resort will forever be associated with King George III, whose seaside holidays in Dorset made history. The king enjoyed his first visit in 1789 so much that he made it an annual habit, returning to Weymouth every time. The stingy Hardy character, Uncle Benjy, complained about high Weymouth ("Budmouth Regis") prices in *The Trumpet Major*. "King George hev ruined the town for other folks". Spending money with abandon, fashionable 18th-century holiday-makers built the terraced Georgian houses that still line the seafront **Esplanade**, now a more plebeian tangle of deck chairs, sun-worshippers and souvenir sellers.

South of Weymouth lies the windswept **Isle of Portland**, a peninsula Hardy characterized as the "Gibraltar of Wessex". This is another important stone-quarrying area, the source of white Portland stone. Hardy locations are thick on the ground here: the ruins of Tudor **Sandsfoot Castle**, where sculptor Jocelyn Pierston trysted over the years with a mother, daughter and grand-daughter called Avice (read *The Well-Beloved*); 19th-century **Pennsylvania Castle** (built for a local governor named Penn), where Pierston lived in the novel; and "**Avice's Cottage**", now a museum of Portland life.

Pulpit Rock at Portland Bill, the tip of the peninsula, offers the ultimate Dorset vantage point. The surf crashes dramatically underfoot as you look out towards the churning water of Portland Race. Fair weather or foul, this can be a treacherous stretch of coast. The 1906 **Portland Bill Lighthouse**, the fourth on the site, keeps shipping a safe distance away from the shore. A second, non-

*S*hips beware! The Isle of Portland—not quite an island—sticks out rather dangerously into the English Channel. The Portland Bill Lighthouse warns shipping to keep away from this treacherous shore.

operational lighthouse serves as a **Bird Observatory and Field Centre**—for a rare, bird's-eye view of the birds: auks, kittiwakes, fulmars and passerines, according to season.

Chesil Bank, a wall of pebbles 29km (18 miles) long, joins Portland to the mainland, and continues west along the coast as far as Abbotsbury. On the lee side of the bank, the **Fleet Lagoon** is the protected haunt of sea birds, mainly cormorants, terns and swans. Abbotsbury's medieval **Swannery** was founded some six centuries ago by monks who raised the birds for their meat. Once there were thousands of swans on the Fleet. Now they number in the hundreds. Also by the lagoon, the **Subtropical Gardens** of Abbotsbury are the unique legacy of an 18th-century landowner. The abbey ruins and 15th-century tithe barn built by the monks can still be seen in the village centre.

Bridport

This old river port lies a mile inland from good swimming, fishing and sailing at **West Bay**. The fabrication of fishing nets is the big local industry, an outgrowth of Bridport's original rope and cord manufacture. For centuries, Bridport had the rope business all sewn up, supplying sailors—and hangmen—countrywide. A "Bridport dagger" was a hangman's noose.

Despite its Saxon foundation, Bridport has a mainly Georgian aspect. The especially wide streets once accommodated the rope-makers, who worked outside. Visit the Perpendicular **parish church** and the little **museum**, full of vintage rope-making paraphernalia.

A 8km (5-mile) detour inland takes you to **Parnham**, an Elizabethan manor

that provides the setting for the furniture designs of John Makepeace, a latter-day Chippendale, who lives and works here. Makepeace creates both one-of-a-kind pieces and limited editions in the Furniture Workshops on the premises (open to the public on Wednesdays). Many articles are on sale—for a price. Makepeace also supervises the School for Craftsmen in Wood, based at Parnham.

Lyme Regis

As picturesque as you might expect it to be, with cliffs to either side and hills behind, this small fishing port and resort has inspired novelists from Jane Austen (*Persuasion*) to John Fowles (*The French Lieutenant's Woman*), who lives nearby. The Regency bustle of **Broad Street** swoops down to **Marine Parade** and the sea. At the western end of the parade, an ancient breakwater known as the **Cobb** protects the harbour.

Cliff walks are particularly exhilarating in the area of Lyme. Head east 6km (4 miles) to **Golden Cap**, at 189m (619ft) the highest cliff on this stretch of the coast. Or walk the rugged **landslip**, a chasm west of town that opened on an eventful Christmas Day last century. To east or west, fossiling is good along the foot of the cliffs (beware of rockfalls), although you should not expect to unearth an ichthyosaurus or pterodactyl as Mary Anning did. Her famous 19th-century finds are displayed at the **museum** in Bridge Street.

The Duke of Monmouth landed here in 1685 to begin his rebellion against James II, an ill-starred enterprise that ended in defeat at Sedgemoor in Somerset.

British Architecture

The buildings of Britain—the cathedrals, thatched cottages, Victorian pubs and imposing 19th-century railway terminals—are as varied as its ways of life.

So-called **Norman** architecture (1050–1150)—the British equivalent of Romanesque—survives in various churches, cathedrals and castles: Durham Cathedral, the crypts of Canterbury and Winchester cathedrals, St John's Chapel and the White Tower in the Tower of London, and Dover Castle. This solid, ponderous style features simple geometric decoration and the plain round arch.

Britain's medieval cathedrals show that great architectural achievement of north European Christianity, the **Gothic** style (1150–1550), at its peak. Spires and steeples give churches a fantastic skyward thrust, enhanced by pointed arches and flying buttresses, stained glass and richly carved ornament. Small details, such as the figure of a toothache sufferer at Wells Cathedral, display a rough medieval humanity.

As on the Continent, the Gothic style divides into three distinct phases. Salisbury Cathedral exemplifies the initial **Early English** phase (to 1280). Also known as the "pointed" style, it has the lancet window as its hallmark. Bristol and Wells cathedrals are typical of the slightly later **Decorated** style (to 1380). Ogee curves and naturalistic plant forms adorn capitals, corbels and pinnacles. Bath Abbey and St George's Chapel, Windsor illustrate the more austere **Perpendicular Gothic** (to 1540), characterized by simpler vertical forms and the panel motif.

Meanwhile, secular buildings across the land—manor houses, guild halls, alms houses—went up in half-timbered "vernacular" style. This perennially popular architecture (with wooden beams and white or buff plaster, or brick) remained in favour beyond the Tudor and Elizabethan eras.

The **Renaissance** manner did not catch on at first in Britain, although crude classical motifs appear on buildings as diverse as Hampton Court Palace in Middlesex (begun 1514) and Longleat House in Wiltshire (under construction from 1572–80). The real rebirth of British architecture came at the beginning of the 1600s, when Inigo Jones (1573–1652) introduced the use of the dome and classical orders. He derived his **classicism** from a study of Palladio, the 16th-century Italian architect, who in turn was influenced by the writings of the Roman architect Vitruvius. There is a down-to-earth, secular grandeur to Jones's work: the Queen's House at Greenwich, the Banqueting House in Whitehall, London, and the church of St Paul's, Covent Garden, London. In the last, an example of classicism at its simplest the primitive Tuscan order proclaims the simplicity of the Reformed Church.

Towards the end of the 17th century, architects, such as Sir Christopher Wren (1632–1723), Sir John Vanbrugh (1664–1726) and Nicholas Hawksmoor (1661–1736), began to mix classical with Gothic and **baroque** elements. Wren's St Paul's Cathedral in London, based on a Gothic plan, with baroque towers and a magnificent classical dome, is the crowning achievement of the age. Among secular buildings, Blenheim Palace, designed by Vanbrugh with Hawksmoor, stands out. Hawksmoor remains a more shadowy figure. There is a vaguely sinister quality to some of his designs, notably St Mary Woolnoth in the City of London, and the Mausoleum at Castle Howard in Yorkshire.

In the 18th century, classicism was domesticated to produce the **Georgian** style (1720–1790), which many people consider the most civilized and practical ever. Robert Adam (1728–92), the leading exponent, also produced refined designs for furniture and interiors (Harewood House, near Leeds; Kenwood, London). Georgian elegance is best appreciated not in single buildings but through an entire ensemble. The planned crescents, squares and terraces of Bath, by John Wood the Elder (1704–54) and Younger (1728–81), and of Edinburgh, are supreme examples.

A generation later, John Nash (1752–1835) carried the architectural ensemble into a grander, **Regency** mode (1790–1830) with his designs for London's Carlton House Terrace and the terraces adjoining Regent's Park. Regency architecture of a very different kind can be seen in the Royal Pavilion at Brighton, remodelled in 1815 by the versatile Nash for the future King George IV. This ornate piece of orientalism displays Indian and Chinese motifs. It was great fun while it lasted, but Queen Victoria wasn't amused.

Blenheim Palace, Oxfordshire.

Victorian architecture (1830–1900) combines high-minded historicism with unprecedented technical know-how. A taste for the Gothic had never really gone away. Sir Charles Barry's (1795–1860) cathedral-like styling of the Houses of Parliament revived it again. Still in his twenties, AWN Pugin (1812–52) collaborated, designing the Gothic details of the façade and interior, including the furniture and fittings. Another example of Victorian historicism in brick and terracotta, the Natural History Museum by Alfred Waterhouse (1830– 1905), harks back to a kind of Romanesque. Not everyone was a Medievalist, however, and a bit of a battle ensued between adherents of the Gothic and classical styles. Sir Robert Smirke (1780–1867), architect of the British Museum—a particularly plain and monumental classical building—took a Greek temple as his model.

New technology made possible such proud Victorian achievements as the tunnels and suspension bridges of Isambard Kingdom Brunel (1806–59) and the magnificent but now vanished Crystal Palace by Sir Joseph Paxton (1801–65), who designed the prefabricated glass and iron structure for the 1851 Great Exhibition. The huge greenhouses at Kew Gardens, London, give some idea of what it was like.

By the end of the 19th century, a reaction to Victorian excess set in, in the person of Charles Rennie Mackintosh (1868–1928). His spare, elegant **Art Nouveau** designs for buildings (the Glasgow School of Art, Sauchiehall Street, Glasgow) and furniture foreshadow the Modernist style.

The British didn't really take to concrete, metal and glass **Modernism**. Suburbia provided the most typical 20th-century form: houses in half-timbered "stockbroker Tudor", complete with stained glass in the hallway and roses in the garden—kitsch or cosy, depending on your point of view. Of course Britain (and the City of London in particular) has its high-rise complexes. Richard Rogers' controversial Lloyd's Building in the City, begun in 1980, shows British Modernism at its most uncompromising. The streamlined style has many critics, in particular Prince Charles, who likened a proposed extension to the National Gallery to "a carbuncle on the face of an old friend". The national mood seems to echo the prince's. In the Post-Modern 1990s, the trend is towards neo-Georgianism, decoration and nostalgia.

Cheddar, Cider and Cream Teas

You are never far from the sea—the open Atlantic or English Channel—in the West Country, England's south-westerly extension. The counties of Somerset, Devon and Cornwall share the peninsula and its long coastline, rugged to the north and west, gentler along the southern, Channel shore. The South-West is relatively remote from the rest of Britain, with a distinct regional character. In the old days, the West Country drank more cider than beer (and still drinks plenty), the visitors consumed a lot of cream teas (and still do). Accents are softer and slower, and outsiders have sometimes assumed that wits are, too—to their cost, often enough.

Avon

Bath

The Romans never could resist a hot spring. When they found one here in AD 44, they established a settlement, calling it *Aquae Sulis* (the "waters of Sul", the local Celtic deity). Their baths can still be seen today near the abbey in the city centre. After the Romans left, no one went in much for bathing until the early

*A*t Bath, steaming spring water gushes from the source. That was all the persuasion the Romans needed to establish their settlement of Aquae Sulis here.

18th century, when a Dr William Oliver built a bath here for sufferers from gout. (His name and his face appear on crunchy Bath Olivers—crackers invented by the good doctor—which some people insist are the best accompaniment to Cheddar or Stilton cheese.) Quite suddenly, taking the waters at Bath became all the rage with fashionable London society, although socializing at soirées, theatre and balls generally took precedence over bathing in, or drinking, the metallic-tasting spa water. Richard "Beau" Nash was appointed Master of Ceremonies in 1704 and dictated for decades the manners and styles of the Bath season. Everybody who was anybody got into a coach and came here, buying houses or taking apartments in the fine new

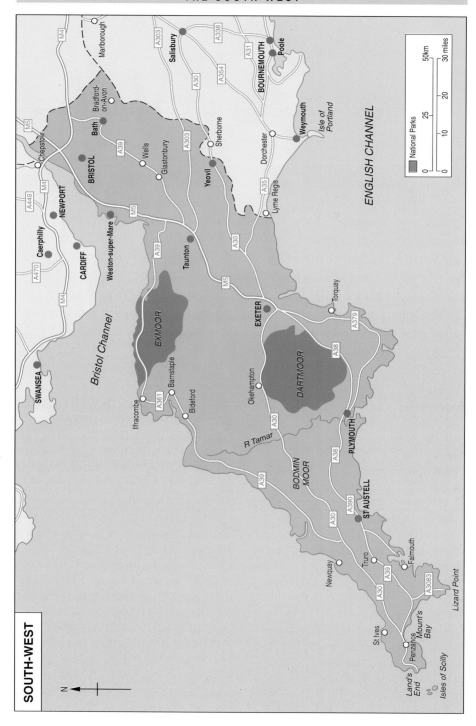

SOUTH-WEST

Georgian terraces. Bath's reign at the pinnacle of fashion lasted fully one hundred years. Jane Austen writes about it in *Northanger Abbey* from her own youthful experience at the end of the 18th century.

The **abbey** in late Perpendicular style seems to warm rather than dominate the centre. Notice the great west window and the stone-carving on the towers. The angels climbing ladders to heaven commemorate a dream in which God commanded a bishop of Bath to restore the church.

The **Pump Room**, opposite, was one of the gathering places for society when Bath was at its zenith. Now tourists queue up to have lunch or tea to the strains of the Pump Room trio. The windows overlook the **King's Bath**, a medieval installation that was the only section of the complex known to Georgian curists.

Excavated in 1878, the **Roman Baths**, below Pump Room level, include the steaming Great Bath and gushing sacred spring. Finds from the adjacent temple complex, revealed in 1983, are on view in a small, on-site museum.

The chief monuments of Georgian Bath lie up the hill from the centre. John Wood the Elder built the terraced houses of **Queen Square** (1728) and the **Circus** (1754) as entities, giving the occupants the feeling of living in something larger. His son, John Wood the Younger, designed the 30 houses of the **Royal Crescent** (1767) to look like a very grand single residence. Now a museum, No. 1 Royal Crescent has been restored and redecorated in late 18th-century style.

The **Assembly Rooms** (1771) near the Circus were *the* place to drink tea, play cards and dance. The basement now houses a costume museum. Other fine examples of Georgian elegance include the terraces of **Duke Street** and **Great Pulteney Street**, but you can wander at will and discover many more. Like Florence's Ponte Vecchio, Robert Adam's little **Pulteney Bridge** incorporates small shops. At the east end of Great Pulteney Street, the **Holburne of Menstrie Museum** displays collections of ceramics and silver from Britain and the Continent. The paintings on view include British portraits from the 18th and 19th centuries.

On a hill to the south, **Prior Park** was built by John Wood the Elder for Ralph Allen, who owned quarries of the "Bath stone" from which all those Georgian houses were built. It is still insisted on today, at least for the facing.

Taking the Cure

Did it work—immersing yourself up to the neck for hours in the warm waters of Bath? Eighteenth-century doctors' records show that 70 to 80 per cent of patients had their aches and pains much relieved. Sceptics might respond "they would, wouldn't they?", but space age research backs up the old claims. Weightlessness speeds up the excretion of liquid, carrying toxins with it, and near immersion in baths has the same effect. Many who came for treatment were suffering from the high lead content of drinks such as the cider of the time, and the cure helped wash lead compounds out of the body. Then, no doubt, the satisfied customers went home and carried on drinking as before.

*S*outh-west England.

*T*he 18th-century Royal Crescent in Bath showed how a row of holiday homes could be built to look like a palace.

Five kilometres (3 miles) east, **Claverton Manor** is the home of the **American Museum in Britain**, featuring rooms furnished with the crafts and antiques of many periods and areas, from colonial New England and French New Orleans to Spanish New Mexico and the Old West. There are displays of American Indian and folk art, as well.

Bradford-on-Avon

This pretty little town of narrow streets and stone houses has three claims to fame. One is the 10th-century **Saxon church**, as well preserved as any in the country and very little altered. That was paradoxically due to the fact that it was put to other uses when the 12th-century parish church went up. The second highlight is a small, domed **chapel** on the old stone bridge, where pilgrims used to pray. Later it became the town lock-up. Across the bridge at Barton Farm, look for the great 14th-century **Tithe Barn**, 51m (168ft) long with massive timbers supporting the roof.

Bristol

"All ship-shape and Bristol fashion", goes the old approving phrase. The city is now one of Britain's largest (over half a million if you include the vast suburbs). It all started around the harbour on the River Avon, several miles from the sea and secure against invaders and storms. Bristol's ships dominated the wine trade with France and Spain, and gave the city's name to a type of sherry. John Cabot of Genoa and his Bristol-born son Sebastian sailed from here, reaching mainland North America in 1497. Wool exports, then tobacco imports, brought prosperity, elegant houses and fine public buildings. In the 20th century, Bristol aircraft and engines led the way from the beginnings of aviation to the supersonic era. Now the city is a major financial centre.

The oldest part of the city lies between Bristol Bridge and Quay Street. Look for the classical **Exchange** building by John Wood the Elder. The brass pillars outside, called the Nails, were used as tables for cash payment: hence, "cash on the nail". What happened to the quay at Quay Street? In the last century this arm of the harbour was partially filled in. The oval **Centre**, a small park, is built on part of it. Just south lies what remains of the channel, with the lively **Watershed** leisure complex on one side and the Arnolfini arts centre on the other.

From the Centre, walk along King Street to the 1766 **Theatre Royal,** which

City plan of Bristol.

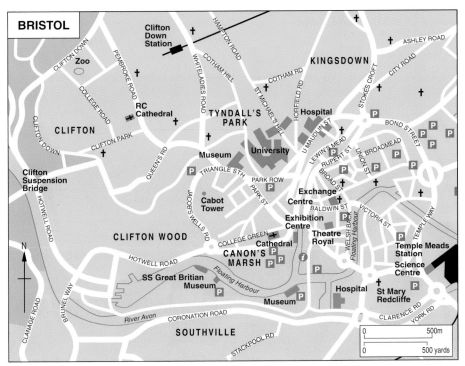

*T*he old port in the centre of Bristol is home to Brunel's SS Great Britain, launched here in 1845 and brought back from the Falklands in 1970 (above).

*N*ot an artificial wave pool, but the Severn Bore, produced by a rare though predictable combination of tide and river flow (below).

miraculously preserves its original lay-out. It is the home of the renowned Bristol Old Vic company. Across the **Floating Harbour** (the main waterway through the city), you can see the 89m (292ft) spire on the tower of **St Mary Redcliffe**, "the fairest, goodliest and most famous parish church in England" according to Queen Elizabeth I. It was founded in the 12th century, and completed in the 19th. Bristol also has a **cathedral**, a fine church in its own right. Notice how much of the city is on two levels: old streets below, bridged by newer ones, with steps between. World War II bombing left some obvious scars; the shopping area of Broadmead is built on the worst-hit part.

Bristol claims two masterpieces of the great engineer Isambard Kingdom Brunel. His 1845 *Great Britain,* the first ocean-going, propeller-driven iron ship, was brought back here in 1970 from the Falkland Islands, where she was abandoned in 1886. You can board the ship, under restoration in the dry dock at the far end of Princes Wharf. Up in the fashionable suburb of Clifton, Brunel's still awe-inspiring 1864 **Clifton Suspension Bridge** spans the 76m (250ft) deep gorge of the Avon. This has been the scene of countless stunts and jumps and daredevil flights.

Somerset

The county name comes from the Saxon word for "lake dwellers". An area of marsh and swamp, the Somerset Levels are England's most extensive wetlands. But Somerset also takes in moorland and hills like the cave-riddled Mendips and the Quantocks.

Wells

From the busy little high street and marketplace, just pass through the gateway into the precinct of the **cathedral** and you arrive in a different world. You could almost be across the Channel, for the cathedral's astonishing **west front** is more like the finest in France than any other in England. Imagine this supreme example of the Decorated style when it was finished, in about 1235, with its 400 figures of apostles and saints, angels and prophets all painted in full colour. Wind and weather, Puritan idol-smashers and ill-judged cleaning have taken their toll, so that some statues are missing and others are unrecognizable. Recent restoration has tried to protect the survivors and, controversially, put in some replicas. Be sure to walk around the outside to the **east end** as well.

Inside, the Early English austerity of the nave makes a strong first impression, enhanced by the bold scissor-shaped arches in the crossing. They represent an unusual solution to a problem: the tower had threatened to collapse when a spire was added in the 14th century. There is a feast of stained glass, wood-carving and modern embroidery in the choir and, in the north transept, a 14th-century **clock** with model axemen striking the quarter hours and knights jousting every hour. Worn steps lead up to the octagonal **Chapter House**, considered to be the most beautiful of its period (around 1300).

Across the green stands the crenellated **Bishop's Palace**. Swans still circle the moat, but not the famous bell-ringing pair, alas. One of them was run over by a car, and its mate ran away in despair. It has proved impossible to

173

train new birds to ring the gatehouse bell at meal times; tourists keep them too well fed.

Wookey Hole

North and west of Wells, the limestone Mendip Hills may look solid, but they are actually honeycombed with holes—Roman lead mines, ancient coal mines and countless caverns cut by rivers and streams that dissolved the rock. Wookey Hole is a group of caves formed where the underground River Axe comes to the surface. Bones found in the caves show they were occupied by Stone Age hunters, when bears, rhinos and mammoths roamed the Mendips. Three caves are open to visitors, and some finds can be seen in the Museum of the Caves. The site has been commercialized for a long time—there is even a waxworks exhibition—but you can get away from the crowds by walking up nearby **Ebbor Gorge**.

Cheddar

Spectacular **Cheddar Gorge**, almost 2km (over a mile) long and up to 137m (450ft) deep, winds down from the ridge of the Mendips through a dramatic gash in the rocks. Several caverns leading off the gorge can be visited. Attractions include stalactites and stalagmites and Stone Age relics. Cheese

*M*oonrise over Wells Cathedral, a great treasure for a small English city. The west front with 293 surviving statues dates from the 13th century. More than 20 bishops are buried here.

from the farms around Cheddar village was so widely imitated that today it is made all over Britain and even as far away as North America and New Zealand. The original, wrapped in cloth and matured for months at Somerset farms, is worth searching for.

Glastonbury

The town is surrounded by a halo of legend so old that lack of evidence hardly matters. One very ancient belief holds that Joseph of Arimathea came here after the Crucifixion, carrying the Holy Grail—the chalice used at the Last Supper—which he buried under the steep hill called the Glastonbury Tor. When he leaned on his staff on nearby Wirrall ("Weary-all") Hill, it took root and grew into the Glastonbury Thorn. (This particular tree was chopped down in the Civil War, but a thorn tree in the abbey grounds is said to have grown from a cutting.) Joseph went on to found Britain's first Christian church in Glastonbury, or so the story continues, and the town became a magnet for pilgrims. Nowadays it attracts adherents of various "alternative lifestyles". **Glastonbury Abbey** is today a romantic ruin set amid beautiful grounds.

In the early days, the land all around Glastonbury would have been marsh and lakes. The second great legend identifies the town as the sacred isle of Avalon, where King Arthur came, and where his body was brought after his death. A plaque marks the supposed burial site before what was once the high altar of the abbey church.

Stroll in the town to see several 14th- and 15th-century buildings, including the handsome **George and Pilgrims Inn**, where prosperous pilgrims used to stay.

The **Abbot's Tribunal** is now a museum with local finds on display from Iron Age villages that once lay hidden in the surrounding swamps.

A walk up the **Tor** is worth it for the superb view. At the summit stands the tower of a ruined chapel. **Chalice Well**, in gardens at the foot of the Tor, marks the site where tradition says the Holy Grail was buried.

Cadbury Castle

If you are fascinated by Arthurian legend, make sure you climb the flat-topped hill crowned with an earthwork called Cadbury Castle, near the village of South Cadbury. Some claim this to be the site of Camelot itself. Excavations revealed the remains of a 5th-century timber hall, so someone of importance lived here.

You could spend a whole holiday visiting sights with an Arthurian connection. If the idea appeals, *see* page 77 in LEISURE ROUTES for a detailed itinerary.

Montacute House
(near Yeovil)
Gabled Montacute, in exemplary Elizabethan style, is one of the most beautiful of England's stately homes. The local Ham Hill stone has weathered to the same honey-gold that gives such warmth to the nearby villages. Montacute narrowly escaped demolition in the 1930s, before the National Trust took the property over. None of the original furniture remains, but a number of valuable period pieces have been loaned or given to the house. The top-floor **Long Gallery** displays a fine collection of pictures of 16th- and 17th-century notables from the National

Portrait Gallery in London, including some portraits of Queen Elizabeth I in magnificently frothy dresses.

Muchelney

This village was once an island in the marshes. In fact, Muchelney means "big island". Benedictine monks founded a monastery here in the 7th century. It was destroyed by Viking raiders in the 9th century, refounded in the 10th and reconstructed in the 15th. Only ruins survive, but the village seems to be built of its stones. Look at the unusual painted ceiling of the parish church, with angels dressed like plump Tudor ladies of the day, around 1600.

Barrington Court

(*Ilminster*)
This early Tudor house has famous spiral chimneys. The sugar baron, Colonel Lyle, who lived here in the 1920s, avidly collected old wood panelling and fittings from all over Europe and installed them in his house, giving it a uniquely eccentric quality. Anyone who loves of gardens will want to see Gertrude Jekyll's formal design.

Taunton

Somerset's lively county town lies in the rich farmland of the Vale of Taunton or Taunton Deane, famous for cider apples and dairy herds. Don't be put off by modern expansion and traffic: there are special flavours to be sampled. Stubborn independence put Taunton on the "wrong" side in several English rebellions. The Duke of Monmouth was proclaimed king here in 1685 before marching off to defeat at Sedgemoor. Ghastly retribution in the form of Judge Jeffreys' Bloody Assize in the Great Hall of the **Norman castle** sent hundreds to the gallows or the plantations of the West Indies. The castle now houses the **County Museum**. Try to get to the Saturday market, and in summer to the County Ground for the cricket—which is a religion here. Search out the tiny side-streets of Georgian houses and bow-windowed shops, and the **Church of St Mary Magdalene**, with its beautiful slim tower and striking interior.

The rolling, wooded Quantock Hills north-west of Taunton are a maze of hidden hamlets which have been the home of writers from Wordsworth to Evelyn Waugh. **Nether Stowey** has a fine old manor house, but it was in the little cottage at 35 Lime Street that Coleridge wrote *The Rime of the Ancient Mariner* and *Kubla Khan*.

The Bristol Channel Coast

For more than 160km (100 miles), the coastline of Somerset and North Devon alternates holiday camps and resorts with some dramatic scenery. **Weston-super-Mare** is the biggest seaside town, with summer throngs and all the traditional entertainments from donkey rides on the beach and Punch and Judy shows to golf and concerts.

Burnham-on-Sea has extensive sands—the tide seems to go almost out of sight—and a church with a leaning tower: biblical advice was ignored and it was built on sand. There is a strange history to the reredos. Designed for Whitehall Chapel by Inigo Jones and carved by Grinling Gibbons, it was installed instead in Westminster Abbey, discarded, and set up here.

Minehead is noisy and cheerful, with an old quay and harbour, more vast beaches at low tide and good cliff and coastal walks. Not far away lies **Selworthy**, a lovely village of thatched cob cottages. Climb up to Dunkery and Selworthy beacons for breathtaking views to seaward and inland, over Exmoor.

Dramatic coastal scenery and spectacular moorland combine in Exmoor, haunt of walkers, wild ponies and red deer. The region is cut by dozens of fast-flowing streams.

Exmoor National Park

Small is beautiful in this favourite of England's many stretches of moorland. Only about 34km (21 miles) from east to west, and no more than 19km (12 miles) north to south, it is nevertheless a region of infinite variety. Red deer, wild ponies and grouse make their home on the high heath and in the hidden valleys. Hardy sheep graze the uplands, and little villages nestle amid the softer cow pastures. This is walking country, but keep an eye on the weather, which can turn bleak.

Lost Art

Cob, a cunning blend of chalk rubble, clay, cow manure and even hair, was once widely used to make walls. They had to be built up slowly, over months or even years, on a plinth of flint—an early damp-proof course, in fact. These days, central heating in the houses dries the cob, so it cracks, and few know how to make a mixture to patch it up.

Exmoor is the memorable setting of RD Blackmore's fateful novel *Lorna Doone,* and fans of the book like to identify the sites that it refers to: Doone Valley itself is placed a few miles north of Simonsbath. **Dulverton** makes a good centre for exploration of the southern part. **Watersmeet**, naturally enough the place where two rivers join in a picturesque valley, is the best starting point for walks in the north of the park. Don't miss the little town of **Dunster**, with its 17th-century octagonal Yarn Market and dramatic castle (though the romantic look is the result of 19th-century additions).

Exmoor meets the sea in some of the finest coastal scenery in Britain, best seen by walking the Somerset and Devon Coast Path, where cliffs and promontories alternate with headlong descents. But the road west from Minehead is spectacular enough. The one-in-four ascents out of **Porlock** and **Countisbury** were considered a great test for cars in the early days of motoring.

Exmoor straddles the county boundary. Clifftop **Lynton**, with **Lynmouth** hundreds of feet below it on the sea, is in Devon. Torrential rains on the moor in 1952 sent disastrous floods through Lynmouth, causing severe loss of life. New channels have since been made.

Devon

The county's charms are no secret to the British holiday-makers who flock to the resorts and crowd the villages of Devon every summer. Take care on the roads: driving can be difficult in the narrow lanes.

North Devon

Ilfracombe is a breezy resort with an old harbour, dozens of shingle beaches and the bonus of **Torrs Walk,** a winding path that seems to hang over the sea. Further west, the more sheltered waters of the Bristol Channel give way at **Woolacombe** to Atlantic swells, to the joy of all surfers. Don't mix up the two old towns of **Barnstaple** and **Bideford**, unless you want to annoy the inhabitants. They were rival ports until silt in the River Taw kept ships from reaching Barnstaple, the main market town of North Devon. Some of England's greatest sea captains came from Devon, and the men of Bideford sailed with the best.

Back on the mainland, **Appledore** is a charming little fishing port and yacht harbour, with steep narrow streets of Tudor cottages climbing from the

Puffins' Perch

You can take a voyage from Bideford (or Ilfracombe in summer) to Lundy Island—its name comes from the Norse word for puffin. The 32km (20-mile) trip can be choppy, so don't forget to take precautions if you're susceptible to seasickness. The island, only 5km (3 miles) long and roughly 1km (half a mile) wide, is a bird sanctuary and perfect for walking. In fact there are no cars, and not many beds either, so make a reservation if you want to stay overnight.

The Devil's Slide on Lundy Island off North Devon. You can take a day trip to Lundy from Bideford or Ilfracombe.

quayside. When it comes to steep streets, however, **Clovelly** takes the medal. Its stepped and cobbled alleys would be quite impossible for cars, so they have to be left at the top. So picturesque and celebrated is Clovelly that the tide of visitors sometimes threatens to swamp it. As an antidote, watch the roaring surf pound grim, jagged rocks at **Hartland Point**.

Exeter

Devon's capital was Roman *Isca*, and the 1st-century walls are still visible along Southernhay and Northernhay. They were uncovered, bizarrely, by the same bombing raid of World War II that burned so much of the old city around the **cathedral**. By some miracle, this, Exeter's glory, was almost unscathed. The two towers are true survivors—having been retained from an earlier Norman building. The main body of the cathedral dates from the 14th century, with wonderful rib vaulting, a minstrel's gallery and massive, canopied bishop's throne. Nearby in Cathedral Close, **Mol's Coffee House** (now an art shop) was once the haunt of Elizabethan captains—Drake, Raleigh and others. They must have felt as if they were at sea in the stern of a great galleon.

From Princesshay, you can enter the underground passages which supplied Exeter, luckier than most medieval cities, with pure spring water. Ask about guided tours at the Tourist Information Centre in the Civic Centre.

Down at the quay by the River Exe, the **Maritime Museum** features a fascinating collection of 100 boats from coracles to sampans, many afloat on the river and the adjoining canal basin.

North of Exeter, the road leads to Exmoor (*see* pages 178–9), but first, at **Bickleigh**, is an old-world village of thatch and cob cottages.

Tiverton, on the River Exe, was once famous for its wool, then for its lace; now it has become quite industrial. Nearby **Knightshayes Court** is worth a visit. William Burges designed this triumph of Victorian Gothic architecture for John Heathcoat-Amory, 19th-century heir to the Tiverton lace fortune. The garden is reckoned to be one of Devon's finest.

*D*ozens of craft, originals and replicas, float on the River Exe at the Maritime Museum, Exeter.

South Devon Resorts

The sheltered south coast dresses itself up as an "English Riviera", with palm trees and rows of white-painted hotels. It got a boost every time there was a European war, from Napoleonic times onwards, and it became difficult to travel abroad. The fashion grew for retiring here, so some of the resorts are pretty sleepy.

Beer has the last chalk cliffs on the Channel coast, with caves that were once used by smugglers, and **Branscombe** is an exceptionally appealing little village of cob and thatch houses. Queen Victoria lived at **Sidmouth** as a baby, and the town retains an air of respectability.

The red cliffs and pebble beach of **Budleigh Salterton** were the setting for *The Boyhood of Raleigh* (the Millais painting and the actuality). The South

Devon Coast Path crosses the clifftops from here to **Exmouth**, which is the oldest resort in the county. People first came to Exmouth for sea bathing early in the 18th century. It's not far to **Teignmouth** from the 518m (1,700ft) long estuary bridge: the former fishing port has been transformed into a vast yacht harbour, as an old resort keeps up with the times.

This is even more true of the biggest and showiest, the Queen of the Coast, **Torquay**, where facilities operate all the year round, and estate agents advertise time-share apartments, just as they do in the Algarve. For contrast, look into **Kent's Cavern** (Ilsham Road), which Stone Age remains show to be one of the oldest inhabited sites in Britain.

Together with Torquay, Paignton and Brixham border beautiful Torbay. At **Paignton**'s little port they still bring in crabs and lobsters, but the fish market to see is at **Brixham** in the early morning. The catch there includes the fish served at dinner in restaurants throughout the south-west.

A few miles inland, **Totnes** has one of the most attractive old town centres in England. A host of 15th- to 19th-

Rows of identical terraced houses are not unique to the little Devon town of Beer. They are everywhere. Look carefully, though; each house has its own individual touches.

century buildings line the main street as it climbs from the River Dart, past the Tudor East Gate to the hilltop Norman castle. Craft and antiques shops are a Totnes speciality. Some of the best of them have a **Butterwalk** address.

The name of **Dartmouth** has become synonymous with the Royal Naval College, but there is much else of interest. As you walk in the old town, keep an eye out for **St Saviour's Church** (1372), noted for its carved stone and woodwork, and **Agincourt House**, home of a 15th-century merchant. The river estuary is beautifully sheltered, and guarded by two castles: they used to haul up a chain between them to keep out enemy ships.

At the southernmost point of Devon, **Salcombe**'s protected waters are perfect for sailing. The locals boast about the mild climate and grow orange and lemon trees to prove it.

Plymouth

The waters of its Sound count as one of the finest natural harbours in the world. No wonder Plymouth has seen so many famous ships and sailors put to sea in peace and war: Sir Francis Drake, finishing his legendary game of bowls on the Hoe before engaging the Spanish Armada in 1588; the *Mayflower* Pilgrims voyaging to the New World in 1620; Captain Cook setting out on his three-year journey around the world in 1768; and battalions joining the 1944 D-Day landings. The city centre was comprehensively smashed in World War II bombing, so buildings are modern rather than historic. The panorama from the top of the high-rise Civic Centre gives you an idea of the layout of this big city, dwarfing any other west of Bristol.

 Some of the old atmosphere survives in the **Barbican** area, between the 17th-century citadel and Sutton Pool, the original harbour that Drake knew. Fishing boats tie up here now. Look for **Island House**, where the Pilgrim Fathers spent their last night in England, and **Mayflower Steps** on the pier, where they embarked. Plaques nearby commemorate the departure of Bermuda's first settlers in 1609, and New Zealand's 230

years later. The Old Customs House by the quay, and taverns like the Ship Inn and Green Lantern, date from Plymouth's Elizabethan heyday.

Take in the view of the Sound from the green expanse of the **Hoe**. Or, better still, go for a harbour cruise. Circular trips take you out past Drake's Island and **Devonport**, longtime home to the grey ships of the Royal Navy.

*O*n Dartmoor, walkers revel in miles of open, heather-covered moorland, punctuated by sparkling streams and weathered granite tors.

When Drake got back from his voyage around the world in 1581, he used some of his store of gold to buy **Buckland Abbey**, 9km (6 miles) north of Plymouth. The Great Hall and wood-panelled drawing room look as they did in his day. On the upper floor, naval displays feature relics of Drake, including the celebrated drum that he took to sea. A legend claims that the drum will beat if England is ever in danger, and that its sound will bring Drake's spirit to the rescue of his homeland.

Stately homes are scattered around the shores of the Sound. **Saltram House**, lying 5km (3 miles) east of Plymouth, is a magnificent Georgian remodelling of a Tudor mansion, with rooms by Robert Adam and Reynolds portraits. **Antony House** lies across the Tamar, near the Torpoint ferry. This classical early Georgian residence in silvery granite has the original furnishings, pictures and famous needlework of the Carew family, whose descendants still live here. You can reach Tudor **Cotehele**, up the Tamar from Plymouth, by boat as well as road. This is a remarkable survival: the Edgecumbe family moved into a newer house (Mount Edgecumbe on Plymouth Sound) and did not modernize this one. The collections of armour and furniture are outstanding, and there is a branch of the National Maritime Museum here, too.

Dartmoor

When you have had your fill of cities, beaches and summer crowds, retreat inland to the wilderness. Dartmoor (a national park) is the least inhabited tract of land in southern England, although it is dotted with traces of medieval tin workings and prehistoric stone circles. Dartmoor is superb pony-trekking and

walking country, but always check the weather forecast: mists can roll in very quickly and it is notoriously easy to get lost. The granite outcrops called "tors" that rear up out of the moor are great landmarks—if you can tell which is which. Beware, also, of bogs, dangerously marshy areas that are not always immediately obvious.

Information is available year-round at the park headquarters in **Bovey Tracey**. In spring and summer, branches are open at **Okehampton**, a good base for the northern moor, and **Tavistock**, the market town to the south-west. The Bronze Age village of **Grimspound** is ringed by a huge wall to keep out wild animals. This is near

Naughty but Nice

Anywhere west of Stonehenge, you will see the "Cream Teas" signs start. What should you get? A pot of tea, of course, not just a cup. Maybe some little sandwiches, and perhaps some cakes too. And most important of all, the scones themselves, served with butter, jam (preferably home-made strawberry) and cream. Thick yellow cream. Devotees will argue till the cows come home whether Devonshire or Cornish (clotted) cream is more toothsome. The first is made by gently heating milk so the cream collects on top, and this is then skimmed off. Cornish cream is heated to concentrate it still further, to the consistency of crumbly butter. Spread the scones with butter, jam and a liberal blob of the cholesterolic cream—and enjoy. You can always skip dinner!

Widecombe-in-the-Moor, known for the September fair that "Uncle Tom Cobbleigh and all" were heading for in the old folk song. When you see the crowd there, you might think that they have finally arrived.

Say "Dartmoor" in a game of word association and most British people will respond "prison". High on the bleakest part of the moor, the famous gaol (jail) originally held POWs from the Napoleonic Wars. Now it holds criminals, and **Princetown** has grown up

The essential ingredients of a cream tea: scones, butter, jam, thick cream and a pot of tea.

around it to house the staff. It all looks depressing and you will not want to linger. **Dartmeet** is far more attractive: an ancient, rough stone "clapper" bridge crosses the bubbling East Dart just north of the modern road bridge.

The unique **Castle Drogo**, built between 1910 and 1930 is the remarkable work of Lutyens. Set high over the gorge of the River Teign, its views of the moor are superb. You feel like a game of croquet on the lawn? No problem, they have equipment for hire.

Cornwall

The River Tamar almost severs Cornwall from the rest of England. It was always a place apart, looking more to the sea than to neighbouring but very different Devon. The separate Cornish language died out, although it has been revived by a few enthusiasts; relics remain in the soft dialect that rolls like the sea swell.

The South Coast
The railway bridge across the Tamar brought the first wave of tourists to Cornwall (1859), but they were as nothing compared with the summer migrations of motorists that followed. **Looe** was the first of the picturesque fishing villages to net a huge catch of visitors, and is still one of the most crowded. It is also the headquarters of English shark fishing. (Don't worry, *Jaws* has never been spotted; swimming is perfectly safe, although you might find the water cold.)

Polperro's little harbour is so narrow at the mouth that it used to be shut off in bad weather. The narrow streets are

*W*ild and rugged it may appear, but hidden beneath the cliffs at Whitsand Bay on Cornwall's south coast are miles of long, golden beaches.

closed to cars and some of the fishermen's cottages seem to stand right in the water. In the Middle Ages, the men of neighbouring **Fowey** (pronounced "foy") used to go in for private enterprise raids on the coast of France. Cross on the ferry to Polruan for the best view of the old waterfront. These days Fowey exports china clay from the

*L*and's End, Cornwall, *the south-western tip of the British mainland.*

diggings near **St Austell**, where spoil heaps pile up like miniature alps. (Britain is one of the world's main producers of the clay, which is used in paper and cosmetics as well as porcelain.) Inland from Fowey, near Lostwithiel, are the romantic ruins of the Norman castle of **Restormel**.

Mevagissey, one of the prettiest of Cornwall's fishing villages, used to send thousands of tons of salted pilchards a year to the Catholic countries of Europe, especially Italy. Now the fishermen take tourists out after sharks.

In **Veryan**, a little way inland, are some curious round houses that were supposed to deny the devil any corner in which to hide. The village is the gateway to **Roseland,** which has nothing to do with roses (the word means "spur" or "heath" in Cornish). This coast has one of the gentlest climates in all England and some have dubbed it the "Cornish Riviera".

The superb harbour of **Falmouth** is a yachting centre and still an important port. Being the first and last call in England once made it the place where urgent transatlantic mail was transferred between ship and shore. Dominating the bay, **Pendennis Castle** formed part of Henry VIII's chain of coastal defences. Continental invasion never came, but the fort saw action in the Civil War: the Roundheads finally captured it after a six-month siege.

The 18th-century merchants of Falmouth who aspired to more genteel surroundings went to live in **Truro**, which soon boasted the most elegant Georgian terraces west of Bath. Fine Regency and Victorian houses were added, although a Georgian aura survives along Boscawen and Lemon streets. Truro's Gothic-revival **cathedral** was begun in 1880, four years after Cornwall gained ecclesiastical independence from Devon. The **museum** is Cornwall's best, noted especially for its display of minerals.

The most southerly point on the English mainland, the pinnacles of the **Lizard** have looked down on countless shipwrecks. The multicoloured serpentine rock here is polished into souvenirs, but you should see it in its natural state—in the cliffs of **Kynance Cove** and around the old smugglers' harbour of **Mullion Cove**.

The extraordinary **St Michael's Mount**, rising out of the sea like a vision, was once crowned by an abbey founded by monks from the remarkably similar Mont-Saint-Michel in Normandy. Later, defence-minded kings decided it would make a fine spot for a castle. You can reach the site for three hours at low tide by a stone causeway. Otherwise take a boat from Marazion or from **Penzance**, the end of the railway line from London and an early seaside resort. Just south, the little fishing harbour of **Mousehole** (pronounced "mowzal") attracts visitors by virtue of its name as much as its charm.

Finally, at the most westerly point of England (though not of Britain), comes the end of the road; the vast car park, worn paths and granite cliffs of **Land's End**. Millions go, just for a geographical fact, though various facilities have now been built to give them something to "do".

Next stop America? Not quite, for 45km (28 miles) south-west of Land's End, the **Isles of Scilly** lie scattered across the turquoise sea like jewels. You reach **St Mary's**, the largest, and that's only 10km² (4 square miles), by boat or helicopter from Penzance. Launches can take you on to the other inhabited islands: **Tresco** noted for its semi-tropical gardens and two castles (one was put in the wrong place so they had to build another); **St Martin's**, with more open heathland and fine walks; tiny **Bryher** and southerly **St Agnes**. Rare birds that have been blown off course alight on the Scillies, bringing a rush of "twitchers" (bird-spotters) to log them. Six kilometres (4 miles) out from St Agnes, **Bishop Rock Lighthouse** signals ships to keep away from the treacherous reefs that wrecked so many craft in the past and now attract divers lured by relics—and by the thought of Spanish gold.

North Cornwall

The north Cornish coast has few harbours to compare with the south. Instead, Atlantic rollers crash on to open sandy beaches or at the foot of dramatic cliffs. **St Just**, near Land's End, was a centre of tin mining: some of the workings, like Botallack, ran far out under the sea. Now the old engine houses make romantic ruins. Geevor, at **Boscaswell**, the last mine to operate in Cornwall, houses a tin mining museum. There's another at **Pool** near Redruth.

 St Ives was once a tin and fishing port, but as these trades declined in the 19th century, a wave of artists, and then a flood of tourists, discovered it. St Ives has survived, almost as pretty as ever, although many cottages have been turned into gift shops and restaurants. The potter Bernard Leach worked here, and his studio still functions. Barbara Hepworth's house is now a museum of her life and sculpture.

Newquay is the main resort, with great sandy beaches that bring surfers from as far away as Australia and Hawaii to ride the rollers that crash in from the Atlantic Ocean. On the cliff-tops, look out for huers' huts, relics of the fishing industry. A huer's job was to spot shoals of pilchards and then signal to the boats.

Padstow's old fishermen's cottages cluster around the quaysides, but the

Newquay's rollers have made the resort a magnet for surfers and the spacious sandy beaches attract a big summer crowd.

Office. Nor the 12th-century castle ruins on the promontory linking Tintagel Head to the mainland. Both were actually built several hundred years too late. And yet, these black cliffs and caves may persuade you.

Boscastle harbour—now sanded up—had such a tricky entrance that vessels had to be "warped through" (towed by rope). The cliffs and country around are magnificent for walks. At **Bude**, north Cornwall signs off with more spectacular scenery, 150m (500ft) cliffs and sandy surf beaches.

Inland, the market towns of **Bodmin** and **Launceston**, once dreaded bottle-necks for traffic, are now by-passed, but are worth a detour. Bodmin has a fine 15th-century church, St Petroc's, and a holy well nearby, which was once recommended as a cure for eye ailments. At Launceston you can see the ramparts of a hilltop Norman castle and the 16th-century church of St Mary Magdelene, almost covered with stone carving. Between the two towns lies the wild upland region of **Bodmin Moor**, most of it only accessible to walkers, which is dotted with prehistoric standing stones and circles. Here, too, is Dozmary Pool, supposed by some to be the lake into which Sir Bedivere threw the sword Excalibur. Compact though it is, at only about 20km (12 miles) across, the moor is easy to get lost in, especially in a mist.

river mouth has silted up. Consequently the harbour is much less important than it was when Sir Walter Raleigh presided at the **Court House** on the South Quay as Warden of Cornwall.

Crowds are drawn to **Tintagel** by the magical name of King Arthur, accepting the legend that claims this was his birthplace. Not the village, which is worth seeing only for the 14th-century house which served as the Old Post

Fertile Land and Fertile Minds

The eastern lowlands are like nowhere else in Britain. There are no big cities, no mountains either, and little sense of connection to the rest of the country. Isolated for centuries by a barrier of marshland and fen, people in this part of eastern England developed a sturdy independence of mind and freedom of spirit. Strictly speaking, three counties make up Britain's eastern bulge: Essex, Suffolk and Norfolk, but neighbouring Cambridgeshire and most of Lincolnshire have similar pastoral landscapes of sprawling farmlands under boundless skies.

Cambridge

The "other place" is smaller than Oxford, and more compact in its charm. Oxford may train more prime ministers and literary men; Cambridge produces physicists, economists and medical researchers. And whereas Oxford is busy with commerce and ringed by industry, in Cambridge the town is the university, with discreet business parks on the outskirts.

The flat lands of eastern England have a lot in common with Holland, and Dutch engineers drained many of the marshes.

Much of the character of the place comes from the River Cam, which flows silently behind the medieval colleges, between green lawns overhung by willows. Take a punt along the delightful stretch of river and garden known as **The Backs** and slide slowly past Queen's and King's colleges, under ancient Clare Bridge and the Venetian-style Bridge of Sighs. The boatyards at Mill Lane (off Trumpington Street) and Quayside (off Magdalene Street) have punts for hire, but you may find it difficult to propel yourself along: poling is not one of those skills you acquire immediately and many beginners have been known to fall in. "Chauffeurpunt" (in Silver Street, behind Queen's College) offers the easy way out, for about the price of a taxi.

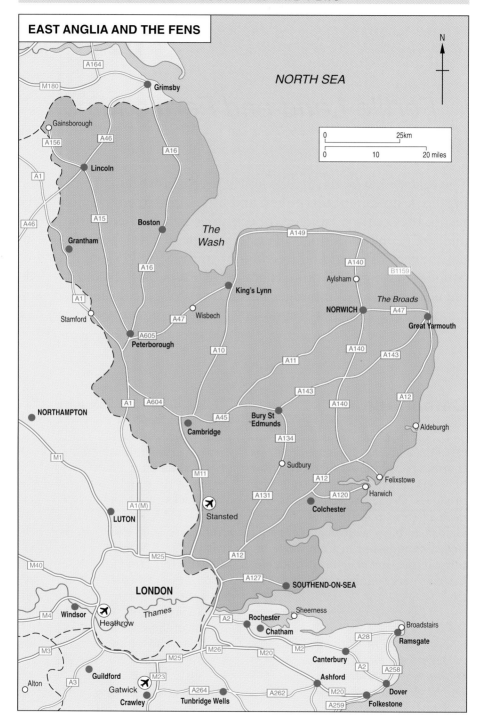

EAST ANGLIA AND THE FENS

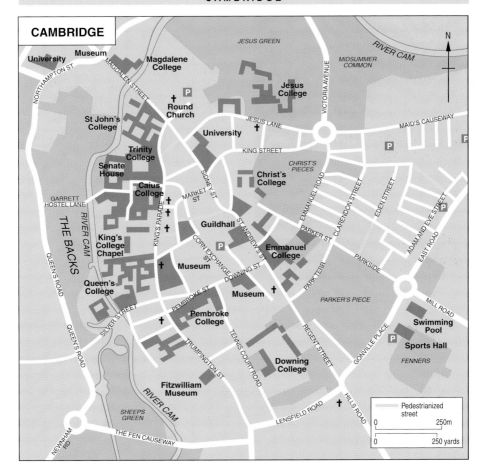

City plan of Cambridge.

Cambridge University began with a handful of students attached to religious and lay teachers. The first college, Peterhouse, was founded in 1284 by the Bishop of Ely, and the newest, Robinson, came into being in 1979, bringing the total to 25. As at Oxford, the colleges follow a monastic design,

East Anglia and the Fens.

with buildings grouped around courts (the equivalent of the Oxford quad). Women were not admitted to the university until the mid-19th century, when Girton, the first women's college, was founded. Today the university has 10,000 undergraduates, more than a third women, and most colleges are open to both sexes.

The colleges lie fairly close together—off the main street known variously as St John's, Trinity, King's Parade and Trumpington. Make your way past the old houses, coffee bars and shops (Heffer's for books is a major land-

The way to see Cambridge is from a punt, if you hire the services of an expert to do the work.

mark) to "KP", King's Parade, in the heart of Cambridge. **King's College Chapel** dominates this stretch, magnificent in its setting of green lawns. A masterpiece of the Perpendicular style, the chapel is bold, structurally simple, yet richly decorated within. Light pouring through the stained-glass windows (25 in all) tints the stone red, violet and gold. Behind the altar, *The Adoration of the Magi* by Rubens swirls with colour, too, while the fan vaulting overhead adds to the overall elaboration. Attend the evensong service at 5.30 p.m. to hear the chapel choir sing.

Narrow King's Lane takes you to **Queens' College**. The name pays tribute to the two founding queens: Margaret, wife of Henry VI, and Elizabeth, wife of Edward IV. Notice the complicated **sundial** in Pump Court, incorporating a rare

moondial as well. Erasmus, the Renaissance scholar and theologian, lodged in the Tower here during a three-year stint as Greek professor from 1510. The half-timbered building by Cloister Court is the President's Lodge. Queens' College extends to the opposite bank of the Cam. Take the **Mathematical Bridge** across. This matchstick construction was made without nails (according to "mathematical" principles) in the 18th century. A hundred years later, some curious students took it apart to see how it was done, and could not put it back together again, so it is now bolted.

North of King's College Chapel, at Gonville and Caius College, called **Caius** (and pronounced "keys"), you can pass through the three gates of student life: the Gate of Humility, the Gate of Virtue and, finally, the Gate of Honour, which leads to **Senate House**. Degree ceremonies take place in this Palladian auditorium designed by James Gibbs.

Trinity is the largest college in the university, with 1,000 students. As you pass through the gateway, look up at the statue of the founder, King Henry VIII. In one hand he holds an orb and in the other, a chair leg—the result of a student prank. The **Great Court** is the largest in Cambridge. Traditionally, students try to run the circuit of this 0.8-hectare (2-acre) expanse while the clock in the chapel tower chimes out the strokes of 12.

Trinity's most distinguished building, the **Wren Library**, stands in Nevile's Court. An arcade runs underneath, giving a view of the river and The Backs—a stroke of genius on the part of the architect, Sir Christopher Wren. Books published before 1820 are kept in the library, along with Sir Isaac Newton's notebook of his Trinity expenses and Lord Byron's college admissions book, recording his pledge of good behaviour. Prince Charles, the first member of the royal family to attend university, was a Trinity man.

Neighbouring **St John's** was the college of William Wordsworth and Cecil Beaton. At the entrance stands a three-storey Tudor gatehouse, decorated with heraldic beasts and Tudor emblems in honour of Lady Margaret Beaufort, mother of Henry VII and patron of the college. The Norman **Round Church** at the top of St John's Street was built by the Knights Templar around 1130.

A student at Cambridge in his day, Samuel Pepys left his library to his old college, **Magdalene** (pronounced "maudlin"), when he died in 1707. Among the books (kept on the original shelves in the original order) was his famous coded diary.

Venerable **Jesus College** (off Jesus Lane) incorporates buildings of the 12th-century nunnery of St Radegund. The old cloister, slightly enlarged, survives as Cloister Court, and the nuns' church serves, with subsequent additions, as the college chapel. The stained-glass windows in medieval spirit were designed by Burne-Jones and others for Morris and Co.

Two other colleges to look for: **Christ's**, in St Andrew's Street, for its gardens (though there is nothing to prove the claim that John Milton planted the legendary mulberry tree); and neighbouring **Emmanuel**, with its Wren chapel and colonnade, where 21 of the Pilgrim Fathers studied.

The university museum, the **Fitzwilliam** (Trumpington Street), admirably fulfils its didactic purpose with collections of Egyptian, Greek and Roman antiquities, European porcelain, rare books, medals, coins and paintings from the Italian Renaissance to the 19th- and 20th-century British school. **Kettle's Yard Art Gallery** (Northampton Street) features paintings and sculpture of the 1920s and thirties in a domestic setting.

Around Cambridge

Literary pilgrims head a couple of miles south to the Old Vicarage at **Grantchester**, home of the World War I poet Rupert Brooke. The village war memorial commemorates his death.

South again is the market town of **Saffron Walden**, famed from medieval times as a centre of the saffron trade. Enjoy the half-timbered charm of the High Street, a quaint medley of old houses and inns like the Cross Keys, inaugurated in 1450. The curious earth maze in the vicinity probably had something to do with pre-Christian fertility rites.

Nearby **Audley End** is the largest Jacobean house ever built. This flagrant example of *folie de grandeur* bankrupted Thomas Howard, Lord Treasurer to James I. James remarked rather pointedly that the house was "too large for a king"—but that didn't stop his grandson Charles from buying it several decades later. Audley End eventually reverted to the Howard family, who spent 40 years cutting it down to size. Two wings were demolished, but what remains is very grand indeed. The Great Hall is decorated with fine wood and plaster work, and the drawing room, done over by Robert Adam, has original furnishings.

North-east of Cambridge, **Anglesey Abbey** has been rebuilt so many times that the house itself holds little intrinsic interest. However Lord Fairhaven's collection of clocks, furniture, paintings and coins is worth seeing, as are the grounds—over forty landscaped hectares (100 acres), with a working watermill that grinds corn.

The A10 takes you the 24km (15 short miles) north of Cambridge to **Ely** (the old Isle of Eels). Treacherous marshland surrounded the island, where Hereward the Wake, "last of the English", held out against William the Conqueror until 1071. Most of the marshland has been drained over the centuries, with the help of Dutch engineers, and hundreds of windmills now replaced by diesel and electric pumps. The small National Trust nature reserve called **Wicken Fen** is much as it was in Hereward's day—half open water, half marsh and often shrouded in mist.

The silhouette of Ely's massive **cathedral** is visible for miles across the flat fenland. Construction began in 1083 on the site of an abbey founded by St Etheldreda. In 1322, the central tower fell, destroying the Norman choir. The choir was rebuilt in Decorated style, and an octagonal lantern tower, the great **Octagon**, was raised. Eight 19m (64ft) oak posts support this tour de force of medieval engineering and haunting beauty. All England was searched for trees of sufficient size.

Some 800 tonnes of wood and lead, the octagon and lantern of Ely Cathedral are a feat of medieval engineering.

Suffolk

With its pink-washed, half-timbered little villages, Suffolk is the gentle face of East Anglia, a county of broad fields, tall churches and placid rivers. By contrast, the coast is busy with ferries and other shipping.

Aldeburgh

This small fishing town provided the inspiration for Sir Benjamin Britten's 1945 opera *Peter Grimes*, based on a poem by a local writer. Britten, a native of Aldeburgh himself, returned the compliment. The Aldeburgh Festival he founded for the première of *Peter Grimes* has gone from strength to strength, but you have to book tickets months ahead for the main June season. The opera house is actually in Snape, a few miles inland.

The Wool Towns

Beyond Dedham Vale the landscape changes subtly. Follow the B1070 road as it weaves through fields and in and out of a series of small towns. Around **Hadleigh**, you may well see men on tractors hard at work, and token flocks of sheep, but this is nothing like the old days when this one-time wool centre was one of the most prosperous towns in the country. The medieval heart of Hadleigh contains the 14th-century **Church of St Mary**; the turreted Tudor gatehouse known as the **Deanery**; and the **Guildhall**, spectacularly overhung by two upper storeys.

Kerse is a typical medieval Suffolk weaving village. Modest weavers' cottages and pastel-tinted, half-timbered dwellings line The Street, as the main thoroughfare is called. This dips down

Constable Country

The country around Dedham Vale is gently undulating and human in scale, planted with sturdy oak trees and slender church towers. This is the terrain that inspired John Constable, the son of a mill owner, to paint some of the most enduring images of the English countryside. "I associate my careless boyhood with all that lies on the banks of the Stour." He wrote, "Those scenes made me a painter."

Constable tourism focuses on the village of Dedham, the largest and most attractive in the Vale, with colour-washed Georgian houses and a 15th-century church that Constable painted time and again. Detailed maps on sale locally pinpoint Constable sights and viewpoints featured in the paintings.

A footpath meanders through the fields from Dedham to the hamlet of Flatford, the inspiration of some of Constable's greatest works (*Flatford Mill* [1817] and *The Haywain* [1821]). The mill Constable's father owned is now on private land, but the National Trust opens the adjacent Bridge Cottage to the public. There is a small Constable exhibition, a book shop and a tea garden by the Stour.

Just a mile away lies East Bergholt, the parish where Constable was born in 1776 and spent much of his youth. Even without so notable a son, it would be worth visiting for its pink half-timbered houses, dating from the time of the Flemish weavers. The church of St Mary hasn't changed since the time the Constable family worshipped here. Money to complete the tower ran out long before John Constable was born and it still stands unfinished today. Stoke-by-Nayland, with its 15th-century church and half-timbered Guildhall, was another Constable subject.

to a ford across a small stream and then rises uphill again to the Perpendicular **Church of St Mary**.

One of the most visited little towns in Suffolk, **Lavenham** has as complete a collection of half-timbered houses as you can find anywhere in England. It is all eminently photographable, from the **Church of St Peter and St Paul**, on its hill, to the old **Guildhall** the clothmakers built. Lavenham was famous for its blue cloth, tinted with woad, the favourite dye of the ancient Britons.

For a village, **Long Melford** really is long—4km (2½ miles) from end to end. Buildings range from the heyday of wool, when the crenellated parish church was erected, to prosperous Victorian times. Turreted **Melford Hall**, the Tudor mansion to the east of the central green, has a good collection of porcelain, period furniture and paintings. It also has a room devoted to Beatrix Potter, who often came to stay.

The painter Thomas Gainsborough was born at **Sudbury** in 1727. **Gainsborough's House**, located in Gainsborough Street—where else?—is the tourist mecca here. The father of the painter joined two Tudor houses and added a Georgian façade. There are some examples of Gainsborough's art on view, all minor works.

Bury St Edmunds

St Edmund is literally buried in Bury, as the locals call the town. Edmund, the young Saxon king of East Anglia, was beheaded by the Danes in 869 for refusing to renounce Christianity. According to tradition, searchers found his head guarded by a wolf, a scene featured on the municipal coat of arms. The abbey that sheltered the martyr's remains was originally founded in 636, rebuilt to take his body in 903, and enlarged in the 11th century as it became a centre for pilgrims who arrived from all over Europe.

After the Dissolution, the abbey fell into ruin and over the centuries, houses were built in the remains. Public gardens surround what remains of the refectory and abbot's house. Two of the gate towers survive intact, the great 14th-century Abbey Gateway, at the entrance to the gardens, and the **Norman Tower**, now the belfry of Bury's Perpendicular Gothic cathedral.

T he perfect little town of Lavenham in Suffolk abounds in picturesque timber-frame houses from the 16th and 17th centuries.

Norfolk

In Norfolk, the fields and pheasant-breeding woodlands give way to flat fens (reclaimed inland swamps) and coastal marshes, interspersed with stretches of open water which are known as the Broads.

Norwich

The university town of Norwich is a fairly quiet place today. It seems odd to think that in the 17th century it was second in size to London. The cathedral is the main sight. The Norman castle (clad in Bath stone a century and a half ago) runs a distant second, with a boat trip through the Broads an attractive excursion.

The **cathedral**'s slender Perpendicular spire is the symbol of Norwich, and is actually the second highest in England after Salisbury's. Massive Norman

pillars in the nave soar into Gothic vaulting, ornamented with 800 intricately carved bosses.

You can enter the Cathedral Close from the old Saxon marketplace, known as **Tombland**, through either of two medieval gates, Erpingham or St Ethelbert's. The grounds run down to the River Wensum at the old watergate of **Pulls Ferry**.

Norwich's town centre includes a network of old alleys, cobbled streets and arcades. **Elm House Street** is one of the finest medieval thoroughfares in Britain. The unusual facing of patterned square flint distinguishes the **Guildhall** on the main Market Square. Similar facing decorates the **Bridewell Museum**, a 14th-century merchant's house which is now a museum of craft and industry. The most interesting museum, however, is installed in the **castle**. Paintings and water-colours by members of the late 18th-century Norwich School (Crome, Cotman and others) are on view.

On the south side of the marketplace stands the **Church of St Peter Mancroft**, one of more than 30 medieval churches in the city, and a particularly good example of the Norfolk style of Perpendicular Gothic.

*E*very region in Britain has its agricultural show when prize cattle parade and there's all the fun of the fair.

Blickling Hall
(near Aylsham)
Built of mellow rose-coloured brick, with imposing corner towers and Dutch-style gables over the windows, Blickling was designed to impress. With its completion in 1625, the Lord Treasurer, Sir Henry Hobart, announced that he had "arrived". The house is set in a vast park, including formal gardens and a crescent lake. Henry VIII's wife, Anne Boleyn, spent her childhood in an earlier house on the site.

King's Lynn
This busy old port—just Lynn to the locals—stands near the mouth of the River Ouse, 45km (30 miles) above its outflow in the great bay known as the Wash. It was near here that luckless King John lost his baggage train, crown jewels and all, when overtaken on the sands by an unexpectedly high tide in October 1216.

The richly decorated chalice known as King John's cup, which is on view in **Holy Trinity Guildhall**, may have been part of the treasure. Interesting in itself, the medieval guildhall is an attractive building faced with chequered stone and flint-work.

There is a concentration of houses from the medieval to Georgian periods in the streets near the quay. Those of particular interest are the **Hanseatic Warehouse** (1428), a reminder of the days when Lynn had the Hansa cities for trading partners, and classical **Custom House** (1683), built down by the sands of King Staithe ("staithe" meaning wharf). Just south, a few steps from the Ouse, **Hampton Court** is a courtyard of half-timbered merchants' homes and warehouses.

Of the several churches in the town, **St Margaret's** (in the Saturday Market Square) is the most imposing, with massive west towers.

Sandringham House

The royal family has houses in the most scenic areas of Britain. The 2,800-hectare (7,000-acre) state of Sandringham, purchased by Queen Victoria for her son and heir Edward in 1861, is no different. You can visit the house and gardens in summer, when the royal family are not in residence. There is nothing remarkable about the Victorian architecture—what draws the crowds is the royal connection. Look out for the vintage car museum in the grounds of the house, and a big game museum of hunting trophies.

Holkham Hall

(near Wells-next-the-Sea)

This severe Palladian mansion rises unexpectedly out of a landscape of dunes and salt marshes. And that is only the first surprise, for the stark exterior conceals some of the most opulent rooms in Britain. The great Marble Hall with its vaulted ceiling and grand staircase sets the tone. William Kent designed the house for Thomas Coke, Earl of Leicester, in collaboration with the great Palladian, Lord Burlington, an architect by avocation. Everything here rates superlatives, including Thomas Coke's magnificent collection of paintings, numerous Poussins and Dughets as well as works by Rubens, Van Dyck and others.

Another Thomas Coke (1752–1842) of Holkham, the great-nephew of the original owner, conducted his pioneering experiments in soil improvement, crop rotation and sheep-breeding on the estate.

The Broads

Between Norwich and the sea extends an area of lagoons, rivers and marshlands known as the Norfolk Broads. The Broads are stretches of open water created in medieval times by villagers digging for peat. Linked by streams, rivers and canals, the Broads provide more than 320km (200 miles) of navigable waterways for sailing, angling and wild-life observation.

Wroxham, the self-styled capital of the Broads, is the centre of the holiday boating industry. Other notable (and quieter) villages in the area include **Ranworth**, whose 15th-century church, St Helen's, is known as the Cathedral of the Broads, and **Horning**, which organizes a summer boat race and regatta. Near Ranworth, the **Broadlands Conservation Centre** maintains a raised walkway through woodland and fens.

Lincolnshire

You might think you were in Holland, what with all the windmills and tulip fields. There is almost no high ground in the south of the county, so the great bulk of Lincoln Cathedral on its hilltop stands out dramatically.

Lincoln

Historic, unspoiled, untouristic—Lincoln is off the beaten path. This was not always been the case: two great highways, Ermine Street and Fosse Way, met here in Roman times. The street called Bailgate ends at **Newport Arch**, the only Roman gateway in England still to straddle a roadway.

The triple-towered **cathedral** is the dominating feature. An earthquake shattered the original Norman structure in 1185, but the magnificent Norman west front remains, decorated with statues, including those of 11 kings from William the Conqueror to Edward III. The rest is Early English and Decorated, scarcely touched since it was completed in 1311. Inside the church, the decorative rib vaults and canopied choir stalls are superbly carved. Beyond the high altar, 30 angels support the roof of the **Angel Choir**. On the last complete column on the north side look for the legendary Lincoln Imp, said to have been turned to stone for his mischief. Two beautiful rose windows light

*W*indpower was first used to grind corn in the Middle Ages. Most of the few windmills still standing have been converted into fanciful houses.

Boston

Not only did Boston generate a transatlantic namesake, it produced a breed of nation-builders to populate it. Those pillars of the Puritan faith, the Pilgrim Fathers, came from Boston and neighbouring towns, but they dreamed of a better life in the New World. In 1607, a group of potential colonists was prevented from making a break for America. They were arrested in Boston and imprisoned in the guildhall. The following year, they went to Holland and most eventually sailed in the *Mayflower* in 1620. A number of sights in the Boston area are associated with the founding of the United States. *See* page 94 in LEISURE ROUTES for a detailed itinerary through Pilgrim Country.

The 83m (272-ft) tower of the **Church of St Botolph** is the town's landmark. Called the Boston Stump, its beacon guided shipping in the treacherous waters of the Wash, a few miles away.

the west transept, the Bishop's Eye and the Dean's Eye.

William the Conqueror gave Lincoln its other landmark, the huge **castle**, in 1068—only two years after he came to power. A 13th-century bastion known as Cobb's Tower housed a prison and gallows right up until the middle of the last century.

Jews were encouraged by the Normans to settle in Lincoln in the 12th century, to help finance trade. Two stone-built houses, among the oldest Norman dwellings to survive in England, testify to the importance of the Jews at this period. One is the **House of Aaron the Jew**, just below the castle. The other, lower down the street called Steep Hill, is simply known as the **Jew's House** (now a restaurant).

Dreaming Spires and Dark Satanic Mills

Here you have the essence of England, the country's very heart. You'll find it in the thatched villages of Shakespeare Country and in Oxford's "dreaming spires", in the rolling Cotswold Hills and the rugged moorlands of the Peak District. The big cities of the Midlands—Birmingham, Nottingham, Derby, Stoke-on-Trent and the rest—which fuelled the expansion of empire are still hard at work. But micro-chips turn the wheels of industry today, and the "dark Satanic mills" of the poet Blake are museums of industrial history.

Oxford

You can't help but be aware that this is the oldest English-speaking university in the world. Its colleges lie timelessly encapsuled within the modern city, their Gothic spires and pinnacles soaring above their cream stone buildings and green quadrangles.

Oxford's origins go back to 1167, when English students from Paris's Sorbonne joined other scholars in this town at the junction of the rivers Cherwell and Thames (here known as the Isis). Originally, college life was based on monastic models, complete with rules and discipline, refectory, cloisters and chapels. Over the subsequent 800 years of learning the number of colleges has increased to 35 and the students to more than 10,000, but the aura of hallowed antiquity and scholarship remains.

If you are making only a short visit to Oxford, concentrate on just a few of the great buildings and try to catch the feel of student life and traditions. Most of the colleges lie off the long curving **High Street**, known as "the High". At Carfax, the main crossroads, stands the 14th-century **Carfax Tower**, once part of St Martin's Church. Climb to the top for a great view of all of Oxford.

Stratford-upon-Avon's Garrick Inn and Harvard House, where the mother of the founder of Harvard University was born.

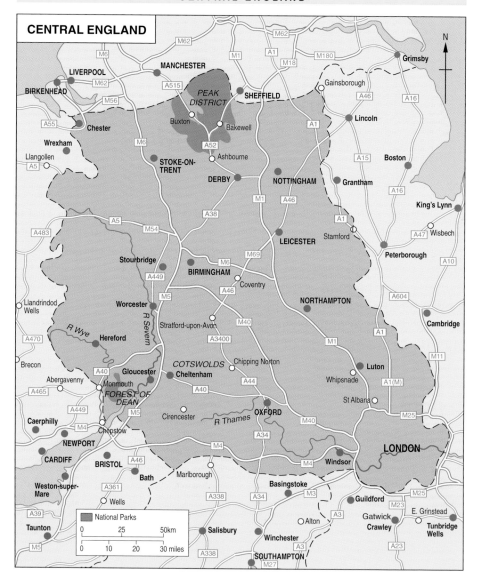

CENTRAL ENGLAND

A short way down St Aldate's from Carfax you come to **Christ Church College**, founded by Cardinal Wolsey in 1515. **Great Tom**, the bell in the tower above the St Aldate's entrance, still chimes 101 times at 9.05 each evening, when the gates closed on the original 101 students.

Central England.

Pass through the gateway into Tom Quad and two other interconnecting "quads", or quadrangles, that make Christ Church one of the biggest col-

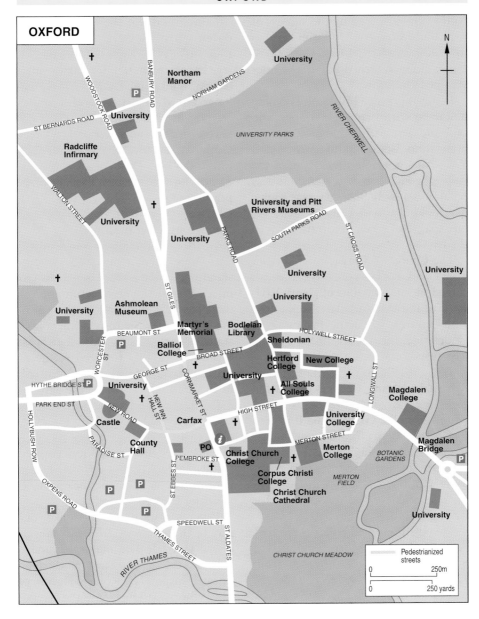

City plan of Oxford.

leges: the middle quad, Peckwater or Peck, is traditionally the haunt of Britain's aristocracy. A mathematics professor named Charles Dodgson (better known as Lewis Carroll) lodged in Canterbury Quad. In between tutorials he dreamed up *Alice in Wonderland,* inspired by Alice Liddell, the young daughter of the dean of the college.

Rather embarrassed by the success of his whimsical book, Dodgson had fan mail addressed to "Lewis Carroll" at the college returned to the sender stamped "unknown".

In the impressive 16th-century dining hall hang portraits of the famous who once ate here as humble undergraduates. John Locke, John Wesley and W H Auden were all members of the college, which has educated countless politicians as well. Students covet rooms overlooking Christ Church Meadow, an expanse of green that runs down to the Isis.

The **Church of Christ**, entered from Tom Quad, has been Oxford's Anglican cathedral since the time of Henry VIII. Parts of the structure date back to the 12th century, when the Priory of St Frideswide, the nucleus of the university, stood on this site.

Take the High as far as Magpie Lane to visit **University College**, one of the earliest. Its origins go back as far as King Alfred the Great in the 10th century, or so college officials claim, though the formal founding date is 1280. The majority of the buildings are 17th-century Gothic. Look for a memorial to the poet Shelley, who was expelled for writing an atheist pamphlet.

Two distinguished colleges are hidden off the High Street in Merton Street. **Merton College** dates from 1264 and its library is one of the earliest in England. The 14th-century Mob Quad was the first college quadrangle. Peer through the gateway of **Corpus Christi College** (1517), opposite Merton, into the handsome Front Quad. The pelican on the 16th-century sundial has been the college mascot for almost 400 years.

Continue down the High to **Magdalen** (pronounced "maudlin"), founded in 1458. Not only does the college have a reputation for flamboyance (Oscar Wilde and Dudley Moore belonged to Magdalen), it is also considered the most beautiful, with extensive lawns, gardens and a deer park, a serene Gothic cloister and Perpendicular bell tower. On May Day, college choristers gather at 6 a.m. to sing a Latin hymn of praise from the tower. The River Cherwell flows past the college and through its water meadows.

North of the High is **New College**. The Perpendicular buildings are outstanding, above all the chapel. Just as interesting as the architecture are the works of art within: an El Greco painting of *St James,* Sir Joshua Reynolds's stained-glass design for the West Window; and the tortured statue of *Lazarus,* sculpted by Sir Jacob Epstein in 1951. The beautiful college gardens contain a section of Oxford's 13th-century city wall.

New College Lane has its own "Bridge of Sighs"—a modern copy of the one in Venice—but Oxford's bridge merely joins two buildings belonging to **Hertford College**.

Pass under the bridge and make your way to Broad Street, the heart of academic Oxford. The major landmark here is the neoclassical **Sheldonian Theatre**, inspired by Rome's Theatre of Marcellus. Designed by the young Christopher Wren (it was his first building), the Sheldonian provides a distinguished venue for academic ceremonies and concerts.

Nearby stands Oxford's world-famous library, the **Bodleian**. A magnificent old room holds the 15th-century

*T*he Sheldonian
Theatre, designed by the young
Christopher Wren, where Oxford
hails in Latin those whom it
wishes to honour.

collection of Humphrey, Duke of Gloucester, the nucleus of the Bodleian's present reserve of 3 million volumes. The Bodleian is entitled to a copy of every book printed in Britain Rare books, including a Shakespeare First Folio, can be seen in the adjoining Perpendicular Gothic building known as the **Divinity School**. Standing alone on a patch of grass, the circular **Radcliffe Camera** (Chamber), originally a science library, now serves as an off-shoot reading room of the Bodleian. James Gibb provided the handsome baroque design.

The "souls" of **All Souls College**, opposite, belong to the soldiers who died in the Hundred Years' War between England and France. This is the only Oxford college that restricts its membership to Fellows, who have teaching or research appointments.

Outside **Balliol College** (famous for classical scholars and statesmen) stands the **Martyrs' Memorial** to the Protestant bishops Cranmer, Latimer and Ridley, who were burned at the stake in Queen Mary's reign.

An important stop on any tour of Oxford is the **Ashmolean Museum**. A Greek-Revival building houses the art and archaeological treasures donated to the university over the centuries, in particular fine works by Rubens, Poussin, Hogarth, Tintoretto and Reynolds. Anglo-Saxon antiquities include the **Alfred Jewel**, a rare portrait in enamel of King Alfred. Some of the spectacular finds from Sir Arthur Evans' excavations at Knossos in Crete and Sir Flinders Petrie's digs in Egypt have also made their way to the Ashmolean.

Blenheim Palace

A residence grand enough for royalty, Blenheim symbolizes England's greatness in the time of Queen Anne. The nation gave the palace to John Churchill, 1st Duke of Marlborough, in gratitude for his victory over the French in the crucial Battle of Blenheim. The duke never saw the place in its finished state, but he chose Sir John Vanbrugh as architect and approved the massive, colonnaded baroque design.

References to Blenheim crop up everywhere: in the **Great Hall**, where a painting shows John Churchill presenting a plan of the Battle of Blenheim to Britannia; in other paintings and tapestries; even in the **park**, where trees were planted according to the disposition of French and English troops on the field. Sweeping vistas extend across landscaped grounds to a towering victory column, monumental bridge and serenely beautiful lake, a Capability Brown creation.

Warwickshire

Stratford-upon-Avon

The birthplace of England's greatest poet and playwright stands at the heart of what has come to be known as Shakespeare Country. The area is overrun with—but not really spoiled by—tourists, who have made the old market town of Stratford a centre of pilgrimage for more than two centuries.

Shakespeare's Birthplace is in Henley Street: the modern Shakespeare Centre alongside is the most prominent building in town. You enter the Birthplace through the Centre, which houses a

> **William Shakespeare**
> Shakespeare was born in Stratford on or about 23 April 1564. His father, John Shakespeare, was a farmer who had moved from the countryside to seek a better life. Turning to glove-making and dealing in wool, he grew rich enough to buy the house in Henley Street where his son was born.
>
> In 1582, William married Anne Hathaway, a woman six or seven years older, with whom he had three children.
>
> By the 1590s, Shakespeare's career as a playwright and actor-manager in London was well on its way. Success brought prosperity as well as fame, and in 1597 the poet bought a rather grand house in Stratford which he named New Place. He also acquired a ten per cent share in the company that built the legendary Globe Theatre in London two years later.
>
> During his own lifetime, Shakespeare was regarded as England's foremost dramatist (an argument against those who claim that someone else wrote the plays). He spent most of his later years in Stratford and died here on 23 April 1616, at the age of 52.

library and archives. Only long tradition maintains that William Shakespeare was born in the bedroom on the upper floor. But the tradition has captured the imagination of writers from Charles Dickens and Sir Walter Scott to Victor Hugo and Herman Melville. Look for their names, scratched into the glass of one of the windows.

The Shakespeare trail leads on to **Judith Shakespeare House**, at the corner of Bridge and High streets. Now Stratford's Tourist Information Centre, this was once the home of William Shakespeare's daughter, who married one Thomas Quiney, a wine merchant by trade.

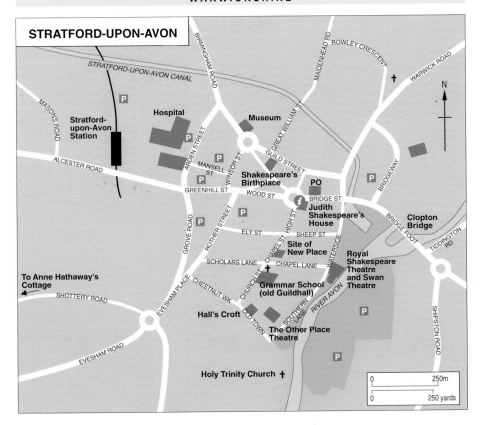

STRATFORD-UPON-AVON

Town plan of Stratford-upon-Avon.

The foundations of William Shakespeare's own house, **New Place**, are visible at the corner of Chapel Street and Chapel Lane. This would have been the focus of Stratford tourism today had it not been for a Reverend Francis Gastrell, who bought the house from Shakespeare's descendants in the 18th century. Something of a crank, he got so fed up with souvenir hunters that he actually burned the place down. All that remains is **Great Garden**, planted with "daisies pied and violets blue".

Nash House, next door on Chapel Street, belonged to Shakespeare's granddaughter, Elizabeth Hall Nash, and her husband Thomas Nash. Of interest here is a collection of 18th-century souvenirs of Stratford: jugs and seals decorated with portraits of the bard.

Near the corner of Chapel Lane, the **Guildhall** of 1417 houses the Grammar School where young Will is thought to have learned his "small Latin and less Greek". Still in use as a school, it is not open to visitors. The **Chapel of the Guild of the Holy Cross**, connected to the Guildhall in the 1400s, serves as the school's chapel.

Hall's Croft, in the street named Old Town, is one of the more charming and

authentic of the Elizabethan houses preserved by the Birthplace Trust. Susanna Shakespeare, William's elder daughter, lived here after her marriage to Dr John Hall. The house is decorated as it would have been when the Halls occupied it 400 years ago. Be sure to have a look at the dispensary, which is furnished in the style of an Elizabethan consulting room. On view is a medical treatise written by Dr Hall, and the type of primitive surgical tools he used to treat "desperate diseases".

Shakespeare remained attached to Stratford all his life, and it was here that he died in 1616. The poet and playwright lies buried in **Holy Trinity Church**, approached down an avenue of trees. A visit to his tomb in the chancel, marked by a simple stone slab, is an obligatory stop for literary pilgrims from all over the world.

the backstage tours, available most days. The **RST Picture Gallery and Museum** contains a fascinating collection of Shakespeariana. Don't overlook the smaller venues, adjacent to the RST in Waterside: the **Swan Theatre**, built in the style of a Jacobean playhouse, stages works by Shakespeare's contemporaries, while The Other Place puts on a variety of classical and contemporary productions. Contact the RST for programmes and tickets.

Shottery

The most photographed of Shakespearean landmarks is undoubtedly **Anne Hathaway's Cottage**. The farmhouse, which is thatched, has a worldwide reputation for picturesque charm. A highlight for many is the "courting settle" by the fire, where William Shakespeare may well have popped the question to Anne Hathaway. In their day, fields and forests intervened between Stratford and the village of Shottery, the site of the cottage. Now a street of detached and semi-detached mock Tudor houses leads the way. It is more pleasant to walk than drive: follow the well-marked footpath that begins at Evesham Place. You can make it there and back in half an hour.

The 1,500-seat **Royal Shakespeare Theatre** in Waterside is another. People book tickets for one of the plays months in advance, although a limited number are available at the box office on the day of the performance. For details write to the RST, Stratford-upon-Avon, Warwickshire CV37 6BB. Call (0789) 269191 for 24-hour booking information. Even if you don't manage to see a performance, you can join one of

Only fragments remain of the **Forest of Arden**, north-west of Stratford, which was the setting for Shakespeare's *As You Like It*.

Warwick Castle

A cast of characters from any of Shakespeare's historical plays would have felt at home in **Warwick Castle**, "the finest medieval castle in England". The battlements dominate the town of Warwick from a steep cliff beside the Avon, north of Stratford. The Beauchamps, the wealthy and powerful medieval earls of Warwick, installed themselves here in the 14th century. Shakespeare described one of them as a "proud setter-up and puller-down of kings". But the reign of the earls came to an end in 1978, when Madame Tussauds acquired the title to the property. Already a fixture on the tourist circuit, the castle has gained in popularity as its tourist potential has been exploited. Wax figures positioned throughout the **private apartments** recreate "A Royal Weekend Party 1898"—an amusing gimmick. Works of art are the big attraction in the carved and gilded **state apartments**: a celebrated equestrian portrait of Charles I by Van Dyck and a painting of two lions by Rubens.

Warwick even has its own ghost, the spirit of Sir Fulke Greville, a 17th-century earl who was murdered by his valet in 1628.

Sulgrave Manor

Not every American knows that the ancestral home of George Washington lies near Banbury. The manor was built on

Continuously occupied for nearly seven centuries, Warwick Castle, like so many great English houses, bears the mark of many different owners.

land purchased by Lawrence Washington from Henry VIII in 1539. The fine period furnishings on display, assembled when the house was restored, include a Gilbert Stuart portrait of George Washington. It was George's great-grandfather, Colonel John Washington, who left here for America in 1656 as mate on a small English ship.

Kenilworth Castle

This awesome ruin recalls 500 years of turbulent history. The thick-walled Norman keep, known as **Caesar's Tower**, went up in 1160, before King John made the fortress his stronghold. Subsequently the castle passed to the dukes of Lancaster. John of Gaunt built the **Strong Tower** and great **Banqueting Hall**, while the Earl of Leicester, one of Elizabeth I's favourites, added the **Gatehouse** and formal gardens, and turned the castle into a palace fit for the queen he hoped to wed. Some of Cromwell's soldiers dismantled the castle in 1649, at the end of the Civil War, although the majority of the massive red sandstone walls and towers were left standing. After the war, the artificial lake and moat were drained.

The Cotswolds

The rolling Cotswold hills, situated between the Thames and Severn valleys, cover an area scarcely 88km (55 miles) long by 40km (25 miles) wide. Pasture alternates with beech woodlands and medieval villages of warm, honey-coloured Cotswold stone.

Farming the thin topsoil was difficult, and agriculture was abandoned in the 13th century in favour of sheep raising. Merchants grew rich in the wool and cloth trades, spending their money to build "wool churches" and country estates. The decline of the wool trade in the 19th century brought an end to such prosperity, but the villages managed to preserve their character and charm, almost untouched by the Industrial Revolution.

Northleach

Flocks of black birds pepper the sky above Northleach, and a quilting of green fields surrounds the town—a fairly sleepy, friendly sort of place. There is a collection of pleasant pubs, some small shops that cater to local trade, and the grand Perpendicular church that all the tourists come to see. Rubbings from Northleach's brass plaques of wool merchants are popular souvenirs. Make your own with paper and crayons from the Cotswold pharmacy in the market square. Look for the monument to John Fortey, whose wealth paid for the nave with its vaulted roof. At the west end of town, across the highway, the **Cotswold Countryside Collection** takes a nostalgic look at local farm life.

Chedworth Roman Villa

This lavish country estate 13km (8 miles) north-east of Cirencester was occupied from the 2nd to 4th centuries AD by prosperous Roman landowners. The best-preserved Roman villa in Britain, it has been partially restored to give an impression of the sophisticated whole—the central heating and sewage systems, elaborate bath complex and dining room, both with fine mosaic pavements. A small **museum** houses artefacts unearthed on the site.

Cirencester

Those Romans who lived in such luxury at Chedworth may have made their fortunes in nearby Cirencester, or *Corinium Dobunnorum*, as it was known to them. Anglo-Saxon warriors sacked the town in the 6th century, but you can still see the amphitheatre and foundations of the forum and basilica. Roman sculptures and frescoes are displayed in the **Corinium Museum** in Park Street.

The affluent Middle Ages endowed Cirencester with its substantial wool church, **St John the Baptist**, the focal point of the central Market Place. The unusual three-storied south porch draws your eye up. Other notable features include the brasses in Trinity Chapel and the elaborate fan vaulting in St Catherine's chapel.

A third age of prosperity in the 18th century provided this capital of the Cotswolds with another asset—direct access into **Cirencester Park**, the extensive grounds of the stately home of the Earl of Bathurst. The park today is a venue for polo matches and its chestnut-lined avenues, footpaths and picnic sites remain open to the public throughout the year.

Bourton-on-the-Water

Visit Bourton in the peak of the tourist season and you may find yourself caught in a tail-back of traffic. People inundate the village—it's just another attraction now, albeit a very beautiful one. The River Windrush flows slowly through the centre, straddled by low-arched bridges of Cotswold stone and flanked by a wide green sward and ancient mellow houses. Where do all the people go? Over to the Motor Museum, Aquarium, old mill and Model Village, and to Birdland (the home of 600 exotic species) and the Butterfly Exhibition.

*T*he pretty villages of the Cotswolds have probably never looked better than they do today.

The Slaughters

There is nothing murderous about the name, it is simply derived from the original Norman landowner, de Scoltre. In Upper Slaughter, a farming village with a medieval look, a cluster of houses is set in rich meadowland. A trout stream much favoured by ducks flows through Lower Slaughter, where there is a picturesque manor house that was once a convent and is now a hotel, and a steepled church.

Stow-on-the-Wold

"Stow-on-the-Wold where the wind blows the cold" perches high on a hill at the junction of several important roads. Gabled shops and inns enclose the spacious **market square**, the site of an annual sheep market. Stocks that were once used to shame offenders still stand in the shadow of the steepled **Town Hall** and the venerable parish **Church of St Edward**.

Cheltenham

To the British mind, Cheltenham symbolizes propriety. Nothing seems amiss in this attractive Regency city. Fame came to Cheltenham in 1715, when an alkaline spring was discovered on the banks of the River Chelt. Visits by Dr Johnson, Handel and King George III, Lord Byron and the Duke of Wellington (who was cured of a liver complaint) gave the spa undeniable cachet. Early in the 19th century, a new town plan created wide avenues and plenty of parks and gardens for exercise—an important part of the cure.

Trees shade the pedestrian **Promenade**, Cheltenham's main shopping thoroughfare, lined with terraced buildings that were private residences in Cheltenham's Regency heyday. Just off the Promenade are the **Imperial Gardens** and **Town Hall**, a venue for concerts during the Cheltenham Music Festival in July.

Further uphill, the shops of **Montpellier Walk**, separated by caryatids, are a highlight of the town's elegant architecture. At the bottom of the Walk stands the **Montpellier Rotunda**, a former pump room where spa water was taken.

Winchcombe

If you look down on Winchcombe from the surrounding hills you will see a huddle of stone roof-tops in a green and wooded valley. The terraced medieval houses of Cotswold stone date from the 16th century, when Winchcombe thrived on tobacco growing. Although the town was originally the capital of the powerful Saxon kingdom of Mercia, only the ruins of an abbey founded by King Kenulf remain. Today, artisans make Winchcombe a centre of creative activity. There is also a small railway museum, with displays of old tickets, uniform buttons, track components and the like. The Perpendicular **Church of St Peter** features 40 grotesque gargoyles.

Broadway

This perfect Cotswold town is the enterprising centre of Cotswold tourism, but unlike some of the villages, Broadway is big enough to contain the crowds. And crowds there are, walking the broad **High Street**, and spilling out of all the tea shops and pubs, antique shops and art galleries—open seven days a week in the tourist season. One of the outstanding buildings, the **Lygon Arms Inn** in the High, served as head-

A common claim is "Queen Elizabeth slept here", but at Sudeley Castle, just outside Winchcombe, it's a well-founded one. She was a frequent visitor.

quarters at different times during the Civil War for both Charles I and Oliver Cromwell. Other Broadway landmarks include the 18th-century Fish Inn, on Fish Hill, and the 12th-century Church of St Eadburgha.

Chipping Campden

The old market ("chipping") town of Chipping Campden calls itself "The Gem of the Cotswold Wool Towns". The curving High Street is terraced with old stone houses, whose doors are painted a showy blue, yellow, black or white. Chipping Campden's woolstaplers (dealers in wool) were among the richest men in England during the 14th and 15th centuries. They sold their fleece at **Woolstaplers' Hall**, the centrepiece of the market square since 1340. An eccentric museum of bygones (from jelly moulds to mantraps) is housed here today.

Gloucester

The Romans called it *Glevum* (but you should say "Gloster"). This manufacturing centre and busy inland port is attractive in parts. The four main streets still form a cross at the centre of town, following the ancient Roman plan. Gloucester claims a variety of historic features, but the glorious **cathedral** remains the chief attraction.

The Perpendicular tower is the most recent addition to this Norman building, which started off as an abbey church. The miracle-working tomb of the murdered King Edward II brought medieval pilgrims to Gloucester. It lies under a pinnacled canopy in the north choir aisle. The alabaster effigy, an idealized portrait, is a masterpiece of 14th-century sculpture.

Henry III was crowned in the cathedral, and the great **east window**—a 22m (72ft) wall of glass—commemorates the Battle of Crécy, fought by his great-grandson, Edward III. Beautiful fan vaulting, the earliest example of it in the country, decorates the **cloisters** and the lavatorium, where the monks washed their hands.

Berkeley Castle

Berkeleys have been living in feudal style here for centuries. There has been a moated fortress at Berkeley since the 12th century, although most of what you see today dated from two hundred years later. Don't miss the grim cell where Edward II was killed in 1327 by a red-hot poker thrust, in revenge for his dependence on court favourites. England's barons met in the **Great Hall** on their way to Runnymede to seal the Magna Carta in 1215.

Slimbridge

The Severn Estuary is famous for migrating wildfowl. At Slimbridge, the Wildfowl Trust, founded by the late Sir Peter Scott, maintains the world's largest and most varied collection of water fowl—literally thousands of wild swans, geese, eiders and others.

Gloucester guarded the lowest crossing over the River Severn. The glorious cathedral is known for its cloisters and the tomb of Edward II, murdered in 1327.

Coalbrookdale started smelting iron with coke in the 18th century. There is also plenty of pastoral beauty on view. To the west, on the border with Wales, lie the rolling Marches, rich in fine Norman castles and attractive half-timbered villages.

Birmingham

The Victorians called the city the "workshop of the world": if it was made of metal, Birmingham made it, from pins to guns to railway engines. They still manufacture textiles, chocolate and car parts here, but the service sector seems to be the wave of the future.

Birmingham's Town Hall, its canals and museums are all legacies of the years of Victorian prosperity and the city's own orchestra in its new home, the remarkable Symphony Hall, is a great source of pride. Urban development has changed the look of the city, bringing Birmingham the doubtful benefits of the Bull Ring Centre, New Street Station, Inner Ring Road and infamous Spaghetti Junction.

The **Museum and Art Gallery**, one of the country's best, has a famous pre-Raphaelite collection. The **Barber Institute of Fine Arts**, a gallery attached to the university, features European painting and sculpture, classical antiquities and oriental and Asian art. Interesting, too, is the **Museum of Science and Industry**, full of the engines

Observation towers and water-level hides give you several different perspectives on the birds.

The Midlands

England's industrial achievements are now as much a part of its history as are the cathedrals and castles. This is where it all began, when the Darby family of

223

that powered the Industrial Revolution. The setting, a converted canalside factory building, could not be more appropriate. Another big attraction for industrial history enthusiasts: the **Gas Street Canal Basin,** in the heart of the city, is the starting point for a walk alongside the canal.

Dudley

In the old days, factory towns like Dudley produced a "plague of smoke" (as Charles Dickens put it) that stained everything black. The open-air **Black Country Museum** brings together period

*T*he Wildfowl Trust at Slimbridge attracts thousands of ducks and geese. Endangered species have been bred here for release into the wild.

buildings of the industrial era and reconstructed workshops (glass cutters' and chain makers').

Iron-Bridge Gorge

The Industrial Revolution started here, along the idyllic banks of the River Severn, when Abraham Darby first smelted iron using coke instead of charcoal. Darby's original blast furnace of 1709 is just one of the historic industrial sites that make up the $15km^2$ (6-square-mile) **Iron-Bridge Gorge Museum.** Others include the world's first iron bridge, cast here in 1779, the old blast furnaces at Coalbrookdale and Blists Hill and the Coalport bone china factory, in operation from the 1790s to the 1920s.

Coventry

Coventry today is predominantly modern, a steel-and-concrete replacement of

the city devastated by German bombs in 1940. The poignant shell of the old 14th-century Gothic cathedral stands at the entrance of the new St Michael's, which rose phoenix-like out of the rubble. Sir Basil Spence provided the angular design in the early 1950s. For the generation that lived through the war, the rebuilding of the **cathedral** symbolized hope in the future. Some of Britain's best modern artists were involved in the project: John Piper designed the immense **stained-glass window** in the baptistry, while Graham Sutherland contributed the *Christ in Glory* tapestry behind the altar. The **Spirit of Coventry** exhibit in the undercroft traces the city's history, using special effects, including laser holographs.

Broadgate garden, the traditional centre of the city, preserves a tenuous link with the obliterated past in the 1949 equestrian **statue** of Lady Godiva. Coventry's history began with the Benedictine abbey her husband founded in her honour in 1043.

The **Museum of British Road Transport** highlights Coventry-made cars,

---

Folk Hero

The 13th-century outlaw who robbed the rich to feed the poor, repeatedly tricked the wicked Sheriff of Nottingham and supported King Richard against his usurping brother John—his legend is too powerful to be dented by lack of evidence. But there certainly was a Robin (or Robert) Hood, and the stories have been around for a long time. How much to believe? It's up to you. The *Tales of Robin Hood* attraction in the city centre takes the romantic view. Not much remains of Sherwood Forest, alas: the last remnants surround the Sherwood Forest Visitor Centre at Edwinstowe, where Robin wed Maid Marian. Nearby Blidworth claims the tomb of his henchman, Will Scarlett.

---

bicycles and motorcycles from the Daimler, Jaguar and Triumph plants.

Nottingham

Lace-making and Robin Hood used to be Nottingham's main claims to fame, but little lace is made now and nothing of Robin's Nottingham remains. The old castle went by the board during the Civil War, and 19th-century industrialization and 20th-century redevelopment have taken their toll. Bicycles, pharmaceuticals and cigarettes are the city's mainstays these days. **Castlegate Museum** has a fine collection of costume and textiles.

Newstead Abbey

Lord Byron's ancestral home preserves a romantic aura befitting the poet. A 12th-century priory, it was converted in 1540 into a house, incorporating the façade of the abbey church. Newstead Abbey was in an advanced state of decay when Lord Byron inherited it, but he was infatuated with the place and

---

Bareback Rider

Everybody has heard of Lady Godiva, but the story behind her famous ride is less well known. As legend would have it, she implored her husband, Leofric, Earl of Mercia, to reduce the high taxes he had levied on the people of Coventry. Unwilling to say no to his wife, he agreed—provided that she rode naked through the town. No one was more astonished than Leofric when Godiva took up the challenge. The townspeople, warned in advance of Godiva's intentions, all closed their shutters, except for Peeping Tom, or so the legend continues, and he was struck blind.

invested a lot of money and energy into restoring it. Mounting debts forced Byron to sell out in 1818. When he left Newstead, he also abandoned England for ever. Ironically, the house has since become a Byron shrine. You can see the table where the poet wrote *Childe Harold* and the memorial to his dog Boatswain, inscribed with Byron's lines.

Hardwick Hall
(*near Chesterfield*)
Elizabeth, Countess of Shrewsbury, aged 70 and four times a widow, began building here in 1590. The magnificent result reflected the wealth of the second-richest woman in the land—Bess of Hardwick, they called her. Her initials, *ES,* stand out along the roofline of the house. "Hardwick Hall, more glass than wall", goes a old rhyme, and indeed the windows grow taller with every storey. The lofty High Great Chamber on the top floor was designed to accommodate the huge tapestries that hang there.

Grantham
The birthplace of Margaret Thatcher is also famous for sausages and ginger-bread. Its buildings , however, embody more ancient history. The **Church of St Wulfram**, with its tall spire, has an old chained library, and there are some historic inns like the **Angel and Royal Hotel**, where King John held court in 1213.

Belvoir Castle
The name of the castle is pronounced, perversely enough, "beaver". Seat of the Dukes of Rutland, this crenellated mock-Gothic extravaganza is famous for its picture gallery. The paintings on

display include works by Rembrandt, Rubens, Holbein, Poussin and Gainsborough—all of them excellent.

Derby
"Darby" is the home of Royal Crown Derby porcelain and Rolls Royce aeroengines. It is also the place where Bonnie Prince Charlie broke off his march on London in the 1745 Jacobite rebellion. **Derby Museum** has a room commemorating his visit, with panelling from the house where he stayed.

The Industrial Revolution brought considerable expansion to Derby, and it is still an important manufacturing centre. The **Royal Crown Derby Works** in Osmaston Road opens its doors to visitors, by prior request. A museum on the premises displays pieces from the company's 18th-century beginnings.

Kedleston Hall
"Ostentatious" was the word Dr Johnson used to describe Kedleston in the century it was built. Robert Adam designed the house on a grand scale: the pavilions alone are larger than many stately homes. However Adam, characteristically, kept things under control, and the effect in the end is awesome but not vulgar.

Stoke-on-Trent
Pottery has been made here since the 16th century, but it was Josiah Wedgwood who put the manufacture of tableware on an industrial footing. He opened the first factory in "The Potteries" in 1769.

The **Stoke Art Gallery and Museum** has a fine collection of Spode, Minton, Copeland and, especially, Wedgwood pieces on display. For a comprehensive look at the industry, visit the enormous **Wedgwood Potters Visitors' Centre** in the factory at Barlaston. The **Gladstone Pottery Museum** at Longton gives a lively explanation of the traditional firing method, using bottle kilns.

Alton Towers, 16km (10 miles) east of Stoke, is a vast, ornate mansion, better known these days for the huge **theme park** in its grounds.

Shrewsbury

For medieval charm, look no further than the cobbled streets and Tudor houses of Shrewsbury (pronounced "shrozebree"), enclosed in a loop of the River Severn. Typical of the local architectural style is the half-timbered warehouse called **Rowley's House** in Baker Street. Now a museum of local history, this landmark dates from the days of the flax and wool trade. Taking you back even further, exhibits on display include artefacts from the excavations at nearby Wroxeter (Roman *Viroconium*).

The Normans saw Shrewsbury's value as a border fortress near the frontier with Wales and built the castle on a rise above the town. There are two outstanding churches: 12th-century **St Mary's** and **Shrewsbury Abbey Church** (Norman to 19th century).

Hereford and the Marches

This is an area of pastoral beauty, the home of cattle and cider. Tranquil half-timbered villages surround the old city of Hereford, but it has not always been so peaceful here. William the Conqueror appointed the Earl of Hereford as one of three barons to quell the turbulent Marches, the borderlands running towards the mountains of Wales.

Today you can tour the border castles, hills and towns north-west of Hereford or walk part of the 224km (140-mile) **Offa's Dyke Path**, which parallels the ancient rampart and ditch built by the Saxons to contain the Welsh tribes (*see* page 237).

Hereford Cathedral, part Norman, part Decorated, with a massive 14th-century tower has a unique **chained library** of 1,500 books, "chained" so that particularly valuable and irreplaceable volumes could not be taken away. Hereford's famous **Mappa Mundi**, a huge 13th-century map of the medieval world, shows Jerusalem at the centre and Paradise at the top. A public outcry recently foiled a bid to sell the map to help pay for the cathedral's upkeep.

Worcester

This cathedral city is famous for gloves, fine porcelain and bottled Worcestershire sauce. The sauce and the town are pronounced alike: "wooster".

Worcester has many attractive faces, none more so than the **cathedral**, built on the banks of the Severn. Once part of a Benedictine abbey, the church has a Norman core overlaid with successive styles of Gothic. The **tomb** of King John (of Magna Carta fame) stands in the chancel. Take a close look at the marble effigy, the earliest existing of any English king. The lion biting the end of John's sword is said to represent the barons curbing his royal power. Near the high altar can be found the tomb of the Tudor Prince Arthur, who died at the age of 15—already a married man. His widow, Catherine of Aragon, went on to marry his younger brother, Henry VIII.

You can tell Worcester was a Royalist city by the **Guildhall** statues of Charles I and Charles II (and by the head of Cromwell nailed by the ears). Worcester was the last town in England to surrender to Cromwell. Visit the **Commandery**, the Royalist headquarters, for an interesting replay of Civil War history. Charles II hid in nearby **King Charles House** after his decisive defeat at the Battle of Worcester in 1651.

The **Dyson Perrins Museum** (Severn Street, adjoining the porcelain factory) is the showcase for an inclusive collection of antique Royal Worcester pieces.

Chester

The continuity of history that you find in so many British cities is clearest of all in Chester. Here, on the banks of the River Dee, the Romans established their major military base of *Deva* in AD 79. They stayed for more than three centuries, guarding the fertile lands of Cheshire from raiders, whether from the Welsh hills or the Irish Sea. Later, this was a Norman stronghold and a launching pad for invasions of North Wales—and it is still a natural gateway if you are heading that way today.

There is no better introduction to Chester than to walk along the top of the best-preserved **ramparts** of any English city. The full circuit is 3km (2 miles), and well worth doing if you can, perhaps dropping down to street level at various points to see some of the sights. Even if you don't go all the way round, be sure to cover part of the northern and eastern stretches where a lot of the original Roman stonework is to be seen. The west and south walls were probably built by the Normans to extend the enclosed area.

If you start at **Eastgate** and head north past the cathedral, you reach King Charles's Tower, at the north-east corner of the ramparts. Charles I is said to have watched from here as his army was defeated at the Battle of Rowton Moor, several miles to the east. Between the tower and **Northgate**, there are stretches of Roman wall as much as 5m (17ft) high. Walk on, and you can look out over the locks of the Shropshire Union Canal—and beyond, to the green hills of North Wales. The west wall overlooks a great open space by the river where the Romans had their harbour. Called the Roodee, the site has served as Chester's racecourse since 1540.

The south-west corner of the wall incorporates **Chester Castle**, largely a Georgian restoration, except for the Norman tower. A military museum is housed within. The wall continues along the banks of the Dee to **Bridge-**

Chester celebrates its Roman past and name of Deva in a modern mosaic.

gate, which leads directly to the Old Dee Bridge. For centuries this was the only dry crossing to the south and to Wales, and the scene of many skirmishes. Look out from **Wolf Gate** over the remains of the largest Roman amphitheatre found to date in Britain, an oval over 96m (310ft) long.

Inside the walled city, the **Rows** are highly unusual shopping arcades one storey up from ground level. The idea seems to date from the 13th century, and it may have developed as townspeople attempted to bypass the Roman rubble in the streets below. That can't have been unique to Chester, but in other places they generally smoothed off the debris and built on top. Perhaps here the remains of Roman stonework were so substantial that it was easier to make new walkways above. Although some of the houses in the Rows have been restored, many 14th- to early 17th-century structures preserve their original timber frames. Sometimes the exposed wood is richly carved. Look for Bishop Lloyd's House and Leche House among the many fine buildings along **Watergate Street**.

Chester's rather unassuming **cathedral** is the church of the former Benedictine abbey, founded in 1092. There is something from every century, though, including the 19th. The superb carving on the **choir stalls** (c. 1390) includes an elaborate Tree of Jesse, displaying the genealogy of Christ.

The Peak District

Right on the doorstep of industrial Manchester, Derby and Sheffield, the

Outdoor types—the gamekeeper of Lord Derby is seen here out with his dogs and gun in the Peak District National Park.

Peak District offers a dramatic change of scenery. The wild landscape of moorland crags and rushing trout streams constitutes England's original national park, covering some 1,165km² (450 square miles). This is prime holiday country for fishing, climbing, pot holing, walking or cycling, as its attractions are remarkably unspoilt.

The ceremony of well dressing began at Tissington, near Ashbourne, in gratitude for an escape from the worst of the Black Death in 1348.

Ashbourne

The gateway to the Peak District, Ashbourne retains much of the quiet charm it must have had when Izaak Walton fished the waters of the River Dove for trout. Except, that is, on Shrove Tuesday every year when the inhabitants turn the town into a football field and play an all-day no-rules game with goals 5km (3 miles) apart.

In rolling farmlands between Ashbourne and Leek, the pretty village of **Tissington** is one of several that still go in for the old custom of "well-dressing". Using flower petals and leaves, villagers create a series of designs around the fonts, as they have every year in May since 1348, when Tissington escaped a severe outbreak of the Black Death.

Matlock

Matlock and its spa at Matlock Bath lie in the narrow wooded gorge of the River Derwent. The setting is beautiful, as Roman and Regency curists appreciated, but the Matlocks have been commercialized, with cable-car rides to the **Heights of Abraham** and the Gulliver's Kingdom and Royal Cave theme amusements. The **Riber Castle Fauna Reserve and Wildlife Park** specializes in rare breeds, both British and European.

Bakewell

A pleasant market town on the River Wye, and the only town within the confines of the Peak District National Park, Bakewell makes a good centre for touring the Peaks. The five-arched medieval bridge over the river is one of the oldest in England. At The Old House museum of country exhibits you can sample the famous Bakewell tart, made with ground almonds.

Chatsworth
(*Bakewell*)
Home of the dukes of Devonshire, palatial Chatsworth is England's answer to Versailles. You can stay on the grounds

in the Devonshire Hotel, one of the Duchess's projects. There is also an adventure playground, and farming and forestry exhibitions.

William Talman, a contemporary of Wren's, designed the baroque mansion for the 1st Duke of Devonshire in the 1680s. At the beginning of the 19th century, Wyatville added a new library, sculpture gallery, ballroom and theatre. At the same time, Joseph Paxton was hard at work in the garden, creating his innovative waterworks and glasshouses. The highlight of a visit to Chatsworth is Talman's **Painted Hall** (decorated with vigorous scenes from the life of Julius Caesar by Laguerre) and his marble and cedar-panelled **chapel**. Up to the 1930s, the entire household gathered every week to pray before the monumental alabaster altar.

Splendid furniture and decorative objects fill the house, but some of the more important paintings may not be on view. The collection of Old Master drawings is accessible only to scholars.

Haddon Hall

(*Bakewell*)
Perfect of its type, medieval Haddon Hall is smaller and less thronged than Chatsworth, but equally worth visiting. The dukes of Rutland, whose house this is, moved to the much grander Belvoir Castle in the 17th century. Haddon Hall was left empty, and intact. The galleried banqueting hall and medieval kitchen are virtually unchanged in 600 years. The house is beautifully set off by its terraced and balustraded Elizabethan rose garden.

Buxton

At 305m (1,000ft), Buxton is one of England's highest spa towns. The place came into its own in the 18th century, when the 5th Duke of Devonshire commissioned the stately **Crescent,** built in columned Palladian style by John Carr. The one-time Pump Room houses the "Micrarium", where microscope images of insects and plants are projected onto large screens.

Scenic roads branch in all directions to cross the Peak District. Fans of the Brontë sisters will head west out of Chapel-en-le-Frith to the attractive little village of **Hathersage**, the setting for Morton in *Jane Eyre*.

Castleton

From commercialized Castleton, a popular touring centre, you can visit **Peveril Castle**'s massive 11th-century keep, as well as a whole range of caves and potholes. Among them are the **Peak Cavern** (in Castleton proper), Derbyshire's largest natural cave, traversed by rope-walks; **Blue John Cavern** west of town, the source of the region's semiprecious Blue John fluorspar stone; and **Speedwell Cavern**, west again, where a short walk and underground boat trip take you to where the waters tumble into the abyss of a huge pot-hole.

Long Walk

North of Castleton, the bleaker High or Dark Peak, with vast tracts of moorland, few villages and still fewer people is traversed by the **Pennine Way**. This challenging footpath starts at **Edale**, below Mam Tor ("Shivering Mountain"), and extends over beautiful but rough terrain for 400km (250 miles) to the borders of Scotland. Stop at Edale's National Park Information Centre for advice about prevailing conditions before you set out.

A Sense of Place: the English Country Town

The English country town is instantly recognizable but hard to define. Even the name is a contradiction in terms, although this might never occur to those who live there. The country towns embody the very essence of England: the traditional values of neighbourliness, courtesy and civic pride that continue to thrive amid the pressures of modern life. Hardly any planning went into the creation of the country town, and the haphazard tangle of roads at its heart offers the driver no favours. It is often preferable to arrive by coach (bus) or train and discover the location on foot. Railway stations are typically situated a little way outside the town centre. Many stations preserve their original Victorian architecture: a neat wooden awning with elaborate eaves over the platform, and a squat redbrick station house, at the top of a street called, unsurprisingly, Station Road.

Street names are a wonderful introduction to a town. Every town plan tells a story of the pattern of influences that make up its history: medieval guilds (Weavers' Row, Coopers' Lane), the pub (White Hart Lane, Red Lion Street), the church (Vicarage Road, Bishop's Walk) and the market-place. But walking for its own sake is rather alien to English town life. There is a saying in Yorkshire: "Never stand when you can sit", which sums up a whole attitude to life, but is also meant literally. After 5.30 p.m., when the shops close, there is a definite lull in activity, and the empty streets leave the visitor free to explore the town at leisure. This is not to say that people stay at home. A busy life goes on behind closed doors in the clubs, classes, voluntary societies and, of course, the pubs.

Castle Combe, Wiltshire.

The pub or inn is a presence in town life almost as ancient as the church or monastery. The oldest pub is thought to be the "Talbot" in the Northamptonshire town of Oundle, which can trace its origins back to a hostel founded by a group of monks in the year 638. The claim is strong, but it could actually be contested by any number of inns. For the pub owes its very existence to the charitable hostelries set up by religious houses.

English towns may appear picturesque, but they were almost invariably constructed on sound pragmatic principles. Until canal transport made it feasible to import raw materials, most towns had to rely on local resources. This has given them the distinctive character that still shines through modern developments. In the south, timber and packed earth were the principal building materials. Flint and brick were used in the east, and stone in the north and south-west. Within these major groups, however, there are myriad subtle distinctions between various tones of brick, different ways of using timber, and assorted qualities of stone. Compare, for example, the Yorkshire town of Haworth with Chester. Haworth uses a warm, red sandstone—making for an atmosphere that is more appealing, if less inspirational to the romantic imagination.

From the low huddle of all these buildings, one more exalted structure invariably soars to catch the eye: the church spire or tower. Many towns even have beautiful cathedrals, set in the middle of that great invention of the English church, the cathedral close. On a more human scale are the smaller churches, often built by local subscription. As communally owned property, they were put to all kinds of uses that today would be regarded as sacrilegious: shelter, celebration and even wassailing. The churchyards, in turn, doubled as a marketplace, but this practice was prohibited in the reign of Edward I, and it was then, around 1285, that many of England's market squares were founded. The tradesmen, it seems, missed the religious atmosphere, and in many of the marketplaces they put up monuments to hold the crucifix, essential for the sealing of contracts and agreements. These "butter

Pub signs—and names—can be plain or fanciful.

crosses", or market crosses, also served as pulpits. Wymondham, in Norfolk, has a very special cross, where miracles were said to have taken place, while Ludlow's Butter Cross is a complete classical building whose upper floor was used as a charity school.

Every town has its own character and sense of place, a memorable individuality acquired gradually over time. No urban planner in his wildest imagination could ever have invented the unique ensemble of buildings of different styles and periods that is the country town.

233

Beyond the Celtic Fringe

The Welsh are different, and proud of it. The distinction crystallized when the Celtic people of Wales fought off the Anglo-Saxons who had taken over England, and the 8th-century Saxon king Offa tried to wall off the recalcitrant Welsh behind a massive earthwork rampart and ditch. You can still see Offa's Dyke stretching for many miles near the present border with England.

Freelance Norman lords came next, licensed by William the Conqueror to keep what they could capture. Some won a foothold around the motte-and-bailey castles they put up across the country, but again the Welsh kept their language and their culture largely intact. Edward I finally broke the power of the Welsh princes in the 13th century. He built a chain of massive castles, using the latest technology learned in the Cru-

*P*oetry in stone: the *roofless and silent shell of Tintern Abbey. A 12th-century Cistercian foundation, it has been abandoned since Henry VIII dissolved the monasteries.*

sades, to hold the people down. Paradoxically, these "Welsh", really English, castles are some of today's biggest attractions for visitors.

The last great rebellion, led by Owain Glyndwr around the year 1400, gave Wales a national hero, but its failure left the country shattered. Then, with Welsh fortunes at their lowest ebb, the twisted patterns of history brought a Welsh-born prince to the English throne as Henry VII, the first of the Tudor kings.

South Wales

If you think only of coal mines, steel works and tin plate, think again. Much heavy industry has gone and all but a

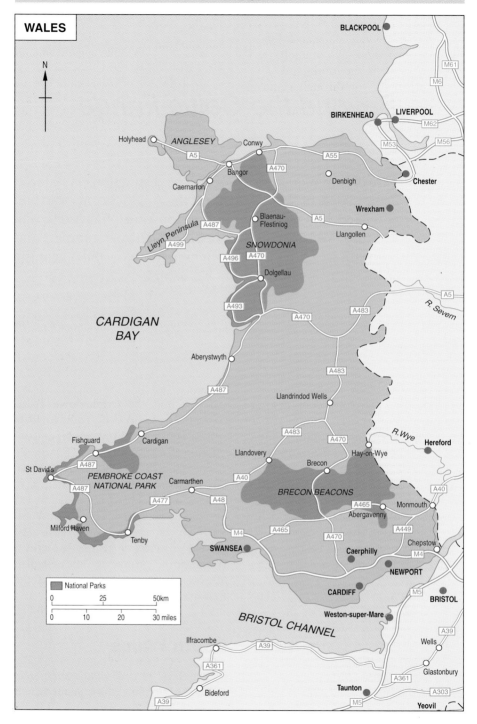

WALES

N

BLACKPOOL

M61

M6

BIRKENHEAD LIVERPOOL

M62

M53

M56

Holyhead ANGLESEY Conwy

A5 A470 A55

Bangor Denbigh Chester

Caernarfon Wrexham

A5 Llangollen

Blaenau-
Ffestiniog

Lleyn Peninsula SNOWDONIA

A487 A470

A499 A496 A470

A493 Dolgellau

A470 A483

R. Severn

CARDIGAN
BAY A5

Aberystwyth

A487 Llandrindod Wells

A483

A483 R. Wye Hereford

Fishguard Cardigan A470

Llandovery Hay-on-Wye

St David's Brecon

A487 PEMBROKE COAST Carmarthen A40 BRECON BEACONS A40

A487 NATIONAL PARK A48 A465 Monmouth

Milford Haven A477 Abergavenny A449

Tenby M4 A465 A470 Chepstow

SWANSEA Caerphilly M4

NEWPORT M5

CARDIFF BRISTOL

Weston-super-Mare A39

BRISTOL CHANNEL Wells

Ilfracombe A39 Glastonbury

A361 A361

Bideford Taunton A303

A39 M5 Yeovil

National Parks

0 25 50km

0 10 20 30 miles

236

few mines have closed. From the green valleys of the Severn, Wye and Usk to the rocky headlands and sandy bays of Pembrokeshire in the south-west, your journey will take you through a land of extraordinary variety.

Wye Valley

The border between England and Wales follows the deep, wooded valley of the River Wye. Sections of **Offa's Dyke**, up to 9m (30ft) high, mark the eastern bank, and the sudden onset of bilingual road signs lets you know you have crossed into Wales.

Whether you come from the northeast by the old Roman road, or over the Severn by the graceful suspension bridge, take a look at **Chepstow**'s mighty Norman castle. It was probably the first to be built in stone after the Conquest, with lines of red Roman tiles robbed from ancient sites nearby. The town still has some of its medieval walls, the 16th-century gate (which houses a museum), and steep, winding streets with little bow-fronted shops.

Up the Wye in a setting of green meadows and wooded cliffs, the eloquent ruins of **Tintern Abbey** moved William Wordsworth to write a poem. Vaulted by the sky, they look as if they were always meant to be like this. Not only the abbey church but parts of many other buildings survive, abandoned when Henry VIII dissolved the monastery in 1536.

Not much remains of the castle at **Monmouth**, where Henry V was born. Longbowmen from the vicinity brought

> **Tongue-twister**
> The Welsh language survives from before the Roman conquest, though it absorbed many Latin words. Only a minority speak Welsh today, but if you hear it used by a poet you will appreciate the power that a spellbinding leader could wield. Maybe the music of the Welsh language explains the number of actors, writers and orators who have come from Wales. Perhaps the marvellous choirs, too, and even the national passion for rugby football, which the Welsh see as a form of poetry. No one will expect you to speak Welsh, but it will help if you can say the place names: *f* sounds like the English *v*, *ff* like *f*, *dd* like *th* in "then", *w* like *u* in "up", and *ll* like a throaty *hl*. *Cymru* (sometimes written Gwmru) means Wales.

him victory at Agincourt, and his statue stands in Agincourt Square beside one of local son Charles Rolls, pioneer aviator and co-founder of Rolls-Royce. The gated bridge over the River Monnow was already a venerable landmark in Henry's day: it is the only Norman bridge still standing in Britain. Lord Nelson stayed for a time in Monmouth during his 1801 progress around the country: the Nelson Museum commemorates the fact.

To the south-west, the nondescript town of **Raglan** is separated from its castle by a busy road, the A40. Take the footbridge across for a closer look. The 15th-century lords of Raglan had social pretensions to satisfy, and their castle puts as much emphasis on decorative effect as impregnability. Still, Raglan held out for months against Parliament in the Civil War. When Cromwell's troops finally broke through the defences, they took the castle apart in vengeance.

*W*ales.

Abergavenny

Lying where the River Usk breaks out of the mountains, Abergavenny is a bleak yet busy market town that likes to call itself the Gateway to Wales. In fact you have a choice of routes. Northward stand the peaceful **Black Mountains**: they are actually red sandstone, and are covered with green gorse and purple heather, but some trick of light makes them look black.

To the west, the Heads of the Valleys road cuts right across the top end of the South Wales coalfield. The grey towns with their tightly packed houses fill the dozen famous mining valleys from Ebbw Vale to the Rhondda. Here you can see the impact of the Industrial Revolution and its aftermath, as the rundown in coal and steel production has forced a search for new roles. Landscaping and tree planting on the former tips (dumps) and slagheaps—and the cleaner air—are transforming the environment.

Blaenavon

The **Big Pit Mining Museum**, in a scarred landscape of lumpy hills, offers a grim look at life in a Welsh coal mine. Until the early 1980s, 1,300 men were still at work here, in continuous shifts. Even now, the mine, a cooperatively run tourist attraction, is Blaenavon's biggest employer. Former miners take you 90m (300ft) down to the old seams, for a look at the boring and haulage equipment, roadways and stables (pit ponies toiled in the mine until as recently as the 1970s).

Crickhowell Area

Carry on up the green vale of the Usk to **Crickhowell**, a little town with fragments of a castle and some fine Georgian houses. **Agen Allwedd**, in the hills to the south-west, is a magnet for cave explorers: the caverns are 22km (14 miles) long.

The round tower of a ruined Norman castle that gave the little village of **Tretower** its name still looks out over a medieval street. Over the gatehouse of Tretower Court you can see not only pistol loops but ducts for pouring something horrible on would-be attackers. The 14th-century house itself has been well restored, especially the woodwork. Sliding wooden shutters seem such a good idea they ought to make a comeback.

Brecon

There is quite an array of craft and antique shops here, in narrow streets dominated by a fine **cathedral**. Notice the chapel dedicated to the shoemakers guild, and the ancient cresset stone whose oil-filled cups used to light the building. The town's wonderful setting, ringed by mountains, makes it a great centre for exploring the **Brecon Beacons National Park** to the south and west, splendid hillwalking country. Six kilometres (4 miles) west of Brecon just off the A470 is a mountain information centre. The peak of the range at Pen-y-Fan, 887m (2,906ft), involves a vigorous walk rather than a real climb, and the views are superb. Weather permitting, you can see 14 counties from the mountains of North Wales to the Bristol Channel and the Malvern Hills. In the south of the Beacons, **Ystradfellte**, a village in a famously pretty area of streams, caves and waterfalls, offers an escape from the industrial landscapes so near to the south.

Uplands and valleys, the interplay of sunlight and shadow in the hill-walking country of the Brecon Beacons in South Wales.

Newport

The River Usk reaches the sea, or rather the mouth of the Severn, at busy Newport. Roman **Caerleon**, where 6,000 soldiers of the 2nd Legion Augusta were based, lies just upstream. Some 20 hectares (50 acres) of remains have been excavated, none more atmospheric than the oval amphitheatre. It was built around AD 90, at about the same time as the Colosseum in Rome. Tradition, if no hard evidence, links Caerleon with King Arthur (Malory's *Le Morte D'Arthur* has him crowned at "*Carlion*"), and it is easy to believe that the town could have stood against the Saxons after the legions left Britain.

Cardiff

The biggest city in Wales is now its capital, despite rival claims. The docks area used to have a wild reputation and its people, descended from the world's sailors, were the most cosmopolitan in Britain. Now an air of respectability hangs about the place, especially the spacious centre.

Cardiff Castle may be the best thing in a rather dull city, architecturally speaking. Although mostly a 19th-century confection—William Burges designed the fantastical interiors—it has a separate moated Norman keep. The **National Museum of Wales**, an institution of national stature, puts Welsh cultural achievements into a British, and European, context. It takes pride in reminding you that Richard Wilson, Edward Burne-Jones and Augustus John were Welsh. Note the remarkable collection of Roman and Romano-British standing stones, some inscribed with the strange Celtic Ogham script.

Llandaff Cathedral, in the north-west of the city, has had its ups and downs. The building was already in an advanced state of decay when Cromwell's soldiers drank in the nave and fed their pigs in the font during the Civil War. Twice restored after that, the cathedral was hit in a World War II air raid and then reconstructed by 1957. See how you react to the modern concrete arch and Epstein's great aluminium figure of Christ.

A near-religion, rugby has its "cathedral" in Cardiff at the National Stadium (Cardiff Arms Park). Try to get a ticket for a big game: nothing can match the atmosphere, and the crowd's singing can equal any opera chorus.

The **Welsh Folk Museum** at St Fagans celebrates the Welsh way of life. In extensive, wooded grounds west of town, a unique collection of buildings from all over Wales has been set up: cottages, farmhouses complete with pigsty, a chapel, tannery, smithy, even a woollen mill. Don't miss the little tollhouse with its list of charges.

Caerphilly
Caerphilly Castle is the biggest in Britain (not counting stately Windsor). It represented the "state of the art" of defence around 1300, with a lake *and* a moat formed by a dam to the east that was itself a massive curtain wall. The

*Y*oung anglers seem oblivious of their historic surroundings. The lake they're fishing forms part of Caerphilly Castle's formidable defence system.

concentric main walls were so devised that even if attackers took the outer wall, they were still dominated by the inner one, and if they got between the two, they could be sealed off and dealt with in an appropriate fashion.

Caerphilly's other claim to fame is a mild, white crumbly cheese that is now made in many other places.

Castell Coch

Landowner and coal baron, the 3rd Marquess of Bute restored Caerphilly Castle and ordered the Victorian additions to Cardiff Castle. Then, on the site of a small ruin by the River Taff, he had his architect, William Burges, create Castell Coch. Complete with a dungeon and working drawbridge, this is a Romantic dream of the Age of Chivalry. The painted murals throughout are astonishing for their detail and meticulous finish. See the drawing room with scenes from Aesop's fables and the whole world of nature.

Swansea

The second city of Wales in numbers (and only in numbers by its own account) has a certain spaciousness, partly because World War II bombs cleared the centre. The decline of the once massive steel and tin plate industries and the coal export trade has left this a cleaner, quieter place. The **Guildhall** (1934) has huge and riotous murals by the Welsh artist Frank Brangwyn that were intended as a World War I memorial for the House of Lords, but rejected as too strong meat by their lordships. Rather than show scenes of horror, Brangwyn depicted the good life Britain's peers had died to preserve—a novel approach. The majority opinion in the House considered the result more appropriate to a nightclub. London's loss was Swansea's gain.

Gower Peninsula

This stretch of land west of Swansea is miraculously unbuilt in spite of pressures from the industrial valleys and towns. Limestone cliffs, sandy bays, marshes that are a haven for birds, caves where the bones of extinct animals have been found: all of these attract walkers and, of course, cars. The traffic on the few roads can be daunting at weekends.

*D*ramatic *coastline around the Gower Peninsula, an area of natural beauty that has remained almost untouched.*

Oystermouth and **The Mumbles**, on the bay nearest to Swansea, have all the Victorian paraphernalia that is associated with old resorts. The railway built round the bay, horsedrawn at first, carried passengers as far back as 1807, making it a world first.

Oxwich has a sandy beach, two castles and a nature reserve—all very pleasant. But the village is too charming for its own good: people, traffic and caravans threaten to overwhelm it. The Gower Society does its best to protect the peninsula, and publishes a full guide to its sights.

Carmarthen Area

Ancient tradition places the cave of the wizard Merlin near the market town of **Llandeilo**, and castle collectors won't want to miss nearby **Carreg Cennen**. If King Arthur and his valiant knights of the Round Table ever rode out of a fortress, it might have looked something like this. Further down the Tywi valley you come to **Carmarthen**, whose Welsh name, *Caerfyrddin*, actually means "Merlin's City". An ancient tree stump in Priory Street is reputed to be the one in his prophecy:

When Merlin's oak shall tumble down,
Then shall fall Carmarthen town.

The citizens take no chances: the tree is held up with iron bands and concrete. One thing is sure, apart from all the legends: this was Roman *Moridunum*, the most westerly of their major British bases. Carmarthen was the scene, too, of "Rebecca riots" in 1843, a protest against extortionate charges at the all-too-numerous toll gates.

Laugharne (pronounced "larn") has some attractive Georgian houses and a romantic ruin of a castle, but these days its fame depends on the memory of the rumbustious poet Dylan Thomas. He lived here with his family, working in the garden shed of the Georgian house called the Boathouse on and off from 1948 to 1953. Thomas died on a tour of the United States, and was brought back for burial in the hillside graveyard of St Martin's Church. He swore that Laugharne was not the model for Llaregyb in *Under Milk Wood*, but that has not stopped anyone looking for resemblances.

Eight kilometres (5 miles) of firm sand at **Pendine** made it the site for world land speed challenges in the 1920s. Sir Malcolm Campbell set successive records of up to 290kph (180mph), and Welsh ace Parry-Thomas was killed here. His car was buried in the sand, but later exhumed and put on display.

Pembrokeshire

The rich farmland of the south-western peninsula of Wales looks not unlike England's West Country. It was settled, too, by English-speakers and used to be a separate county, Pembrokeshire, known as "Little England beyond Wales". Almost the whole of the coast falls within the boundaries of a national park and the 269km (167-mile) Pembrokeshire Coast Path takes you out along the cliffs. The sandy beach of Amroth is the starting point; here at low tide you can see the stumps of a 1,000-year-old sunken forest.

Fashionable early in the 19th century, when bay-windowed Regency hotels rose above the little harbour and along the cliffs, **Tenby** is still popular for holidays. You will soon see why: the original town inside the best-preserved

Quiet days on the Welsh Riviera: old-fashioned relaxation is on offer at scenic Tenby, the prime resort of the Pembrokeshire Coast.

old walls in Wales; the choice of beaches; and plenty of things to see and do in the vicinity.

Less than 5km (3 miles) offshore, **Caldey Island** has been the site of a Cistercian monastery since 1929. The order actually revived an ancient abbey, which stood here for many centuries up to the Dissolution of 1534. Take a launch trip and see how the monks have put the old buildings back into use, how they farm their tiny island and produce scents from the island's flowers.

Along the coast in the castle at **Manorbier**, about the year 1146, was born one of the greatest scholars, travellers and, above all, writers of his time: Giraldus Cambrensis ("Gerald of Wales"), half-Norman, half-Welsh. The record of his travels is the best account we have of what the country was like in the Middle Ages.

Mighty **Pembroke Castle**, with water on three sides, dominates the town of Pembroke. Climb the keep for the view and look inside at the great stone domed roof. A spiral staircase leads down from the North Hall into a great cave called "the Wogan", which must have been a shelter for narrow boats. The defences were designed by William Marshal, who once unhorsed Richard the Lionheart but spared his life. Harri Twdwr (better known as King Henry VII, first of the Tudor dynasty) was born here in 1457.

Intriguingly, the port of **Pembroke Dock** was built with money acquired by one man (Charles Francis Greville) through trading away his mistress to another (his uncle, Sir William Hamilton). The woman in question was Emma Hart, later Lady Hamilton, who was to return to Wales with Lord Nelson on his 1801 tour. The natural harbour of **Milford Haven**, across the water, is one of the best in Britain. The town of the

same name grew up after Sir William Hamilton got permission from Parliament to build the docks.

Haverfordwest ("harford", as the locals say it) was the centre of English settlement in these parts and, a fascinating anomaly, used to be a county all by itself. Its castle is "one of the ruins that Cromwell knocked about a bit", as the old song goes. Within the walls is a museum of local history.

It is worth making for the end of the neck of land at **Dale**, a sheltered yachting centre with beaches on either side of the peninsula. It was on the sandy western shore that Henry Tudor landed in 1485, so near his childhood home of Pembroke, to begin the triumphal march that led to Bosworth Field, victory over Richard III, and the crown.

Marloes has much older memories: you can clamber over Iron Age

Next stop Ireland. St David's Head on the Pembrokeshire coast, southwest Wales.

ramparts and see, offshore, the islet of Gatehold, with traces of a hundred prehistoric huts. A mile or two out to sea lie the islands of **Skomer** and **Skokholm**, the former with more mysterious relics of an old settlement, both with squadrons of seabirds. Boats to the isles set sail from Dale or Martin's Haven.

Follow the sweep of St Bride's Bay to **St David's**—a cathedral city, but one no bigger than many villages. **St David's Cathedral** almost hides in a hollow, probably on the site chosen by the patron saint of Wales himself in the 6th century. (The concealment was inten-

tional in the days when raiders usually arrived by sea.) In contrast to the severe exterior, there is plenty of decorative detail within the Norman church. Look out for the humorously carved misericords on the 15th-century choir stalls: laughter was a weapon against the devil.

More boat trips beckon, to **Ramsey Island**, a nature reserve just offshore, or **Grassholm**, 19km (12 miles) out to sea, home to thousands of gannets.

Up the coast, **Fishguard** is the ferry port for sailings to Rosslare in Ireland. If you think the docks look oversized for the purpose, you are quite right. There were hopes, long ago, of attracting Atlantic liners and whisking the passengers to London by train. Still earlier excitements included a raid by the American John Paul Jones during the War of Independence, and the "French invasion" of 1797, when a ragtag force led by the Irish-American Colonel Tate

246

landed in the hope of igniting a peasants' revolt. It was the last notable hostile landing on the British mainland, and it is said that the raiders first got drunk and then surrendered to Welsh women, mistaking them in their red dresses for redcoats of the army.

Inland, the rolling uplands of **Mynydd Preseli** were the source of the massive "bluestones" that Bronze Age Britons set up at Stonehenge, all of 386km (240 miles) away.

Cardigan Area

Aberteifi ("Mouth of the Teifi") is the Welsh name for **Cardigan**, a dynamic little town. An old bridge spans the river that once brought sea-going ships to the harbour, before it silted up. There is some memorable fishing along the Teifi: salmon make the run upriver to spawn.

A few miles inland, **Cilgerran** is a fishing centre for salmon and trout. You may still see coracles on this stretch of the river. The small wickerwork and canvas boats were traditionally used by local fishermen, and every August Cilgerran holds a coracle regatta. The ruin of Cilgerran's Norman castle looms above the gorge of the river.

Mid-Wales

Genteel spas and gentle hills merge almost imperceptibly with rural England to the east; lovely valleys drop to meet the long curve of Cardigan Bay to the west. In between, on remote and empty moors and hills, you will see more sheep than people. This narrow waist of Wales has its own personality and an atmosphere more restful than the heavyweights of north and south.

Aberystwyth

Far from other big towns, the Queen of Cardigan Bay cultivates her independence. Victorian railway-builders made it easy to get here, and package-holiday pioneer Thomas Savin made it cheap, providing a week's free board for the price of a ticket in the 1860s. He lost a fortune, and his grand hotel on the promenade was a failure, but it provided the University of Wales with its original building. A **museum** of decorative and folk art is housed here now.

Welsh scholars do their research at Aberystwyth's **National Library of Wales** (*Llyfrgell Genedlaethol Cymru*), the largest collection in Welsh in the world. Formerly in splendid isolation on a hill above the town, the library is surrounded by the new buildings of the much expanded university.

On a promontory by the sea, only fragments remain of another of Edward I's many powerful castles.

Welsh Waters

Now for that test of your Welsh pronunciation: Llandrindod Wells, Builth Wells, Llangammarch Wells and Llanwrtyd Wells came to be fashionable in the 18th century in the manner of Bath. People arrived to take the waters, and pump rooms, hotels, even gaming rooms sprang up. Llandrindod, the largest, remains a spa but adds golf and fishing. It also makes a convenient touring centre for the whole area. So does Builth, a market town on a beautiful stretch of the Wye. Llangammarch waters contain barium, said to be good for the heart, and Llanwrtyd's were thought to be invigorating after an 18th-century vicar claimed the local frogs to be exceptional jumpers.

Vale of the Rheidol

The journey is half the fun on the narrow-gauge steam railway that runs up the wooded valley of the Rheidol to **Mynach Falls**. The River Mynach meets the Rheidol in spectacular waterfalls hundreds of feet high, and three bridges stand one above the other over a vertiginous gorge. The lowermost, Devil's Bridge, dates from the 12th century and, far from being built by the devil, ought to be credited to the monks of Strata Florida Abbey (which lies in ruins to the south).

The **Plynlimon** range looks deceptively gentle. In fact, the hills rise to over 732m (2,400ft). Trek to the top for some superb views over Cardigan Bay, but first check the weather forecast. Stay on firm tracks: boggy morasses lurk beneath innocent-looking green moss and reeds, and thick mists can roll

centre for fishing, walking, pony-trekking and antiquing. Search in craft and antique shops for the Welsh dresser you have always wanted.

The **Elan Valley** has long been flooded as a reservoir for Birmingham. If the water level is not too high it can be eerie to look down on the few remaining stones of Shelley's cottage in Elan Village, remembering that the poet's first wife, and in the end he, too, drowned in boating accidents.

New Radnor

The town is anything but new: the question is whether it was founded by Saxon King Harold when he was Earl of Hereford or by the Normans. Don't assume that Radnor Forest had many trees, either—though there are plantations now. It was a forest in the old sense, meaning moorland used for hunting, and is still rich in wildlife.

Hay-on-Wye

Hay's old toll bridge straddles the border with England, a remarkably tranquil landscape of green hills, though the castle ruins recall the days when this was a hostile frontier. Today Hay is noted for literary pursuits, not past disputes. The town hosts an annual literary festival of national stature, and local bookshops (mainly concentrated in the area of Castle Street) just happen to stock the *world's* biggest

in and mystify even those who consider they know these moors. On the south-west face of the hills, the Wye and the Severn start their serpentine paths to the Bristol Channel.

Rhayader

There's water, water, everywhere if you head down the Wye to Rhayader and on to a chain of nostalgic spas in the heart of mid-Wales. Rhayader is a good stock of second-hand books. Collectors come from far afield to browse through hundreds of thousands of volumes on sale.

Llandovery to the Coast

The busy market town of **Llandovery** can be your base for forays to the Black Mountain (not to be confused with the Black Mountains—plural—to the east). Tough mountain walkers head for the crest between two lakes that look as lovely as their names sound, Llyn y Fan Fawr and Llyn y Fan Fach.

If you walk in the hills, you will be able to take old drovers' tracks by which sheep and cattle were once herded to English markets. In places these tracks follow even more ancient paths paved by Roman legionaries. The Romans were not just empire-building: it was gold that lured them here. You can visit authentic Roman gold mines at **Dolaucothi** near Pumpsaint. The Visitor Centre sets out the history of the mines in background displays.

Probably the most exciting thing, however, is to go underground into the Roman adits, or tunnels, which honeycomb the slope—though this is not advised for the less agile or sufferers from claustrophobia.

A few miles south, **Talley Abbey** is a peaceful ruin of graceful arches and walls set among lakes and woods. Beautiful country surrounds **Lampeter**, a small market and college town, and **Tregaron**, the starting point for hiking and pony-trekking excursions into the Cambrian Hills.

From here you can return to the coast, to the sailing centre of **Aberaeron**, a planned port and town that was built by newly rich Thomas and Susannah Jones: it gives away its age by the street names, such as Waterloo Street and Regent Street.

Machynlleth

Up the Dyfi valley, Machynlleth stood at a major coaching crossroads. All 24 inns clustered around the market cross where a Victorian clock tower stands today. Most of the inns have been converted to other uses, but it is not hard to identify them. Walk down Doll (Toll) Street to see a table of charges levied in the days of turnpike roads. Even sheep were not exempt, as this was, and still is, a sheep market town. The years of glory, though, are long gone; Machynlleth was once the capital of Wales, and here in 1404, at the height of his success, Owain Glyndwr was proclaimed king.

Welshpool

An evocative title for border lands, the Marches bring echoes of raid and counter-raid, but Welshpool (*Trallwng* in Welsh) is peaceful enough now. Nearby **Powis Castle,** once a bastion, was turned into a Georgian palace. Capability Brown's lush gardens are reckoned a national treasure, and if you are interested in India, you will revel in the Clive Museum in the castle.

In the hills that beckon to the northwest, **Lake Vyrnwy** (*Llyn Efyrnwy*) looks natural enough now, but it was created in the 1880s to provide the city of Liverpool with water. Llanwddyn village near the dam is equally new, built for the people whose houses were submerged as the waters rose. Take a boat trip (you can hire a rod, and the fishing is excellent) or walk in the forests and on the moors.

North Wales

To climbers and lovers of mountains, this part of Wales means Snowdonia National Park, with some of Britain's most challenging rock climbing and wild scenery. Railway buffs want to ride the historic narrow-gauge railways, and an increasing number of visitors are fascinated by the industrial history on view in the slate quarries.

Llangollen

Every corner of the valley fills with song and dance in July when the International Musical Eisteddfod attracts choirs and folk groups from around the world. Competitors all wear their national costume. Above the town, engineering genius Thomas Telford tamed the falls of the River Dee to feed his Shropshire Union Canal. The canal swoops over the river on a 300m (1,000ft) aqueduct of cast iron, some 37m (120ft) up in the air.

Right on the border, with Offa's Dyke passing through the grounds, massive **Chirk Castle** was an archetypal fortress of the Marcher lords. It seems to have been an unlucky place, six owners being hanged or beheaded in medieval times. Then by changing sides at the wrong time in the Civil War, yet another owner managed to fall foul of the Roundheads *and* the Cavaliers: Chirk was wrecked by both. The castle itself was later turned into a magnificent Georgian stately home. The wrought-iron gates, as intricately fashioned as lace, took the local Davies brothers 15 years to make.

Walkers should head south-west along the lovely Vale of Ceiriog and into the Berwyn hills.

Erddig

(near Wrexham)
When the National Trust acquired this great house, built around 1700, it was something like a time capsule. Rooms had been left unchanged for a hundred years, some storerooms and outbuildings for even longer. The laundry, for example, retained all the original 18th-century equipment, including a hand-cranked box mangle. Farming on the estate used traditional techniques that had died out elsewhere.

North from Ruthin

At the hilltop market town of **Ruthin**, where Owain Glyndwr's uprising began in 1400, you can see fine half-timbered buildings that would have been standing even then. You can also stay in the castle: this 19th-century construction on the site of the old fortress is now a hotel.

Nearby in **Denbigh**, the museum inside the ruined castle has some relics of the explorer H M Stanley, famous as the man who found Dr Livingstone, who was born in a cottage below the walls in 1841.

18th-Century Scandal

Plas Newydd (New Place) was home for 50 years to the unconventional "Ladies of Llangollen". These two Irish aristocrats ran away together and bought a cottage here in 1778, eventually expanding it into this long black-and-white timbered curiosity. Polite society cut the odd couple, and their families disinherited them, but less conventional acquaintances came to call—including William Wordsworth and the Duke of Wellington. Guests were expected to bring a gift of carved oak, and you can see the result inside.

*T*he Hon. Sarah
Ponsonby and Lady Eleanor
Butler caused quite a stir when
they set up home together at Plas
Newydd in Llangollen in the 18th
century.

Down the valley of the River Clwyd,
the mainly 15th-century cathedral of **St
Asaph** is no larger than many village
churches, but it does mark the site of
one of the earliest monasteries in Wales,
founded in 537.

North Coast

Holiday crowds flock to brash
Prestatyn and **Rhyl** from Liverpool
across the bay, attracted by the flat
sandy beaches and the funfairs.

Five kilometres (3 miles) upriver
at still impressive **Rhuddlan Castle**,
Edward I of England, after years of
campaigns intended to crush their independence, announced to Welsh leaders that he was naming as their prince
one who was "born in Wales and could
speak never a word of English". He was
referring to his baby son, who had just
been born at Caernarfon.

Colwyn Bay has no such echoes of
history: it grew up as a rather ordinary
resort with a long sandy beach and
promenade. On a hill above the town,
you can see free-flying birds of prey at
the Welsh Mountain Zoo.

Llandudno is the giant among Welsh
seaside spots, with a sweep of hotels and
guest houses along the north shore
sands. A cable railway and toll road
lead to the top of 207m (679ft) **Great
Orme Head**, west of town, for vast
views of Anglesey and Snowdonia.

In his master plan to subdue the
Welsh, Edward I had to secure the
crossing of the River Conwy, and his
Conwy Castle survives as a perfect
example of medieval fortification.
Take a walk around the battlements
and the walls of the town. Telford's suspension bridge of 1826 leading to the
castle gate is a graceful addition, par-
alleled by Robert Stephenson's 1848
railway bridge.

Facing Anglesey across the Menai Strait, **Bangor** is home to a branch of the University of Wales. The venerable look of the cathedral is deceptive: it is mainly the result of 19th-century restoration.

Nearby **Penrhyn Castle** is no restoration, but a complete fake. As if there were not enough Norman castles in Wales already, sugar and slate baron Lord Penrhyn had another built in the 1820s and thirties. These days the castle belongs to the National Trust, and is home not only to the original "Norman" furniture (don't miss the outsize, slate state bed—Queen Victoria slept here), but to the disparate collections (locomotives to dolls).

The **Penrhyn slate quarries** lie a few miles inland at Bethesda, a village that took the name of its Nonconformist chapel in place of the original Glan

Ogwen. You can tour the quarry and see how "queens", "duchesses" and other fine "ladies" (the different slate sizes) in blue, red and green are cut from a 300m (1000ft) deep gash in the mountainside.

Anglesey

Ynys Môn in Welsh, *Mona* to the Romans, the island is flatter than any other part of Wales, but with rugged cliffs and sandy beaches. The tireless Thomas Telford built the 1826 **Menai Bridge** from the mainland. It was the first practical, heavy-duty suspension bridge ever constructed—177m (579ft) from pier to pier, and 30m (100ft) above the water at the highest tide (by order of the Admiralty, to let navy ships through).

Llanfair PG is the short form for a 58-letter name that was probably a 19th-century joke: Llanfairpwllgwyngyllgogerychwyrndrobwllllantysiliogogogoch (literally, St. Mary's by the White Aspen over the Whirlpool and St Tysilio's by the Red Cave). The old railway station sign is on display in Penrhyn Castle.

Beaumaris (Norman French for "beautiful flat land") is rich in fine old houses, and the **castle**, with a sea moat lapping at its outer walls, is one of the finest designs of Edward I's master builder, James of St George.

Sadly, many travellers see little of Anglesey as they hurry to the ferry port of **Holyhead**. They might be surprised to hear that seaborne trade with Ireland has been going on by this route for 4,000 years, since gold and axe heads were first imported. The port is actually on **Holy Island** (reached by a causeway), the seat of Celtic saints. Try to make time to take the road to the western tip of the island, where South Stack is the site of a lighthouse, bird sanctuary and caves where grey seals breed.

Caernarfon

The name means "the fort on the shore", rather an understatement for this last and most dominating of Edward I's castles in Wales. His son, the first English Prince of Wales, was born

*A*n Anglesey name, complete with pronunciation guide, that is nearly as long as the train.

here in 1284. (The investiture of the present prince took place here in 1969.)

The walled town was built for English merchants and settlers; it is intensely Welsh today, and you will hear plenty of Welsh spoken. Take the dizzying walk around the battlements for some expansive views of Anglesey, across the Menai Strait, and mountainous Snowdonia.

Did Edward I know of the remains of the Roman fort of **Segontium**, less than a kilometre (only half a mile) away? Those earlier intruders arrived about AD 78 and stayed 300 years. Then the legions, led by Magnus Maximus, departed for Gaul and brief glory before disappearing into the darkness of disintegrating empire. Around this event, Welsh bards wove legends of the hero Macsen Wledig, second only to King Arthur in splendour.

The Lleyn Peninsula

A coast of rocky coves, fishing harbours and sandy beaches; whitewashed slate-roofed cottages; low, windswept hills covered with heather and gorse; cliffs at "Land's End"—doesn't it all sound a little bit like a miniature Devon and Cornwall? Never the less it is very Welsh, though quite unlike any other part of Wales you may have seen.

Wales has never lacked visionaries. In the early 19th century, William Madocks saw the need for a port for the shipping of slate from local quarries and mines, so he had the twin Regency-style towns, **Tremadog** and **Porthmadog** built (the names derive from his own). As you'll see, the plans anticipated an expansion that never quite happened. T E Lawrence ("Lawrence of Arabia") was born in Tremadog in 1888. Perhaps

his early interest in castles was triggered by first-hand knowledge of some of the greatest here in North Wales.

Just along the coast, **Criccieth**'s ruined fortress dominates the little town and beaches from its high headland. Walk up and around it for views of Snowdonia and the Lleyn.

Close by to the west, **Llanystumdwy** was the boyhood home of David Lloyd George—dubbed the "Welsh Wizard" for his oratory—statesman and British Prime Minister during World War I. His grave is here, along with a memorial and museum designed by Williams-Ellis, who was also the architect of the unusual village of Portmeirion.

Mention **Pwllheli** and many people will think of the huge holiday camp, but that is some way from the old town with its harbour full of yachts and powerboats. From little **Abersoch** you can sail round St Tudwal's Islands, which are bird sanctuaries.

The last bay on the south of the Lleyn Peninsula shelters **Aberdaron**, where countless pilgrims used to embark for **Bardsey Island**, across Bardsey Sound. The isle is site of ancient monasteries and the purported burial place of 20,000 "saints" (in the sense of "believers"). Less than one square mile (about 2km^2) in area, this is another bird sanctuary.

Nefyn is the main resort on the north coast of the Lleyn, but its popularity hardly new. Edward I organized a tournament here in 1284 to celebrate his successful Welsh campaign. Six kilometres (4 miles) north is an impressive Iron Age site with 100 hut-circles, but Bronze Age burial places show the peninsula to have been inhabited considerably earlier.

Snowdonia

Snowdonia National Park covers over 2,000km² (about 800 square miles) of mountains, hills and coastline between Conwy, Bala, Aberdovey and Bangor. National Park Information offices in Llanberis and Betws-y-Coed sell maps and guides and organize guided day walks. Just because you can "climb" to the 1,085m (3,560ft) peak of **Snowdon** on a Swiss-type rack railway, don't think that these mountains are easy, or

safe. There are plenty of challenging routes, and the first expedition to reach the top of Mount Everest trained here.

Llanberis is where you catch the Snowdon train—or start the most straightforward walk to the summit, which will give you 8km (5 miles) of aerobic exercise, plus a great feeling of superiority over the rail passengers. Either way, the views are worth the trip.

Back at Llanberis, the narrow-gauge Lake Railway follows the shore

Snowdonia National Park attracts both walkers and serious mountaineers. Snowdon itself is the highest peak in Wales (and tops any in England).

serve at **Crafnant** attracts specialists from all over the world.

Betws-y-Coed can be crowded, and the traffic brought to a standstill by the daily influx of tourists and excursion coaches attracted to this famous beauty spot. Get away from the roads by walking the forest paths. Three valleys meet here, the Conwy, Lledr and Llugwy, all with waterfalls (including the celebrated Swallow Falls and Conwy Falls).

Everything seems to be made of slate at **Blaenau Ffestiniog**, a small town set splendidly in a steep horseshoe of mountains that have been cut, sliced and mined by the slate quarriers. Dress up warmly—you will be given lights and safety helmets—for a grim descent into the **Nyth y Gigfran** quarry. Or go on the tourist route at **Llechwedd** slate mines. You can ride an electric train through the labyrinth of old tunnels and buy things you never imagined could be made from slate.

Most of the "Great Little Trains of Wales" began as industrial services, transporting slate. The **Ffestiniog Railway** is no exception. The steam-hauled, narrow-gauge line runs through a glorious section of Snowdonia National Park on its 21km (13-mile) journey from the market town of Ffestiniog to Porthmadog on the coast (*see* page 255). Inaugurated in 1836, this is the oldest passenger-carrying light railway in the world, restored by enthusiasts after a period of neglect.

of wildly scenic Llyn Padarn. The round trip takes 45 minutes, leaving sightseers plenty of time to visit the Welsh Slate Museum on the site of the old Dinorwic quarry, where workings rise in terraces to 550m (1,800ft).

A dramatic road south-east over Llanberis Pass leads to **Pen-y-Gwryd**, the climbers' inn which is now a centre offering courses in all kinds of mountain activities. There is a similar centre at **Capel Curig**. The alpine nature re-

257

Harlech

Every Welsh child can sing the rousing song "Men of Harlech". Practically a second national anthem, it immortalizes the defence of Harlech's awe-inspiring castle by the Constable of Wales, Dafydd, at the end of the Wars of the Roses. Like so many heroes in Welsh history, he was on the losing side, but Harlech had been a last refuge before. Owain Glyndwr made the fortress his headquarters in 1408 and his family was captured here by the future Henry V of England. On the losing side again in 1647, Harlech was the last bastion to withstand Parliamentary attack in the Civil War. Consequently the fortress suffered some destructive "slighting" to ensure no repetition of such defiance.

Barmouth

Sands and sheltered waters, plus countless sights to see if the weather drove them off the beach, drew families to Barmouth when the railway arrived in the 19th century. The terraced Victorian town remains a popular holiday centre. If your travels have made you a supporter of the great work of the National Trust, you might like to walk up **Dinas Oleu**, the hill behind the harbour. It was the first piece of land ever acquired by the Trust, in 1895.

Upriver, **Dolgellau**'s dark slate houses match the cliffs around. This is a tradition-minded area, and Welsh tends to be spoken. Visitors use the town as a base for exploring and climbing in the **Cadair Idris** range of mountains that fill the southern horizon. Do head for the hills—but don't miss the walks around Dolgellau itself. "Precipice Walk" is not at all hair-raising, despite the name, and there are fine views.

Tywyn

The **church** of Tywyn is part-Norman, but the famous St Cadfan's Stone it shelters is much older, perhaps 7th or 8th century, and inscribed in Welsh. Arguments rage about what it actually says, but scholars agree that it is the oldest known example of the Welsh language.

You may have seen the Talyllyn narrow-gauge steam railway in half a dozen films and TV series. Opened in

1865 and in continuous operation ever since, the steep little line starts from Tywyn and does not quite reach the enchanting lake that gives the line its name. Disembark at Nant Gwernol and walk through forested country to the lake. Nearby **Aberdovey** (*Aberdyfi* in Welsh) didn't actually have any bells when an 18th-century song "The Bells of Aberdovey" spread its name round the world. They were supposed to come from a drowned city under the waves,

*U*nassuming enough now, Dolgellau was the site in 1404 of the last Welsh parliament of Owain Glyndwr, who led a popular uprising against English rule.

perhaps a folk memory from the distant past—tree stumps thousands of years old are sometimes visible in the sand at low tide, so the sea has indeed risen.

Lakes, Moors—and Industrial Powerhouse

Most European countries have a north–south divide: England is no different. Southerners can't help seeing the north in terms of grim, smoke-blackened cities. It was never true of more than a small fraction, and still less is it true in these days of clean air and soot-free buildings. Most of the north remains what it was, the most varied and beautiful, as well as the most rugged landscape in England. All over the north there are abbeys and fortresses with stirring tales to tell. There is an infectious warmth to the big cities, too, and a new pride in their industrial history.

Northern Cities

A swathe of great manufacturing centres runs across the north of England from Manchester and the mill towns of Lancashire to Sheffield, Bradford and Leeds in Yorkshire. Motorways link the cities and surrounding towns into one immense industrial network. Splendid recreational tracts of open country, moorland and valley lie near at hand, on both sides of the Pennines.

A mid the bracken and heather of the Nidderdale moors, near Pateley Bridge, wind and rain carved out the fantastic shapes of Brimham Rocks.

Liverpool

Who hasn't heard of this rowdy, rebellious seaport city? Kids the world over used to reel off the names of Liverpool's football (soccer) stars. For their parents' generation, Liverpool meant the Beatles. Earlier, emigrants to the New World sailed from here in their millions, and in World War II this was the landfall in Europe of many G I s. Since then, the Atlantic trade that made the city rich has mostly gone elsewhere, leaving miles of docks derelict and whole areas depressed. Now people are beginning to see the magnificence of some of the Victorian and Edwardian architecture on the waterfront. Imaginative schemes have restored quayside warehouses, as fine in their way as the palazzos of Venice.

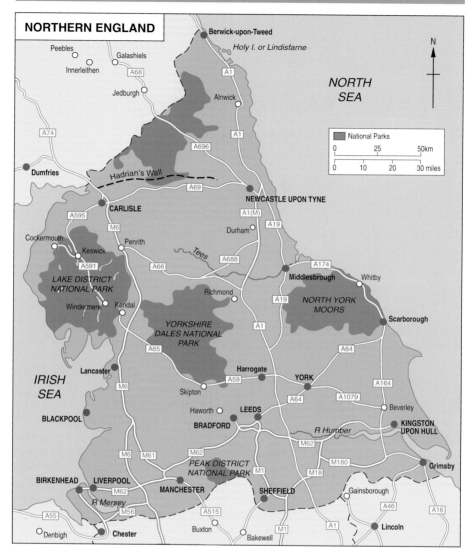

NORTHERN ENGLAND

Berwick-upon-Tweed

Peebles
Innerleithen
Galashiels
A68
Jedburgh
Holy I. or Lindisfarne
A1
Alnwick
A1
A696

N

NORTH
SEA

National Parks

0   25   50km

0   10   20   30 miles

Dumfries

Hadrian's Wall

A69

CARLISLE

A595

Cockermouth

Keswick

A591

LAKE DISTRICT
NATIONAL PARK

Windermere   Kendal

M6

Penrith

A66

Tees

Richmond

A688

A174

Middlesbrough   Whitby

A19

NORTH YORK
MOORS

Scarborough

NEWCASTLE UPON TYNE

A1(M)

A19

Durham

IRISH
SEA

Lancaster

M6

Skipton

YORKSHIRE
DALES NATIONAL
PARK

A65

A59

Harrogate

A1

YORK

A64

A164

Haworth

LEEDS

BRADFORD

Beverley

A1079

BLACKPOOL

M6

M61

M62

PEAK DISTRICT
NATIONAL PARK

M1

M62

R Humber

KINGSTON
UPON HULL

M180

M18

Grimsby

BIRKENHEAD   LIVERPOOL

M62

MANCHESTER

SHEFFIELD

Gainsborough

A46

A16

R Mersey

M56

A55

Denbigh   Chester

A515

Buxton

M1

A1

Lincoln

Bakewell

*T*he North of England.

The best view of the **waterfront** would
be from a ship—not so easy to arrange
now that most of the ferry services have
been superseded by tunnels and bridges
across the Mersey. (Ferries still operate
to the Isle of Man and Ireland from

here.) You can't miss the two towers of
the Royal Liver (pronounced "lyver")
Building, with mythical "liver" birds on
top—at 90m (295ft) they are the
tallest thing around.

A short walk south brings you to the
showpiece of the docks renewal. The
buildings around **Canning Dock** have
been converted to house the **Merseyside
Maritime Museum**, along with part of

First sight of England for GIs in World War II, last sight for many emigrants, the waterfront of Liverpool.

the magnificent colonnaded **Albert Dock**. Trendy shops, offices and restaurants fill the rest. Another warehouse here has been taken over by the **Tate Gallery, Liverpool**, for the display of modern art from the collections of the Tate in London.

From the waterfront, Water Street leads inland past the Georgian Town Hall, designed by John Wood the Elder of Bath fame. Almost a mile from the Mersey, is the city's cultural centre of gravity, a cluster of 19th-century palaces near Lime Street railway station. Massive, classical **St George's Hall**—law court and concert hall—is the grandest of the lot.

Liverpool Museum, strong on natural history and archaeology, does not quite stand up to the London competition, but the **Walker Art Gallery** is world class. Begin with the early Italian and North European section (Simone Martini to Cranach), or concentrate on the Flemish and Dutch masters. A memorable self-portrait of Rembrandt as a young man stands out. Gainsborough, Constable, Romney, Reynolds and Turner are well represented in a comprehensive British collection. The gallery's Pre-Raphaelite and later Victorian works (Millais, Holman Hunt, Watts and many more), disparaged for decades, have at last come into their own—none more so than the celebrated *And When Did You Last See Your Father?* by the almost forgotten name of W F Yeames. Among British painters of the 20th century, don't miss that brilliant recorder of the industrial north, L S Lowry.

More Pre-Raphaelite and Victorian art is on view across the Mersey at the model village of **Port Sunlight**, built for the workers of Lord Lever's Sunlight soap factory. The **Lady Lever Art Gallery** specializes in these dramatic, romantic, narrative pictures.

Two cathedrals crown Liverpool's skyline. The **Anglican Cathedral** by Sir Giles Gilbert Scott, completed in 1978, was seven decades in the building. It is one of the last—and among the

263

biggest—ever constructed in Gothic style—rivalling Rome's St Peter's in size. The 1960s Roman Catholic **Metropolitan Cathedral** could hardly be more different. Dubbed the "tea cosy" by the locals, it's circular, with a conical roof topped by a tower of coloured glass and slender pinnacles.

Beatles fans will be more interested in the **"Beatles' Magical History Tour"**, leaving Albert Dock at 2.20 p.m. or the Welcome Centre (Clayton Square shopping centre) at 2.30 p.m. daily. It takes in the key places in the early lives of the quartet: where they were born, went to school, the Cavern nightclub where they got their start, Strawberry Fields… and all this to a background of Beatles hits.

Manchester

"What Manchester thinks today, London thinks tomorrow", self-confident cotton bosses used to declare. The textile industry has declined now, but Victorian pride survives. That was the

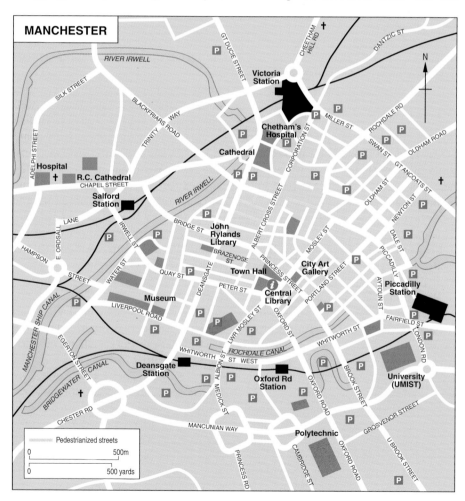

quality which drove the Manchester Ship Canal 58km (36 miles) through to the sea in 1894, turning the inland city into a port for ocean-going vessels. The same attitude demanded that the self-proclaimed northern capital should have public buildings, educational institutions, museums, theatres and an orchestra (the Hallé) the equal of—or better than—London's.

World War II bombing, the demolition of mills and slums, and piecemeal modern development changed the character of the city, and not always for the better. But clean-air laws and the removal of decades of grime have certainly brightened things up. The financial sector burgeoned as cotton declined: Manchester still means business.

The Gothic-revival **Town Hall** (1877) on Albert Square sets the tone with its murals of commerce, industry and Christianity by Pre-Raphaelite painter Ford Madox Brown. A civic building on a grand scale, the massive **Central Library** opposite is one of the world's largest lending libraries.

The **City Art Gallery** (Princess Street) displays a rich collection of the High Victorian painting that is returning to fashion after decades of disregard, and much more besides. Special emphasis is given to Manchester's own L S Lowry (1887–1976), painter of industrial and slum landscapes. There is a sampling of Lowry's work, as well as a reconstruction of his modest living-room and studio.

While Manchester boomed in the 19th century, the factory hands strug-

gled in deplorable conditions. Friedrich Engels described their plight in his 1845 book *The Condition of the Working Class in England.* Engels did his writing in the library of **Chetham's Hospital** (a medieval charitable institution) on the north side of town near the 15th-century cathedral. You can see the desk he shared with Karl Marx when they teamed up to denounce the exploitation of the cotton workers.

The city's wealth of art seems limitless. In the university area south of the centre, the **Whitworth Art Gallery** has superb water-colours, modern art and historic textiles in the kind of collection that would do credit to an international capital.

Castlefield was the site of the Roman fort of *Mancunium* (Manchester people are still called Mancunians), as well as the one-time terminus of the earliest canal and railway systems. Now it is home to the **Museum of Science and Industry**, the **Air and Space Museum** and an **Urban Heritage Park** with constantly changing exhibits. The **Granada TV Studios** let you stare at the stars and walk around the set of the oldest British "soap" of them all, *Coronation Street.*

Sheffield

The name has been synonymous with cutlery since the Middle Ages. The miller in Chaucer's 14th-century *Canterbury Tales* was carrying a Sheffield knife (visit the City Museum in Weston Park to see implements like it). Unfortunately, steel-making meant pollution, and by the 18th century Sheffield had become appallingly grimy. Horace Walpole declared it "the foulest town in England in the most charming situation". Today's city boasts clean air, a

City plan of Manchester.

largely new centre and good shopping in traffic-free complexes. Sadly, Sheffield cutlery is almost a thing of the past.

Leeds

The bold commercial capital of Yorkshire can hardly be ignored, even if it is not a feature on many tourist routes. You might come here for the cricket at Headingley, the scene of Yorkshire and England triumphs and as many disasters. Or for the music: the International Piano Competition is one of the most important in the world, although the local vote might be for the brass band championships.

The public buildings speak of Victorian self-confidence, led by the imposing classical **Town Hall**, opened by Queen Victoria herself in 1858. The banks of the River Aire, long hidden by derelict warehouses, are now being imaginatively redeveloped. The **City Art Gallery** concentrates on English painting of the 19th and 20th centuries and on the work of English sculptors—two of the greatest of these, Henry Moore and Barbara Hepworth, both studied art here in Leeds.

Many of the Old Masters from the city's collection are on view at **Temple Newsam**, a severe Jacobean house on the eastern outskirts of Leeds, acquired by the municipality in the 1920s. The enormous park was designed by the indefatigable Capability Brown, although he might now be surprised by the golf courses.

Harewood House

Capability Brown laid out the park here, too, for Edwin Lascelles, whose family had grown rich on West Indian sugar. His descendant, the Earl of Harewood, a cousin of the queen, lives on at Harewood. The interiors represent some of the best work of Robert Adam. Everything carries the Scotsman's stamp, from ceilings to carpets, chimneypieces to mirrors. He even designed furniture for Thomas Chippendale to make. The elegant **Gallery** is the best room in the house, and provides a perfect setting for a formidable collection of pictures by Titian, El Greco, Bellini and Turner.

Bradford

If, a few years ago, you had said you were including Bradford on a holiday itinerary, you would have been met with blank incomprehension. However, the home of "worsted" (a type of tightly-woven wool) has made a major effort to attract visitors. The city is used to arrivals from overseas: so many came from India and Pakistan to work here that you might think you are on another continent—with the appropriate shopping and restaurant options.

Some of the mill buildings are models of industrial architecture. The slim Florentine chimney—smokeless now of course—at **Manningham Mill** rivals the campanile of the neo-Gothic **City Hall**. Bradford has gone out of its way to cater to the growing interest in industrial history. You can learn about wool and worsted at the **Bradford Industrial Museum**. There is a transport collection there, too, and another at the **West Yorkshire Transport Museum**.

Housed appropriately in a former cinema, the **National Museum of Photography, Film and Television** is compulsive viewing, with its lively displays and film shows on the stunning, several-storeys-high IMAX screen.

Yorkshire Dales and Pennine Moors

First-timers here or elsewhere in the industrial north are invariably amazed by the proximity of open country to inner-city streets. Windswept moors and idyllic valleys, called dales in these parts, are never far away. No coincidence this, for it was water from the high Pennines, soft for washing and fast-flowing for power, that the mills needed. When steam power replaced the waterwheels, there was plenty of coal to generate it. The towns became smoke-blackened, but the countryside stayed pristine. Climbers, pot-holers and hikers head for the hills and dales, and some of the more accessible roads can become processions of traffic on summer weekends.

Wharfedale

One of the most attractive of the valleys which cut the eastern side of the Pennines, Wharfedale gets more scenic as you head up it. You can start at **Ilkley**, a one-time Victorian spa where "curists" treated every ill from rheumatism to melancholia with a freezing plunge bath. History goes back much further. **All Saints** parish church has the shafts of three Anglo-Saxon crosses, and the **Manor House Museum** displays Roman relics from its own back yard. The Panorama Stone in the public gardens dates from the same Bronze Age period as the Twelve Apostles stone circle on the moors above the town. South-west of Ilkley, on Addingham Moor, the unique **Swastika Stone** may be a religious relic of the Iron Age. The folksong, "On Ilkla Moor baht 'at" (that is, without a hat) is practically Yorkshire's national anthem.

Brontë Country

At the top of the steep, cobbled main street of Haworth stands the parsonage where the brilliant, tragic Brontë family settled in 1820. Here at the edge of the bleak moors that so often feature in the sisters' writing, Charlotte, Emily and Anne Brontë and their brother Branwell spent most of their lives. Charlotte published *Jane Eyre* in 1847, and Emily's *Wuthering Heights* soon followed. Anne's *The Tenant of Wildfell Hall* appeared in 1848, but within months, and before their worth was recognized, Emily and Anne had died. With Branwell dead, too, Charlotte was left alone with her father.

In 1854, Charlotte Brontë married the curate, Arthur Nicholls, in **Haworth Church**, where you can see the family vault in which all were buried except Anne. Charlotte herself died only nine months after her wedding. The church is largely a later reconstruction, but the **parsonage** has been restored to the way it was in the Brontës' time. It is filled with memorabilia—look out for Branwell's portraits of the family—and the **museum wing** has a fine collection of letters and manuscripts. In the village, which can be overrun by visitors in summer, you can still find the **Black Bull**, the inn where Branwell Brontë, already ill, drank away his days.

A diversion into Airedale, the next valley to the south, takes you to **Skipton Castle**, former stronghold of the powerful Cliffords. It was restored by the energetic Lady Anne Clifford after the Civil War and survives little changed. She planted the yew tree which dominates Conduit Court. In Skipton itself, the **Craven Museum** has Bronze Age relics, including cloth from a tomb, and tells the story of the lead boom of the 18th and 19th centuries.

Much of upland Britain is a patchwork of small enclosures bounded by dry (mortarless) stone walls, home to insects, snails and hedgehogs.

The little streets of **Grassington** can be busy in summer. It was a centre for lead mining, and former miners' cottages now house the Upper Wharfedale Folk Museum. Over the river in the village of **Linton** you will see the ancient pack-horse bridge and tinkling "beck" (the local word for stream). A few miles west, **Malham** is set in rugged limestone country, and Malham Cove is a celebrated natural theatre of cliffs rising to a height of 90m (300ft). The little lake of Malham Tarn inspired Charles Kingsley to write *The Water Babies*, and it is now the centre of a 1,620-hectare (4,000-acre) nature reserve owned by the National Trust.

Wensleydale

Don't look for a river called the Wensley, although there is a sleepy village of that name with a fine old church. This green valley is watered by the River Ure. At **Aysgarth**, the river tumbles down a photogenic succession of falls crossed by an ancient bridge. In the hills to the north-east, **Bolton Castle** (not to be confused with Bolton Priory or Abbey) was one of the first fortresses to serve as a prison for Mary Queen of Scots after her flight to England in 1568. Climb the battlements for the same views she had, over Wensleydale and the high moors beyond.

Further downriver, the massive Norman keep survives at **Middleham Castle**, "Windsor of the North". Early each morning, see the stable lads and lasses taking the racehorses trained near here for exercise on the moor near the castle. It was probably the monks of nearby **Jervaulx Abbey** who started horse-breeding in this area, and the tradition survived the dissolution of the abbey in 1537. Credit for producing the first Wensleydale cheese also goes to them.

You will undoubtedly have to share the little market town of **Hawes** in

Upper Wensleydale with local farmers and their livestock every Tuesday. Any day it makes a good centre for touring and walking. The long-distance north-south trail called the Pennine Way funnels hikers through here. You can join them on a short walk to **Hardraw Force**, where water cascades 30m (99ft) over a limestone ledge. In town, the **Upper Dales Folk Museum** occupies the station building of the defunct railway. A line that does still exist, after years of running battles between preservationists and accountants, sweeps over the famous **Ribblehead Viaduct**, 14km (9 miles) (south-west, on its way across the high moors from Settle to Carlisle. Building the 24 soaring arches is said to have cost the lives of 100 men. The marshy ground beneath was supposedly stabilized with the fleece of sheep.

The best-known caves in the Pennines are reached through the village of **Clapham** (with a National Park Information Centre). A short walk leads to **Ingleborough Cave**, which goes half a mile into the hillside. Another mile up the hill you will come to the mouth of **Gaping Ghyll**, the most dramatic of Yorkshire's pot-holes, where a waterfall flings itself 110m (360ft) to the ground. For cavers, that is just the start of one of the most exciting labyrinths in Europe. Claustrophobes will cringe at the idea, and instead could make the easy climb to the summit of **Ingleborough**, 724m (2,373ft).

Upper Swaledale

In deeper and wilder valleys than those to the south, the fast-flowing Swale and its tributaries burrow under windswept fells where hardy Swaledale sheep live out all winter. Remote villages here can be cut off by snow, and the farms are some of the loneliest in Britain.

You can join Upper Swaledale by the road from Hawes over Buttertubs Pass. Head for **Keld**, a pretty greystone village where footpaths follow the Swale as it tumbles down roaring cataracts. Downstream, at **Reeth**, the river is joined by Arkle Beck flowing out of Arkengarthdale—on a grey day, this is as dark, mysterious and Nordic as its name. There is a National Park Information Centre here, as well as the Swaledale Folk Museum.

At **Richmond**, the Swale emerges from the hills and begins a gentler journey across the Vale of York. The fine old town is dominated by the Norman castle, with its 12th-century keep towering over the gatehouse. (Climb to the

Inspecting the stock— hill farmers compare notes in Swaledale (Yorkshire Dales National Park).

top for the views of the town and the moors.) Eighteenth-century prosperity left the big, sloping, cobbled market-place surrounded by good Georgian buildings, including the remarkable little **theatre** with its boxes and gallery. Built in 1788, it was closed in 1848 and became an auction room, warehouse and finally a rubbish tip, before restoration in 1962. It is one of only two theatres of the period left (the other being in Bristol).

York

History is packed into the ancient walls of this jewel of English cities. Narrow streets twist and turn like a maze around the splendid Minster, which is perhaps the greatest medieval cathedral in northern Europe. As *Eboracum*, York was the headquarters of Roman

City plan of York.

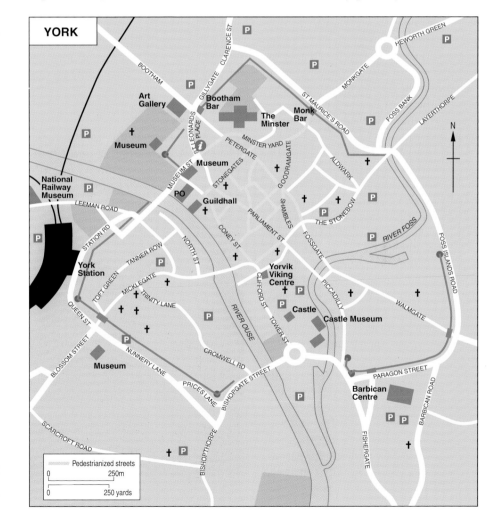

emperors—Hadrian came here in 121, Septimius Severus, born in North Africa, died in York in 211 and Constantine the Great was proclaimed emperor here in 306.

After the Romans left, the city was for a time capital of Deira, kingdom of the Angles. Then it came under the sway of Saxon Northumbria. Invading Danes captured the city in 867, calling it Jorvik (whence is derived the name York). They stayed for a century, developing the town as a trading port on the River Ouse. The Normans, for their part, expanded the walls and built two castles. In the Middle Ages, York was England's second city, grown rich from the wool trade. For long periods the affairs of the north were run from here, scarcely influenced by king or Parliament in London.

York Minster, despite its vast size, has a warmth and beauty unsurpassed in English cathedrals. A wonderful harmony of style was achieved, although it took from 1220 until about 1475 to build. Make an early visit if you can, to enjoy the atmosphere before the crowds arrive, and hope for a sunny morning to see the stone glowing honey-gold. The Minster's glory is its fabulous **stained glass**, which has somehow survived civil wars, religious turmoil and the ravages of several fires—including one in 1984 that destroyed part of the roof of the south transept. It has now been rebuilt, and the 40,000 pieces of the rose window weakened in the blaze have been painstakingly remounted. The west window dates from 1338, while the great east window was completed 70 years after that. At 186m² (2,000ft²), it is the largest expanse of such early stained glass in the world.

The 15th-century stone **rood screen** between the nave and choir supports a parade of stern statues of the English kings up to that time.

From the north transept, with its **Five Sisters Window** in grisaille, go through the vestibule to the 13th-century **Chapter House**—and look up. The vaulted wooden roof is original, and the stone carving incorporates amusing grotesques and grisly vignettes. In the **undercroft** and **crypts** you can see Norman and even Roman foundations, as well as fine displays of York silver.

Outside, take time to walk in the little streets around the Minster: Low Petergate, Stonegate, Goodramgate and

*P*ride of the north, York Minster has the biggest and finest array of medieval stained glass of any cathedral in Britain.

The Shambles, where the medieval buildings seem almost to meet overhead.

Off the modern Coppergate shopping complex, the **Jorvik Viking Centre**, a Disney-style recreation of the 9th-century Viking settlement—complete with appropriate noises and smells—is one of those tourist attractions that people love or loathe. It is not all ersatz: the actual excavations of Coppergate are on view, along with finds from the site.

The curators of the prize-winning **Castle Museum** in the former women's prison (opposite the Norman Clifford's Tower) use more orthodox methods to bring the past to life. All parts of the folk collections are fascinating, but the highlight is a 19th-century "street" with fully stocked shops, a prison, post office and fire station.

A million visitors a year descend on the **National Railway Museum** alone. Next to the railway station, former engine sheds house gleaming locomotives from the earliest days right up to the last mighty behemoths produced before boring diesel and electric power took over. A prize exhibit is the *Mallard*, a world record-breaker at 203kph (126mph) in the 1930s. Carriages on show include Queen Victoria's lush, plush saloon car.

Beverley

They love their horse racing in these parts, and Beverley is no exception. This charming market town, predictably enough, has one of Yorkshire's most attractive courses. While you are here, be sure to see the **Minster**, bigger and more magnificent than some cathedrals. The stone carving of the **Percy tomb** is exceptionally beautiful, as is the wood carving of the **misericords**, all 68 of them—the greatest number in any English church.

Harrogate

An elegant spa which is now a leading conference centre, this attractive town managed to make the change without losing its appeal. In fact, the extra vitality and facilities have added to Harrogate's advantages, both as a destination and as a touring base.

Parks and flower gardens everywhere, hosts of small shops both antique and boutique, and a variety of restaurants and tearooms make it perfect for idling. The dignified **Royal Pump Room** (1842) now houses a museum of local history and dress.

Ripon

One of England's smaller cities, Ripon has one of its smaller cathedrals, a 12th- to 15th-century edifice on Saxon

---

Walking York

Narrow streets, traffic and parking limitations will test your sanity if you try to drive, and York is the perfect size to see on foot anyway. You can orient yourself and enjoy the views by walking the **city walls**, a 5km (3-mile) circuit. If you only go part of the way, be sure to include the section nearest to the Minster, between Bootham Bar and Monk Bar. (No drinks at these "bars": they are the old city gates.) The little streets have kept their medieval names, most derived from the trades that were practised there: The Shambles (from Flesh-ammels, or slaughterhouses; and Colliergate, the street of the charcoal dealers ("gate" coming from the Norse word for street). In the short Whip-ma-Whop-ma-gate, petty criminals were tied to a post and given a public thrashing.

foundations. The local woodcarvers' guild created the striking Perpendicular choir stalls. Notice the misericords under the seats, with portraits of Samson and Jonah and a fox and geese. Every night at 9 p.m. the City Hornblower in tricorn hat "sets the watch", as he has, so they say, for 1,000 years.

Fountains Abbey

The poignantly beautiful ruins of what was once the greatest monastery in England stand in wooded Skelldale near Ripon. Fountains Abbey was begun in the 12th century, and profits from wool enabled the Cistercian monks to buy more farms, employ farm

workers—and to build on a noble scale. Their **church** extends for a considerable 110m (360ft), its walls remarkably complete. At the east end, the remains of the soaring 13th-century **Chapel of the Nine Altars** make a tremendous impression.

Walk round the cloisters with a ground plan, to see how such a complex

In 1132, 13 Cistercian monks opted for a life of austerity on the banks of the Skell. Paradoxically, Fountains Abbey became one of the richest in the land.

community lived. The **lay brothers' refectory** is amazingly preserved: their dormitory would have been on the floor above. The opulence of such religious houses was in the end to lead to their downfall, when Henry VIII dissolved them and sold their property.

A lot of the credit for the survival of so much of Fountains Abbey goes to the 18th-century landowner William Aislabie, who bought the ruins—a convenient source of stone—and protected them from dispersal. (Some of the stone had already gone into Fountains Hall nearby.) His father John established the formal gardens of **Studley Royal**, diverting the River Skell into water gardens and building classical temples and follies. The gardens and deer park make a perfect approach to the abbey, and are now all in the care of the National Trust.

Castle Howard
(*near Malton*)

If it looks familiar, that's probably because it *is* familiar as the setting for the British TV production of *Brideshead Revisited*. In real life the Howard family, not the Marchmains, reside here.

Charles Howard, the 3rd Earl of Carlisle, chose Sir John Vanbrugh to design the place in 1699, which was curious, because Vanbrugh was a playwright, not an architect. He in turn picked Nicholas Hawksmoor, a pupil of Wren, as clerk of works and together they produced this baroque tour de force. Everything is on a monumental scale, outside and in, from the Great Hall, with its painted dome, to the vaulted Antique Passage, a gallery of classical statuary.

Walk in the vast park and gardens to the haunting Mausoleum and Temple of The Four Winds. The stables house a notable **costume museum**.

The North York Moors

North of York and the lush green Vale of Pickering, the land rises suddenly to a surprisingly wild plateau. There is a scattering of villages in the hills and deep valleys that cut through the heather-covered uplands. Bronze and Iron Age stone circles suggest that people then may have preferred the vulnerability of the open moors to the dangers that lurked in lowland forests. This is good walking country: one of England's long-distance trails follows the western and northern heights for 145km (90 miles). The Romans marched this way too, and you can still trace sections of their road across Wheeldale Moor. Some more recent roads are remarkably steep and a test for lungs and cars alike.

Thirsk, below the western edge of the moors, makes a possible starting point. The town is a magnet in itself for fans of the writer-vet James Herriot, whose stories are set here and in the countryside around.

The road east climbs to the top of **Sutton Bank**, a 214m (700ft) escarpment irresistible to hang-glider aces, who leap off into the prevailing south-west wind.

Helmsley is one of North Yorkshire's prettiest towns, with a big market square and ruined Norman castle. But connoisseurs of romantic ruins will travel on for a couple of miles to the glorious shell of **Rievaulx Abbey** (pronounced "reevo") in Ryedale. Like Fountains, it was a rich Cistercian monastery dating from the 12th century and dissolved in the 16th. The lofty

*T*he graceful Humber Bridge was unkindly said to go from "nowhere to nowhere" when it opened. There's plenty of traffic now.

choir (1225) soars over a whole range of remains of the monastery's domestic buildings. For a heart-stopping view, climb to **Rievaulx Terrace**, above the ruins to the east.

The market town of **Pickering** is a good base for exploring the eastern moors. Before heading off, you can get a drink or a snack in one of the friendly pubs. Take a look in the church to see the rare 15th-century wall paintings that were found beneath layers of whitewash. One scene shows the murder of 9th-century King Edward the Martyr. The **Beck Isle Museum** celebrates Victorian ingenuity with exhibits that range from a foot-powered lemon squeezer to "Moule's Automatic Earth Closet".

The North Yorkshire Coast

Scarborough enjoys a magnificent setting, on two bays separated by a headland crowned by a **Norman castle**. From its walls, you can look out over the old town and fishing harbour of **South Bay**, 90m (300ft) below. Make your way there, down the steep streets and steps, and you'll find all the fun of the fair, from cockle stalls to bingo halls. Seabathing began in Scarborough in the mid-18th century, as early as anywhere else in Britain. Quite a masochistic exercise, you may think, if you test the water temperature.

Northward up the coast, **Robin Hood's Bay** is a former fishing (and smuggling) village, now a popular and crowded resort. The houses squeeze into a picturesque cove and up its steep slopes, trying to avoid the fate of many along this shore which have been washed away by the encroaching sea.

Whitby is the gem of the north-east coast. Its pretty red-roofed houses are stacked up the steep sides of the busy harbour, where the River Esk reaches the sea. Walk through the old town and, if you have the energy, do as the parishioners have to, and climb the 199 Church Stairs to **St Mary's Church** at the top of East Cliff. Up there on the breezy heights, you will be drawn to the gaunt ruins of 13th-century **Whitby Abbey**, founded in 657 by St Hilda for both monks and nuns.

The explorer Captain James Cook served an apprenticeship in Whitby, and it was from here that he sailed for

Captain James Cook's gaze is turned landwards for a change, towards Whitby's medieval abbey. The great explorer sailed from here on his first expedition.

The Great Navigator

Like many English sailors before and since, James Cook came from the Cleveland coast of north-east England. With eight years' experience aboard North Sea traders carrying Tyne coal to London and lumber from the Baltic, he volunteered for the Royal Navy. Rapidly recognized for superb seamanship, he was given his first command at the age of 29 and saw action with Wolfe at Quebec. When peace came, he made his name by accurately surveying the coasts of Newfoundland and Labrador.

In 1768, the Royal Society appointed him to carry some of their members to Tahiti, and then to establish whether there was a *Terra Australis*, a great southern continent. He sailed from the port of Whitby which he knew so well from his apprentice days, in the Whitby-built *Endeavour*. Not only was the expedition carried safely to Tahiti (where Cook appears to have been unique in resisting the attractions of free-loving Tahitian women), but the whole coast of New Zealand was charted for the first time. Then Cook made a landfall on the south-east coast of Australia and charted the east coast including the hazardous Great Barrier Reef.

Remarkably, through Cook's insistence on a varied diet, not a single member of his crew died of scurvy, which usually claimed a large fraction of the crews of such long voyages.

During a second amazing expedition, he sailed round the world further south than anyone had done before. On his third, in 1776–77, he explored the coasts of Oregon, Alaska and eastern Siberia before making a fatal landing on the island of Hawaii in 1779, when he was killed by the local Polynesians. He was 50, and he left a new map of the world.

Tahiti in the locally built *Endeavour*. The house in Grape Lane where he lived is now the **Captain Cook Memorial Museum**. The municipal museum also displays memorabilia of Cook and other local sailors.

From Whitby, you can drive up the coast through Runswick to the charming fishing village of **Staithes** (pronounced "steers"). Park your car at the top of the cliff and make the precipitous descent on foot; although the road is paved, your car might never make it back up again. At the bottom, on the sea's edge, is the higgledy-piggledy cluster of stone cottages, beloved of local Sunday painters.

Whitby also offers a glorious drive across the gorse- and heather-clad moors via Grosmont and Castleton to **Guisborough**, a cheerful market town dominated by the ruins of an Augustinian priory.

Lake District

The most popular scenic region of England draws 12 million visitors a year. Only 56km (35 miles) across and scarcely more from north to south, its astonishingly varied landscapes and countless sights are so concentrated that you could spend a lifetime exploring them. Glance at a map and you will see that the lakes radiate roughly to the points of the compass. They formed at the end of the Ice Age when the rivers running off a dome of ancient rocks were blocked by glacial debris. Even the largest, Lake Windermere, is only 16km (10 miles) long, and the mountains are hardly on an alpine scale. Yet the scenery can be just as awe-inspiring.

There are few roads, so weekend and summer traffic can be reduced to a crawl. In any case, the most beautiful parts of the Lake District can only be reached by walking. Fortunately, plenty of short walks suggest themselves: if you intend to make longer hikes make sure you prepare for severe weather. This is, by the way, one of the wettest parts of England.

Kendal

A gateway to the Lakes, the market town of Kendal made its name for woollen cloth, then shoes. Not much is left of the castle, birthplace of Catherine Parr, Henry VIII's last wife. The portrait painter George Romney (1734–1802) worked in Kendal before leaving for London, fame and fortune. The **Abbot Hall Art Gallery**, in a Georgian house by the river, displays several of his works, and fine watercolours by other artists who loved the Lakes. The stables of the house have been converted into a Museum of Lakeland Life.

Windermere

On the long narrow lake of the same name, Windermere town merges with busy Bowness—two fixtures on the holiday circuit. The scenery is gentle rather than dramatic. Consequently, the climb up **Orrest Head** (230m/754ft), the classic lookout view, is not too hard. Windermere's **Steamboat Museum** exhibits some fine old craft, but there are plenty still in action to take you for a cruise. At times there are so many boats on the water you might think you could walk to the other side. In fact, a car ferry runs from Bowness, and if you were brought up on *Peter Rabbit* and the rest of the stories of Beatrix Potter

279

In the 1720s Daniel Defoe called the Lake District scenery "barren and frightful". Yet by 1800, writers and artists were in raptures over the same landscape.

(1866–1943), you might like to take it. From the landing stage on the west side of the lake, it is only a couple of miles to **Hill Top**, the farm cottage near the little lake of Esthwaite Water where the writer lived in the early 1900s.

Lakeland is for ever associated with the poet William Wordsworth. From 1779 until 1787 he went to school at **Hawkshead**, near the head of Esthwaite Water. Apart from the crowds of literary tourists on his trail, the village probably looks much as it did then, though the school is now a museum. You can still see the desk on which the poet carved his initials. There is a fine view from Hawkshead Hill, and good walking can be found in Grizedale Forest.

Coniston

Set below the 804m (2,635ft) Old Man of Coniston, this is a fine centre for climbing and walking, but take care if you go exploring in the old copper mines near the village. The little lake of **Tarn Hows**, 3km (2 miles) to the northeast, is a favourite excursion.

The writer and art historian John Ruskin is buried in Coniston churchyard, and if you take the road along the east side of Coniston Water you can visit his house, **Brantwood**. Ruskin lived here from 1871 until he died in 1900, preaching his gospel of beauty and of the value of hand-made things. He was a champion of the Pre-Raphaelites, and

some of their work—and his own—is still in the house.

Ambleside

Walkers and climbers crowd the town, a natural centre for the southern Lakes. Nearby is a Roman fort: the east-west road of the Romans went through here on its way to Wrynose and the steep Hardknott Pass. Some would like to believe that the rush-bearing ceremony

and floral procession held here in July has come down from Roman times, but a medieval origin is more likely.

Not quite so old, **Bridge House** is a curiosity built entirely over a river—not, as the joke goes, by a canny Scot to avoid ground rent, but as an 18th-century summer-house. The building has the distinction of being the National Trust's oldest information centre and its smallest shop.

A short walk will take you to the waterfall of **Stock Ghyll Force**, but for the more energetic who want to forge on farther, there are no limits except time, equipment and weather. The truly fit locals go in for fell running, racing up and—even more hazardously—down the steep hill-sides.

Although William Wordsworth lived just north of Ambleside at **Rydal Mount** from 1813 until his death in 1850, the crowds of literary pilgrims go on a little further, to **Grasmere**. Just outside the village and near Grasmere Lake lies their objective: white **Dove Cottage**, where the poet set up house with his sister, Dorothy, then with his wife and growing family, from 1799 to 1808. The little cottage shows how simply the penurious Wordsworths lived. The barn opposite is now a museum of the life and times of Wordsworth and his friend Samuel Taylor Coleridge. Typical Lakeland events feature at Grasmere Sports festival, held in mid-August. Crowds pour in to see fell races, local styles of wrestling and "trailing", in which hounds follow a scent trail laid across open country.

Keswick

The kingpin of the northern lakes lies below the towering mass of Skiddaw. Keswick retains its charm while pursuing a long-standing devotion to the tourist business. Here, as elsewhere in Lakeland, it started with the poets: first Coleridge, then Southey lived at **Greta Hall**, now part of a school. The quaint **Pencil Museum** recalls the much earlier industry of graphite mining, and **Fitz Park Museum** exhibits range from local geology to literary manuscripts by Keswick's famous residents, to paintings by Ruskin and Turner. Right in the centre, **Moot Hall** (1813), with its odd one-handed clock, now houses a useful information centre.

*T*he English Lake District has captivated poets and painters since Wordsworth lived here, and draws countless visitors today.

The walks near Keswick are superb. **Castle Head** just to the south gives a glorious view of **Derwentwater**, where wooded slopes and rocky crags descend to the shore. The lakeside road leads to steep-sided **Borrowdale**, celebrated as one of the most beautiful valleys of them all. You can take the trail to the famous viewpoint of **Friar's Crag**, or make a side-trip over Ashness Bridge through woods and past grazing sheep to prospects that sent the Romantic poets into rhapsodies.

The road through Borrowdale climbs steeply to the top of **Honister Pass**, where black-faced sheep pick their way through forbiddingly rocky terrain. From here, 359m (1,176ft) up, there is a vigorous 5km (3-mile) walk south to the top of **Great Gable** (899m/2,949ft), affording one of the finest panoramas in England.

Cockermouth

The handsome pink Georgian house in Main Street, **Wordsworth House**, was where William was born in 1770. The elegant furnishings, though not family originals, are typical of the time. While admiring the Turner painting, the Sheraton table and Hepplewhite chairs in the dining room, you may be drawn by appetizing smells to the copper-gleaming kitchen, where cooks in costume make cakes for the tearoom.

It is pleasant to walk through the town, with its colourfully painted houses, to the castle, largely in ruins. Cockermouth has more claims to fame than the Wordsworths. Fletcher Christian, leader of the mutiny on the *Bounty*, and John Dalton, who formulated the atomic theory, were born on the outskirts of Cockermouth. And the town gave its name to the cocker spaniel.

You can return to Keswick by way of the quite gentle Whinlatter Pass, which transits Thornthwaite Forest. The most direct route follows the west side of **Bassenthwaite Lake**. The road was built despite the protests of conservationists, who said it would destroy the atmosphere. In hindsight, they were right, and this most northerly of the lakes is best seen from the east side, at the foot of Skiddaw.

Ullswater

The favourite lake of many, Ullswater snakes south between higher and higher fells. Boats crowd the water, and roads along the shore can be congested, too. The roads do not make a complete circuit, so to escape the traffic, walk the shore path between **Howtown** and **Glenridding**. If you don't want to undertake that 10km (6-mile) hike, try one of the motor launches that cruise the lake, touching at all the main points. From Glenridding or nearby Patterdale, hardy hikers set out to climb **Helvellyn**, at 951m (3,118ft) not the highest, but arguably the most striking, of the Lakeland peaks. It is about 5km (3 miles) to the top, a trek that takes some two hours. No actual climbing is involved on this route, but you need to be equipped for fell walking, and to have a good head for heights on the 2km (1-mile) long, sharp Striding Edge that leads to the top. Check the weather forecast before you set out, and take advice from the National Park Information Centre at Glenridding.

Penrith, a few miles north-east of Ullswater, is practically out of the Lake District, although it can make a useful base. The historic market town is within striking distance of Scotland—as Scots raiders proved whenever they sacked it in the Middle Ages. The view from **Penrith Beacon** west to the lakes is worth the walk up, whether this is your first or last look.

Carlisle

The capital of Cumbria and a railway junction, this busy industrial centre was England's fortress at the western end of the border. Before that it was Rome's—Hadrian's Wall passes nearby. Such a frontier position meant that Carlisle had 17 of the most violent centuries of any English city, right up to 1745 when Bonnie Prince Charlie's army captured the town and held it for a few weeks.

The **castle** has a suitably grim look, especially the massive Norman keep where you will be shown marks cut in the walls by some of the many prisoners held here. None were made by the most famous, Mary Queen of Scots, who had her quarters in another tower when she was confined here in 1568.

Carlisle's **cathedral** dates in part from the 12th century, but much of it was in ruins by the time a Scottish army tore a large part down during the Civil War. So now, though restored, it is England's smallest cathedral, but there is some fine wood-carving to be seen, and original painting on the backs of the 15th-century choir stalls.

The North-East

Nothing happened by halves up here in a part of England much nearer Edinburgh than London. There was almost perpetual war or raiding across the Scottish border, from Roman times until the Union of the Crowns. Dukes and prince-bishops reigned like kings with scarcely a glance to the south. When industry came, it came in an extreme form, but most of the land was left as wild and remote as ever. The economic wind can blow as cold as the one off the North Sea, but the people have a sense of humour second to none—if you can understand the accent.

Durham

The setting is one of the most thrilling in Britain. The River Wear makes such a great bend that it almost cuts off a steep bluff of sandstone, like a moat. Crowning its wooded banks, the magnificent cathedral and the castle face each other across Palace Green. It makes a sight worth gazing on from every direction.

Monks fleeing from Viking raids on Lindisfarne eventually ended up in

Durham in 995, carrying the coffin and remains of St Cuthbert. The church they built as his shrine was replaced by the present Norman **cathedral**, begun in 1093. This masterpiece creates an impression of enormous strength and antiquity. The bronze Sanctuary Knocker on the North Door is a replica of the one (in the Treasury) to which criminals once clung to claim immunity from pursuers. Inside are several architectural "firsts": the ribbed stone vaulting of the choir roof, earliest in northern Europe, and the pointed transverse arches of the nave, the first hint of Gothic in England. The nave itself is lined with massive columns deeply cut with geometric designs.

St Cuthbert's shrine lies behind the high altar, but parts of his wooden coffin, carved in the 7th century, are in the **Treasury**, off the fine 14th-century cloisters. The tomb of the equally revered Venerable Bede, the famous 8th-century historian, is in the wonderfully light, 12th-century **Galilee Chapel**. The Washington family came from these parts, too, as you will be reminded, by a plaque in the cloisters to Prior John Washington (1416–46), "whose family has won an everlasting name in lands to him unknown".

The bishops of Durham were so powerful that they ruled not only the church but the county, as prince-bishops. Granted the right to keep an army, they ran a kind of buffer state

*D*urham Cathedral is *a fine example of Norman and Gothic; the rose window in the Chapel of the Nine Altars was remodelled in the 18th century.*

against the Scots. The headquarters of these potentates, the Norman **castle**, stands on the peninsula, completing its defences. Now restored, it belongs to Durham University, but the chapel, Norman gallery, Great Hall and huge kitchens are open to the public.

To see how modern architects meet the challenge, stroll on to **Kingsgate** footbridge (1962) from Palace Green. From the bridge itself, you can see the university's Dunelm House. Five minutes from the centre of the city on Elvet Hill, the **Oriental Museum** is also part of the university. This is modern, pleasant and small enough for you to take in most of the outstanding pieces, from the Near and Far East, that are on display.

Beamish

The **Open Air Museum** here has won many awards for its re-creation of the

In 1829, six Quakers set up the coal-exporting community of Middlesbrough. Two years later iron was discovered in the Cleveland Hills, and the city boomed.

dominates: Billingham has a main plant of mighty I C I; Middlesbrough, on the opposite bank, was an important centre of shipbuilding and the steel industry. The history of transport was changed in 1825 when George Stephenson's *Locomotion* pulled the first-ever passenger train from Stockton-on-Tees to **Darlington** at the hair-raising speed of 19kph (12mph). That actual locomotive is on show, along with many more relics, in Darlington's **Railway Centre and Museum**.

At **Barnard Castle**, the land begins to rise towards the High Pennines. At the west end of town stands a huge 19th-century French château, the **Bowes Museum**. John Bowes and his wife, a French actress, formed a superb collection of art works, ceramics and furniture, but sadly they both died before they could see their dream museum completed. Don't miss the paintings by El Greco, Goya and Boucher, and the magnificent tapestries.

Further up the Tees valley is the picturesque little town of **Middleton-in-Teesdale**, a centre for walking. Head especially for some of the most spectacular waterfalls in England, **High Force** and **Caldron Snout**.

town and country scene at the end of the 19th century. There is a working farm, a drift mine and miners' cottages and the whole street scene with horse-drawn vehicles, a pub, a bakery and shops of the period.

Tees Valley

If you like contrasts, travel up the valley of the Tees, south of Durham. Near the coast, industry at its heaviest

Newcastle-upon-Tyne

The bridges over the Tyne gorge are a fine sight as you approach from the south. Newcastle has come a long way since it was a fort near the end of Hadrian's Wall. The "new" castle in the name is the one the Normans built in 1080. For centuries Newcastle was engaged in warfare with the Scots. A port for coal exports (hence the expression "coals to Newcastle"), the town experienced explosive growth as a shipbuilding and engineering centre. Recently it has been hard-hit by the decline of heavy industry, but the "Geordies" with their sing-song accent are irrepressible.

You can still find vestiges of the medieval town near the quayside, and the Victorians gave Newcastle a fine city centre. Queen Victoria opened the vast central railway station in 1850. The **Laing Art Gallery** has good collections of the decorative arts and of British painting from the 18th-century portraitists to modern times.

The Northumberland Coast

The north-east has its share of seaside resorts, although sea bathing is only for the hardy. The coast is visually impressive and marked by formidable fortresses like the dramatic ruin of **Warkworth.** Most were built, or at some time held, by members of the powerful Percy family, which wrote its own rules in these remote lands for most of the Middle Ages.

Alnwick (pronounced "annick") is a picturesque old town dominated by a huge castle, the seat of the Percys, who were earls and later dukes of Northumberland. It fell into ruin before 1600, so today's fine sight is a restoration. The 19th-century Italian Renaissance-style interior is worth a look for curiosity value and paintings by Titian, Canaletto, Van Dyck and Turner. There is an archaeological museum in the Postern Tower, with Roman objects

Hadrian's Wall

The greatest testimony to the Roman presence in Britain snakes for 118km (73 miles) across the width of northern England. Still as much as 4m (14ft) high in places, and faced with dressed square stones, the wall once stood 6m (21ft) high, including its battlements. Add to that a ditch on the north side and you have an impressive barrier. The Emperor Hadrian had the wall built to mark and defend the north-west extremity of Rome's empire. He actually came to Britain himself in the year 122 and seems to have decided on a strategy of active defence, not so much using the wall as if it were a castle but sending cavalry out from its forts to cut off any attackers.

There was a "milecastle" every Roman mile (1,480m/1,620yds), and 17 larger forts stood 5–11km (3–7 miles) apart. The garrisons ranged from 500 to 1,000 men. Each fort had its own bath house and steam rooms, which may have gone some way to make up for the harsh climate. It is strange to think of soldiers from the Mediterranean serving on these bleak moors—it can hardly have been a popular assignment.

You can walk along the line of the wall today, and roads follow quite near it for most of the way for those without the time or energy. The best-preserved parts are in the middle, near **Winshields Crags**, where the wall climbs to 375m (1,230ft) above sea level. The most impressive of the forts, **Housesteads**, is here, too: you can see the outline of storehouses, hospital, even latrines. The model in the museum gives a still clearer idea. East, at **Chesters**, are the elaborate bath houses used by the cavalry who were stationed here on and off until the wall was finally abandoned in about 383.

that will be of interest if you have visited Hadrian's Wall.

Up the coast at Seahouses, you can vary the diet of castles with a boat ride out to the **Farne Islands**, a couple of dozen rocky islets that were once the haunt of hermits, and now of seals and seabirds. The Victorian heroine Grace Darling was 23 when she rowed out with her father, then keeper of the Longstone Lighthouse on one of the more remote islands, to rescue the survivors from a shipwreck. The boat is now in a little museum in **Bamburgh**, where another massive Norman castle dominates the shore. You will have a fine view of the Farne Islands from its upper terraces.

It was the Newcastle industrialist Lord Armstrong who paid for the late 19th-century restoration of Bamburgh Castle. His remarkable house, **Cragside**, lies inland near the little market town of Rothbury, and is a triumph of Pre-Raphaelite decoration allied to Victorian technology. This was the first house in the world to be lit by electricity, and it also has central heating and a lift. The fascinating power-houses which provided the energy for all this innovation have been restored.

Off the coast north of Bamburgh, low-lying **Lindisfarne**, or Holy Island, was one of the cradles of Christianity in Britain. A 5km (3-mile) causeway connects the isle to the mainland, but make sure you consult the tide tables at either end; you cannot cross from two hours before high tide to at least three hours after. St Aidan came here from Iona in 635 to convert the people of Northumbria. St Cuthbert, Lindisfarne's bishop, was buried here until Viking raiders forced the monks to flee, carrying his

coffin with them (*see* page 284). You can see the ruins of the later Norman priory and a church, and also visit the castle, built in 1550 and restored by Lutyens in 1902.

The border town of **Berwick-upon-Tweed** looks well worn within its walls, which are 16th century, unusually late. This place was long a bone of contention between England and Scotland, being sold, sacked, ransomed or captured by one side or other at least 13 times in the Middle Ages. Finally accepted as English, it was still looked on as separate and used to be listed specially in Acts of Parliament. Berwick claims, bizarrely enough, to be at war with Russia, having been listed in the declaration of the Crimean War but not in the peace treaty!

St Aidan came from Iona in 635 to found a monastery on Lindisfarne island as a base for converting the pagan Northumbrians.

A World of Difference

Constitutionally entwined with England for nearly three centuries, Scotland is in many ways still a nation unto itself, with its own bank-notes and special postage stamps (Bank of England notes and plain UK stamps are valid as well), independent educational and judicial systems and its own church. Added to that, the Scots quite often speak in ways the English find hard to decipher. Scotland's economy received a welcome boost from North Sea oil, and the electronics industry has partly filled the gaps left by the decline of ship-building and other heavy engineering. Tourism is a major earner, trading on Scotland's special attractions, from kilts and bagpipes to salmon-fishing and whisky.

Edinburgh

Proud, cultured and increasingly lively, Scotland's capital surprises and pleases—particularly when the sun shines. International attention focuses on the city for three weeks every summer, when the August–September Edinburgh Festival showcases innovative dance, opera, theatre and music from around the world—fringe events, too—with performances in every possible venue, including in the street.

In the romantic loneliness of Scotland's far north, the ruins of Varrich Castle overlook the Kyle of Tongue.

Most of Edinburgh's principal sights are located within easy walking distance of each other.

Edinburgh Castle

The castle dominates the city from its great crag, the stump of an extinct volcano. It was a royal residence from the 11th century, and medieval Edinburgh grew up along the ridge that runs from here to Holyrood. Kilted guards from the Royal Scots Regiment are posted by the gate at the end of the Esplanade, the parade ground where the Military Tattoo is held. On **Half-Moon Battery** you will see the cannon which is fired every weekday at 1 p.m. Why not at noon? "Remember where you are", quip the guides. "One shot at one o'clock is much cheaper than 12 at noon."

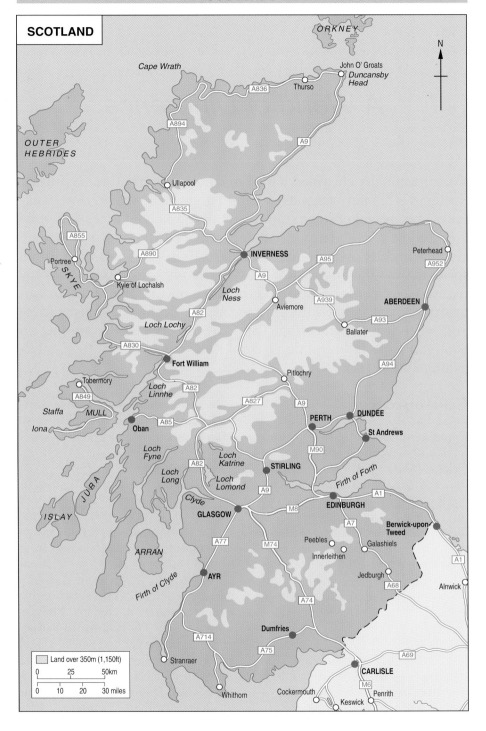

SCOTLAND

N

ORKNEY

Cape Wrath

Duncansby Head
John O' Groats
A836
Thurso

A894

A9

OUTER HEBRIDES

Ullapool

A835

A855

A890
INVERNESS
Peterhead
Portree
A95
A952
SKYE
A9
Kyle of Lochalsh
Loch Ness
ABERDEEN
A82
Aviemore
A939
Loch Lochy
A93
Ballater

A830

A94
Fort William
Pitlochry
Tobermory
A82
Loch Linnhe
A827
A849
A9
Staffa MULL
A85
PERTH
DUNDEE
Iona
Oban
St Andrews

Loch Fyne
Loch Katrine
STIRLING
A82
M90
Loch Long
JURA
Loch Lomond
Firth of Forth
A9
A1
Clyde
ISLAY
M8
EDINBURGH
GLASGOW
A7
Berwick-upon-Tweed
A77
M74
Peebles
Galashiels
ARRAN
Innerleithen
A1
Jedburgh
AYR
A68
Alnwick
A74

Firth of Clyde
Dumfries
A714
A75
A69
Stranraer
CARLISLE
M6
Whithorn
Cockermouth
Penrith
Keswick

Land over 350m (1,150ft)

0   25   50km

0   10   20   30 miles

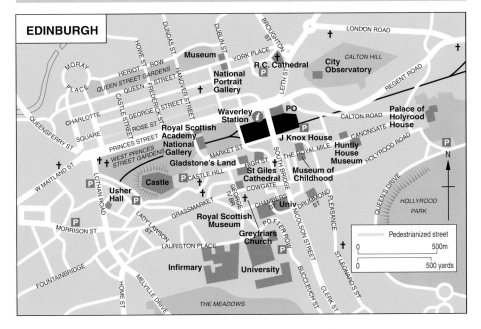

EDINBURGH

City plan of Edinburgh.

Scotland (left).

Tiny **St Margaret's Chapel**, only 8m (26ft) by 3m (10ft), may well be the oldest building in Edinburgh. Honouring the saintly Queen Margaret who died in 1093, it has survived every assault on the fortress. It was also the only structure spared when Robert Bruce captured the castle from the English in 1313. The terrace in front of the chapel commands one of the best views over the crescents and squares of the Georgian New Town.

The residential section of the castle faces Crown Square. On the east side, the **royal apartments** include the claustrophobic little chamber where Mary Queen of Scots gave birth to the future James VI (James I of England) in 1566. The Crown Chamber in the same building houses the **Honours of Scotland**—the ancient Scottish crown jewels, comprising crown, sceptre and sword. Among the oldest crown jewels in Europe, they were successfully hidden from Oliver Cromwell, who destroyed all the royal regalia he could lay his hands on.

On the south side of Crown Square, the **Great Hall** of 1502 has one of Britain's finest hammerbeam roofs, while the military museums to the west highlight the history of Scotland's regiments. Another relic of the military past can be seen in the old prisons below the Crown Square building: **Mons Meg**, a massive cannon given to James II of Scotland in the 15th century. He was killed by an exploding cannon, and this one burst too, when firing a royal salute in 1680.

The Royal Mile

A little more than a mile—Scottish miles were longer—this is a gentle downhill stroll along the Old Town's famous main street from the castle to The Palace of Holyroodhouse. Start near the top with a visit to the **Camera Obscura**, in the Outlook Tower. This piece of Victorian technology projects a 360-degree view of the living, moving city on to a white table—when the weather is bright enough.

The street and the wynds (alleys) and courtyards leading off the Mile must have been smelly and hazardous in the days when citizens threw the contents of their chamber-pots out of the windows. Some of the 17th-century tenements were a surprising six storeys high. One of these, **Gladstone's Land**, has been beautifully restored as a shop, with living quarters (open to view) on the first floor. The painted ceilings are original, and the furniture is typical of the period.

Take a detour down across George IV Bridge to see the statue of **Greyfriars Bobby**. This famous Skye terrier waited faithfully by his master's graveside in Greyfriars Churchyard for 14 years, until he died of old age himself in 1872. In adjoining Chambers Street, the **Royal Scottish Museum** features world arts and crafts, science and the history of transport.

Back on the Royal Mile, **St Giles Cathedral** doesn't look its age (15th

century). Refaced in the 19th century, the High Kirk of Scotland retains its famous spire, the **Crown of St Giles**, a replica in stone of the Scottish crown. The present church is probably the third on the site. Elements survive from the previous, Norman, structure—notably the piers supporting the central tower. But most of the side chapels were destroyed in the Reformation, along with the relic and statue of St Giles. The Reformer John Knox was minister here: his statue is inside the church. The 1911 **Thistle Chapel** has a stall for the sovereign and one for each of the 16 Knights of the Thistle, Scotland's oldest order of chivalry.

Further down the Royal Mile, here called High Street, the **Museum of Childhood** displays all kinds of toys and games. The 15th-century **John Knox House**, now a museum of Knox's life and times, may not itself have had much to do with the great reformer.

*M*onument to patience: Bobby the terrier waited by his master's grave in Greyfriars churchyard for 14 years.

Double Life

Genteel though their reputation may be, Edinburgh's citizens can still relish stories of villains of the city's past. Brodie's Close in the Old Town recalls one: Deacon Brodie was a respected city official and carpenter by day, a burglar by night. Finally arrested in 1788 and condemned to be hanged, he thought to cheat death by wearing a steel collar under his shirt. He was wrong, the gallows which he himself had designed, worked. Brodie's life inspired Edinburgh writer Robert Louis Stevenson's *Dr Jekyll and Mr Hyde*.

The **Palace of Holyroodhouse** began life as a guest residence for the adjacent abbey. Around 1500, James IV began the alterations that transformed the residence into a royal palace. The Reformation and Civil War took their toll, and Charles II gave the order to rebuild. His architect, Sir William Bruce, incorporated part of James IV's building in a new Palladian design. The so-called **Historic Apartments** include the rooms occupied by Mary Queen of Scots. A plaque marks the spot where her secretary, Rizzio, was stabbed to death at the instigation of her husband, Lord Darnley.

New Town

As old Edinburgh became increasingly crowded and unhealthy, pressure for expansion mounted. Architect James Craig was still in his twenties when he won a competition to design a new residential area in 1767. He proposed a rectangular grid of streets, with spacious terraces linking two squares (Charlotte and St Andrew). It was Craig's idea to build on only one side of Princes and Queen streets, the outer streets of the grid.

A fetid stretch of water called Nor' Loch was drained and turned into **Princes Street Gardens**, the city's attractive centrepiece for more than two centuries now. The pinnacled **Scott Monument** was added to the cityscape in the 1840s. You can climb to the top—287 narrow steps wind their way up—for a wide-angle view of the gardens (see the huge floral clock).

A sloping road called the Mound crosses the gardens. The **National Gallery of Scotland**, to one side, houses a distinguished collection. A pleasure to visit, the museum is manageable in size, and all the works are laid out in chronological order. Look for Velázquez's striking *Old Woman Cooking Eggs*, the Rembrandt portraits and Van Dyck's early *Lomellini Family*, with its superb detail of costume. Gainsborough's ravishing *The Honourable Mrs Graham*, Reynolds' *Ladies Waldegrave* and several works by Edinburgh's own Sir Henry Raeburn take pride of place among the British portraits.

At first the New Town began to grow piecemeal, but Robert Adam set an

The Body Snatchers

Edinburgh's famous medical schools attracted so many students in the early 19th century that they had a problem in obtaining enough bodies for dissection in anatomy classes. William Burke and William Hare set about filling the need, by digging up recently buried corpses. When extraordinary measures to defend new graves made this sort of "resurrection" too hazardous, they turned to murder. Travellers were lured into Hare's lodging house, filled with drink and suffocated. Eventually caught, Hare turned king's evidence and incriminated Burke, who was hanged in 1829.

example of unified development in noble **Charlotte Square**. The Georgian house at **No. 7** has been restored and furnished in the style of the period. Take a look at the marvellous old medicine chest and antique sanitary arrangements in the bedchamber, and the kitchens and National Trust for Scotland shop downstairs.

Along Inverleith Row are the 30-hectare (75-acre) **Royal Botanic Gardens**. These have one of the world's best rhododendron collections, huge plant houses and a great, meticulously tended rock garden.

At the famous **Zoo** in the western suburb of Corstorphine, the park setting and lack of bars allow both visitors and animals to get a good, long look at each other.

Firth of Forth

Hopetoun House, an outstanding country manor on the south shore of the Forth, preserves its original furnishings and paintings. The core of the building, completed in 1703 to Sir William Bruce's design, was expanded and altered by William Adam, beginning around 1720. After William's death in 1748, the work went forward under the talented supervision of his sons Robert and James, who had already begun to decorate the interior. The **Yellow** and

A triumph of 19th-century engineering, the railway bridge over the Firth of Forth was built to last.

Red Drawing Rooms, with gilded plasterwork and specially commissioned furniture, are fine early examples of the Adam style.

Not far from here are the huge spans of the **Forth Bridges**, road and rail, that lead to the north. Cross over, if you have enough time, to the lovely little town of **Culross**, with its steep cobbled streets and 16th-century houses.

Border Country

South in the Borders region, the River Tweed and the streams that feed it cut picturesque valleys through the green hills. Sheep wander nonchalantly across the minor roads, and their wool still goes into the local knitwear and—naturally—tweed.

City plan of Glasgow.

Peebles is a wool town, but its coat of arms shows three salmon: this is prime fishing country. **Traquair House** near Innerleithen claims to have sheltered 27 Scottish and English monarchs in its 1,000-year history. It is full of intriguing things from secret stairs and a private brewery to family needlework, 400 years old but still in brilliant, original colours.

Abbotsford, on the Tweed near Galashiels, was the home of Sir Walter Scott for the last 20 years of his life. The novelist personally designed the study where he worked, as well as many other features of this Scottish baronial-style house—as romantic as the novels. Scott was buried at **Dryburgh Abbey** nearby, his favourite of the four great 12th-century Border abbeys, the others being **Jedburgh** (roofless but complete), **Melrose** (famous for the decorative sculpture around the outside) and **Kelso**, once the largest, now largely in ruins.

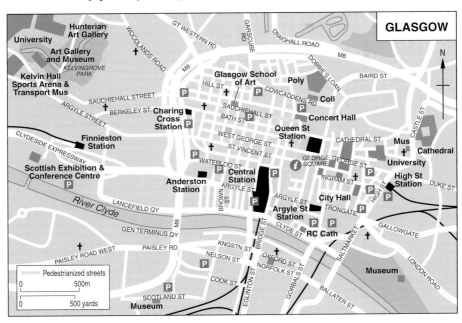

Victorian brick buildings stand side by side with the superstructure of a vast modern shopping centre in Glasgow.

Jedburgh and Kelso were destroyed in English raids during the 1500s; Melrose gradually decayed.

Two generations of Adams worked on **Mellerstain**, near Kelso. William designed the simple, square wings in 1725, while his son, Robert, planned the palatial main block 45 years later. A sophisticated simplicity characterizes Robert Adam's contribution, the greater in every way, the neoclassical interiors showing him at his most accomplished. In the beautifully detailed **library**, the same theme recurs again and again, in the bookcases, fireplaces, door cases and friezes.

Glasgow

There is no denying the eternal rivalry between Scotland's two great cities and near neighbours. With almost a million people, Victorian Glasgow is twice the size of Georgian Edinburgh. It has much more industry, too, despite the decline of the once-mighty shipyards. For a long time people tended to perceive Edinburgh as Scotland's cultural centre. Now Glasgow has struck back, providing a home for Scottish Opera and Ballet, and for the world-class Burrell Collection. Recognized by the European Community as a City of Culture, "Glasgow's Miles Better", the ad men proclaim.

Urban expressways slash through the city, and the major sights are scattered. But you can get around easily enough by bus or the small underground railway (subway), nicknamed the "Clockwork Orange" for its colour.

The heart of Glasgow today is pleasant **George Square**, surrounded by the grand stone buildings of Glasgow's 19th-century prime. The Tourist Information Centre lies nearby in St

Vincent Place. For orientation, you might take a city bus tour from here. Cathedral Street leads to the Gothic **cathedral**, a rare medieval survival among so much Victoriana. The crypt holds the tomb of 6th-century St Mungo, the city's patron. See also the Early English choir, with its crisply carved capitals and corbels.

Head west along pedestrian-only Sauchiehall Street to the **Glasgow School of Art**, a milestone in the history of modern architecture by the Glasgow-born Charles Rennie Mackintosh (1862–1928). Tours of the interior are on offer mornings and afternoons.

West again, beyond the centre, the eclectic collections of the **Art Gallery and Museum** in Kelvingrove Park grew with the bequests of Glasgow's 19th-century magnates. Exhibits include items of scientific and historic, as well as

By the bonny, bonny banks o' Loch Lomond, a short drive but a far cry from Glasgow.

artistic interest. However, the Old Masters steal the show: Rembrandt's powerful *Man in Armour*, the Ruisdael landscapes, Van Gogh's 1887 portrait of Glasgow art dealer Alexander Reid, some penetrating Raeburn portraits… Don't overlook the work of Scotland's own artists, the late 19th-century Glasgow Boys—James Guthrie, E A Walton, W Y MacGregor—who wanted to get away from Victorian sentimentality and out into the open air—and the early 20th-century Colourists.

As if this were not enough, a stone's throw away stands the university's **Hunterian Art Gallery** with more fine Old Masters, portraits by Romney and Reynolds, and the highly original works of Scotland's own William McTaggart (1835–1910). The Hunterian boasts a definitive James McNeill Whistler collection and an entire wing devoted to Charles Rennie Mackintosh—furniture and objects are displayed in rooms

reconstructed from the pioneer designer's Glasgow home.

The cultural renaissance of this city was crowned by the opening in 1983 of the **Burrell Collection**, in a purpose-built gallery in Pollok Park, south of the River Clyde. Scottish shipping magnate Sir William Burrell spent the half-century up to his death in 1958 amassing thousands of works of fine and decorative art with the intention of presenting them to the city. After years in packing cases, they went on display, to universal acclaim. Burrell concentrated on certain fields: Chinese bronzes, jade and ceramics (notably the Ming Dynasty figure of a *Lohan*), European tapestries (like the Flemish *Peasants Hunting Rabbits with Ferrets*), stained glass (including the superb 12th-century *Prophet Jeremiah* window from St-Denis), and French 19th-century painting (*The Rehearsal* by Degas, *The Ham* by Manet). The works are so compelling and the displays so attractive that you may find yourself developing an interest in things you have never considered before. What better accolade for a museum?

Loch Lomond

Britain's largest freshwater lake runs about 37km (23 miles) north to south. It lies so near to Glasgow that traffic can be heavy at weekends. To get off the roads, take one of the steamers that cruise the loch, starting from Balloch. They will take you to the north end, past majestic Ben Lomond, 974m (3,192ft).

Ayrshire Coast

Famous golf links (Troon and Turnberry) and breezy resorts line the coast south-west of Glasgow, a traditional playground for folk who live in the crowded metropolis.

This is Burns Country, too, where the beloved national poet Robert Burns was born, lived most of his very full 37 years and died in 1796. In **Alloway**, near Ayr, visit his birthplace, a whitewashed cottage with thatched roof. You can still see the little box bed where Burns and three of his brothers slept as small children. The original of *Auld Lang Syne* and many other Burns documents are on display in the adjacent museum.

After you finish at the birthplace, wander down to the River Doon and the 13th-century **Auld Brig o' Doon**, the bridge mentioned by Burns in his narrative poem *Tam o' Shanter*, where Tam escapes the warlocks and hags. Nearby in the **Land o' Burns Centre** you can decide how much more of the Burns Heritage Trail to follow.

Further down the coast, **Culzean Castle** (pronounced "culain"), a National Trust for Scotland property, towers above the sea. The present structure dates mostly from the 18th century, when it was rebuilt by Robert Adam, whose elegant classical designs grace the interior. Dwight D Eisenhower had the use of an upstairs apartment for his lifetime, a mark of Scotland's gratitude for his contribution to the Allied victory in World War II. An Eisenhower exhibition details the general's wartime career.

W hen Scottish lairds raised private armies, they had the wherewithal to equip them. This display is at Culzean Castle.

Dumfries and Galway

Unjustly neglected by most visitors, the south-western corner of Scotland has beautiful shorelines, moors and forests and a mild climate. That helps to make the **Logan Botanic Garden**, on the peninsula called the Rhinns of Galloway, one of the best collections in the country, with palms, tree ferns and rare magnolias.

On a hill half-way down the peninsula, a chapel houses the ancient Christian **Kirkmadrine Stones**: three tombstones with Latin inscriptions dating back to the 5th century. A string of peaceful old fishing villages leads to the tip of the next peninsula to the east. Here, at **Whithorn**, is the true cradle of Scottish Christianity. The ruins of a 13th-century priory adjoin the probable site of St Ninian's 4th-century chapel.

Robert Burns lived his last five years in **Dumfries**, and here he wrote some of his best-known verses. Burns tourism focuses on the bard's house, in Burns Street, a shrine and museum of manuscripts and mementoes. The Burns Mausoleum in nearby St Michael's churchyard contains his tomb. There is also a Burns Centre in Mill Road.

The brief detour north is worthwhile for a look at the dashing, turreted roofline of **Drumlanrig Castle** (open to the public in summer). This 17th-century residence still has the feel of a family home, which it is—that of the dukes of Buccleuch. It is, however, a palatial one, furnished with outstanding French and Flemish pieces as old as the house. Among the paintings, look for Holbein's portraits and Rembrandt's *Old Woman Reading*. Pictures of Buccleuch ancestors include the unlucky, or misguided, Duke of Monmouth.

Arran

Offshore in the Firth of Clyde, the Isle of Arran offers a little bit of the loveliest things Scotland has to offer: mountains, glens and lochs, and a rugged coastline. This is pre-eminently hill walkers' country. An amazing ten summits rise to over 600m (2,000ft), headed by 874m (2,866ft) Goat Fell. Car-ferries link Ardrossan on the Ayrshire coast to Brodick; in summer, services connect Claonaig on the Kintyre peninsula with the north of Arran.

Brodick, the "capital", is just a little village, and all Arran's inhabitants together number only about 3,500. Almost as many red deer roam wild on this unspoiled isle. **Brodick Castle**, a 19th-century baronial residence, houses priceless silver, porcelain and paintings by Watteau and Turner. Thousands of rhododendrons bloom in a magnificent garden that covers 26 woodland hectares (65 acres) between the castle and **Brodick Bay**.

The main sightseeing route takes you right around the coast—a distance of 80km (50 miles). You may spot seals basking on the rocks offshore, as well as herons and gannets.

Central Scotland

This scenic area of lakes, hills and fertile fields lies on Glasgow's northern doorstep, and is also within minutes of Edinburgh, via the M90 and M9 motorways.

Bannockburn

An epic victory here in 1314 confirmed Scotland's independence. The hero of the hour, Robert Bruce faced and routed an English army three times the size of his own. Shown in chain mail and on horseback, his statue stands on the field today.

The National Trust for Scotland's centre on the site features a clear explanation of the complex Wars of Independence. "We fight not for glory nor for wealth nor for honour, but only and alone we fight for freedom, which no good man surrenders but with his life," declared Bruce.

Legend recounts that while in hiding on the Irish island of Rathlin, he watched a spider try six times to affix its web; on the seventh attempt, it succeeded. Impressed by the spider's perseverance, Robert Bruce was encouraged to resume his own fight.

Stirling

The town commands the main route between the Lowlands and the Highlands and over the centuries saw some of Scotland's most savage warfare. The strategic **castle** on a 76m (250ft) crag was a prize worth fighting for. Guides tell of sieges, betrayals and dastardly murders within the massive walls. Call at the Visitor Centre for an audio-visual outline of local history before climbing to the clustered buildings of the fortress itself.

James V built the **palace** in the early 16th century, and he made it the most sumptuous in Scotland. An early example of the Renaissance style, it has been decorated with rather strange classical carvings outside and in. (Local workmen probably copied the motifs from pattern books.) Look out for the "Stirling Venus", cherubs and demons on the Upper Square façade and, inside the palace, in the Queen's Outer and

The unforgettable sight and sound of Scotland, a pipe band in all its glory.

Own Halls, the "Stirling Medallions", a series of portrait medallions that depict a number of historical and mythological personages.

The **Great Hall** (c. 1500) was once Scotland's grandest Gothic chamber, fit for sessions of parliament, but later it suffered two centuries as a military barracks. Now this section of the castle is being restored.

The Trossachs

Romanticized by Sir Walter Scott in *The Lady of the Lake* and *Rob Roy*, the Trossachs is a region of lovely glens, lochs and lochans. The word "trossachs" probably means "bristly places", after all its wooded crags. It is easy to get off the beaten track here, since beaten tracks are few. Try the road past Loch Arklet to Inversnaid on Loch Lomond (such a memorable dead end that you won't mind retracing your route). Reached via the wild ravine country south of Loch Katrine, in the heart of the Trossachs, this is the inspiration for Sir Walter Scott's poems *Rob Roy* and *The Lady of the Lake*. Salmon may be leaping up the falls of Leny near the small Regency town of Callander.

Argyll

There is a storybook quality to Inveraray Castle, near Loch Fyne, home to the dukes of Argyll, chiefs of Clan Campbell and "uncrowned kings of the Highlands". The present edifice, with its decorative towers and keep, dates from the 18th century, when the Campbells felt secure enough to dispense with fortifications. They held on to the old armoury, though, just for show—enough axes, broadswords, halberds and ancient firearms to equip a small army.

To the west, near Kilmartin, among many Stone Age and Bronze Age remains, stands **Nether Largie North Cairn**, a ritual stone chamber used nearly 3,000 years ago. Clambering down, you should be able to make out dozens of cup marks and carved axeheads. West again, on the coast, lies **Oban**, a busy ferry port with connections to several islands.

Glen Coe

The spectacular scenery of Glen Coe, complete with red deer, even golden eagles, attracts thousands of hikers and climbers every year. In the steep valley, a memorial commemorates the 1692 massacre of over 40 Macdonalds by Campbell soldiery.

More often than not, clouds obscure the rounded and not very dramatic summit of **Ben Nevis**, at 1,344m (4,406ft) the highest mountain in the British Isles. Although best seen from the north, the easiest climb is actually from the bustling touring centre of Fort William. Caution is advised: bad weather can close in quickly.

Glen Garry

East–west roads are few when you get this far north, and from Fort William to Blair Atholl there is really only one route. How fortunate then, that it follows beautiful Glen Garry down to Robert Burns' favourite **Falls of Bruar**.

Not far beyond, the white-harled and pinnacled **Blair Castle** is the seat of the Duke of Atholl, who commands the last "private army" of Highlanders—most of them in reality his peaceable estate workers. Brussels tapestries, Sèvres porcelain

The bens and glens— mountains and valleys—of the Scottish Highlands have a magic all their own. This is Loch Achtriochtan in Glen Coe.

and fine period furniture decorate the castle, built in the 13th century, renovated in the 18th and "baronialized" in the 19th. Look for the portrait of Lord George Murray, the member of the family who, as Bonnie Prince Charlie's lieutenant general, found himself having to besiege this, his own home.

Pitlochry

The main road now bypasses the picturesque **Pass of Killiecrankie**, so make a diversion to learn about the battle near here in 1689, when Jacobite Highlanders fought a successful holding action. The crowded riverside resort of Pitlochry also lies off the main road. The Pitlochry Festival Theatre runs a long summer season of plays and music. On stage, too, are the thousands of salmon that leap up special ladders by the local power station (the observation room gives you a ringside view) to reach their spawning grounds up-river.

Dunkeld

Notice the splendidly restored little houses from the 17th century, on the way to the grand old cathedral. This stands, part ruined, part restored, by the River Tay. From the grounds, you can see Thomas Telford's fine 1809 stone arched bridge.

Scone Palace

This ancestral home of the earls of Mansfield stands at or near the site of the abbey where once was kept the Stone of Destiny or Stone of Scone, on which the Scottish kings were

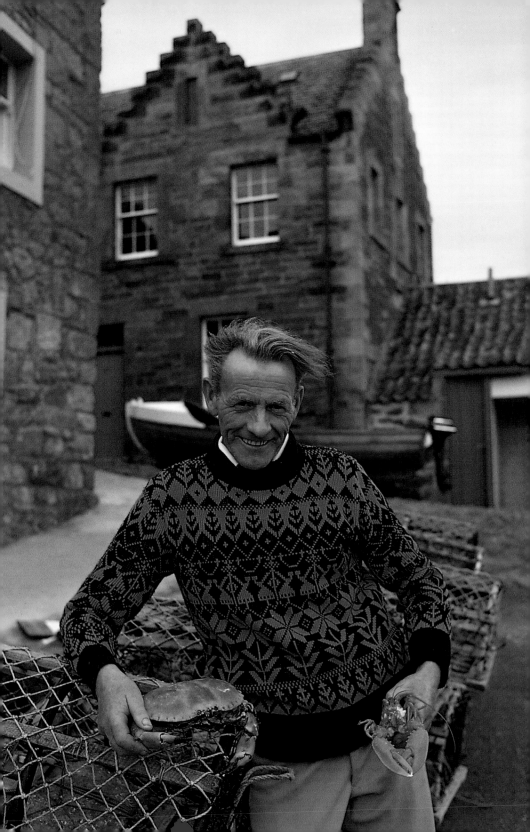

crowned—until Edward I of England appropriated it in 1296. (Some say the stone now in the Coronation Chair in Westminster Abbey is only a replica, and that the real one is hidden somewhere in Scotland.)

The great house that you see today contains fine, mostly French furniture, acquired by the 2nd Earl, who served as Britain's ambassador to the court of Louis XVI. In the **Long Gallery**, notice the rare Vernis Martin objects, which may look like china, but are actually varnished papier-mâché. They were made in Paris in the 18th century by the Martin brothers.

Vast grounds surround the palace. With stately cedars, California sequoias, Japanese silver firs and other conifers, the Pinetum alone covers 20 hectares (50 acres).

St Andrews

Out on the Fife coast, St Andrews is known worldwide as the home of golf. The game, or something like it, has been played here for over 500 years; in 1457 an Act of Scottish Parliament utterly condemned it as a threat to church attendance. Today, anyone can tee off on the Old Course at the **Royal and Ancient Golf Club**, where so many epic championships have been held.

Charming seaside St Andrews also claims Scotland's oldest university (1411), as well as the great ruin of the country's largest-ever cathedral. The old castle features a blood-chilling, escape-

*T*he little stone-built fishing village of Crail in Fife's East Neuk is noted for fresh crab and lobster.

proof "bottle dungeon" cut 7m (24ft) down into the rock.

East Neuk

Picturesque fishing villages with little harbours and red-tiled cottages are strung like beads along Fife's south-east coast. The locals call the area the East "Neuk", or corner. On two levels, **Crail** comprises the quaint port still used by lobster boats and the upper town, with its marketplace and 16th-century tolbooth (courthouse-jail). The weathervane on the belfry takes the form of a gilded copper haddock.

Learn something about the history of the fishing industry at the Scottish Fisheries Museum in **Anstruther** (pronounced "anster"). Here, you can see how the fisherfolk lived and worked—displays illustrate traditional and modern fishing methods—and there are some magnificent model ships. These days, most fishing boats sail from **Pittenweem** and bring in enticing catches to the quayside market.

In good weather, take a boat excursion to the **Isle of May**, a seabird sanctuary with 76m (250ft) cliffs.

North-East Scotland

North of Perth and east of the A9 motorway, you are in the North-East. The region claims Aberdeen, the Grampian castles (including Balmoral) and Aviemore, Scotland's premier ski resort. Here, too, is the Whisky Trail, featuring tours and tastings.

Aberdeen

The "Granite City" of grey stone buildings is anything but sombre when the crystalline granite sparkles in the sunshine. Aberdeen may lie farther north than Moscow, but a million roses and countless other flowers planted along the roads and in the parks discount the latitude. Aberdeen won the Britain in Bloom award so many times that it had to be excluded from the competition.

Scotland's third city (pop. 210,000) is still a fishing port, though the emphasis has changed from the North Sea and herring to more distant waters, white fish and modern methods. The **fish market** down at Commercial Quay is the best show in town: try to get there any weekday soon after the 7 a.m. opening. Battered trawlers land fish by the ton for inspection by canny buyers. Halibut, skate, dogfish, cod, haddock and the rest—it does not take long for the day's catch to be auctioned off to nationwide retailers and to local processors for freezing, smoking or canning.

Fishing, however, is only one of Aberdeen's vocations, and not the most important. The "Offshore Capital of Europe" struck oil servicing all the rigs that extend across the North Sea, halfway to Norway. The influx of oil people has brought a surprising cosmopolitanism to Aberdeen: the Texans you hear on Union Street are probably local residents.

In medieval Shiprow, not far from the harbour, the **Maritime Museum** occupies two 16th-century town houses. Exhibits honour the Aberdeen builders of some of the fastest tea clippers afloat, before steam, while the survey of offshore oil technology brings you right up to date with modern developments.

Where Union Street widens into Castlegate, see the 1686 **mercat cross** (as market crosses are called in Scotland),

topped by the Scottish unicorn and decorated with portrait medallions of ten Stuart monarchs, from James I to James VII (James II of England). The impressively austere walls of 17th-century **Provost Skene's House** (in Guestrow, off Broad Street) hide rather elegant rooms, which probably appealed to the Duke of Cumberland when he stayed here (before the Battle of Culloden, where he defeated Bonnie Prince Charlie).

In Broad Street itself, the 1905 **Marischal College** is claimed by some to

King's College in Aberdeen, granite city of the north. The stone crown on the chapel tower is a characteristically Scottish device.

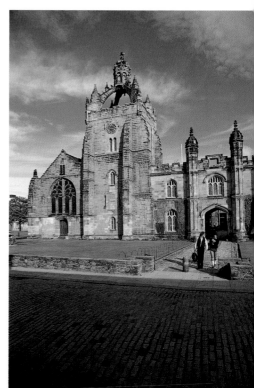

be the finest granite building in the world: it is certainly one of the biggest and most elaborate. For a long time a separate foundation, now it has become part of Aberdeen University. Another and even older part, King's College, stands a few hundred yards away in **Old Aberdeen**. Have a look at the Gothic **King's College Chapel**: the superb carved wood rood screen and stalls are medieval originals. The famous Crown Tower, however, had to be rebuilt after a storm in 1633.

High Street leads to Aberdeen's **Cathedral of St Machar**. The fortified, undecorated exterior, especially the stern west front, reflects a time when religion and war were two sides of the same coin. Inside, the brightly painted heraldic ceiling of around 1520 contains a lesson in ecclesiastical power politics. The arms of the pope, prince of the Church, take precedence over those of mere kings, while the arms of the King of Scots are placed higher than those of the King of England.

The **Aberdeen Art Gallery** (Schoolhill Street) houses a notable contemporary collection and a fine assembly of portraits of artists, mostly by themselves.

Grampian Castles

North and west of Aberdeen, gently rolling farmland gives way to more dramatic scenery. In the plains and hills alike, lovers of castles, ruined or perfectly preserved, have about 70 to choose from.

Crathes Castle, on the River Dee, has dramatic gardens with giant yew hedges centuries old. Within the 16th-century tower house you will probably spend half the time looking up at the painted ceilings, which include vigorous representations of the Nine Nobles

(Alexander the Great to Charlemagne), and Seven Virtues. Robert Bruce gave the ivory **Horn of Leys** in the Hall to an ancestor of the Burnett family in 1322 to symbolize his tenure of the property. (Burnetts lived at Crathes until 1951, when they donated the castle to the National Trust for Scotland.)

The A980 leads on to **Craigievar Castle**, a fairy-tale extravaganza finished in 1625 and little changed since. The clustered six- and seven-storey castellated towers and conical-roofed turrets are the last word in Scottish baronial. Inside, ornate plaster ceilings

R̲ugged Highland cattle are well used to the hard winters of the Cairngorms, north-east Scotland.

and pine panelling grace the Great Hall and many of the other rooms. Among the unusual objects on display: the "scold's bridle", a metal collar used to silence nagging wives, and three rare long "Craigievar tables" for gaming.

Alternatively, you can follow the long, picturesque valley of the River Dee west from Crathes. Queen Victoria loved the Deeside area and often came to stay at **Balmoral Castle**, which her consort Prince Albert bought and rather ponderously refashioned in a Germanic version of Scottishness. In summer, you can visit the grounds provided royalty are not in residence. When they are, crowds gather at little **Crathie Church**, where the queen and her family attend Sunday service.

North near Udny, **Pitmedden Garden** is a re-creation of a 17th-century formal sunken garden in elaborate geometric designs. Some 37,000 annuals are planted out each summer, so the optimum time to view is in July and August; but the subtle colours at other seasons have their own appeal.

In contrast to this disciplined version of nature, the often stormy coastal waters crash against plunging cliffs south of Peterhead. Don't go too near the edge at the **Bullers of Buchan**, caverns and clefts where the waves seem to boil and the screams of gulls cut through the roar of the sea. Visiting Scotland with Dr Johnson in the 18th century, Boswell called this sight a "monstrous cauldron".

Speyside

Along the lovely valley of the River Spey, fishermen cast their lines into the rushing waters to entice their prey, the elusive salmon. The slate-roofed houses

> **Whisky Trail**
> Enthusiasts will soon notice familiar names on the signposts: Glenlivet, Glenfiddich, Glenfarclas, Balvenie, Knockando and the rest. Some of the companies open their doors to tourists and around Keith and Dufftown they have actually organized a 112km (70mile) circuit that takes in seven distilleries. You will be shown the time-honoured methods of malting and mashing and can observe the subtle processes of fermentation and distillation, which go on as they have done for centuries. Then you will very likely be invited to taste a wee dram. The word whisky, incidentally, comes from the Gaelic *uisge-beatha*, meaning "water of life".

with pagoda-like chimneys, almost hidden in the trees, are the old distilleries, generating some of the finest of Scotch whiskies.

Cairngorms

Up the Spey at **Aviemore**, one of Scotland's ski centres has turned into a year-round resort with sports and entertainment, day and night. On a clear day, take the chair-lift ride into the high Cairngorms. The view from the terminal, 1,100m (3,600ft) up, is superb, but the footpath to the summit of Cairn Gorm, 1,246m (4,084ft), puts you right on top of the world. At **Carrbridge**, the Landmark Visitor Centre features a multi-screen film about the life and landscape of the Highlands.

At the excellent **Highland Wildlife Park** further upriver near Kincraig you can drive through, just like an African game park—except for the animals around you. Herds of red deer, European bison, wild horses, ibex, shaggy Highland cattle and mouflons (wild ancestors of domestic sheep) roam free. In

*B*eginners try the nursery slopes at Glenshee, one of Scotland's ski areas. Neither snow nor sun is guaranteed.

the walk-through areas you can spot wildcats, badgers, arctic foxes and wolves and many of the native birds.

The Highlands

Scotland's mountains might not stand up in size to the Andes or the Alps, but they contrive to be just as awe-inspiring. Snow-capped peaks and hills purple with heather reflect in deep, silent lochs. The moors and forests are home to birds and mammals found nowhere else in Britain: the wildcat, pine marten, golden eagle and turkey-like capercaillie. Ruined crofts and castles are reminders that the population was once larger than today's small numbers. Roads are few, though this means that summer traffic is concentrated on them: you really need to walk or climb to experience the solitude of Britain's northern wilderness.

Inverness

The town has been known as capital of the Highlands since ancient times. For a useful introduction to Highland history, visit the **Museum and Art Gallery** in Castle Wynd. Road and rail links from the south funnel through here, so it is hard to avoid in any case.

So, too, are all the souvenirs of the local submarine celebrity presumed to inhabit the deeps of **Loch Ness** to the south-west. The Loch Ness Monster (dubbed "Nessie" on the T-shirts) has a long history of supposed sightings, as well as some persuasive photographs. Murkiness caused by peat particles washed in by the rivers that feed the loch has defeated underwater cameras. Sonar equipment has picked up some echoes that could be anything. If there *are* descendants of the dinosaurs or giant eels down there, they have got plenty of room to hide: the water is 300m (1,000ft) deep in some parts. Excursion boats make regular monster-spotting cruises down the loch.

Loch Ness is only the beginning of the **Great Glen**, a fissure that cuts right across Scotland. The lochs that stretch along it were linked up in the early 19th century (by one of Britain's greatest engineers, Thomas Telford) to form the Caledonian Canal. You can go through on an excursion boat, or take the time to hire one yourself and make the trip, working your way through the 29 locks on the canal. (No need to go all the way back; you can start from either end and drop the boat off at the other.)

Culloden

Bleak Culloden Moor saw the defeat of Bonnie Prince Charlie's Highlanders in 1746. The victorious Duke of Cumberland's army lost only 76 men, compared to the Highlanders' 1,200 dead. His treatment of the injured, the prisoners and captured fugitives earned him the title of "Butcher" Cumberland. A stirring film at the battlefield Visitor Centre recounts the story of the '45.

Kilts and Tartans

For many Scots, Highland dress is not just an item of folklore to be brought out of mothballs on ceremonial occasions. For some it is everyday wear and it is also the standard uniform of certain Scottish regiments. Pipe and drum bands arrayed in kilted splendour are a frequent sight.

Daytime Highland dress consists of knee-length kilt, matching tweed jacket, long knitted hose with a dirk (knife) stuck in the right stocking, and garters. The kilt is held up by a belt, and a sporran (purse) hangs from the waist. Sometimes a plaid, a sort of tartan rug, is flung over the shoulder.

Authentic tartans are registered designs. Each clan—originally a loose organization based on a family—had its own pattern. As the years went by and the clans subdivided, many variations (setts) of the tartans were produced. Today, it is estimated that there are more than a thousand setts.

While a certain amount of commercialism surrounds the tartan business, you may in fact have a genuine clan connection—even if your family name seems far removed from Campbell, Macdonald or Stewart.

Cawdor Castle

You might feel the presence of ghosts at Cawdor Castle if you took all the legends seriously. But here, you're not really expected to. If you recall your Shakespeare, Macbeth was promised by the witches that he would be Thane of Cawdor and a king. Some say that it was at this castle that he had King Duncan murdered, but the historical Macbeth lived much earlier than the 14th-century date of the castle, and the whole story owes rather more to Shakespeare's imagination than Scottish history.

Today, the grounds have fine gardens and a nature trail. Inside the castle, the walls are hung with 17th-century tapestries. Beautiful, but practical too, in keeping rooms a bit less cold and draughty. The **Thorn Tree Room** encloses a 600-year-old hawthorn, the legendary reason for choosing this spot for the building.

West of Inverness

A narrow road, or one of the most dramatic railway lines in Britain, can take you through the mountains to the west coast. The train journey ends at Kyle of Lochalsh, where you can cross to the Isle of Skye (see page 316). Minor roads lead north around the dramatic shores of remote sea lochs: **Loch Carron, Loch Torridon** and **Loch Gairloch.** The diversion inland to mountain-girt **Loch Maree** will bring you to some

*U*rquhart Castle is a vantage point for seeking a glimpse of the elusive—and possibly mythical—Loch Ness Monster.

breathtaking views. But most of this wild land is accessible only to well-equipped walkers (carrying tents if they want to penetrate far).

At Loch Ewe, the Gulf Stream works its magic in the luxuriant **Inverewe Gardens**, a riot of colour in spring and early summer when azaleas and magnolias bloom. The founder, Osgood Mackenzie, clearly relished a challenge. Frost-free it may be, but salt-laden gales blasted the rocky site when he started the gardens in 1862, and this is the same latitude as Juneau, Alaska.

Ullapool

Near the seaward end of Loch Broom, Ullapool is a busy fishing port and the terminal of the car ferry to Stornoway in the Outer Hebrides. Boats will take you deep-sea fishing, too, or out to the lovely **Summer Isles**, once the home of

fisherfolk, now abandoned to countless birds. At the head of Loch Broom, the **Falls of Measach** plunge 60m (200ft) into the awesome chasm called Corrieshalloch Gorge.

The Far North

Scotland's most memorable scenery is probably the north-west coast above Ullapool. Where you can, take the secondary road closest to the shore, wind-

The north-eastern tip of Scotland, Duncansby Head is too exposed for settlement, but sheep thrive on the grass and seabirds perch on the cliffs.

ing past lochs and tiny lochans. The rare little fishing villages of no more than a handful of houses were given a new lease of life by the fish-farming industry. You can reach the north-western tip of the mainland, **Cape Wrath**, by ferry and minibus in summer. You need a clear day: then the cliffs, the seascapes and the birdwatching are superb.

Smoo Cave near Durness is a set of limestone caverns, the outer one reached from the seaward side through a huge spectacular arch (the inner ones being for serious potholers only). Having come so far, you should try to make the journey along the north coast, via the glorious scenery of the **Kyle of Tongue**. An exhibition in Farr Church, at Bettyhill, tells the story of the vicious "Highland Clearances" of the 18th and 19th centuries, when crofters were mercilessly turned off their land to make way for sheep.

Dunnet Head, the northernmost point in mainland Scotland, is less famous than **John O'Groats**, which is as far as you can get (874 miles, the sign says) from Land's End by road. If you like making these geographical points, **Duncansby Head** is the furthest northeast you can go without getting your feet wet, and it is quite impressive. Should you hanker for still more northern latitudes, the Orkney Isles are in view on a clear day; the Shetlands are quite a bit further. Car ferries sail for both from Scrabster (and from Aberdeen).

Islands

Scotland's islands are counted in hundreds—great and small, legendary and unknown. A complex network of steamers, car ferries, little fishing boats, even some planes can get you to a surprising number of them.

Skye

Extravagantly beautiful, Skye is rich in history and in myth, and it seems harder here than anywhere to tell which is which. There is no disagreement about the size: 80km (50 miles) long, with a coastline so indented that nowhere is more than 10km (6 miles) from the sea. Or the weather—when the rain and mists clear, make the most of it.

The rugged **Cuillins** in the south are a hikers' and climbers' paradise, with a string of peaks over 900m (3,000ft). Getting to the hills involves a well-prepared expedition and a trek, or a boat from Elgol. Some call **Loch Coruisk**, ringed by peaks, the prettiest lake in Britain. The hills of the north are more accessible: inland from the precipitous coast near Staffin, the road crosses them on the way to Uig, which is the ferry terminal for the Outer Hebrides.

No castle in Scotland has been lived in by the same family for as long as **Dunvegan Castle**, the stronghold of the chiefs of Clan MacLeod for more than seven centuries. One of their treasures, a faded square of spotted silk, is the fabled Fairy Flag, said to have been given to the 4th chief in the 14th century. It saved the MacLeods in clan battles twice, they say, and has the power to do it once more.

At **Kilmuir,** you can visit the grave and monument of Skye's heroine, Flora Macdonald, who smuggled the fugitive Bonnie Prince Charlie to safety dressed as her maid. Anywhere in the north you are likely to hear the lilting Gaelic language spoken. Portree and Broadford are the main touring centres, but you will easily find somewhere quieter and more atmospheric to stay.

Mull

Peaceful moorland glens and dramatic peaks, forests and little crofting villages, and a varied coastline combine to make Mull an ideal island. It is also a stepping stone, to Iona and Staffa. Ferries from Oban sail to Craignure on Mull, and if you want to continue north by a different route, cross the Sound of Mull from Fishnish.

Tobermory, the charming "capital" (pop. 700), clusters round its harbour, ringed by wooded hills. Small it may be, but this is Scotland, so it has its own golf course, and the bay is often filled with sailing boats. Somewhere deep in the mud of the sea bottom lies the wreck of one of the greatest galleons of the Armada, said to be laden with treasure when it blew up and sank in 1588. Salvage attempts have failed to produce more than a tantalizing doubloon or so.

Little **Calgary**, to the south-west, with one of the best of Mull's sandy beaches, inspired the name of the Canadian city about a century ago. If you have the time, take the winding coast road bordering **Loch Na Keal**, perhaps returning through Glen More. This is single track and slow going, and dozing sheep only reluctantly get up and out of your way.

Two of Mull's castles, both visible from the Oban ferryboat, are open to visitors. **Duart** on its promontory is the restored home of the chiefs of Clan Maclean; parts date back to the 13th century. **Torosay Castle** was built in the 19th, with showpiece Italian and Japanese gardens and a water garden.

Iona

Precious to Scots and revered by Christians worldwide, this tiny island lies off the south-west tip of Mull. Here from Ireland in 563 came St Columba and a handful of followers to establish a monastery, with the ultimate mission of converting all Scotland.

It takes seven minutes by sometimes bumpy passenger ferry (no cars are allowed on Iona) from Mull, and excursion boats make the journey from Oban. All the main sights are within an easy walk of the pier. The entire island measures less than 3km (2 miles) across and 6km (4 miles) long.

Nearest the pier, the early nunnery was restored in the 19th century. The mostly 15th-century abbey doubtless stands on the site of St Columba's original. **St Oran's Chapel** is the oldest surviving building on the island, with a notable Norman west door, and next to it, a graveyard said to be the burial place of many early Scottish kings and lords of the Isles. The carved stone Celtic St Martin's Cross near the abbey dates from as early as the year 800.

Most of Iona's 100 or so inhabitants live near the ferry landing. They raise a few sheep or cattle, but in summer most of their time is taken up with the throngs of visitors and pilgrims. Religious scholars come too, to spend time with the active abbey community.

Staffa

From Iona you can take an hour's boat trip around Staffa, the small uninhabited island whose dramatic **Fingal's Cave** inspired Mendelssohn to write his "Hebrides" overture. Columns of smooth black basalt stand out of the sea like organ pipes as the sound of the waves echoes in the cave. (Excursion boats usually circle Staffa. Only in very calm weather is it possible to land.)

Never a Dull Moment

Monuments and museums are only the beginning of a holiday in Britain. Along with the sightseeing, try to participate in the nation's rich cultural life. Innovative theatre, opera and ballet, concerts (symphony and rock) flourish in London and the other big cities. Elsewhere country pursuits come into their own—from active sports to leisurely walks.

Sports

The British invented just about every game worth playing except basketball. There's not much in the way of sports you can't do, or see, during a stay in their country.

For Spectators

Major events are usually televised; something to bear in mind if you cannot get tickets for Wimbledon or Wembley.

Compared to the leviathans of American football, rugby players play their vigorous contact sport relatively unprotected.

Cricket was born at a place called, quaintly enough, Broadhalfpenny Down near Hambledon in Hampshire, and even today much of England's cricketing strength is drawn from the south. The game, described as "chess on grass", is bound to mystify the uninitiated at first, but the rules aren't hard to pick up. Just remember that there are two teams of 11 players, both wearing the same white trousers and shirts. The two players on the field holding bats belong to one team, all the others to the second, whose object is to remove the batsmen. The cricket season runs from late April to the end of September. In London, important county and test (international) matches are played at Lord's Cricket Ground and The Oval.

*E*nglish summer weekends wouldn't be the same without a cricket match on the village green.

The most unlikely people get excited about **football** (soccer). Professional clubs play each Saturday between August and May to crowds of chanting supporters. Cup Finals take place at London's Wembley Stadium. A small proportion of rowdy fans has given British football a bad name, but the game itself as played here is followed the world over. If you would like to see a match, avoid the standing areas on the terraces (which are being phased out), where trouble is more likely.

Rugby is said to have originated when a soccer player at Rugby School in Warwickshire picked up the ball and ran with it. Rather than disqualifying him, those present saw the beginning of a new sport. Two variants of "rugger" are played in Britain: Rugby League (13-a-side) and Rugby Union (15-a-side), with slightly differing rules. Rugby League is mostly played by professionals and has a big following in the north of England. Rugby Union, the amateur version, has its English headquarters at Twickenham, near London, the place to see major matches, including internationals. Scottish rugby fans have their mecca at Murrayfield in Edinburgh, and the Welsh at Cardiff Arms Park. The Five Nations Tournament, between England, Scotland, Wales, Ireland and France, is rugby's focus from January to April.

Horse-racing is the sport of kings— and Britain's queen, a knowledgeable horse breeder. Watch the thoroughbreds run at Epsom (Surrey), Ascot (Berkshire), Goodwood (Sussex), Newmarket (Suffolk), Doncaster (Yorkshire) and many other courses around the country. The Epsom Derby and Royal Ascot in June are just two highlights of the long and eventful flat racing season (March to early November). National Hunt steeplechasing events are scheduled from late August to early June. Cheltenham is the venue for the National Hunt Festival Meeting in February or March, while the most famous of steeplechases, the Grand National, takes place in spring at Aintree near Liverpool.

The major **show jumping** events of the year are held at Wembley: the Royal International Horse Show in July and the Horse of the Year Show in October.

A network of ancient footpaths and bridleways lets walkers and riders enjoy the countryside.

Polo matches—highly social occasions—are held at weekends between April and August at some 20 clubs across the country, including Windsor (Berkshire), Cowdray Park (Sussex) and Cirencester Park (Gloucestershire).

Motor Racing. Silverstone in Northamptonshire hosts the British Grand Prix for Formula One racing in July. The circuit is also used most weekends for motorcycle or car races, as is Brands Hatch in Kent.

Tennis fans descend on London at the end of June for the Wimbledon Lawn Tennis Championships, still played on grass. Tickets for Centre Court matches are hard to come by, especially for the finals, but you may be able to see some young hopeful take on one of the greats in an earlier round.

Rowing events take place on the Thames: the hotly contested Oxford and Cambridge University Boat Race in spring (between the London suburbs of Putney and Mortlake) and the Head of the River race, the largest assembly of river craft in the world. Of the 250 regattas held each year, the most important is the Henley Royal Regatta in July; crews from all over the world come to compete.

Highland Games are a Scottish summer tradition, especially the Braemar Gathering, attended by the Royal Family. Watch the kilted titans grunting through tugs-of-war and tossing the famous caber.

Active Sports

Walking

You can get away from traffic and people on canal and river towpaths and other marked footpaths. Walkers often have legal right of way over privately owned property, provided that they respect the laws against trespassing, damage or misuse. Local and regional tourist offices publish suggestions for short walks and longer, cross-country jaunts. You can also get information and advice from the Ramblers' Association, 1–5 Wandsworth Road, London SW8 2XX.

Hiking

For those with time and stamina, two feet can be a feasible means of transport. A number of cross-country paths transit some eminently walkable regions of Britain, including the North and South Downs Way and Ridgeway Path in South-East England, the Coastal Paths of the South-West, Central England's Cotswold Way, the Cleveland Way and Pennine Way in the North of England, and the Pembrokeshire Coastal Path in South Wales. You can join one of the excursions conducted by trained naturalists familiar with the terrain: week-long treks over moors and glens include food and accommodation, as well as the services of a guide.

Mountain Climbing

Combine physical challenge with scenic thrills in England's Peak District or Lake District, the Snowdonia region of Wales or the Scottish Highlands, on the peaked ridges of Arran and the Cuillins on Skye. Information centres in mountain regions have a stock of maps and guide books for sale. For advance information, contact the British Mountaineering Council, Crawford House, Precinct Centre, Booth Street East, Manchester M13 9RZ.

Despite safety campaigns, significant numbers of climbers continue to get into trouble, many. having to be brought down by mountain rescue teams. Always get local advice on weather and conditions, plan your route so as to be back before dark and never go alone.

Cycling

Join a tour (for beginners or advanced riders, according to your stamina) or go it alone. The flatlands of Essex and Suffolk are ideal for gentle cycling in rural surroundings. More demanding routes follow the contours of the Downs, the Cotswolds, the Dorset hills, the dales and moors of Yorkshire, and the Scottish Borders. Keep to the minor and unclassified roads and cross-country paths designated as bridleways to avoid traffic.

Horse Riding and Pony Trekking

You can ride by the hour, half-day or full day at centres across Britain. Instruction is often available. Many centres also organize pony trekking holidays (touring at a walk or gentle trot)—a great way to explore the countryside, whatever your level of skill. Choose from a variety of weekend and week-long tours in different parts of the country. Or opt for a weekly package programme with accommodation, setting out from the same base on a different ride each day. Establishments affiliated to the British Horse Society have been inspected and approved. For details write to British Horse Society, British Equestrian Centre, Stoneleigh, Kenilworth, Warwickshire.

Golf

Britain has some of the finest and most varied courses in the world—1,800 in all. The surprise is that it is cheaper and easier to play here than in most countries. Scotland, where the game was devised, claims the historic St Andrews Royal and Ancient Golf Club's Old Course, Carnoustie, Royal Troon, Turnberry and Gleneagles.

Fox hunting

Hunting on horseback with a pack of hounds arouses strong feelings, pro and con. A lot of people follow the hunts on Saturdays in winter, circling the fields on foot or in cars.

Shooting

Grouse, pheasant and other game-birds may be shot on specially supervised estates, with a closed season. You must have a certificate for your shotgun, issued by the police.

Fishing

This is one of the favourite sports in the land. England's most famous trout river, the Trent, flows through Hampshire—a haunt of Izaak Walton, author of the 17th-century classic, *The Compleat Angler.* The best salmon and trout rivers in Wales are the Severn, Usk and Wye, matched by Scotland's Spey, Tay and Tweed. In Scotland you will need only a local permit to fish, but in England and Wales a general licence is required. Apply to the regional water authority, or the nearest tackle shop or fishing hotel.

Most fishing is fly, though occasionally a spinner or bait may be used. Closed season for salmon or trout runs from early October to mid-March; for salmon rod-fishing from sometime in October until January or February. Coarse fishing for perch, pike and the like is allowed year-round and can be very good, particularly in southern waters. Deep-sea fishermen land dogfish, mackerel, conger eel, pollack and shark. Trips run from many ports in south-west England, on the Scottish mainland and in the islands. The fishing can be good from beaches and shoreline perches as well. You do not need a

Too busy getting out of the sand to enjoy the view. Many golf courses are set in idyllic scenery.

licence unless you are planning to fish for sea trout in tidal estuaries.

Boating

Britain's extensive network of inland waterways, developed during the early days of the Industrial Revolution, now serves recreational purposes. Charter a traditional narrowboat (barge) and cruise the rivers and canals of England, Wales and Scotland at a leisurely pace. The rental company will show you how to steer and operate the locks along the way. Or hire a motorboat or houseboat and cruise the inland waterways of the Norfolk Broads in East Anglia.

Sailing

Opportunities abound in maritime Britain, notably along the south coast. Chichester (Sussex), Poole (Dorset), Salcombe and Plymouth in Devon, and Falmouth (Cornwall) are big yachting centres, not forgetting Cowes on the Isle of Wight. The Cowes Week races at the beginning of August attract international participation. Also popular for sailing are the Norfolk Broads.

For information about all aspects of sailing and a list of the recognized teaching centres in Britain, contact the Royal Yachting Association (RYA) headquarters at Victoria Way, Woking, Surrey GU21 1EQ.

Swimming

Quite a few of the better country hotels have pools, many of them heated and under cover. Pools in the large urban hotels often belong to an indoor fitness centre. Leisure complexes with pools, slides and wave machines have opened up in some of the old seaside resorts. There is swimming at beaches around the coast, though the traditional resorts like Brighton, Blackpool and Clacton are unlikely to have a magnetic appeal for a tourist. The remoter West Country beaches are attractive, but currents here can be treacherous. And nowhere is the water warm.

Cold water doesn't deter rugged watersports enthusiasts and wetsuits have extended the season to most of the year.

Surfing

The Cornish coast is the ideal place, especially off Newquay. Boards can be hired here and at various other resorts. There is also year-round surfing off the west coast of Wales. Bring along your wet suit.

Windsurfing (boardsailing)

You will never be far from a suitable stretch of water, be it the sea, a lake or reservoir. Equipment is available for hire in larger towns and resorts.

Skiing

You will find instructors, chair-lifts, tows and mushrooming accommodation at Scotland's three developed ski areas: Aviemore, Glenshee and Glen Coe. There is usually snow on the slopes from December to May.

Shopping

The provincial centres may be good for certain specialities but they can't approach the selection available in London. If you are planning to do some serious shopping, a couple of days there at the end of your trip could be time well spent. London's discount outlets offer bargains equal to any you'll find at the source of most items—there is no advantage in buying Wedgwood in Stoke-on-Trent, or cashmere in Scotland. Antiques may be an exception. London dealers do their own buying at country fairs and auctions where prices are appreciably lower.

Shopping Hours

Most shops open from 9 or 9.30 a.m. to 5.30 or 6 p.m., from Monday to

---

VAT

Practically all goods and services in Britain—except for food, transportation, books and children's clothes—are subject to value added tax (effectively a sales tax and currently set at 17.5 per cent). As an overseas visitor you may be able to avoid paying, or to reclaim, the VAT on larger purchases of merchandise, but not on services such as hotels and car hire.

Department stores and many specialist shops can help you if your purchases exceed a stipulated amount and you show them your passport or national identity card.

There are three ways to avoid paying VAT:

1) Stores can send goods directly to your home address free of VAT.

2) When you make your purchases, ask for the VAT 407 form, completed and stamped by the shop. Present it with the goods to the customs officer on duty at your point of departure within three months of purchase. After the officer has certified the form, seal it in the envelope provided and put it in the letter box at the customs desk. In due course, the shop will forward you a sterling cheque for the VAT (minus a small administration fee). To avoid bank charges, you can have it transferred to your credit card account.

3) Buy from a shop displaying the "Tax Free For Tourists" sign. You'll be given a voucher for validation by customs on leaving the country. Return it in the envelope issued by the shop, to Tourist Tax Free Shopping. The VAT will be refunded in your own currency by banker's draft (minus a service charge) or to your credit card account. Tourist Tax Free Shopping has an advisory service at the British Travel Centre, 12 Regent Street, London.

Saturday. Department stores tend to stay open late—until 7 or 8 p.m.—one day a week. Conversely, most small-town shops usually close one midweek afternoon.

British Shopping From A to Z

Antiques. From classical antiquities to Beatles memorabilia, the British market caters to the most diverse interests. The weekly *Antiques Trade Gazette* announces all the auctions and shows in London and around the country. The better dealers display the seal of the professional associations: LAPADA and BADA.

Books. Big booksellers in London include Foyles (Charing Cross Road); Dillons, London University's bookshop (Malet Street, London WC1); and Hatchard's (Piccadilly) and branches of Waterstone's. For antiquarian books, roam the area between Charing Cross Road and the British Museum. In Oxford, Blackwell's is the traditional haunt of the bibliophile. The Welsh border town of Hay-on-Wye is a world-famous centre for secondhand books.

China. Spode, Wedgwood, Minton and Royal Doulton are some of the names to look for. The department stores carry a wide selection of patterns and makes. London's Reject Shops stock seconds and ends of series at bargain prices.

Clothing. Made-to-measure elegance is a British speciality. London's Savile

New, angular variations on traditional porcelain designs. Fine china was one of the first products of the industrial revolution in the 18th century.

Row and Jermyn Street fill most masculine requirements from head (Locke, the hatters) to toe (Lobb, the cobblers). King's Road and Covent Garden suit the trendy. For women, the choice ranges from couture classics to the latest fads. The chain stores offer fair quality with economy.

Fabrics. The selection ranges from tweeds, cashmeres and Viyella to Liberty lawn, fine cotton in garden party prints. John Lewis and Liberty's in London have the largest stocks.

Fine Foods. Take home a taste of Britain: handmade jams and marmalade (flavoured with whisky in Scotland), cheese (Stilton sealed in stoneware jars, or some farmhouse Cheddar), biscuits, mustards and traditional Christmas puddings.

Glassware. Several lines of handmade glassware are manufactured in Scotland: Edinburgh and Stuart Crystal and Caithness Glass, with distinctive thistle or star designs. Other names in British glass: Royal Brierley and Webb.

Perfumes and pot-pourri. The British go in for traditional scents like lavender, rose, English bluebell and Scottish heather. Penhaligon's and Floris are the specialists.

Pottery. Craftsmen around the country work in traditional and contemporary styles. The West Country, Wales and Scotland seem to attract the most creative talents.

Rainwear. The British, who know as much about rain than anybody, gave the world the umbrella, the trenchcoat and wellington (rubber) boots. The best selection of all-weather clothing can still be found here.

Scottish Souvenirs. Look for the heraldic shield or tartan that denotes your clan. Half a dozen suppliers in Edinburgh alone will sell you a kilt or even bagpipes.

Sports gear. You will find hunting, riding and fishing equipment, golf clubs and cricket bats and all kinds of sportswear (although it may be imported).

Teas. An inexpensive souvenir of the British way of life, and easily portable. Specialized merchants sell the widest range of blends in the western world.

Tobacco. Connoisseurs far and wide know two famous London shops—Dunhill and Fribourg & Treyer, both in St James's. They carry notable pipe mixtures and the best imported cigars.

Toys. Britain is the home of Paddington Bear, Peter Rabbit—and Hamleys, London's superstore for toys.

Whisky. Although Scotch is probably no cheaper in Scotland, you will come across far more brands than you ever thought existed; experts rave about the best Highland and island malts.

Woollens. Cardigans, shawls and scarves come in cashmere, Shetland and lambswool. Harris tweed (from the Outer Hebrides) is hand loomed. Other fine tweeds are from mainland Scottish and Welsh sources.

Shopping in London

The West End is the obvious place to start. Bond Street, Piccadilly, and Regent and Jermyn Streets offer the best in antiques, fine art, jewellery, leather goods and clothing. Oxford Street has the chain stores and the crowds. Battle your way through to the busy main branch of Marks and Spencer for well-styled woollens and underwear at popular prices. The comprehensive Selfridges is convenient

for one-stop shopping. John Lewis has one of the biggest selections of household goods.

Knightsbridge sends up a big challenge to the West End. Harvey Nichols and Harrods, one of the world's great department stores, dominate the scene. The emphasis is on high fashion along nearby Sloane Street and Beauchamp Place, while Chelsea offers the contrasts of King's Road excess and Fulham Road chic, and Walton Street has some very attractive small shops for home furnishings and clothes. Over in Kensington, the High Street proves only slightly less frenetic than Oxford Street. Veer off into Kensington Church Street and have a look at the antique shops.

London Street Markets

Market traders set up their stalls before dawn, year-round, fair weather or foul. The main markets:

Portobello Road (W11), Saturday. General antiques, collectibles. Begin at the Notting Hill end in the covered arcades.

Bermondsey (New Caledonian Market), south of the river off Tower Bridge Road (SE1), Fridays. General antiques, collectibles.

Camden Passage (Islington, N1), Wednesdays and Saturdays. General antiques, collectibles.

Camden Lock, by Regent's Canal (Chalk Farm, NW1), Thursdays, and especially Sundays. Crafts and collectibles.

There is not much of interest at Petticoat Lane, the Sunday market in the East End, nor at Club Row nearby, now that the animal market has closed.

Entertainment

Craft markets abound in oddities, like flowers made from wood-shavings.

London dominates the nation's entertainment but does not monopolize it. Theatre, opera, concerts, even nightclubs prosper in the provinces as well as the capital. In London the choice is so great you might consult one of the events magazines like *What's On*, *Time Out* or *City Limits* to plan your entertainment for the week ahead.

Theatre. For many London visitors, the theatre comes first. It can be divided into three categories: repertory, commercial West End, and "fringe" (experimental). The National Theatre (South Bank Arts Centre) stages innovative productions of the classics and the best contemporary pieces. At the modern Barbican Centre, the highly respected Royal Shakespeare Company puts the accent on England's greatest playwright. For both venues, some tickets are available from 10 in the morning for performances the same day. If you fancy something avant-garde or alternative, Royal Court (SW3) or Riverside Studios (Hammersmith W6).

West End theatres—including the distinguished Theatre Royal in Haymarket and that old London institution, the Palladium—feature comedies and musicals, as well as some drama. In many theatres, drinks are served during the interval (intermission). To avoid the crush at the bar, order and pay before the performance begins.

Booking

For some productions you can buy tickets at the box office just before the performance. But to be sure of a seat at the more popular shows and events, especially in London, you should book in advance through British Airways offices abroad, travel agencies abroad with representatives in Britain, or through a booking agency (the commission normally amounts to 10 or 15 per cent). Look in the *Yellow Pages* for booking agencies.

In London, theatre tickets priced at £5 or more may be available at half price (plus a service charge) *on the day of performance* from the Half-Price Ticket Booth in Leicester Square (open Monday to Saturday from noon to 2 p.m. for matinee tickets and from 2.30 to 6.30 p.m. for evening performances). In Edinburgh, try at the Waverley Centre, 3 Princes Street.

Most cities in Britain have at least one legitimate theatre; there are hundreds nationwide. Some, like the Palace Theatre in Manchester, the Theatre Royal, Nottingham and the Bristol Old Vic, are historically important buildings. National touring productions and local professionals keep audiences across the country entertained, sometimes trying out productions in the provinces before they go to London's West End.

In tourist circles the best known theatre outside London is the Royal Shakespeare in Stratford-upon-Avon. Tickets can be hard to come by, but returns are sometimes available at the box office on the day of a performance. Attached to the Royal Shakespeare Theatre is the Swan Theatre, which concentrates on works by Shakespeare's contemporaries and also showcases new plays. The company also performs plays by authors classical and modern in a small experimental theatre, a former warehouse called The Other Place.

Opera. The Royal Opera House, in London's lively Covent Garden, is the home of the Royal Opera. Over at the Coliseum, just off Trafalgar Square, the excellent English National Opera sings in English. A night at the opera might also feature the Scottish Opera, based in Glasgow but often on the road. The New Theatre in Cardiff is home for the Welsh National Opera, one of the most adventurous of Britain's opera companies.

Choral groups such as the Royal Choral Society and the Bach Choir give frequent concerts, often in conjunction with the big symphony orchestras.

Ballet. Be it classical or contemporary, ballet in London can be superb. The Royal Ballet appears at the Royal Opera House, alternating with the opera company. Tickets may be out of the question unless you are willing to queue for a seat the same day. One ticket per person may be available from 10 a.m. If that fails, try to see the Royal Ballet's sister company, the Birmingham Royal Ballet (in London at Sadler's Wells Theatre), or for modern repertory, the London Contemporary Dance Theatre.

Concerts. London enjoys Europe's busiest concert scene. Local orchestras of international repute, such as the Royal Philharmonic, the London Philharmonic, the Philharmonia and the BBC Symphony, all perform here, as do guest orchestras, chamber groups and soloists from around the world. The prime concert halls are at the South Bank Arts Centre (Royal Festival Hall and two smaller houses), the Barbican (home to the London Symphony Orchestra), Royal Albert Hall (South Kensington) and intimate Wigmore Hall (W1). In London between July and September, try for the informal Henry Wood Promenade Concerts, the Proms. Holders of cheap tickets (on sale one hour before-hand) sit, stand, even lie down while the orchestra plays. Another London tradition is the lunchtime concert—perhaps a chamber orchestra or an organ recital in St Martin-in-the-Fields (Trafalgar Square) or St John's (Smith Square, SW1).

An unusually vigorous concert life goes on around the rest of the country, too. Among world-class orchestras based beyond London: The City of Birmingham Symphony, the Hallé Orchestra of Manchester and the Scottish National Orchestra. Thanks to TV licence fees, the BBC can afford to run good regional orchestras.

Jazz. The great showcase in London is Ronnie Scott's (Frith Street in Soho), where the biggest names in the business let loose. There are other clubs, big and small. Look out for jazz events in less intimate but more prominent places like the Festival Hall, Royal Albert Hall and Hammersmith Odeon. Elsewhere in London and beyond, jazz is performed in many a pub.

Folk and rock. Big halls like the Wembley Arena and Hammersmith Odeon in West London host the big names, but countless pubs and clubs around Britain showcase other groups. You may "discover" the next George Michael or Elton John. All over Scotland, *ceilidhs* or folk nights are held, featuring dancers, pipers and fiddlers.

Nightclubs. The more exclusive London clubs like Annabel's and Tramps restrict admission to members. At other night spots, entrance is at the discretion of the management. Nightclubs and discos in all the provincial cities offer late night entertainment, or at least some music and company.

Cinema. The London film scene includes the big West End houses, featuring first-run films; the neighbourhoods, showing movies on release; and the art cinemas, screening classic and foreign films. Things are quieter in the provinces, where television and video have conspired to wipe out many cinemas. Still, the British Film Institute and related organizations subsidize filmmakers and regional movie theatres.

The Right Place at the Right Price

Broadly, it has to be said that Britain's hotels are expensive. They can be superb; take the famous luxury establishments of London or the great country house hotels. Smaller establishments may be prized for their historical associations, or for their charm, character or cuisine.

Here, we have made a selection of hotels and restaurants in London and points around the country, based on price, attraction and location and listed by region and then alphabetically by town. Most entries are hotels with restaurants; those which are hotels only are indicated with an **H**; restaurants only are marked with an **R**. Don't leave finding a bed for the night until too late in the day. For a small fee, many tourist offices arrange accommodation throughout Britain, through the "Book a Bed Ahead" scheme. With a confirmed booking, you'll be given detailed directions to your destination if you ask for them.

The hotels listed below are categorized according to the price of a double room with bath. Prices given are only broad indications.

Hotels
Ⅰ	up to £60
Ⅱ	£60–120
Ⅲ	over £120

Restaurants
(for a three-course dinner)
Ⅰ	below £15
Ⅱ	£15–£25
Ⅲ	above £25

The London Area

Waterside Inn   Ⅲ
Ferry Road, Bray-on-Thames
Berkshire SL6 2AT
(Reading 21km/13 miles)
Tel: (0628) 20691;
fax: (0628) 784710

Elegant riverside restaurant with 5 rooms. Outstanding French cuisine. Closed Tuesday lunch, Sunday evenings in winter, Monday and 6 weeks from 26 December.

Amsterdam (H)   Ⅰ
7 Trebovir Road
Earl's Court
London SW5 9LS
Tel: (071) 370 2814;
fax: (071) 244 7608
20 rooms. Pleasant bed-and-breakfast hotel.

L'Arlequin (R)   Ⅲ
123 Queenstown Road
Battersea
London SW8 3RH
Tel: (071) 622 0555
Good French cuisine. Relaxed atmosphere. Closed Saturday, Sunday, 3 weeks in August– September and 1 week at Christmas.

Athenaeum   Ⅲ
116 Piccadilly
Mayfair
London W1V OBJ
Tel: (071) 499 3464;
fax: (071) 493 1860
112 rooms. Luxury hotel overlooking Green Park. Good French cuisine.

The Berkeley   Ⅲ
Wilton Place
Knightsbridge
London SW1X 7RL
Tel: (071) 235 6000;
fax: (071) 235 4330
160 rooms. Modern luxury hotel with traditional standards. Indoor swimming pool. Good restaurant.

Forte Crest Bloomsbury   Ⅱ
Coram Street
Bloomsbury
London WC1N 1HT
Tel: (071) 837 1200;
fax: (071) 837 5374

284 rooms. Modern. Carvery restaurant.

Bombay Brasserie (R)   Ⅱ
Courtfield Close
140 Gloucester Road
South Kensington
London SW7 4QH
Tel: (071) 370 4040
North Indian and other authentic regional Indian dishes. Elegant setting.

Brown's   Ⅲ
29–34 Albemarle Street
Mayfair
London W1A 4SW
Tel: (071) 493 6020;
fax: (071) 493 9381
130 rooms. Solidly traditional British hotel, almost like a club.

Capital   Ⅲ
22–24 Basil Street
Knightsbridge
London SW3 1AT
Tel: (071) 589 5171;
fax: (071) 225 0011
48 rooms. Elegant modern hotel with atmosphere. Good restaurant.

Central Park   Ⅱ
Queensborough Terrace
Bayswater
London SW2 3SS
Tel: (071) 229 2424;
fax: (071) 229 2904
250 rooms. Modern hotel with attractive restaurant Sauna, solarium.

Claridge's   Ⅲ
Brook Street
Mayfair
London W1A 2JQ
Tel: (071) 629 8860;
fax: (071) 499 2210
190 rooms. Distinguished luxury hotel favoured by royalty and VIPs.

Connaught ▯▯▯
16 Carlos Place
Mayfair
London W1Y 6AL
Tel: (071) 499 7070;
fax: (071) 495 3262
*90 rooms. Luxury hotel with
traditional comfort and excellent
cuisine.*

Dan's (R) ▯
119 Sidney Street
Chelsea
London SW3 6NR
Tel: (071) 352 2718
*English and French. Simple, good-
quality food. Closed Saturday
lunch, Sunday, Bank Holidays and
1 week at Christmas.*

Duke's ▯▯▯
35 St James's Place
St. James's
London SW1A 1NY
Tel: (071) 491 4840;
fax: (071) 493 1264
*64 rooms. Hotel in fine Edwardian
house. Roof garden. Good cuisine.*

Durrants ▯▯
26–32 George Street
Marylebone
London W1H 6BJ
Tel: (071) 935 8131;
fax: (071) 487 3510
*96 rooms. Converted Georgian
house. Traditional comfort.*

Ebury Court ▯▯
28 Ebury Street
Victoria
London SW1W 0LU
Tel: (071) 730 8147;
fax: (071) 823 5966
*46 rooms. Old-fashioned, friendly,
compact hotel near Victoria Coach
Station.*

Edward Lear ▯
30 Seymour Street
Marylebone
London W1H 5WD
Tel: (071) 402 5401;
fax: (071) 706 3766
*31 rooms. Georgian town house
with informal atmosphere.*

Elizabeth (H) ▯
37 Eccleston Square
Victoria
London SW1V 1PB
Tel. (071) 828 6812
*23 rooms. Quiet hotel behind
Victoria Station. Friendly
atmosphere. No restaurant.*

Food for Thought (R) ▯
31 Neal Street
London WC2H 9PR
Tel: (071) 836 0239
*Imaginative vegetarian food at
economical prices. Unlicensed, but
you can take in your own wine.*

Le Gavroche (R) ▯▯▯
43 Upper Brook Street
Mayfair
London W1P 1PF
Tel: (071) 408 0881
*Outstanding French cuisine. Closed
Saturday, Sunday, Bank Holidays,
and 23 December to 4 January.*

Goring ▯▯▯
15 Beeston Place
Grosvenor Gardens
Victoria
London SW1W 0JW
Tel: (071) 396 9000;
fax: (071) 834 4393
*90 rooms. Traditional English hotel
with good restaurant.*

Halkin ▯▯▯
Halkin Street
Belgravia
London SW1X 7DJ
Tel: (071) 333 1000;
fax: (071) 333 1100
*41 rooms. Remarkable innovative
design. Excellent Italian
restaurant.*

Hilaire (R) ▯▯
68 Old Brompton Road
South Kensigton
London SW7 3LQ
Tel: (071) 584 8993
*Good French cuisine. Relaxed
atmosphere. Closed Saturday
lunch, Sunday, Christmas and
Bank Holidays.*

Kensington Close ▯▯
Wright's Lane
Kensington
London W8 5SP
Tel: (071) 937 8170;
fax: (071) 937 8289
*530 rooms. Large and busy. Indoor
swimming pool, sauna, solarium,
squash, fitness centre.*

Lanesborough ▯▯▯
Hyde Park Corner
London SW1X 7TA
Tel: (071) 259 5599;
fax: (071) 259 5606
*95 rooms. Elaborate, luxurious
hotel, within classical walls of
former hospital. Fine restaurants.*

London Ryan ▯▯
Gwynne Place
Kings Cross Road
Finsbury
London WC1X 9QN
Tel: (071) 278 2480;
fax: (071) 837 3776
*211 rooms. Modern hotel with well-
equipped rooms.*

Ma Cuisine (R) ▯▯
113 Walton Street
Brompton
London SW3 2EP
Tel: (071) 584 7585
*Good French cuisine. Small,
well appointed. Closed Saturday
lunch, Sunday, and Bank
Holidays.*

Martin's (R) ▯▯
239 Baker Street
Marylebone
London NW1 6XE
Tel: (071) 935 3130
*English cuisine. Contemporary
decor. Closed Saturday lunch,
Sunday and Christmas.*

Novotel London ▯▯
1 Shortlands
Hammersmith
London W6 8DR
Tel: (081) 741 1555;
fax: (081) 741 2120
*640 rooms. Modern
facilities. Business and group-
oriented hotel on western outskirts
of town.*

Odin's (R) ▯▯
27 Devonshire Street
Marylebone
London W1N 1RJ
Tel: (071) 935 7296
*Good English cuisine. Closed
Saturday lunch, Sunday and Public
Holidays.*

Poon's of Russell Square (R) ▯
50 Woburn Place
Bloomsbury
London WC1H 0JZ
Tel: (071) 580 1188
*Authentic Cantonese and Szechuan
cuisine. Closed Christmas.*

Red Fort (R) ▯
77 Dean Street, Soho
London W1V 5HA
Tel: (071) 437 2525
*Indian cuisine. Varied regional
dishes. Closed 25 and 26
December.*

Rue St Jacques (R)   ▌▌▌
5 Charlotte Street
Bloomsbury
London W1P 1HD
Tel: (071) 637 0222
Good French cuisine. Closed Saturday lunch, Sunday, Bank Holidays and Christmas–New Year.

Santini (R)   ▌▌▌
29 Ebury Street
Victoria
London SW1W 0NZ
Tel: (071) 730 4094
North Italian cuisine. Closed Saturday lunch, Sunday lunch and Bank Holidays.

The Savoy   ▌▌▌
Strand
Covent Garden
London WC2R 0EU
Tel: (071) 836 4343;
fax: (071) 240 6040
200 rooms. Grand, impressive luxury hotel, famous for its excellent restaurants.

Smollensky's Balloon (R)   ▌
1 Dover Street
London W1X 3PJ
Tel: (071) 491 1199
Family restaurant with entertainment. Children's shows and menus at weekend lunchtimes.

Sutherlands (R)   ▌▌▌
45 Lexington Street
Soho
London W1R 3LG
Tel: (071) 434 3401
English and French. Good cuisine. Stylish restaurant. Closed Saturday lunch, Sunday and Bank Holidays.

La Tante Claire (R)   ▌▌▌
68 Royal Hospital Road
Chelsea
London SW3 4HP
Tel: (071) 352 6045
Fine French cuisine. Closed Saturday, Sunday, 10 days at Christmas, and Bank Holidays.

Runnymede   ▌▌
Windsor Road
Egham
Surrey TW20 0AG
Tel: (0784) 436171;
fax: (0784) 436340
172 rooms. Modern hotel with many facilities: swimming pool, sauna, solarium, gymnasium, tennis. Convenient for Heathrow Airport. Choice of restaurants.

Oakley Court   ▌▌▌
Windsor Road
Water Oakley
Windsor
Berkshire SL4 5UR
Tel: (0628) 74141;
fax: (0628) 37011
91 rooms. Part Gothic manor house on bank of the Thames 2 miles (3km) west of London on A308. Good restaurant.

South-East England

Norfolk Arms   ▌▌
22 High Street
Arundel
West Sussex BN18 9AD
Tel: (0903) 882101;
fax: (0903) 884275
34 rooms. 18th-century coaching inn. Centre of country town, full of character.

Netherfield Place   ▌▌
Battle
East Sussex TN33 9PP
Tel: (04246) 4455;
fax: (04246) 4024
13 rooms. Country house and gardens near site of Battle of Hastings. Good restaurant. Tennis. Closed Christmas to mid-January.

Old Ship   ▌▌
King's Road
Brighton and Hove
East Sussex BN1 1NR
Tel: (0273) 29001;
fax: (0273) 820718
152 rooms. Pleasant hotel on seafront. Traditional services.

St Catherine's Lodge   ▌▌
Kingsway
Hove
East Sussex BN3 2RZ
Tel: (0273) 778181;
fax: (0273) 774949
50 rooms. Well-established seafront hotel opposite King Alfred Leisure Centre, Hove.

Whitehaven   ▌▌
34 Wilbury Road
Hove
East Sussex BN3 3JP
Tel: (0273) 778355;
fax: (0273) 731177
17 rooms. Friendly hotel in quiet residential area of Hove. Solarium.

Falstaff   ▌
8–12 St Dunstan's Street
Canterbury
Kent CT2 8AF
Tel: (0227) 462138;
fax: (0227) 463525
25 rooms. 15th-century coaching inn. Central.

The Dolphin & Anchor   ▌▌
West Street
Chichester
West Sussex PO19 1QE
Tel: (0243) 785121;
fax: (0243) 533408
49 rooms. Combination of two old inns. Central location opposite the cathedral.

Cliffe Court   ▌
25–26 Marine Parade
Dover
Kent CT16 1LU
Tel: (0304) 211001;
fax: (0304) 201667
25 rooms. Central location on the seafront. Friendly.

White Cliffs   ▌
Sea Front
Dover
Kent CT17 9BW
Tel: (0304) 203633;
fax: (0304) 216320
54 rooms. Good view of the harbour. Closed 24–26 December.

Gravetye Manor   ▌▌▌
near East Grinstead
West Sussex RH19 4LJ
Tel: (0342) 810567;
fax: (0342) 810080
18 rooms. Fine Elizabethan manor house, superb gardens. Good restaurant. Croquet.

Downland   ▌
37 Lewes Road
Eastbourne
East Sussex BN21 2BU
Tel: (0323) 73268
14 rooms. Warm atmosphere. Home cooking.

Grand   ▌▌▌
King Edward's Parade
Eastbourne
East Sussex BN21 4EQ
Tel: (0323) 412345;
fax: (0323) 412233
161 rooms. Victorian seafront hotel. Swimming pools, sauna, solarium.

Lansdowne ⌷⌷
King Edward's Parade
Eastbourne
East Sussex BN21 4EE
Tel: (0323) 725174;
fax: (0323) 739721
127 rooms. Seafront hotel close to theatres and shops. Closed New Year and early January.

Garden House ⌷
142 Sandgate Road
Folkestone
Kent CT20 2BL
Tel: (0303) 252278;
fax: (0303) 241376
42 rooms. Refurbished Victorian house. Central location.

Star & Eagle ⌷⌷
High Street
Goudhurst
Kent TN17 1AL
Tel: (0580) 211512
11 rooms. Fine old inn in an attractive village. Good simple food.

Beauport Park ⌷⌷
Battle Road
Hastings
East Sussex TN38 8EA
Tel: (0424) 851222;
fax: (0424) 852465
23 rooms. Georgian house in formal gardens. Riding, golf, tennis, squash, croquet, swimming pool.

Imperial ⌷⌷
Princes Parade
Hythe
Kent CT21 6AE
Tel: (0303) 267441;
fax: (0303) 264610
100 rooms. Victorian seafront hotel. Golf, tennis, squash, croquet, pool, sauna, solarium, gymnasium.

Mermaid Inn ⌷⌷
Mermaid Street
Rye
East Sussex TN31 7EU
Tel: (0797) 223065;
fax: (0797) 226995
28 rooms. Famous inn rebuilt in 1420. Good cooking. Attractive, characterful rooms.

South of England

Bridge House ⌷⌷
Prout Bridge
Beaminster
Dorset DT8 3AY
Tel: (0308) 862200;
fax: (0308) 863700
14 rooms. Historic house in pretty town centre. Home cooking of fresh local produce.

Montagu Arms ⌷⌷
Palace Lane
Beaulieu
Hampshire SO42 7ZL
Tel: (0590) 612324;
fax: (0590) 612188
24 rooms. Attractive Tudor-style building. Formal and informal restaurants.

Chinehead ⌷
31 Alumhurst Road
Bournemouth
Dorset BH4 8EN
Tel: (0202) 752777;
fax: (0202) 751734
21 rooms. Westbourne area. Friendly atmosphere. Good home cooking. Closed January.

Cliffeside ⌷⌷
32 East Overcliff Drive
Bournemouth
Dorset BH1 3AQ
Tel: (0202) 555724;
fax: (0202) 294810
62 rooms. Panoramic view. Swimming pool.

Carey's Manor ⌷⌷
Lyndhurst Road
Brockenhurst
Hampshire SO42 7RH
Tel: (0590) 23551;
fax: (0590) 22799
80 rooms. Extended manor house. Gardens. Indoor swimming pool, sauna, solarium.

Alexandra ⌷
Pound Street
Lyme Regis
Dorset DT7 3HZ
Tel: (0297) 42010;
fax: (0297) 443229
26 rooms. 18th-century house. Panoramic view over Lyme Bay. Garden. Closed Christmas to early February.

Stanwell House ⌷⌷
High Street
Lymington
Hampshire SO41 9AA
Tel: (0590) 677123;
fax: (0590) 677756
35 rooms. Pleasant Georgian hotel in sailing centre. Traditional cooking.

Parkhill ⌷⌷
Beaulieu Road
Lyndhurst
Hampshire SO43 7FZ
Tel: (0703) 282944;
fax: (0703) 283268
20 rooms. Georgian mansion with antique furniture. Fine view. Swimming pool and croquet lawn.

Chewton Glen ⌷⌷⌷
Christchurch Road
New Milton
Hampshire BH25 6QS
Tel: (0425) 275341;
fax: (0425) 272310
58 rooms. Celebrated luxury retreat with many facilities: health club, pools, sauna, solarium, croquet. Fine restaurant.

Mansion House ⌷⌷
11 Thames Street
Poole
Dorset BH15 1JN
Tel: (0202) 685666;
fax: (0202) 665709
28 rooms. Attractive 18th-century town house. English cooking. Central location.

Marriott ⌷⌷
Southampton Road
North Harbour
Portsmouth
Hampshire PO6 4SH
Tel: (0705) 383151;
fax: (0705) 388701
170 rooms. Indoor swimming pool, sauna, solarium, gymnasium, squash.

King's Arms ⌷
9 St John's Street
Salisbury
Wiltshire SP1 2SB
Tel: (0722) 327629;
fax: (0722) 414246
15 rooms. Part 13th- and part 15th-century inn near centre.

Rose & Crown ⌷⌷
Harnham Road
Harnham
Salisbury
Wiltshire SP2 8JQ
Tel: (0722) 327908;
fax: (0722) 339816
28 rooms. Characterful 14th-century inn out of city centre on the banks of the River Avon.

Forte Post House ▯
Herbert Walker Avenue
Southampton
Hampshire SO1 0HJ
Tel: (0703) 330777;
fax: (0703) 332510
128 rooms. Modern. Swimming
pool, sauna, solarium, gymnasium.
Central.

Star ▯
26–27 High Street
Southampton
Hampshire SO9 4ZA
Tel: (0703) 339939;
fax: (0703) 335291
45 rooms. Friendly, family-run
hotel. Central location. Closed
Christmas.

Plumber Manor ▯▯
Sturminster Newton
Dorset DT10 2AF
Tel: (0258) 72507;
fax: (0258) 73370
16 rooms. Jacobean country house
3km (2miles) south of Sturminster
Newton on road to Hazelbury
Bryan, family-run. Good English
cooking. Tennis, croquet. Closed
February.

Streamside ▯
29 Preston Road
Overcombe
Weymouth
Dorset DT3 6PX
Tel: (0305) 833121;
fax: (0305) 832043
15 rooms. Charming mock-Tudor
hotel and restaurant.

Lainston House ▯▯▯
Sparsholt
Winchester
Hampshire SO21 2LT
Tel: (0962) 863588;
fax: (0962) 72672
38 rooms. Elegantly furnished
Georgian manor house in a park
5km (3 miles) north-west by A272.
Good cuisine. Riding, croquet.

South-West England

Downrew House ▯▯
Bishop's Tawton
Barnstaple
Devon EX32 0DY
Tel: (0271) 42497;
fax: (0271) 23947
12 rooms. Extended 17th-century
country house 3km (2 miles) south
on A377. Golf, tennis, swimming
pool, solarium. Closed January.

Pratts ▯▯
South Parade
Bath
Avon BA2 4AB
Tel: (0225) 460441;
fax: (0225) 448807
48 rooms. Attractive Georgian
house near centre of city.

The Priory ▯▯▯
Weston Road
Bath
Avon BA1 2XT
Tel: (0225) 331922;
fax: (0225) 448276
21 rooms. Elegant hotel in 19th-
century Gothic house. Good
restaurant. View, garden,
swimming pool.

Royal Crescent ▯▯▯
16 Royal Crescent
Bath
Avon BA1 2LS
Tel: (0225) 319090;
fax: (0225) 339401
42 rooms. Luxury hotel in exquisite
18th-century town house. Excellent
cuisine. View, garden, spa pools,
croquet.

Durrant House ▯▯
Heywood Road
Northam
Bideford
Devon EX39 3QB
Tel: (0237) 472361;
fax: (0237) 421709
120 rooms. Georgian and
modern hotel 1.6km (1 mile)
north on A386. Swimming pool,
sauna, solarium. Closed early
January.

Yeoldon House ▯▯
Durrant Lane
Northam
Bideford
Devon EX39 2RL
Tel: (0237) 474400;
fax: (0237) 476618
10 rooms. Country house
overlooking the River Torridge
1.6km (1 mile) north on A386.
Sauna, solarium.

Mason's Arms ▯
Branscombe
Devon EX12 3DJ
Tel: (0297) 80300;
fax: (0297) 80500
21 rooms. 14th-century
thatched inn 18km (11 miles)
from Lyme Regis. Renowned
restaurant.

Clifton ▯
St Paul's Road
Clifton, Bristol
Avon BS8 1LX
Tel: (0272) 736882;
fax: (0272) 741082
63 rooms. In attractive suburb
close to city centre.

Markwicks (R) ▯▯
43–45 Corn Street
Bristol
Avon BS1 1HT
Tel: (0272) 262658
Stylish French–English restaurant.
Closed Saturday lunch, Sunday,
Bank Holidays and 2 weeks in
August.

Marriott ▯▯▯
2 Lower Castle Street
Old Market
Bristol
Avon BS1 3AD
Tel: (0272) 294281;
fax: (0272) 225838
290 rooms. Indoor swimming pool,
sauna, solarium, gymnasium.
Central location.

Unicorn ▯▯
Prince Street
Bristol
Avon BS1 4QF
Tel: (0272) 230333;
fax: (0272) 230300
245 rooms. Modern. Central
location.

Quayside ▯▯
41–49 King Street
Brixham
Devon TQ5 9TJ
Tel: (0803) 855751;
fax: (0803) 882733
29 rooms. Old-established hotel
overlooking the harbour. Sailing.

Hartland ▯
Hartland Terrace
Bude
Cornwall EX23 8JY
Tel: (0288) 355661
29 rooms. Overlooking the beach.
Swimming pool. Closed December
to February.

Carved Angel (R) ▯▯▯
2 South Embankment
Dartmouth
Devon TQ6 9BH
Tel: (0803) 832465
French and English cuisine.
Quayside location. Closed Sunday
evening, Monday, Christmas and
January.

Royal Castle 🎂🎂
11 The Quay
Dartmouth
Devon TQ6 9PS
Tel: (0803) 830033;
fax: (0803) 835445
*25 rooms. Former 17th-century
coaching inn. Central. View.*

Buckerell Lodge 🎂🎂
Topsham Road
Exeter
Devon EX2 4SQ
Tel: (0392) 52451;
fax: (0392) 412114
*54 rooms. Modern hotel on
outskirts of city.*

St Olaves Court 🎂🎂
Mary Arches Street
Exeter
Devon EX4 3AZ
Tel: (0392) 217736;
fax: (0392) 413054
*15 rooms. Attractive centrally
located Georgian hotel with good
restaurant.*

White Hart 🎂
65–66 South Street
Exeter
Devon EX1 1EE
Tel: (0392) 79897;
fax: (0392) 50159
*58 rooms. Part 14th-century inn
with 15th-century wine room and
bars.*

Royal Beacon 🎂🎂
The Beacon
Exmouth
Devon EX8 2AF
Tel: (0395) 264886;
fax: (0395) 268890
*35 rooms. Georgian posting house
overlooking the sea. Tennis.*

Penmere Manor 🎂🎂
Mongleath Road
Falmouth
Cornwall TR11 4PN
Tel: (0326) 211411;
fax: (0326) 317588
*32 rooms. Overlooking Falmouth
Bay. Swimming pools, sauna,
solarium, gymnasium, croquet.*

George & Pilgrims 🎂🎂
1 High Street
Glastonbury
Somerset BA6 9DP
Tel: (0458) 831146;
fax: (0458) 832252
*14 rooms. Historic hotel, the
nucleus being a 15th-century inn.*

Housel Bay 🎂🎂
Housel Cove
The Lizard
Cornwall TR12 7PG
Tel: (0326) 290417;
fax: (0326) 290359
*23 rooms. Breathtaking seaviews.
Quiet location. Closed
January–mid-February.*

Hewitt's 🎂🎂
North Walk
Lynton
Devon EX35 6HJ
Tel: (0598) 52293;
fax: (0598) 52489
*9 rooms. Victorian country house
on clifftop. Quiet location.*

Benares 🎂
Northfield Road
Minehead
Somerset TA24 5PT
Tel: (0643) 704911;
fax: (0643) 706343
*20 rooms. Home cooking. Gardens.
Closed November to end-February,
except Christmas.*

Kings Arms 🎂
Bishopston
Montacute
Somerset TA15 6UU
Tel: (0935) 822513;
fax: (0935) 826549
*11 rooms. 16th-century inn,
charming village setting 8km (5
miles) from Yeovil.*

Trebarwith 🎂🎂
Trebarwith Crescent
Newquay
Cornwall TR7 1BZ
Tel: (0637) 872288
*41 rooms. View of bay and coast.
Fishing, indoor swimming pool,
sauna, solarium. Closed October to
Easter.*

Old Custom House 🎂
South Quay
Padstow
Cornwall PL28 8ED
Tel: (0841) 532359
*26 rooms. Pleasant harbourside
inn, good seafood restaurant.
Closed January and February.*

Tarbert 🎂
11–12 Clarence Street
Penzance
Cornwall TR18 2NU
Tel: (0736) 63758
*12 rooms. Georgian house. Central.
Closed Christmas to end January.*

Copthorne 🎂🎂
Armada Centre
Armada Way
Plymouth
Devon PL1 1AR
Tel: (0752) 224161;
fax: (0752) 670688
*135 rooms. Modern. Good
restaurants. Indoor swimming pool,
sauna, solarium, gymnasium.
Central location.*

Novotel Plymouth 🎂
270 Plymouth Road
Plymouth
Devon PL6 8NH
Tel: (0752) 221422;
fax: same as tel. (ask for fax)
*101 rooms. Modern. Out of city
centre. Swimming pool.*

Boscundle Manor 🎂🎂
Tregrehan
St. Austell
Cornwall PL25 3RL
Tel: (0726) 813557;
fax: (0726) 814997
*11 rooms. 18th-century manor in a
park 3km (2 miles) east on A390.
Golf, croquet, swimming pool,
gymnasium. Closed mid-October to
Easter.*

Tides Reach 🎂🎂
South Sands
Salcombe
Devon TQ8 8LJ
Tel: (0548) 843466;
fax: (0548) 843954
*42 rooms. Fine view of the estuary.
Good cooking. Indoor swimming
pool, squash, sauna, solarium,
gymnasium. Closed December to
March.*

Littlecourt 🎂🎂
Seafield Road
Sidmouth
Devon EX10 8HF
Tel: (0395) 515279
*21 rooms. Regency house in a
garden. Central location.
Swimming pool. Closed November
to March.*

Victoria 🎂🎂
The Esplanade
Peak Hill
Sidmouth
Devon EX10 8RY
Tel: (0395) 512651;
fax: (0395) 579154
*61 rooms. Elevated gardens.
Superb beachfront view. Swimming
pools, tennis, sauna.*

337

Ston Easton Park ▮▮▮
Ston Easton
Bath
Somerset BA3 4DF
Tel: (0761) 241631;
fax: (0761) 241377
19 rooms. Stately home in parkland, now a luxury hotel. Fine restaurant. Croquet.

Castle ▮▮▮
Castle Green
Taunton
Somerset TA1 1NF
Tel: (0823) 272671;
fax: (0823) 336066
35 rooms. Family-run hotel. Part 12th-century building with Norman garden and castle keep. Central. Excellent cuisine.

Homers ▮▮
Warren Road
Torquay
Devon TQ2 5TN
Tel: (0803) 213456;
fax: (0803) 213458
15 rooms. Family-run hotel. Panoramic view. Closed January.

Kistor ▮▮
Belgrave Road
Torquay
Devon TQ2 5HF
Tel: (0803) 212632;
fax: (0803) 293219
56 rooms. Central, near beach. Indoor swimming pool, sauna, solarium, gymnasium.

Orestone Manor House ▮▮
Rockhouse Lane
Maidencombe, Torquay
Devon TQ1 4SX
Tel: (0803) 328098;
fax: (0803) 328336
18 rooms. Georgian house in peaceful countryside 5km (3 miles) N of Torquay on A379. Sea view. Good cooking. Pool. Closed January.

Crown ▮
Market Place
Wells
Somerset BA5 2RF
Tel: (0749) 673457;
fax: (0749) 679783
21 rooms. 15th-century inn. Central. Squash.

Watersmeet ▮▮
Mortehoe
Woolacombe
Devon EX34 7EB
Tel: (0271) 870333;
fax: (0271) 870890

24 rooms. Country-house hotel. Views. Swimming pool, tennis. Good home cooking. Closed mid-December to mid-February.

East Anglia and The Fens

Austins ▮▮
High Street
Aldeburgh
Suffolk IP15 5DN
Tel: (0728) 453932;
fax: (0728) 453668
7 rooms. Comfortable, personal service. Theatre memorabilia and antiques. Notable restaurant (closed Monday). Hotel closed late January/early February.

White Hart ▮
Bridge Foot
Boston
Lincolnshire PE21 8SH
Tel: (0205) 364877;
fax: (0205) 355974
23 rooms. Regency-style building.

Angel ▮▮
3 Angel Hill
Bury St Edmunds
Suffolk IP33 1LT
Tel: (0284) 753926;
fax: (0284) 750092
40 rooms. A coaching inn since the 15th century. Good cuisine. Central.

Ounce House ▮▮
Northgate Street
Bury St Edmunds
Suffolk IP33 1HP
Tel: (0284) 761779
4 rooms. Lavishly equipped rooms in a Victorian mansion. Home cooking (restaurant closed Sunday, Monday.)

Arundel House ▮
53 Chesterton Road
Cambridge
Cambridgeshire CB4 3AN
Tel: (0223) 67701;
fax: (0223) 67721
88 rooms. Overlooking the river. Central location. Closed December 25–26.

Garden House ▮▮▮
Granta Place
Cambridge
Cambridgeshire CB2 1RT
Tel: (0223) 63421;
fax: (0223) 316605
118 rooms. Modern. Riverside gardens. Central location.

Maison Talbooth (H) ▮▮▮
Stratford Road
Dedham
Essex CO7 6HN
Tel: (0206) 322367;
fax: (0206) 322752
10 rooms. Luxuriously converted Victorian house 13km (8 miles) from Colchester. Garden, croquet. Restaurant Le Talbooth is a short drive away.

Le Talbooth (R) ▮▮▮
Gun Hill
Dedham
Essex CO7 6HP
Tel: (0206) 323150
English and French cuisine. Charming cottage on the banks of the River Stour 13km (8 miles) from Colchester.

Duxford Lodge ▮▮
Ickleton Road
Duxford
Cambridgeshire CB2 4RU
Tel: (0223) 836444;
fax: (0223) 832271
16 rooms. Extended Georgian house in village noted for air museum. Fine restaurant (closed 25–26 December, 1 January).

Cliff ▮
Marine Parade
Dovercourt
Harwich
Essex CO12 3RE
Tel: (0255) 503345;
fax: (0255) 240358
28 rooms. Victorian hotel on seafront.

Hintlesham Hall ▮▮▮
Hintlesham
Ipswich
Suffolk IP8 3NS
Tel: (047387) 268;
fax: (047387) 463
33 rooms. 16th-century country house hotel in a park 8km (5 miles) from Ipswich by A1214 on A1071. Excellent cuisine. Tennis, fishing, riding, swimming pool, croquet.

Congham Hall ▮▮
Lynn Road
Grimston, King's Lynn
Norfolk PE32 1AH
Tel: (0485) 600250;
fax: (0485) 601191
14 rooms. Georgian country house hotel 10km (6 miles) north-east of King's Lynn. View. Good cooking. Tennis, croquet, swimming pool.

Angel ▯
Market Place
Lavenham
Suffolk CO10 9QZ
Tel: (0787) 247388
*7 rooms. Friendly, central and
historic pub: building is part-
medieval, part-Tudor. Simple food.*

The Swan ▯▯
High Street
Lavenham
Suffolk CO10 9QA
Tel: (0787) 247477;
fax: (0787) 248286
*50 rooms. Hotel formed of linked,
picturesque houses in beautiful old
town 35km (22 miles) from
Colchester.*

Hillcrest ▯▯
15 Lindum Terrace
Lincoln
Lincolnshire LN2 5RT
Tel: (0522) 510182;
fax: same as tel., ask for fax
*17 rooms. Former Victorian
rectory. View, garden. Closed
Christmas and New Year.*

The White Hart ▯▯
Bailgate
Lincoln
Lincolnshire LN1 3AR
Tel. (0522) 526222;
fax: (0522) 531798
*50 rooms. Early Georgian house
near the cathedral.*

Arlington ▯▯
Newmarket Road
Norwich
Norfolk NR2 2DA
Tel: (0603) 617841;
fax: (0603) 663708
42 rooms. In quiet residential area.

Maids Head ▯▯
Tombland
Norwich
Norfolk NR3 1LB
Tel: (0603) 761111;
fax: (0603) 613688
*80 rooms. Part 13th-century
coaching inn opposite the
cathedral. Good restaurant.*

George of Stamford ▯▯
71 St Martin's
Stamford
Lincolnshire PE9 2LB
Tel: (0780) 55171;
fax: (0780) 57070
*47 rooms. Characterful historic
coaching inn. Central. Croquet.
Good cooking.*

Central England

Bell Inn ▯▯▯
Aston Clinton
Buckinghamshire
HP22 5HP
Tel: (0296) 630252;
fax: (0296) 631250
*21 rooms. Charming old coaching
inn 6km (4 miles) from Aylesbury.
Converted stables. Rose gardens.
Notable cuisine. Croquet.*

Copthorne ▯▯▯
Paradise Circus
Birmingham
West Midlands B3 3HJ
Tel: (021) 200 2727;
fax: (021) 200 1197
*215 rooms. Modern, central.
Indoor swimming pool, sauna,
solarium.*

Plough & Harrow ▯▯
135 Hagley Road
Edgbaston
Birmingham
West Midlands B16 8LS
Tel: (021) 454 4111;
fax: (021) 454 1868
*44 rooms. Traditional hotel not far
from centre. Sauna.*

Sloan's (R) ▯▯
Chad Square
27/29 Hawthorne Road
Edgbaston
Birmingham
West Midlands B15 3TQ
Tel: (021) 455 6697
*Well-known French-style
restaurant. Closed Saturday lunch,
Sunday, Bank Holidays and New
Year.*

Buckland Manor ▯▯▯
Buckland
Broadway
Worcester WR12 7LY
Tel: (0386) 852626;
fax: (0386) 853557
*10 rooms. Hotel in old Cotswold
country house 3km (2 miles)
south-west of Broadway by B4632.
Good cuisine. Tennis, swimming
pool, croquet.*

Lygon Arms ▯▯▯
High Street
Broadway
Worcester WR12 7DU
Tel: (0386) 852255;
fax: (0386) 858611
*64 rooms. Well-known hotel—part
is a 15th-century inn. Good cuisine.
Tennis.*

Portland ▯
32 St John's Road
Buxton
Derbyshire SK17 6XQ
Tel: (0298) 71493;
fax: (0298) 27464
*25 rooms. Converted Victorian
houses in spa town.*

De La Bere ▯▯
Southam
Cheltenham
Gloucestershire GL52 3NH
Tel: (0242) 237771;
fax: (0242) 236016
*57 rooms. Tudor manor house 5km
(3 miles) north-east of Cheltenham
on A46. Good restaurants. Tennis,
squash, swimming pool, sauna,
solarium.*

Greenway ▯▯▯
Shurdington
Cheltenham
Gloucestershire GL51 5UG
Tel: (0242) 862352;
fax: (0242) 862782
*19 rooms. Fine 16th-century
Cotswold manor house. Good
cuisine. Croquet. Closed early
January.*

The Chester Grosvenor ▯▯▯
Eastgate Street
Chester
Cheshire CH1 1LT
Tel: (0244) 324024;
fax: (0244) 313246
*86 rooms. Traditional luxury hotel.
Central. Notable cuisine. Sauna,
solarium.*

Crabwall Manor ▯▯
Parkgate Road
Mollington
Chester
Cheshire CH1 6NE
Tel: (0244) 851666;
fax: (0244) 851400
*32 rooms. Luxurious country house
hotel with 16th-century origins 3km
(2 miles) north-west of Chester on
A540. Good restaurant. Croquet.*

Green Bough ▯
60 Hoole Road
Chester
Cheshire CH2 3NL
Tel: (0244) 326241;
fax: (0244) 326265
*17 rooms. Comfortable, family-run
hotel. Closed Christmas period.*

Cotswold House ▯▯
The Square
Chipping Campden
Gloucestershire GL55 6AN
Tel: (0386) 840330;
fax: (0386) 840310
*15 rooms. Regency house in centre
of attractive town. Croquet.*

Fleece ▯▯
Market Place
Cirencester
Gloucestershire GL7 4NZ
Tel: (0285) 658507;
fax: (0285) 651017
*25 rooms. Tudor inn, centre of
historic town. Closed 24 and 25
December.*

De Vere ▯▯
Cathedral Square
Coventry
West Midlands CV1 5RP
Tel: (0203) 633733;
fax: (0203) 225299
*190 rooms. Modern. Central loca-
tion near cathedral. Restaurant.*

Old Mill ▯
Mill Hill
Baginton
Coventry
West Midlands CV8 3AH
Tel: (0203) 303588;
fax: (0203) 307070
*20 rooms. Attractively converted
mill 5km (3 miles) south by A444
off A45. Restaurant.*

Midland ▯▯
Midland Road
Derby
Derbyshire DE1 2SQ
Tel: (0332) 45894;
fax: (0332) 293522
*100 rooms. Expanded, modernized
railway hotel with restaurant.*

Pennine ▯▯
Macklin Street
Derby
Derbyshire DE1 1LF
Tel: (0332) 41741;
fax: (0332) 294549
100 rooms. Modern. Central.

Hatton Court ▯▯
Upton St Leonards
Gloucester
Gloucestershire GL4 8DE
Tel: (0452) 617412;
fax: (0452) 612945
*45 rooms. Former 17th century
manor house 5km (3 miles) south-
east on B4073. View across Severn
valley. Swimming pool.*

**Le Manoir aux
Quat' Saisons** ▯▯▯
Church Road
Great Milton
Oxfordshire OX9 7PD
Tel: (0844) 278881;
fax: (0844) 278847
*19 rooms. Elegant 15th- and
16th-century manor house 19km
(12 miles) from Oxford.
Outstanding cuisine. Gardens.
Riding, tennis, croquet, swimming
pool.*

The Green Dragon ▯▯
Broad Street
Hereford
Hereford and Worcester HR4 9BG
Tel: (0432) 272506;
fax: (0432) 352139
*88 rooms. Traditional. Central
location near cathedral.*

Belmont House ▯▯
De Montfort Street
Leicester
Leicestershire LE1 7GR
Tel: (0533) 544773;
fax: (0533) 470804
*68 rooms. Victorian, since
enlarged. Good restaurant. Closed
Christmas.*

Riber Hall ▯▯
Riber
Matlock
Derbyshire DE4 5JU
Tel: (0629) 582795;
fax: (0629) 580475
*11 rooms. Attractive Elizabethan
manor house 5km (3 miles) south-
east of Riber by A615. Peaceful.
Tennis.*

Lime Trees ▯
8 Langham Place
Barrack Road
Northampton
Northamptonshire NN2 6AA
Tel: (0604) 32188;
fax: (0604) 233012
*20 rooms. Friendly, family-run
hotel, away from city centre.
Closed 25–26 December.*

Swallow ▯▯
Eagle Drive
Northampton
Northamptonshire NN4 0HW
Tel: (0604) 768700;
fax: (0604) 769011
*122 rooms. Modern. Indoor
swimming pool, sauna, solarium,
gymnasium.*

Bestwood Lodge ▯▯
Bestwood Lodge Drive
Arnold
Nottingham
Nottinghamshire NG5 8NE
Tel: (0602) 203011;
fax: (0602) 670409
*36 rooms. 19th-century hunting
lodge 5km (3 miles) north off
A60.*

Stakis Victoria ▯▯
Milton Street
Nottingham
Nottinghamshire NG1 3PZ
Tel: (0602) 419561;
fax: (0602) 484736
*167 rooms. Former railway hotel.
Central location.*

Bath Place ▯▯
4–5 Bath Place
Holywell Street
Oxford
Oxfordshire OX1 3SU
Tel: (0865) 791812;
fax: (0865) 791834
*10 rooms. Created from old
cottages. Compact but well-
equipped. Notable restaurant
(closed Sunday evening and
Monday).*

The Randolph ▯▯▯
Beaumont Street
Oxford
Oxfordshire OX1 2LN
Tel: (0865) 247481;
fax: (0865) 791678
*109 rooms. Old-established Gothic-
style traditional hotel. Central
location.*

Welcome Lodge ▯
Peartree Roundabout
Woodstock Road
Oxford
Oxfordshire OX2 8JZ
Tel: (0865) 54301;
fax: (0865) 513474
*100 rooms. Modern hotel on
northern outskirts. Carvery
restaurant.*

The Lion ▯▯
Wyle Cop
Shrewsbury
Shropshire SY1 1UY
Tel: (0743) 353107;
fax: (0743) 352744
*59 rooms. Modernized Georgian
inn. Central.*

The North Stafford ▯▯
Station Road
Stoke-on-Trent
Staffordshire ST4 2AE
Tel: (0782) 744477;
fax: (0782) 744580
70 rooms. Friendly. Opposite the
railway station.

Grapewine ▯▯
Sheep Street
Stow-on-the-Wold
Gloucestershire GL54 1AU
Tel: (0451) 830344;
fax: (0451) 832278
23 rooms. Charming. Good
restaurant. Closed Christmas to
mid-January.

The Shakespeare ▯▯
Chapel Street
Stratford-upon-Avon
Warwickshire CV37 6ER
Tel: (0789) 294771;
fax: (0789) 415411
63 rooms. Famous 16th-century
timbered inn. Central.

Welcombe ▯▯▯
Warwick Road
Stratford-upon-Avon
Warwickshire CV37 0NR
Tel: (0789) 295252;
fax: (0789) 414666
76 rooms. Fine historic mansion.
View, park. Quiet location. Golf,
croquet, tennis.

The White Swan ▯▯
Rother Street
Stratford-upon-Avon
Warwickshire CV37 6NH
Tel: (0789) 297022;
fax: (0789) 268773
37 rooms. 15th-century inn.
Central location.

Feathers ▯▯
Market Street
Woodstock
Oxfordshire OX7 1SX
Tel: (0993) 812291;
fax: (0993) 813158
17 rooms. Central. Hotel formed
from 17th-century houses. Good
cuisine.

Brown's (R) ▯▯
South Quay
Worcester
Hereford and Worcester WR1 2JN
Tel: (0905) 26263
French/English cuisine in converted
riverside cornmill. Closed Saturday
lunch, Sunday evening, Bank
Holidays and Christmas week.

Fownes Resort ▯▯
City Walls Road
Worcester
Hereford and Worcester WR1 2AP
Tel: (0905) 613151;
fax: (0905) 23742
61 rooms. Converted glove factory.
Good cooking. Sauna, gymnasium.

Ye Olde Talbot ▯
Friar Street
Worcester
Hereford and Worcester WR1 2NA
Tel: (0905) 23573;
fax: (0905) 612760
29 rooms. Traditional 13th-century
former coaching inn. Central.

Wales

Plas Penhelig ▯▯
Aberdovey
Gwynedd LL35 ONA
Tel: (0654) 767676;
fax: (0654) 767783
12 rooms. Edwardian country house
in terraced gardens. Tennis, croquet.
Closed January and February.

Wellington ▯
The Bulwark
Brecon
Powys LD3 7AD
Tel: (0874) 625225;
fax: (0874) 623223
21 rooms. Georgian hotel in
pleasant town centre.

Copthorne ▯▯
Copthorne Way
Culverhouse Cross, Cardiff
South Glamorgan CF5 6XJ
Tel: (0222) 599100;
fax: (0222) 599080
135 rooms. Modern, convenient to
M4 motorway. Pool, sauna,
solarium, gymnasium.

Lincoln ▯
118 Cathedral Road
Cardiff
South Glamorgan CF1 9LQ
Tel: (0222) 395558;
fax: (0222) 230537
18 rooms. Small, friendly, centrally
located near National Stadium.

La Chaumiere (R) ▯▯
44 Cardiff Road
Llandaff, Cardiff
South Glamorgan CF5 2XX
Tel: (0222) 555319
Good French cuisine. Closed
Saturday lunch, Sunday evening,
Monday and 1–14 January.

Royal ▯
St Mary Street
Cardiff
South Glamorgan CF1 1LL
Tel: (0222) 383321;
fax: (0222) 222238
63 rooms. Victorian. Central
location.

Old Black Lion ▯
Lion Street
Hay-on-Wye
Powys HR3 5AD
Tel: (0497) 820841
10 rooms. Ancient inn in town
noted for second-hand bookshops.
Home cooking.

The Metropole ▯▯
Temple Street
Llandrindod Wells
Powys LD1 5DY
Tel: (0597) 823700;
fax: (0597) 824828
121 rooms. Centre of spa town.
Indoor swimming pool, sauna,
solarium.

Bodysgallen Hall ▯▯
Llandudno
Gwynedd LL30 1RS
Tel: (0492) 584466;
fax: (0492) 582519
28 rooms. Elegant 17th-century
country house in terraced gardens.
Good cuisine. Tennis, croquet.

Dunoon ▯
Gloddaeth Street
Llandudno
Gwynedd LL30 2DW
Tel: (0492) 860787;
fax: (0492) 860031
70 rooms. Central location in
seaside resort. Solarium. Closed
November to mid-March.

Lake ▯▯
Llangammarch Wells
Powys LD4 4BS
Tel: (05912) 202;
fax: (05912) 457
19 rooms. Victorian mansion in
parkland. Fine cooking using local
produce. Tennis, shooting. Closed
January.

Tre-Ysgawen Hall ▯▯
Capel Coch
Llangefni, Anglesey
Gwynedd LL77 7UR
Tel: (0248) 750750;
fax: (0258) 750035
19 rooms. Fine Victorian manor
house with extensive grounds. Good
restaurants. Pool, shooting.

Llangoed Hall ▦▦▦
Llyswen, Brecon
Powys LD3 0YP
Tel: (0874) 754525;
fax: (0874) 754545
*23 rooms. Magnificent country
mansion, turned into a luxury hotel
by Sir Bernard Ashley. Superb art
and antiques. Fine cuisine. Tennis.*

Portmeirion ▦▦
Portmeirion
Gwynedd LL48 6ET
Tel: (0766) 770228;
fax: (0766) 771331
*35 rooms. Unusual hotel in remark-
able Italian-style village. Good
locally-based cooking. Pool, tennis,
croquet. Closed January.*

Ruthin Castle ▦▦
Corwen Road
Ruthin
Clwyd LL15 2NU
Tel: (08242) 2664;
fax: (08242) 5978
*58 rooms. 15th-century castle.
Gardens. View. Fishing.*

St Brides ▦▦
St Brides Hill
Saundersfoot
Dyfed SA69 9NH
Tel: (0834) 812304;
fax: (0834) 813303
*45 rooms. Hotel with sea view 5km
(3 miles) from Tenby. Pool, sauna,
solarium, sailing. Closed 1 January
to mid-January.*

Windsor Lodge ▦
15 Mount Pleasant
Swansea
West Glamorgan SA1 6EG
Tel: (0792) 642158;
fax: (0792) 648996
*19 rooms. Georgian town house.
Sauna. Closed 25–26 December.*

Parva Farmhouse ▦
Tintern
Gwent NP6 6SQ
Tel: (0291) 689411;
fax: (0291) 29298
*9 rooms. Converted old farm.
Simple home cooking.*

North of England

Kirkstone Foot Country House ▦▦
Kirkstone Pass Road
Ambleside
Cumbria LA22 9EH
Tel: (05394) 32232;
fax: (05394) 32232

*15 rooms. Attractive 17th-century
manor house. Traditional English
cuisine. Closed December and
January (except Christmas and
New Year).*

Rothay Manor ▦▦
Rothay Bridge
Ambleside
Cumbria LA22 OEH
Tel: (05394) 33605;
fax: (05394) 33607
*15 rooms. Elegant late-Georgian
house. Attractive interior. Croquet.
Closed January to mid-February.*

Lord Crewe Arms ▦
Front Street
Bamburgh
Northumberland NE69 7BL
Tel: (06684) 243
*25 rooms. Peaceful location near
castle. Closed November to Easter.*

King's Arms ▦▦
43 Hide Hill
Berwick-upon-Tweed
Northumberland TD15 1EJ
Tel: (0289) 307454;
fax: (0289) 308867
36 rooms. Impressive stone building.

Central Plaza ▦▦
Victoria Viaduct
Carlisle
Cumbria CA3 8AL
Tel: (0228) 20256;
fax: (0228) 514657
*84 rooms. Victorian hotel. Central
location.*

Swallow Hilltop ▦▦
London Road
Carlisle
Cumbria CA1 2PQ
Tel: (0228) 29255;
fax: (0228) 25238
*92 rooms. Modern. Golf, indoor
swimming pool, sauna, solarium,
gymnasium.*

Royal County ▦▦
Old Elvet
Durham
Durham DH1 3JN
Tel: (091) 386 6821;
fax: (091) 386 0704
*150 rooms. Historic hotel
overlooking the river. Swimming
pool, sauna, solarium, gymnasium.*

Michael's Nook ▦▦▦
Grasmere
Cumbria LA22 9RP
Tel: (05394) 35496;
fax: (05394) 35765

*14 rooms. Peaceful Lakeland
country house hotel. Antique
furnishing. Good cuisine.*

Ayton Hall ▦▦
Low Green
Great Ayton
North Yorkshire TS9 6BW
Tel: (0642) 723595;
fax: (0642) 722149
*9 rooms. Historic country house.
Antique furniture. Tennis.*

Gables ▦
2 West Grove Road
Harrogate
North Yorkshire HG1 2AD
Tel: (0423) 505625;
fax: (0423) 561312
*9 rooms. Converted Victorian
house. Home cooking. Central
location.*

Studley ▦
28 Swan Road
Harrogate
North Yorkshire HG1 2SE
Tel: (0423) 560425;
fax: (0423) 530967
*40 rooms. Attractive hotel near
Valley Gardens. Good cuisine.
Closed Christmas.*

Black Swan ▦▦
Market Place
Helmsley
North Yorkshire YO6 5BJ
Tel: (0439) 70466;
fax: (0439) 70174
*44 rooms. Picturesque 16th-century
inn and houses. Croquet.*

Garden House ▦
Fowling Lane
Kendal
Cumbria LA9 6PH
Tel: (0539) 731131;
fax: (0539) 740064
*10 rooms. Regency house. Garden.
Closed Christmas to mid-January.*

Grange Country House ▦
Manor Brow
Ambleside Road, Keswick
Cumbria CA12 4BA
Tel: (07687) 72500
*10 rooms. Pleasant hotel with pan-
oramic view. Home cooking. Closed
mid-November to mid-March.*

42 The Calls ▦▦▦
42 The Calls
Leeds
West Yorkshire LS2 7EW
Tel: (0532) 440099;
fax: (0532) 344100

39 rooms. Superb conversion of riverside warehouse to luxury hotel. Brasserie restaurant next door at No 44.

The Queen's ▊▊
City Square
Leeds
West Yorkshire LS1 1PL
Tel: (0532) 431323;
fax: (0532) 425154
188 rooms. Impressive building. Good restaurants. Central location.

Liverpool Moat House ▊▊
Paradise Street
Liverpool
Merseyside L1 8JD
Tel: (051) 709 0181;
fax: (051) 709 2706
250 rooms. Modern. Central. Indoor swimming pool, sauna, solarium, gymnasium. Near Albert Dock development.

St George's ▊▊
St John's Precinct
Lime Street
Liverpool
Merseyside L1 1NQ
Tel: (051) 709 7090;
fax: (051) 709 0137
155 rooms. Modern business-oriented hotel. Opposite Lime Street Station.

Mitre ▊
Cathedral Gates
Manchester M3 1SW
Tel: (061) 834 4128;
fax: (061) 839 1646
28 rooms. Family-run hotel near the cathedral.

Portland Thistle ▊▊
3–5 Portland Street
Piccadilly Gardens
Manchester M1 6DP
Tel: (061) 228 3400;
fax: (061) 228 6347
205 rooms. Modern hotel with restored warehouse façade. Indoor swimming pool, sauna, solarium, gymnasium.

Teesdale ▊
Market Place
Middleton-in-Teesdale
Durham DL12 0QG
Tel: (0833) 40264
13 rooms. Friendly central hotel in small market town.

Fisherman's Lodge (R) ▊▊▊
Jesmond Dene
Jesmond
Newcastle-upon-Tyne
Tyne and Wear NE7 7BQ
Tel: (091) 281 3281;
fax: (091) 281 6410
Good cuisine. Seafood. Closed Saturday lunch, Sunday, Bank Holidays.

Gosforth Park Swallow ▊▊
High Gosforth Park
Newcastle-upon-Tyne
Tyne and Wear NE3 5HN
Tel: (091) 236 4111;
fax: (091) 236 8192
178 rooms. Modern hotel in woodland setting. Indoor pool, sauna, squash, solarium, gymnasium.

Holbeck Hall ▊▊
Seacliff Road, South Cliff
Scarborough
North Yorkshire YO11 2XX
Tel: (0723) 374374;
fax: (0723) 351114
28 rooms. Victorian house. Panoramic view. Good cooking.

Red Lea ▊
Prince of Wales Terrace
South Cliff
Scarborough
North Yorkshire YO11 2AJ
Tel: (0723) 362431;
fax: (0723) 371230
67 rooms. Traditional. Sea view. Swimming pool, sauna, solarium.

Wrea Head ▊▊
Scalby
Scarborough
North Yorkshire YO13 0PB
Tel: (0723) 378211;
fax: (0723) 371780
21 rooms. Victorian country house. Landscaped gardens. Quiet location 5km (3 miles) north-west by A171. Good English food.

Beauchief ▊▊
161 Abbeydale Road
Sheffield
South Yorkshire S7 2QW
Tel: (0742) 620500;
fax: (0742) 350197
41 rooms. Part old inn, part modern. Riverside setting. Sauna, solarium, gymnasium.

Sharrow Bay ▊▊▊
Pooley Bridge, Ullswater
Cumbria CA10 2LZ
Tel: (07684) 86301;
fax: (07684) 86349

28 rooms. Lakeside hotel in country house, furnished with antiques. Gardens. View. Excellent cuisine. Closed December to February.

Langdale Chase ▊▊
Windermere
Cumbria LA23 1LW
Tel: (05394) 32201;
fax: (05394) 32604
31 rooms. Fine old house in landscaped gardens 5km (3 miles) north-west on A591. Lake and mountain views. Tennis, rowing boats, croquet.

Miller Howe ▊▊
Rayrigg Road
Windermere
Cumbria LA23 1EY
Tel: (05394) 42536;
fax: (05394) 45664
13 rooms. Exceptional view of lake and mountains. Good cuisine. Closed mid-December to early March.

Willowsmere ▊
Ambleside Road
Windermere
Cumbria LA23 1ES
Tel. (05394) 43575
13 rooms. Family-run hotel. Home cooking. Closed December to February.

Grange ▊▊
Clifton
York
North Yorkshire YO3 6AA
Tel: (0904) 644744;
fax: (0904) 612453
29 rooms. Elegant Regency town house just outside city. Fine cuisine.

Holiday Inn ▊▊
Clifford Tower
1 Tower Street
York
North Yorkshire YO1 1SB
Tel: (0904) 648111;
fax: (0904) 610317
128 rooms. Central, modern and comfortable.

Kilima ▊▊
129 Holgate Road
York
North Yorkshire YO2 4DE
Tel: (0904) 625787;
fax: (0904) 612083
15 rooms. Restored Victorian rectory. Good cooking. Garden.

Middlethorpe Hall ▮▮
Bishopthorpe Road
York
North Yorkshire YO2 1QP
Tel: (0904) 641241;
fax: (0904) 612176
31 rooms. Fine 17th-century house.
Charming interiors. Notable
restaurant. Gardens. Croquet.

Savages ▮
15 St Peters Grove
York
North Yorkshire YO3 6AQ
Tel: (0904) 610818;
fax: (0904) 627729
18 rooms. Victorian house. In quiet
Clifton area, near centre. Closed 25
December.

Scotland

Caledonian Thistle ▮▮
10 Union Terrace
Aberdeen
Grampian AB9 1HE
Tel: (0224) 640233;
fax: (0224) 641627
80 rooms. Central. Victorian
building with modern facilities.
Executive rooms. Sauna, solarium.

New Marcliffe ▮
51–53 Queen's Road
Aberdeen
Grampian AB9 2PE
Tel: (0224) 321371;
fax: (0224) 311162
27 rooms. West end of city.
Comfortable.

Farleyer House ▮▮
Weem, Aberfeldy
Perthshire PH15 2JE
Tel: (0887) 20332;
fax: (0887) 29430
11 rooms. Country house 1.6km (1
mile) west of Weem on B846, near
Loch Tay. Good restaurant. Golf,
gardens. Closed early December
and February.

Arisaig House ▮▮▮
Beasdale
Arisaig
Highland PH39 4NR
Tel: (06875) 622;
fax: (06875) 626
15 rooms. Fine hotel in old
mansion. Magnificent setting above
Loch nan Uamh, 5km (3 miles)
south-east on A830. Croquet.
Excellent cuisine. Closed
November to end-March.

Tullich Lodge ▮▮
Ballater
Grampian AB3 5SB
Tel: (03397) 55406;
fax: (03397) 55397
10 rooms. Pleasant hotel in
Victorian country house. View of
the Dee Valley. Closed November
to March.

Banchory Lodge ▮▮
Banchory
Grampian AB31 3HS
Tel: (03302) 2625;
fax: (03302) 5019
23 rooms. Family-run hotel in
Georgian country house. Scottish
home cooking. Fishing, sauna,
solarium. Closed mid-December to
end-January.

The Peat Inn ▮▮▮
Peat Inn
by Cupar
Fife KY15 5LH
Tel: (033484) 206;
fax: (033484) 530
8 luxury rooms in hostelry 10km (6
miles) south-east of Cupar on
B940. Celebrated restaurant with
cuisine based on fresh local
produce, especially seafood. Closed
Sunday, Monday, part November,
part January.

Cairn ▮▮
10–18 Windsor Street
Edinburgh
Lothian EH7 5JR
Tel: (031) 557 0175;
fax: (031) 556 8221
52 rooms. Friendly atmosphere.
East of the city centre.

Caledonian ▮▮▮
Princes Street
Edinburgh
Lothian EH1 2AB
Tel: (031) 225 2433;
fax: (031) 228 6632
238 rooms. Distinguished luxury
hotel. Central location near
Edinburgh Castle.

Channings ▮▮
South Learmonth Gardens
Edinburgh
Lothian EH4 1EZ
Tel: (031) 315 2226;
fax: (031) 332 9631
48 rooms. Comfortable hotel in
quiet Georgian terrace, convenient
for city centre. Brasserie.

Kalpna (R) ▮
2–3 St Patrick Square
Edinburgh
Lothian EH8 9EZ
Tel: (031) 667 9890
Fresh and attractive Indian
vegetarian cuisine. Non-smoking.
South side of city. Closed Saturday
lunch and Sunday.

L'Auberge (R) ▮▮
56 St Mary's Street
Edinburgh
Lothian EH1 1SX
Tel: (031) 556 5888
Inventive French-style
cooking. Notable seafood, game and
desserts. Close to Royal Mile.
Closed 25–26 December, early
January.

Martins (R) ▮▮
70 Rose Street
North Lane
Edinburgh
Lothian EH2 3DX
Tel: (031) 225 3106
Inventive menu. Cheerful. Closed
Saturday lunch, Sunday, Monday,
Christmas to mid-January.

Roxburghe ▮▮
38 Charlotte Square
Edinburgh
Lothian EH2 4HG
Tel: (031) 225 3921;
fax: (031) 220 2518
75 rooms. Traditional. In elegant
Georgian square close to Princes
Street.

Inverlochy Castle ▮▮▮
Fort William
Highland PH33 5BN
Tel: (0397) 702177;
fax: (0397) 702953
16 rooms. Luxury hotel in
Victorian castle 5km (3 miles)
north-east on A82. Splendid
views of the loch and
mountains. Fine cuisine. Tennis,
fishing. Closed mid-November to 1
March.

Forte Crest ▮▮
Bothwell Street
Glasgow
Strathclyde G2 7EN
Tel: (041) 248 2656;
fax: (041) 221 8986
250 rooms. Modern hotel with
view. Central location.

Jimmys' (R)   ▯
1 Victoria Road
Eglinton Toll, Glasgow
Strathclyde G42 7AD
Tel: (041) 423 4820
Celebrated for fish and chips, a
large place southwest of the city.

La Parmigiana (R)   ▯▯
447 Great Western Road
Glasgow
Strathclyde G12 8HH
Tel: (041) 334 0686
Fresh and authentic Italian cuisine.
West of city centre. Closed Sunday.

Marriott   ▯▯
500 Argyle Street, Anderston
Glasgow
Strathclyde G3 8RR
Tel: (041) 226 5577;
fax: (041) 221 9202
300 rooms. High-rise. Central
location. Indoor swimming pool,
sauna, solarium, squash.

One Devonshire Gardens   ▯▯▯
1 Devonshire Gardens
Glasgow
Strathclyde G12 0UX
Tel: (041) 339 2001;
fax: (041) 337 1663
27 rooms. Luxury hotel adapted
from Victorian mansion houses.
Fine creative restaurant.

The Triangle (R)   ▯▯
37 Queen Street
Glasgow
Strathclyde G1 3EF
Tel: (041) 221 8758
Imaginative and varied menu.
Central.

Dalmunzie House   ▯▯
Spittal of Glenshee
Tayside PH10 7QG
Tel: (025085) 224;
fax: (025085) 225
16 rooms. Mountain lodge with fine
views 29km (18 miles) north of
Blairgowrie on A93. Good home
cooking. Fishing, golf, tennis. Near
ski slopes.

Greywalls   ▯▯▯
Duncar Road
Muirfield
Gullane
Lothian EH31 2EG
Tel: (0620) 842144;
fax: (0620) 842241
22 rooms. Attractive Lutyens
house, Jekyll gardens. Good res-
taurant. Views. Golf, tennis, cro-
quet. Closed November to March.

Culloden House   ▯▯▯
Culloden
Inverness
Highland IV1 2NZ
Tel: (0463) 790461;
fax: (0463) 792181
20 rooms. Georgian house near site
of the 1746 battle 5km (3 miles)
Eon A82. Tennis, sauna, solarium.

Kingsmills   ▯▯
Culcabock Road
Inverness
Highland IV2 3LP
Tel: (0463) 237166;
fax: (0463) 225208
79 rooms. Landscaped gardens.
Golf, squash, indoor swimming
pool, sauna, solarium, gymnasium.

Port Askaig   ▯▯
Port Askaig
Isle of Islay
Strathclyde PA46 7RD
Tel: (049684) 245;
fax: (049684) 295
10 rooms. Old-world pub and hotel
on pretty island. Simple cooking.
Views. Fishing.

Sunlaws House   ▯▯
Heiton
Kelso
Borders TD5 8JZ
Tel: (05735) 331;
fax: (05735) 611
22 rooms. Charming Victorian
country mansion 5km (3 miles)
south-west by A698. Good cuisine.
Views. Tennis, croquet, fishing.

Ardsheal House   ▯▯▯
Kentallen
Highland PA38 4BX
Tel: (063174) 227;
fax: (063174) 342
13 rooms. Historic house in lochside
setting 27km (17 miles) from Fort
William. Good cuisine. Tennis.
Closed November to Easter.

Kildrummy Castle   ▯▯
Kildrummy
Alford
Grampian AB3 8RA
Tel: (09755) 71288;
fax: (09755) 71345
15 rooms. Country house built in
"baronial castle" style. Fishing.
Closed January.

Champany Inn (R)   ▯▯▯
Champany
Linlithgow
Lothian EH49 7LU
Tel: (050683) 4532

Acclaimed for steaks and wine
cellar. Fine restaurant (with a
more informal "Chop & Ale
House" adjoining: ▯▯).

Green Park   ▯
Clunie Bridge Road
Pitlochry
Tayside PH16 5JY
Tel: (0796) 473248;
fax: (0796) 473520
37 rooms. Quiet country-house
hotel. View of loch and mountains.
Fishing. Closed November to end-
March.

Knockinaam Lodge   ▯▯
Portpatrick
Dumfries and Galloway DG9 9AD
Tel: (077681) 471;
fax: (077681) 435
10 rooms. Pleasant hotel. Victorian
lodge in a park. Fine sea view.
Quiet location. Excellent cuisine.
Fishing, croquet. Closed January to
Easter.

Rufflets   ▯▯
Strathkinness Low Road
St Andrews
Fife KY16 9TX
Tel: (0334) 72594;
fax: (0334) 78703
23 rooms. Country house in
splendid gardens. Scottish home
cooking. View. Closed January.

St Andrews Old Course Hotel   ▯▯▯
St Andrews
Fife KY16 9SP
Tel: (0334) 74371;
fax: (0334) 77668
125 rooms. Modern luxury hotel
adjoining the historic golf course.
Good restaurants. Swimming pool,
health spa.

Terraces   ▯
4 Melville Terrace
Stirling
Central FK8 2ND
Tel: (0786) 72268;
fax: (0786) 50314
18 rooms. Georgian town house.
Close to the shopping centre.

Ceilidh Place   ▯▯
14 West Argyle Street
Ullapool
Highland IV26 2TY
Tel: (0854) 612103;
fax: (0854) 612886
15 rooms. Friendly atmosphere.
Arts and music centre. Popular
restaurant.

Index

References to illustrations are in *italic*; those in **bold** refer to main entries; those with an asterisk refer to maps.

Aberaeron 250
Aberdeen 307–9
  airport 12
  Art Gallery 309
  cathedral 309
  King's College *308*, 309
  Marischal College 308–9
  Maritime Museum 308
Aberdovey 259
Abergavenny 238
Abersoch 255
Aberystwyth 247
Abbotsbury 163
Abbotsford 297
accommodation 25–7
air travel 10–12, 15
Aldeburgh 199
Alloway 301
Alnwick 288–9
Alton Towers 23, **227**
Amberley 139
Ambleside 280–1
American Museum in Britain,
  Claverton Manor 170
Anglesey, Isle of 86, 254, **254**
Anglesey Abbey 199
Anstruther 307
Appledore 179
architecture, British 164–5
Arden, Forest of 215
Argyll 304
Arran, Isle of 302
art, British 124–5
Arthur, King 55
  sites 77–8, 176, 191, 243
Arundel 138–9, *138–9*
Ashbourne 230
Audley End 83, **197**
Austen, Jane **149–50**, 163,
  169
Avebury *46*, 51, 75
Aviemore 310
Avon 167–73
Aysgarth 268
Ayrshire 301

Bacon, Francis 125
Bakewell 90, **230**
ballet 330
Balmoral Castle 310

Bamburgh 289
Bangor 253
banks 14, 32
Bannockburn 59, **302–3**
Bardsey Island 255
Barmouth 258
Barnard Castle 287
  Bowes Museum 287
Barnstaple 179
Barrington Court, Ilminster
  177
Bassenthwaite Lake 283
Bath *166*, 167–70, *170*
  abbey 169
  Roman sites 76, 169
  Claverton Manor 170
  Georgian area 169
  Prior Park 169
  Pump Room 169
Battle Abbey, Kent 134–5,
  135
Beachy Head *126*, 135
Beaconsfield miniature town
  23
Beamish Open Air Museum
  95, **286–7**
Beaulieu Motor Museum and
  House 23, **146–7**
Beaumaris Castle 86, **254**
Beer 181, *182–3*
Beltring Whitbread Hop
  Farm 23
Ben Nevis 304
Berkeley Castle 222
Berwick-upon-Tweed 289
Betws-y-Coed 257
Beverley 273
Bickleigh 180
Bideford 179
Birmingham 94, **223–4**
  International Airport 12
  Museum and Art Gallery
    223
  Museum of Science and
    Industry 223–4
Bishop Rock Lighthouse,
  Cornwall 189
Black Country Museum,
  Dudley 224
Black Mountains 238
Blaenau Ffestiniog 257
Blaenavon Big Pit Mining
  Museum 238
Blair Castle, Scotland 304–5
Blake, William 124
Blickling Hall, Norfolk 202
Blenheim Palace 83, 164, *165*,
  212

boating and sailing 18, 20,
  27, 203, 324
Bodiam Castle, Kent 133
Bodmin 191
Bodmin Moor 78, *191*
Bolton Castle, Yorks 268
Borrowdale 282
Boscastle 191
Boscaswell 189
Boston 94, **205**
Bournemouth 154–5
Bourton-on-the-Water 219
Bovey Tracey 185
Bradford 95, **266**
  National Museum of
    Photography, Film and
    TV 266
Bradford-on-Avon 170
Branscombe 181
Brecon 238
Brecon Beacons National
  Park 238, *239*
Bridport 163
Brighton 135–8
  Museum and Art Gallery
    137
  Palace Pier 138
  Royal Pavilion *136*, **137**,
    164
Bristol 171*, 171–3
  Clifton Suspension Bridge
    173
  SS Great Britain 172, 173
  St Mary Redcliffe 173
Brixham 181
Broadlands Conservation
  Centre, Norfolk 203
Broadstairs 130
Broadway 220–1
Brontë family 231, 267
Brownsea Island 156
Buckler's Hard Maritime
  Museum 147
Buckland Abbey, Devon 84,
  184
Bude 191
Budleigh Salterton 181
Builth Wells 247, *248–9*
Bullers of Buchan 310
Burnham-on-Sea 177
Burns, Robert 301, 302
Bury St Edmunds **200–1**,
  233
Buxton 90, **231**
Byron, George Gordon Lord
  225–6

Cadair Idris range 258

Cadbury Castle, Somerset 78, **176**
Caerleon 76, 78, 86, **239**
Caernarfon 76, **254–5**
  Castle 58, 86, **254–5**
Caerphilly Castle 85, *241*, **241–2**
Cairngorms 310–11
Caldey Island 244
Caldron Snout, Teesdale 287
Calgary 317
Cambridge 193–7, 195*
  The Backs 193
  Caius College 196
  Christ's College 198
  Emmanuel College 198
  Fitzwilliam Museum 197
  Jesus College 198
  Kettle's Yard Art Gallery 198
  King's College 196
  Magdalene College 197
  Queens' College 196
  Round Church 197
  St John's College 197
  Senate House 196
  Trinity College 196–7
camping and caravanning 26–7
Canterbury 127–30, 129*
  cathedral 58, 86, **129**
Capel Curig 257
car hire 15–16
Cardiff 239–41
  airport 12
  Castle 85, **239**
  Llandaff Cathedral 241
  National Museum of Wales 239
  Welsh Folk Museum 241
Cardigan 247
Carisbrooke Castle, Isle of Wight 146
Carlisle 283–4
Carmarthen 78, **243**
Carrbridge 310
Carreg Cennen 243
Carron, Loch 312
Castell Coch 85, **242**
Castle Combe *232*
Castle Drogo, Devon 187
Castle Howard, Yorks 84, 164, **276**
Castleton 90, **231**
Central England, map of 208*
Channel Tunnel 131
Cerne Abbas 159, *160*

Chatham 23, **92**
Chatsworth House, Derbys 90, **230–1**
Chawton 149
Cheddar Gorge 174–6
Chedworth Roman Villa 76, **218**
Cheltenham 220
Chepstow Castle 86, **237**
Chesil Bank 163
Chessington World of Adventures 23
Chester 76, **228–9**, 233
  Castle 228
  cathedral 229
  ramparts 228
  The Rows 229
Chichester 140
children's activities 23
Chipping Campden 221
Chirk Castle, Wales 251
Cilgerran 247
cinema 331
Cinque Ports 130–2
Cirencester 76, **219**
Clapham, Yorks 270
climate 9
climbing 322
Clovelly *25*, 180
coach/bus travel 14–15, 17–18, 20
Cockermouth 283
Colwyn Bay 252
complaints 30–1
Coniston 280
Constable, John 124–5, 200
Conwy Castle 58, 86, **252**
Cook, Capt James 278–9
Corfe Castle 158
Cornwall 187–91
Coruisk, Loch 316
Cotswolds 218–21
Coventry 224–5
  cathedral 225
  Museum of British Road Transport 225
Crafnant Alpine Nature Reserve 257
Cragside, Northumberland 289
Craigievar Castle, Grampian 309–10
Crail *306*, 307
Crathes Castle, Grampian 309
Criccieth Castle 58, **255**
cricket 319, *320*
Crickhowell 238

crime, guarding against 31
Cuillins, Skye 316
Culloden 89, **312**
Culross 88, **297**
Culzean Castle 301, *301*
customs controls 13
cycling 15, **322**

Dale 245
Darlington 287
Dartmeet 187
Dartmoor 90–1, *184–5*, **184–7**
Dartmouth 182
Deal 131
Dedham Vale 200
Denbigh 251
Derby 226
Derbyshire 89–90, 229–31
Derwentwater 282
Devil's Dyke, Sussex 138
Devon 179–87
Dickens, Charles 91–2, 130
disabled visitors, information for 22
distance chart 45
Dolaucothi 250
Dolbadarn Castle, Wales 86
Dolgellau 258, *258–9*
Dorchester 93, **158–9**
Dorset 92–3, **154–63**
Dorset Coastal Path 158
Dover 131
driving 15–17
Drumlanrig Castle, Dumfries 302
Dryburg Abbey 297
Duart Castle, Mull 317
Dudley 224
Dulverton 179
Dumfries 302
Duncansby Head *315*, 316
Dunkeld 305
Dunnet Head 316
Dunster 179
Dunvegan Castle, Skye 316
Durham 284–6
  cathedral 87, 164, **284**, *285*

East Anglia *192*, 194*, 193–205
East Bergholt 200
East Neuk *306*, 307
Eastbourne 135
eating and drinking 33–40
Edinburgh 291–6, 293*
  airport 12
  Camera Obscura 294

Castle 87, **291–3**
Greyfriars Bobby statue 294, *294*
Holyroodhouse 87, 89, **295**
John Knox House 294
Museum of Childhood 23, **294**
National Gallery of Scotland 295
New Town 295–6
Royal Botanical Gardens 296
Royal Mile 294
Royal Scottish Museum 294
St Giles Cathedral 294
Scott Memorial 295
zoo 296
Elan Valley 249
electric current 31
Ely cathedral 87, **199**
embassies and consulates 24–5
emergencies 31
Erddig 251
Eton College 122
Exeter 86, **180**, *181*
Exmoor *10–11*, *178*, 178–9
Exmouth 181

Falmouth 188
Farne Islands 289
festivals and events 41–3
Ffestiniog Railway 257
Fingal's Cave 317
Fishbourne Roman Villa 76, 140
Fishguard 246–7
fishing 323–4
football (soccer) 320
Forth Bridge *296*, 297
Fountains Abbey, Yorks 274–6, *274–5*
Fowey 78, **187**

Gainsborough 94
Gainsborough's House, Sudbury 200
Gairloch, Loch 312
Galloway, Rhinns of 302
Gaping Ghyll 270
Gatwick 12
Glasgow 297*, *298*, 298–300
airport 12
Art Gallery and Museum 299–300
Burrell Collection 300
cathedral 299

Hunterian Art Gallery 300
School of Art 165, **299**
Glastonbury 78, **176**
Glen Coe 304, *305*
Glen Garry 304–5
Gloucester 221, *222–3*
Glyndebourne 137
golf 322, *323*
Goodwood House and Park 140–1
Gower Peninsula *242*, 242–3
Grampian 309–10
Grantchester 197
Grantham 226
Grasmere 282
Grassington 268
Great Gable 282
Great Glen 311
Grimspound 185
Guildford 141
Guisborough 279

Haddon Hall, Derbys 90, **231**
Hadleigh 199
Hadrian's Wall *54*, 55, 77, **288**
Hampshire 143–50
Hardraw Force, Yorks 269
Hardwick Hall, Derbys 226
Hardy, Thomas 92–3, 154–5, 158, **159**
Harewood House, Yorks 84, 164, **266**
Harlech Castle 58, 86, **258**
Harrogate 273
Hartland Point 180
Hastings 134–5
Hatfield House 83, **123**
Hathersage 231
Haverfordwest 245
Hawes 268–9
Hawkshead 280
Haworth 233, **267**
Hay-on-Wye 249–50
health care 24
Heathrow 11–12
Helmsley 276
Helvellyn 283
Henry VIII 60–1, *62*
Hereford 227
Hever Castle, Kent 83
High Force, Teesdale 287
Highland Wildlife Park, Cairngorms 310
Highlands, Scottish 311–16
Hilliard, Nicholas 124
hitchhiking 15
Hockney, David 125

Hogarth, William 124
Holbein, Hans, the Younger 124
Holkham Hall, Norfolk 203
Holyhead 254
home exchange scheme 26
Honister Pass 282
Hood, Robin 225
Hopetoun House, Queensferry 87, **296–7**
Horning 203
horse-racing 320
horse-riding 322
Humber Bridge *277*
hunting and shooting 322–3
Hythe 131–2

Ilfracombe 179
Ilkley 267
Ingleborough 270
Inverewe Gardens, Loch Ewe 314
Inverness 311
Iona 317
Iron-Bridge Gorge Museum, Shropshire 95, **224**
Isle of Wight 146

Jedburgh Abbey, Borders 297–8
Jervaulx Abbey, Yorks 268
John O'Groats 316

Kedleston Hall, Derbys 226
Keld 270
Kelso Abbey, Borders 297–8
Kendal 279
Kenilworth Castle 218
Kent 91–2, **127–33**
Kent and East Sussex Railway 133
Kerse 199–200
Keswick 282
Killiecrankie, Pass of 305
Kilmuir 316
King's Lynn 202–3
Knightshayes Court, Devon 180
Kyle of Tongue 316
Kynance Cove 189

Lake District **279–84**, *280–1*, 282
Lampeter 250
Land's End *188*, 189
Laugharne 243
Launceston 191
Lavenham 200, *201*

Lawrence of Arabia 158
Leeds 266
Leeds Castle, Kent 83, *133*
Leicester 76
Lincoln 76, 87, 94, **205**
Lincolnshire 205
Lindisfarne 289, *289*
Linton, Yorks 268
Liverpool 261–4, *263*
  Beatles tour 264
  cathedrals 263–4
  Liverpool Museum 263
  Merseyside Maritime
    Museum 262
  St George's Hall 263
  Tate Gallery 263
  Walker Art Gallery 263
  waterfront area 262–3
Lizard Point 189
Llanberis 286–7
Llandeilo 243
Llandovery 250
Llandrindod Wells 247
Llandudno 252
Llanfair PG 254, *254*
Llangollen 251
  Plas Newydd 251, *252–3*
Llanystumdwy 255
Lleyn Peninsula 255
Lomond, Loch *300*, 301
London 80–1*, 98–9*,
    97–121
  accommodation 26
  Admiralty 104
  Apsley House 82, **112**
  Bank of England 108
  Banqueting House **104**,
    164
  Belgravia 112
  Big Ben *96*, 102
  Bloomsbury 114
  boat travel 18, 20
  Bond Street 112
  Buckingham Palace 79,
    101
  Burlington Arcade 111
  buses 17
  Cabinet War Rooms 104
  Carnaby Street 114
  Changing the Guard 101
  Chelsea 116
  children's activities 23
  Chinatown 114
  Chiswick House 82
  Churches
    St Andrew by the
      Wardrobe 82
    St Anne 114

St Bride 82, 106
St Clement Dane 82
St James Garlickhythe
    82
St James Picadilly 111
St Paul's, Covent Garden
    114, 164
St Peter-upon-Cornhill
    82
St Stephen Walbrook 82
City Airport 12, 110
City of London
    105, 105–10
Cleopatra's Needle 104
clubs, gentlemen's 113
Covent Garden 114
Crown Jewels 110
Docklands 110
Downing Street 104
Dr Johnson's House 106
Fleet Street 105–6
Fortnum & Mason 111–12
Gray's Inn 106
Green Park 79, 112
Greenwich 79, 119–20
guided tours 19
Guildhall 108–9
Ham House 82
Hampton Court Palace
    78, **121**, 164
Harrods 115, *116*
Highgate Cemetery 119
Horse Guards 104
Houses of Parliament
    (Palace of Westminster)
    102
Hyde Park 79, **113**
Kenilworth Castle **218**
Kensington 115–16
Kensington High Street
    116
Kensington Palace and
    Gardens 79, **115–16**
Kenwood House **82**, 164
Kew Palace and Gardens
    79, **120–1**, *120*
King's Road 116
Knightsbridge 115
Leicester Square 111
Lincoln's Inn 106
Lloyd's **109**, 165
London Pavilion 111
Lord Mayor's Show 104
Madame Tussaud's 118
Mall, The 100
Mansion House 108
Marble Arch 113
Marble Hill House 83

Mayfair 112–13
Monument 82
museums and galleries
  Barbican Arts Centre
    108
  British Museum 114,
    117, 165
  Courtauld Institute
    Galleries 79, **104**
  Hayward Gallery 105
  Museum of London 108
  Museum of Mankind
    112
  Museum of the Moving
    Image 105
  National Army Museum
    117
  National Gallery 100,
    117–18
  National Maritime
    Museum 119–20
  Natural History Museum
    116, *117*, 165
  Queen's Gallery 101
  Royal Academy 111
  Royal Armories 110
  Saatchi Collection 118
  Science Museum 116
  Sir John Soane's
    Museum 82
  Tate Gallery 103, 118
  Theatre Museum 114
  Transport Museum 114
  Victoria and Albert
    Museum 116
  Wallace Collection 118
  Wellington Museum 112
Osterley Park House 82
Oxford Street 113
Park Lane 113
Picadilly 111
Picadilly Circus 110–11,
    111
Regent Street 113
Regent's Park 79, **113**
Richmond Park 79
Roman sites 76, 108
Royal Hospital, Chelsea
    116
Royal Naval College 120
Royal Observatory 119
Royal Opera House 114
St Katharine's Dock 110
St James's 113
St James's Palace 101
St James's Park 79, 100
St Paul's Cathedral 82,
    106–8, *107*, *108*, 164

Savile Row 112
Shepherd Market 113
shopping 328
Soho 113–14
Somerset House 79, **104**
Sotheby's 112
South Bank Arts Complex 105
Speaker's Corner 113
Strand 104
Syon House 83
taxis 18
Temple 106
Thames Barrier 120
Tower Bridge 110, *110*
Tower of London 78, *109*, **109–10**
Trafalgar Square 100
Travelcard 19–20
Trocadero 111
underground 17, 100*
Westminster, Palace of 78, *101*, **102**, 165
Westminster Abbey 102–3
Westminster Cathedral *103*
Westminster Hall 102
Whitehall 104
zoo 113, 119
Long Melford 200
Longleat House, Wilts 84, **153–4**, 164
Losely Park 141
lost property 31
Looe 187
Lulworth Cove 158
Lundy Island 179, *180*
Luton Hoo 123
Lyme Regis 163
Lynmouth 179

Machynlleth 250
Malham 268
Maree, Loch 312
Manchester 264*, 264–5
  art galleries 265
  Central Library 265
  Granada TV Studios 265
  International Airport 12
  Museum of Science and Technology 95, 265
  Town Hall 265
Manorbier Castle, Pembrokeshire 244
maps 22
Margate 130
Marloes, Pembrokeshire 245–6
Matlock 89, **230**

May, Isle of 307
Measach, Falls of, Loch Broom 315
Mellerstain, Kelso 298
Melrose Abbey, Borders 297–8
Menai Bridge, Anglesey 254
Mevagissey 188
Middleham Castle, Yorks 268
Middlesbrough *286–7*, 287
Middleton in Teesdale 287
Midlands 223–9
Milford Haven 244–5
Minehead 177
money 14
Monmouth Castle 86, **237**
Montacute House, Somerset *1*, 84, **176–7**
Moore, Henry 125
motor-racing 321
Mousehole 78, **189**
Muchelney 177
Mull 317
Mullion Cove 189
Mumbles, The 243
music 330
Mynach Falls, Mid Wales 248
Mynydd Preseli, South Wales 247

Na Keal, Loch 317
Nefyn 255
Ness, Loch 311–12
Nether Stowey 177
New Forest 146, *147*
New Radnor 249
Newcastle-upon-Tyne 287–8
  Laing Art Gallery 288
  Museum of Science and Technology 95
Newport, Gwent 86, **239**
Newquay 190, *190–1*
newspapers and magazines 29
Newstead Abbey, Notts 225–6
Nidderdale *260*
night-clubs 331
Norfolk 201–4
Norfolk Broads 203
North-Eastern England 284–9
north of England, map of 262*
North York Moors 276–7
Northleach 218

Northumberland Coast 288
Norwich 201–2
  Castle Museum 202
  cathedral 201–2
Nottingham 225

Oban 304
Offa's Dyke 237
Offa's Dyke Path 227
Okehampton 185
Old Harry Rocks, Dorset *156*
opening hours 32, 325
opera 330
Osborne House, Isle of Wight 146
Oxford 207–11, 209*
  All Souls College 211
  Ashmolean Museum 211
  Balliol College 211
  Bodleian Library 210–11
  Carfax Tower 207
  Christ Church College 208–10
  Corpus Christi College 210
  Hertford College 210
  High Street 207
  Magdalen College 210
  Merton College 210
  New College 210
  Radcliffe Camera 211
  Sheldonian Theatre 210, *211*
  University College 210
Oxwich 243
Oystermouth 243

Padstow 190–1
Paignton 181
parking regulations 17
passports and visas 13
Peak District 89–90, 229–31
Peebles 297
Pembroke Castle 244
Pembrokeshire 243–7
Pendennis Castle, Cornwall 189
Pendine 243
Pennine Way 231, 269
Penrhyn Castle and quarries 253–4
Penrith 283
Penzance 189
Petworth House 139–40
Pevensey Bay 76, **135**
pharmacies 24
Pickering 277
Pilgrim Fathers' sites 94, 183, 197, 205

Pitlochry 305
Plynlimon range 248–9
Plymouth 182–4
    Antony House 184
    Cotehele House 184
    Saltram House 84, 184
polo 321
Polperro 187
Pool, Cornwall 189
Poole, Dorset 155–6
Port Sunlight 263
Porthmadog 255, 257
Portland, Isle of 162
Portland Bill *162*, 162–3
Portsmouth 143–5
    Royal Dockyard 143–5
post offices 28, 32
Potter, Beatrix 279–80
Powis Castle, Wales 250
Pre-Raphaelite movement
    125, 263, 280
Princetown 91, 186–7
public holidays 32–3
pubs 32, 33, 233
Purbeck, Isle of 158
Pwllheli 255

quarantine regulations 13

radio 29
Raglan Castle 86, **237**
Ranworth 203
Reculver Roman Fort, Kent
    130
Reeth 270
religious services 30
Restomel Castle, Cornwall
    188
Rhayader 249
Rheidol Valley 248
Rhuddlan Castle 252
Ribblehead Viaduct, Yorks
    269
Richborough 131
Richmond 270–1
Rievaulx Abbey, Yorks
    276–7
Ripon 273–4
Robin Hood's Bay 277
Rochester 92
Roman Britain 52, 55
    sites 76–7, 130, 140, 169,
    218, 219, 228–9, 250, 255,
    288
Romney, Hythe and
    Dymchurch Railway 132,
    132
Romney Marsh 132

Romsey 147–8
Roseland 188
rowing 321
Royal Tunbridge Wells 133
rugby *318*, 320
Ruskin, John 280
Ruthin 251
Rye 132, *133*

Saffron Walden 197
St Andrews 307
St Asaph 252
St David's 246
    Cathedral *42*, 246
St David's Head *246*
St Ives 190
St Margaret's Bay, Kent 131
St Michael's Mount 189
St Just 189
Salcombe 182
Salisbury 75, 150–2, *152*
    cathedral 86, **150–2**
    Old Sarum 75, **150**
Salisbury Plain *150–1*, 152–3
Sandringham House, Norfolk
    203
Sandwich 130–1
Scarborough 277
Scilly, Isles of 189
Scone Palace, Perth 87,
    305–7
Scotland 88*, 291–317, 292*
    air travel 12, 18–19
    Bonny Prince Charlie sites
    89, 316
    food specialities 38
    Highland Games 321
    islands 316–17
    money 14
    skiing 310, *311*, 325
    tartans 312
    train travel 18
    travel passes 18–19
    whisky *39*, 40, 310
Scotney Castle, Kent 133,
    134
Selworthy 178
Seven Sisters cliffs 135
Severn Bore *172*
Sidmouth 181
Shakespeare, William 91,
    212–15
Sheffield 265–6
Sherborne 159–60
    abbey church 159, *161*
    castles 160
shopping 325–8
show-jumping 320

Shrewsbury 227
Sissinghurst Castle, Kent 133
skiing 310, *311*, 325
Skipton Castle, Yorks 267
Skomer and Skokholm
    islands 246
Skye 89, **316**
Slaughter, Upper and Lower
    220
Slimbridge 222–3, *224*
Smoo Cave, Durness 316
Snowdon 256
Snowdonia 256–7, *256–7*
Somerset 173–9
Somerset and Devon Coastal
    Path 179
South Downs Way 137
South-East England, map of
    128*
South-West England, map of
    168*
Southern England, map of
    144*
Southampton 146
speed limits 16–17
Speyside 310
sport 319–25
Staffa 317
Staithes 279
Stansted airport 12
Stirling 87, **303–4**
Stock Ghyll Force, Cumbria
    281
Stoke-on-Trent 226–7
Stonehenge 51, *52–3*, 75,
    152–3
Stonor Park, Henley 83
Stourhead, Wilts 84, 154
Stow-on-the-Wold 220
Stratford-upon-Avon 91,
    206, **212–15**, 213*, *215*
    Anne Hathaway's Cottage
    215
    Guildhall (Grammar
    School) 213
    Hall's Croft 213–14
    Holy Trinity Church 214
    Judith Shakespeare's
    House 212
    Nash House 213
    New Place 213
    Shakespeare's Birthplace
    212
    Shottery 215
    theatres **214–15**, 330
Studley Royal, Yorks 276
Sudbury 200
Sudeley Castle, Glos *221*

Suffolk 199–201
Sulgrave Manor, Oxon 217–18
Summer Isles, Scotland 314–15
Surrey 141
Sussex 134–41
Sutton Bank 276
Swaledale *270*, 270–1
Swanage 158
Swansea 242

Talley Abbey, Wales 250
Talyllyn Railway, Wales 258–9
Tarn Howes, Cumbria 280
Taunton 177
Tavistock 185
Tees Valley 287
Teignmouth 181
telephones 28–9
television 29–30
Temple Newsam, Leeds 266
Tenby 243–4, *244–5*
tennis 321
Tenterden 133
theatre 329–30
Thirsk 276
Thomas, Dylan 243
time differences 10
Tintagel 77–8, **191**
Tintern Abbey *234*, 237
tipping 40
Tissington 230, *230*
Tiverton 180
Tobermory 317
toilets 41
Torosay Castle, Mull 317
Torquay 181
Torridon, Loch 312
Totnes 181–2
tourist information centres 20–2
tours 19–20
train travel 14, 18
Traquair House, Inverleithen 297

Tregaron 250
Tremadog 255
Tretower 238
Trossachs 304
Truro 189
Turner, JMW 118, **125**, 139
Tywyn 258

Uffington, St Mary's Church *30*
Ullapool 314
Ullswater 283
Urquhart Castle *313*

Varrich Castle *290*
VAT 325
Veryan 188
Victory, HMS 142, 143–5
Vyrnwy, Lake 250

Wales 85*, 235–59, 236*
   airport 12
   food specialities 38
   language 237
   Tourist Board 22
walking 323–4
Walmer Castle, Kent 131
Wareham 156
Warkworth Castle, Northumberland 288
Warwick Castle *216–17*, 217
Washington, George 218
Watersmeet 179
water sports 324–5
Weald and Downland Open-Air Museum, Singleton 141
weights and measures 41
Wells 173–4
   Bishop's Palace 173–4
   cathedral 86, 164, 173, *174–5*
Welshpool 250
Wensleydale 268–9
Weston-Super-Mare 177
Weymouth 162

Wharfedale 267–8
Whipsnade Wild Animal Park 122
Whitby 277–9, *278*
Whithorn 302
Whitsands Bay *187*
Whitstable 130
Wicken Fen, Cambs 199
Widecombe-in-the-Moor 90, **186**
Wilmington Long Man, Sussex 137
Wilton House, Wilts 84, **152**
Wiltshire 150–4
Winchcombe 220
Winchester 78, 148–9
   cathedral 86, *148*, **148–9**
Windermere 279–80
Windsor Castle 121–2, *122*
Wisley RHS Gardens, Ripley 141
Woburn Abbey 83, **122–3**
Wookey Hole, Somerset 174
Woolacombe 179
Worcester 227–8
   cathedral 227
Wordsworth, William 280, 281–2, 283
Wrath, Cape 316
Wroxham 203
Wye Valley 237

York 271*, 271–3
   Castle Museum 273
   city walls 273
   Jorvik Viking Centre 273
   Minster 87, **272**, *272*
   National Railway Museum 273
   Roman remains 77
Yorkshire Dales 267–71, *268–9*
youth and student accommodation 26
Ystradfellte 238